Ethnic Business

The role of ethnic Chinese business in Southeast Asia in catalyzing economic development has been hotly debated – and often misunderstood – throughout cycles of boom and bust.

This book critically examines some of the key features attributed to Chinese business: business–government relations, the family firm, trust and networks, and supposed 'Asian' values. The in-depth case studies that feature in the book reveal considerable diversity among these firms and the economic and political networks in which they manoeuvre.

With contributions from leading scholars and under the editorship of Jomo and Folk, *Ethnic Business* is a well-written, important contribution to not only students of Asian business and economics, but also professionals with an interest in those areas.

Jomo K. S. is Professor of Applied Economics at the University of Malaya, Kuala Lumpur, Malaysia. Other books he has edited include *Manufacturing Competitiveness in Asia* and *Southeast Asian Paper Tigers?*, both published by Routledge.

Brian C. Folk is a Ph.D. Candidate, Sociology Department, at the University of California, Berkeley, USA.

RoutledgeCurzon Studies in the Growth Economies of Asia

1   **The Changing Capital Markets of East Asia**
    Edited by Ky Cao
2   **Financial Reform in China**
    Edited by On Kit Tam
3   **Women and Industrialization in Asia**
    Edited by Susan Horton
4   **Japan's Trade Policy**
    Action or reaction?
    Yumiko Mikanagi
5   **The Japanese Election System**
    Three analytical perspectives
    Junichiro Wada
6   **The Economics of the Latecomers**
    Catching-up, technology transfer and institutions in Germany, Japan and South Korea
    Jang-Sup Shin
7   **Industrialization in Malaysia**
    Import substitution and infant industry performance
    Rokiah Alavi
8   **Economic Development in Twentieth Century East Asia**
    The international context
    Edited by Aiko Ikeo
9   **The Politics of Economic Development in Indonesia**
    Contending perspectives
    Edited by Ian Chalmers and Vedi Hadiz
10 **Studies in the Economic History of the Pacific Rim**
    Edited by Sally M. Miller, A.J.H. Latham and Dennis O. Flynn
11 **Workers and the State in New Order Indonesia**
    Vedi R. Hadiz
12 **The Japanese Foreign Exchange Market**
    Beate Reszat
13 **Exchange Rate Policies in Emerging Asian Countries**
    Edited by Stefan Collignon, Jean Pisani-Ferry and Yung Chul Park
14 **Chinese Firms and Technology in the Reform Era**
    Yizheng Shi
15 **Japanese Views on Economic Development**
    Diverse paths to the market
    Kenichi Ohno and Izumi Ohno
16 **Technological Capabilities and Export Success in Asia**
    Edited by Dieter Ernst, Tom Ganiatsos and Lynn Mytelka
17 **Trade and Investment in China**
    The European experience
    Edited by Roger Strange, Jim Slater and Limin Wang
18 **Technology and Innovation in Japan**
    Policy and management for the 21st century
    Edited by Martin Hemmert and Christian Oberländer

19 **Trade Policy Issues in Asian Development**
   Prema-chandra Athukorala

20 **Economic Integration in the Asia Pacific Region**
   Ippei Yamazawa

21 **Japan's War Economy**
   Edited by Erich Pauer

22 **Industrial Technology Development in Malaysia**
   Industry and firm studies
   Edited by Jomo K. S., Greg Felker and Rajah Rasiah

23 **Technology, Competitiveness and the State**
   Malaysia's industrial technology policies
   Edited by Jomo K.S. and Greg Felker

24 **Corporatism and Korean Capitalism**
   Edited by Dennis L. McNamara

25 **Japanese Science**
   Samuel Coleman

26 **Capital and Labour in Japan**
   The functions of two factor markets
   Toshiaki Tachibanaki and Atsuhiro Taki

27 **Asia Pacific Dynamism 1550–2000**
   Edited by A.J.H. Latham and Heita Kawakatsu

28 **The Political Economy of Development and Environment in Korea**
   Jae-Yong Chung and Richard J. Kirkby

29 **Japanese Economics and Economists since 1945**
   Edited by Aiko Ikeo

30 **China's Entry into the World Trade Organisation**
   Edited by Peter Drysdale and Ligang Song

31 **Hong Kong as an International Financial Centre**
   Emergence and development 1945–1965
   Catherine R. Schenk

32 **Impediments to Trade in Services**
   Measurement and policy implication
   Edited by Christopher Findlay and Tony Warren

33 **The Japanese Industrial Economy**
   Late development and cultural causation
   Ian Inkster

34 **China and the Long March to Global Trade**
   The accession of China to the World Trade Organization
   Edited by Alan S. Alexandroff, Sylvia Ostry and Rafael Gomez

35 **Capitalist Development and Economism in East Asia**
   The rise of Hong Kong, Singapore, Taiwan, and South Korea
   Kui-Wai Li

36 **Women and Work in Globalizing Asia**
   Edited by Dong-Sook S. Gills and Nicola Piper

37 **Financial Markets and Policies in East Asia**
   Gordon de Brouwer

38 **Developmentalism and Dependency in Southeast Asia**
   The case of the automotive industry
   Jason P. Abbott

39 **Law and Labour Market Regulation in East Asia**
Edited by Sean Cooney, Tim Lindsey, Richard Mitchell and Ying Zhu

40 **The Economy of the Philippines**
Elites, inequalities and economic restructuring
Peter Krinks

41 **Private Enterprise in China**
Edited by Ross Garnaut and Ligang Song

42 **The Vietnamese Economy**
Awakening the dormant dragon
Edited by Binh Tran-Nam and Chi Do Pham

43 **Restructuring Korea Inc.**
Jang-Sup Shin and Ha-Joon Chang

44 **Development and Structural Change in Asia–Pacific**
Globalising miracles or end of a model?
Edited by Martin Andersson and Christer Gunnarsson

45 **State Collaboration and Development Strategies in China**
Alexius Pereira

46 **Capital and Knowledge in Asia**
Changing power relations
Edited by Heidi Dales and Otto van den Muijzenberg

47 **Southeast Asian Paper Tigers?**
From miracle to debacle and beyond
Edited by Jomo K. S.

48 **Manufacturing Competitiveness in Asia**
How internationally competitive national firms and industries developed in East Asia
Edited by Jomo K. S.

49 **The Korean Economy at the Crossroads**
Edited by MoonJoong Tcha and Chung-Sok Suh

50 **Ethnic Business**
Chinese capitalism in Southeast Asia
Edited by Jomo K. S. and Brian C. Folk

Ethnic Business

Chinese capitalism in Southeast Asia

**Edited by
Jomo K. S. and Brian C. Folk**

RoutledgeCurzon

Taylor & Francis Group

LONDON AND NEW YORK

First published 2003
by RoutledgeCurzon
11 New Fetter Lane, London EC4P 4EE

Simultaneously published in the USA and Canada
by RoutledgeCurzon
29 West 35th Street, New York, NY 10001

RoutledgeCurzon is an imprint of the Taylor & Francis Group

Typeset in Bembo by
HWA Text and Data Management, Tunbridge Wells
Printed and bound in Great Britain by
Antony Rowe Ltd, Chippenham, Wiltshire

British Library Cataloguing in Publication Data
A catalogue record for this book is available from the British Library

Library of Congress Cataloging in Publication Data
Ethnic Business: Chinese capitalism in Southeast Asia / [edited by]
Jomo K. S. & Brian C. Folk.
    p. cm. – (RoutledgeCurzon studies in the growth economies of Asia;
    p. 49)
Includes revised papers presented at a workshop held at the University
of Malaya in 1997.
Includes bibliographical references and index.
1. Minority business enterprises–Asia, Southeastern. 2. Chinese–Asia,
Southeastern–Economic conditions. 3. Entrepreneurship–Asia,
Southeastern. I. Jomo K. S. (Jomo Kwame Sundaram) II. Folk, Brian C.
(Brian Cameron), 1960– III. Series.

HD2358.5.A785E85 2003
338.6′422′0959–dc21   2003046516

ISBN 0-415-31011-3

Contents

Illustrations   ix
Contributors   x
Acknowledgements   xi
Abbreviations   xii

1   **Introduction**   1
    BRIAN C. FOLK WITH JOMO K. S.

2   **Chinese capitalism in Southeast Asia**   10
    JOMO K. S.

3   **The politics of 'seeing Chinese' and the evolution of a
    Chinese idiom of business**   26
    ALEX G. BARDSLEY

4   **The cultural limits of 'Confucian capitalism': power
    and the invention of the family among Chinese traders
    in Sarawak**   52
    YAO SOUCHOU

5   **All are flexible, but some are more flexible than others:
    small-scale Chinese businesses in Malaysia**   73
    DONALD M. NONINI

6   **The leading Chinese–Filipino business families in
    post-Marcos Philippines**   92
    TEMARIO C. RIVERA

7   **Pre-1997 Sino–Indonesian conglomerates, compared
    with those of other ASEAN countries**   105
    JAMIE MACKIE

8   Determinants of business capability in Thailand   129
    AKIRA SUEHIRO

9   De-mythologizing Charoen Pokphand: an
    interpretive picture of the CP Group's growth and
    diversification   153
    PAUL HANDLEY

10 Telecommunications, rents and the growth of a
    liberalization coalition in Thailand   182
    SAKKARIN NIYOMSILPA

11 Japanese transnational production networks and
    ethnic Chinese business networks in East Asia:
    linkages and regional integration   211
    KIT G. MACHADO

    Glossary   235
    Index   237

Illustrations

Figure

8.1 Thailand: strategic alliances among business groups in the
     telecommunications industry   143

Tables

7.1 Major business groups in Indonesia, 1993   108
7.2 Malaysian business groups, 1995–6   117
7.3 Market capitalization of KLSE and SEJ, 1983–96   118
8.1 Assets from leading politicians on grounds of corruption   130
8.2 Thailand: distribution of top 100 ranked firms in terms of
     total sales, classified by capital ownership, 1979, 1985 and 1992   132
8.3 Thailand: concessions to private firms in the telecommunications
     industry, 1986–93   137
8.4 Thailand: major business groups in the telecommunications
     industry, 1994   140
8.5 Development of the Shinawatra Group, 1982–93   145
10.1 Thailand: revenue from the mobile telephone business, 1987–95 194
10.2 Thailand: mobile cellular telephone services, 1986–94   194
10.3 Thailand: comparison of proposals for the three-million-line
     telephone project   197
11.1 Portion of listed firms controlled by ethnic Chinese and
     number and market capitalisation of top 500 ethnic Chinese
     listed firms in East Asian countries, 1994   214
11.2 Main activities of top 500 ethnic Chinese firms in East Asia,
     top 20 in each East Asian country and all Japanese firms in
     East Asia   215
11.3 Sources of FDI in ASEAN-4, Vietnam and China   216
11.4 Japanese and ethnic Chinese specialized manufacturing TNCs   224

Contributors

Alex G. Bardsley is a freelance writer and editor based in Washington, DC.

Brian C. Folk is a Ph.D. candidate in the Sociology Department at the University of California, Berkeley.

Paul Handley is a journalist who was based in Thailand from 1987–2001, reporting for *Far Eastern Economic Review*, *Institutional Investor* and *Newsweek*.

Jomo K. S. is Professor, Applied Economics Department, University of Malaya, Kuala Lumpur, Malaysia.

Kit G. Machado is Professor Emeritus of the Political Science Department, California State University, Northridge.

Jamie Mackie is Professor Emeritus in the Economics Department, Research School of Pacific and Asian Studies (RSPAS), Australian National University, Canberra, Australia.

Sakkarin Niyomsilpa is Senior Analyst at KASIKORN Research Center, Bangkok, Thailand.

Donald M. Nonini is Professor of Anthropology at the University of North Carolina, Chapel Hill.

Temario C. Rivera is Professor of International Relations at the International Christian University of Tokyo and editor of the *Philippine Political Science Journal*. He was formerly professor of political science and department chair at the University of the Philippines.

Yao Souchou is Senior Lecturer in the Anthropology Department, University of Sydney.

Akira Suehiro is Professor at the Institute of Social Science, University of Tokyo.

Acknowledgements

On 23–25 June 1997, a week before the East Asian financial crisis began with the Thai baht float on 2 July 1997, a workshop on 'Chinese Business in Southeast Asia' was held at the Faculty of Economics and Administration, University of Malaya in Kuala Lumpur. This meeting was part of a larger project on Chinese business in Southeast Asia undertaken with financial support from the Chiang Ching Kuo Foundation in Taipei. With separate support from this grant, two papers presented at the workshop by E. Terence Gomez and Rajeswary A. Brown have since been expanded into and published as books (Gomez 1999; Brown 2000). Additional support for this workshop was provided by the Southeast Asian Studies Regional Program (SEASREP) based at the University of the Philippines in Diliman, MetroManila.

After the conference, progress was disrupted by a number of developments. Four of the more historical essays have been published together in the June 2002 issue of the *Journal of Southeast Asian Studies* (Loh 2002; Post 2002; Trocki 2002; Visscher 2002). Many of the remaining papers have been heavily revised, updated and edited for inclusion in the present volume. Two other papers (by Sakkarin and Suehiro) were solicited for inclusion in this book. Hence, this volume is far from being the proceedings of that workshop, but nonetheless seeks to critically engage a very complex and constantly mutating subject. Thus, despite the circumstances of its origins, the chapters in this volume collectively offer a multi-faceted critique of the dominant discourse on Chinese business in the Southeast Asian region that emerged in the 1980s and 1990s.

We are grateful to all the contributing authors for their efforts, patience and cooperation, and to Alex Bardsley for his earlier role in preparing the manuscript for publication despite his own difficult circumstances. Alex Bardsley initially helped Jomo with the editorial work for this volume, while Brian Folk took over in 2001 after it became clear that Bardsley could not go on. As always, Foo Ah Hiang has been helpful.

Jomo K. S.
University of Malaya, Kuala Lumpur, Malaysia

Brian C. Folk
University of California, Berkeley

January 2003

Abbreviations

ASEAN	Association of Southeast Asian Nations
AT&T	American Telephone and Telegraph
BMB	Bangkok Mercantile Bank
BOI	Board of Investment (Thailand)
B-O-T	build-operate-transfer
BOT	Bank of Thailand
BT	British Telecoms (UK)
CAT	Communications Authority of Thailand
CCC	Counter Corruption Commission (Thailand)
CDC	China Development Corporation
CP	Charoen Pokphand (Thailand)
DoS, MTI	Department of Statistics, Ministry of Trade and Industry (Singapore)
EIU	Economist Intelligence Unit
FDI	foreign direct investment
FEER	*Far Eastern Economic Review*
GCC	global commodity chain
GDP	gross domestic product
GTDC	General Telephone Directory Company
HPAEs	high-performing Asian economies
IBM	International Business Machines
IC	integrated circuit
IEC	International Engineering Company (Thailand)
IMF	International Monetary Fund
IQF	individual-quick-freezing
JETRO	Japan External Trade Organization
JPRI	Japan Policy Research Institute
KLSE	Kuala Lumpur Stock Exchange
LDC	less developed country
LSE	large-scale enterprise
MBA	Masters of Business Administration
MITI	Ministry of International Trade and Industry

MMC	Mitsubishi Motor Corporation
MNC	multinational corporation
MoF	Ministry of Finance
MOTC	Ministry of Transport and Communications (Thailand)
NASA	National Aeronautics and Space Administration (USA)
NEC	Nippon Electric Corporation
NEP	New Economic Policy (Malaysia)
NESDB	National Economic and Social Development Board (Thailand)
NIC	newly industrializing country
NIE	newly industrialized economy
NPKC	National Peace Keeping Council
NSO	National Statistical Office (Thailand)
NTT	Nippon Telegraph and Telephone Corporation
ODA	official development assistance
OEM	original equipment manufacturing
PAL	Philippine Airlines
PAP	Peoples' Action Party
PC	personal computer
PCIB	Philippine Commercial and International Bank
PNB	Philippine National Bank
PPP	purchasing power parity
PTD	Postal and Telegram Department (Thailand)
SEASREP	Southeast Asian Studies Regional Program
SEJ	Jakarta Stock Exchange
SET	Stock Exchange of Thailand
SME	small- and medium-sized enterprise
TAC	Total Access Communication Plc (Thailand)
TBG	Thai Business Group
TFB	Thai Farmers Bank
TMT	Toyota Motor Thailand
TNC	transnational corporation
TOT	Telephone Organization of Thailand
TPE	Thai state-owned or public enterprise
TT&T	Thai Telephone and Telecommunication
UCOM	United Communication Industry Public Company Limited
UK	United Kingdom
UMNO	United Malays National Organization
UNCTAD/	United Nations Conference on Trade and Development,
DTCI	Division on Transnational Corporations and Investment
US(A)	United States (of America)
VCR	video cassette recorder

1 Introduction

Brian C. Folk with Jomo K. S.

This volume has its origins in a workshop on 'Chinese Business in Southeast Asia', held a week before the East Asian crisis began in July 1997. The debacle brought an end to the region's 'economic miracle', and for several years virtually required everybody working on business in Southeast Asia to address the origins and nature of the crisis, regardless of the relevance of one's own research to answering that important question. East Asian, especially Chinese, business organization and practices – once celebrated for their dynamism and contribution to the regional miracle – were increasingly denounced as the source of the malaise as business journalists and some researchers lamented corporate governance practices in the region without bothering to establish how they caused the crisis. Close business-government relations, the family firm, trust and supposed Asian values were rapidly transformed from being portrayed as the keys of the region's miracle to the villains responsible for its debacle. With rapid, V-shaped recovery from 1999 – after 1998, the year of severe recessions in the region – the passage of time has allowed a more considered analytical balance to re-assert itself.

Chinese capitalism – debates, constructions, projections

The study of ethnic Chinese capitalism in Southeast Asia has served as a kind of canvas upon which various paradigmatic approaches have been projected in different historical periods. As we shall see below in greater detail, these conceptions have typically contained strong normative overtones. In its oscillations from praise to blame, and sometimes back again, this discourse was basically essentialist. It implied or suggested, and sometimes explicitly claimed, a certain common but unique Chineseness to the organization, culture, norms and practices of businesses owned and managed by ethnic Chinese in the Southeast Asian region, if not throughout the world. With the possible exception of Singapore and sometimes Thailand, ethnic Chinese businesses are assumed to have similar, if not identical, characteristics throughout the region. This is usually attributed to their common condition as ethnic minorities, often subjected to discrimination and exclusion by hostile states dominated by indigenous majorities. Some variations to this basic theme have had to be admitted to accommodate the obvious variety of ethnic Chinese business experiences in the region. Sometimes, genetic differences were implied, if not openly acknowledged (see Chan and Chee 1984), but more often than not, cultural differences were emphasized.

Confucian and other ostensibly Chinese values, once denounced for their backwardness and responsibility for Chinese poverty on the mainland, became celebrated as the surrogate for the Protestant ethic in the East Asian miracle.[1] Some East Asians took great pride in turning Max Weber on his head in his grave, to replace now ostensibly decadent Western values with Asian – usually Confucian – values. This ostensibly Confucian heritage – previously denounced by progressive Chinese intellectuals, of the May Fourth Movement of 1919, for instance – became the common denominator for explanations of the East Asian miracle, especially in Japan and the first-tier East Asian newly industrialized economies of Taiwan, South Korea, Hong Kong and Singapore.

Several recent collections have usefully surveyed research on Chinese businesses in Southeast Asia (Gomez and Hsiao 2001) as well as the extent and distinctiveness of globalization processes affecting Chinese business firms (Yeung and Olds 2000). Some of the most active and salient recent debates in the literature have dealt with the divergent tendencies, manifest in the workings of ethnic Chinese businesses, prevalent under conditions of deepening liberalization in the period leading up to the crisis.

A positive account of the beneficial effects of risk-taking, entrepreneurialism, government connections, and the conglomerate structure typical of Chinese businesses under what used to be considered 'normal' conditions of national economic growth in Southeast Asia is outlined by Lim (2000). On the other side of this coin, however, were tendencies towards what are now seen as 'excessive borrowing', 'over-investment' and related-party lending without sufficient measures to attend to risk management. Thus, 'the very practices which contributed to rapid growth when macro-economic fundamentals were strong led to financial collapse when they weakened, creating excess capacity in the industrial and property sectors along the way' (Lim 2000: 9).

The general line of argument here is that with secular trends towards institutional development and foreign direct investment (FDI) liberalization, and the demographic diminution of the older generations, ethnic Chinese business reliance upon family-sourced labour, capital and management becomes intrinsically uncompetitive. The result is an inexorable tendency towards declines in traditional social networks and personalistic patron-client linkages. Nevertheless, as Yeung (1999: 1) argues, 'globalization presents opportunities for such social institutions as Chinese business firms to take advantage'. As can be seen in the case of crisis-induced relaxation of equity ownership stipulations in Malaysia (itself a consequence of earlier policy interventions), this provides an opening for 'cash-rich Malaysian Chinese' to benefit, albeit indirectly and unintentionally, through opportunistically capitalizing on fire-sale restructuring projects (Yeung 1999: 20–1). And Tan's (2000: 75–6) explication of 'political *guanxi*' shows how the patronage-based strategic alliances between Chinese business networks and state elites are premised upon uninterrupted growth to underwrite the distribution of largesse, and that these relationships can come under severe strain when favourable conditions do not obtain. These developments serve usefully as reminders that while economic and political *guanxi* networks are often (correctly) seen as informally institutionalized strategies facilitating exchange relations and accumulation within the context of weak formal institutions, these arrangements are always contingent, precarious, and subject to re-negotiation.

Understanding Chinese capitalism historically

In the following chapter, Jomo's contribution begins with an overview of the debates explaining Chinese capitalism in Southeast Asia. While various shibboleths supporting and attacking the Weberian thesis' applicability to the question of Chinese capitalism and the supposed role of Confucianism have been advanced over the years, Jomo makes it clear that a more fruitful analytical strategy lies elsewhere. Rather than debating ahistorical, essentialist over-generalizations, it is only through careful historical analysis of the political economy and distinctive institutions of Southeast Asian societies that the variegated forms of what he terms the 'distinct idioms of Chinese capitalism' can be understood.

The chapter highlights two main arguments. First, the norms and institutions associated with Chinese communities and businesses in Southeast Asia are presumed to condition the development of both individual family-based enterprises as well as the broader structures of Chinese business networks. Specifically, in the context of weak formal institutions and vulnerability due to politically sanctioned suspicion or hostility, idiomatic, informally institutionalized relationships based on trust and reciprocity – which reduce transaction costs and socialize risk over longer time horizons – have developed. While these may bolster Chinese family-based enterprise, the limitations and weaknesses of this archetypal institution are also apparent, especially in terms of scope for expansion and highly centralized intra-family decision-making.

Second, the discussion makes the case for the centrality of state-business relations, given the overwhelming importance of state-sponsored development projects, and the complex, potentially explosive inter-ethnic redistribution agendas that have typified some 'plural' or multi-ethnic Southeast Asian societies. With the weakness of both corporatist-type links and national bourgeoisies, compared with the Northeast Asian economies, the nature of key policy factors, such as industrial policy and liberalization, can be expected to play an important role in determining the incentive structure that confronts Chinese business. In some cases, a stance of 'benign neglect' on the part of the state has allowed some scope for manoeuvre for certain fractions of Chinese capital. More typically, however, highly uncertain business environments and capricious governments have served to induce a 'short-termist' calculus among businesses, often at the expense of longer-term commitments and more productive investments within national economies.

Alex Bardsley sets out to de-familiarize the notion of 'Chineseness' in its various usages in the literature on ethnic Chinese business. He argues that such conventional abstractions as 'the Chinese' and 'capital' have been used carelessly, made monolithic and reified, in ways that obscure as much as they illuminate. Focusing on the common, if implicit, presumption that 'the Chinese dominate business' in Southeast Asia, the author suggests that the assumption that capital can be neatly divided along the lines of the supposed political loyalties or national interests of its owners is problematic. Given the importance of state-building projects by local political elites, control over capital per se – not just the stereo-typically 'suspect' nature of Chinese-controlled capital – is a vital political and economic concern. Nevertheless, 'indigenism' is propagated by hegemonic or aspiring political elites in post-colonial societies, conflated with constructions of ethnic identity, and used as a political weapon to conjure up the bogeyman of 'Chinese-dominated' industries or national economies.

The author nicely outlines how the legitimacy of various (racially categorized) groups engaging in particular economic roles has its roots in the colonial division of labour. These new frameworks of social organization served as crucibles for upward mobility, besides spurring the evolution of new, culturally distinctive institutions within Chinese communities. In this context, Bardsley argues that the issue of a Chinese idiom of business can best be grasped by considering 'how Chinese (style) business employs capital', focusing on how resources are mobilized 'in a system of communally accepted legitimacy'. The transition from the colonial order to post-colonial regimes occasioned the dislocation of Chinese businesses, with the increasing unpredictability of the new environment, resulting in rising anxiety and mistrust between them and the local political elites. In response, Chinese business network organizations helped organize the distribution of credit and facilitated a kind of networked flexibility that linked and supported individual firms in the context of weak formal market and political institutions.

With the consolidation of increasingly interventionist states, certain Chinese businesses, especially large groups, found it advantageous to strategically cultivate rent-generating political connections as a basis for further expansion and diversifi-cation. At the same time, more recently, Bardsley argues, Chinese business groups have tended to incorporate Western-style corporate forms and norms as well as impersonal management practices. This development reflects the increasing necessity of business-friendly state policies, in the context of heightened regional and global competition, and is further driven by the spread of local capital markets. Much like 'traditional' transnational corporations, Chinese-controlled conglom-erates are being spurred to reinvent existing networks as flexible production systems within competitive industries. In this way, the practices of Chinese business groups can be understood as merging the need to accommodate still-prevalent personalistic social relations in Southeast Asia with the strictures and opportunities presented by the current phase of international capitalism.

Contradictions of small-scale Chinese businesses and the myths of 'Confucian familism'

Two of our studies focus on small-scale Chinese businesses, a sphere which has been conspicuously under-represented in the literature. These ethnographies are especially valuable in bringing to the fore issues of contestation and power relations at the day-to-day micro level within and across small Chinese enterprises. Yao Souchou examines management practices among Chinese traders in Sarawak, especially the use of family labour in the workplace. Yao argues that the idea of 'Chinese economic familism' – which emphasizes consensus between management and workers, especially those recruited from among kin – is a cultural myth. Based on anthropological fieldwork in the township of Belaga in Sarawak, he describes various management practices that attempt to reproduce 'family relations' in the shops in order to bind workers in a relationship of obligation and control. Instead of articulating a 'perfect matching of expectations of management and workers', as is so often argued, the cultural invention of the family is designed to institute and maintain structural differences between workers as outsiders and members of the owner's family.

The second thread of Yao's chapter describes and analyses worker responses to this mode of management control. Introducing the notion of resistance, the discussion focuses on the management practice of *kan dian* or 'watching the shop': a visual surveying of workers' performance in order to monitor and check recalcitrant behaviour. *Kan dian* is a logical outcome of the necessity for surveillance on the part of management – one that nonetheless opens the way for workers' resistance. Overall, Yao argues against the pitfalls of 'cultural determinism' which underpins the works of Gordon Redding, Wong Siu-lun and others. By showing both the enabling capabilities and impotence of Chinese cultural values with regards to the family, the chapter contributes to the critique of current understandings of the *modus operandi* of Chinese business enterprise.

Donald Nonini discusses small-scale Chinese businesses in Peninsular Malaysia based on ethnographic fieldwork in 1978–80, 1985 and 1991–3. There are several major findings. First, subcontracting among small-scale Chinese businesses is the crucial arrangement through which they are articulated with large-scale enterprises in the Malaysian economy. Second, *guanxi* or 'particularistic relationships' is only one of several ways in which small-scale Chinese businessmen interact with these enterprises, with one another, and with their employees: certain interactions are market-driven and relatively impersonal, even hostile. Third, patriarchal power within the family base of small-scale Chinese businesses comes into contradiction with their low level of capitalization, generating a petty accumulation trap that leads to the business' eventual demise. Finally, small-scale Chinese businesses and the families around which they are organized engage in strategic transnational traversals-staged moves out of Malaysia in response to the business politics of ethnicity and labour markets in Southeast Asia.

Chinese big business groups

Temario Rivera's chapter provides straightforward accounts of the development of the six most prominent Chinese–Filipino business families in the Philippines. Despite the long history of ethnic Chinese in the national economy, the families analyzed here represent new money, virtually all of them having become prominent within the last few decades. These groups have maintained their essential character as 'family firms,' retaining familial control over the lead companies even while floating stocks or bonds, and expanding their operations along the lines of diversified modern conglomerates. Each group has flagship operations in banking and finance, as well as real estate development.

Having outlined the mode of development of these groups, Rivera argues that critical to their expansion has been the cultivation of links and partnerships with key Filipino political elites. Rivera documents, in some detail, the pantheon of key political figures that have been recruited to serve as powerful executives or partners in the leading groups. While this distinctive style of management and expansion has heretofore served the family firms well, a series of new challenges now confronts these groups. These include the issue of inter-generational succession; increasing dependence on the skills of professional managers; the relative diffusion of political power; and the necessity of adapting to a more harshly competitive regional and international business environment. Rivera concludes that the families have addressed succession and management issues through advanced professional training abroad and supplementary recruitment measures, and that the families are well placed to adapt to new economic conditions and to maintain their collective hegemonic position in key sectors of the domestic economy.

Jamie Mackie's chapter shows that the differences between various groups of Southeast Asian Chinese and the socio-political contexts in which their businesses have operated are as illuminating as the similarities among them in explaining the reasons for their commercial success and the patterns of business–government relations they have encountered. Indonesian big business groups differ strikingly from those of Malaysia, Thailand, the Philippines and Singapore in many ways. Few of them were prominent before 1970. Nearly all have grown rapidly under the Soeharto regime, especially since deregulation of the economy accelerated in the 1980s. The patterns of their dependence on state and private banks and on the stock exchange for capital and credit were very different from those of their counterparts in other ASEAN countries. Political connections with Soeharto and his entourage were crucially important for some of the largest business groups, to a far greater degree than their counterparts in Malaysia and Thailand. Such connections were much less important for the smaller ones, although most Sino-Indonesian business firms have had to buy political protection from officials of all kinds.

The character of the political system has been crucial in this process: highly patrimonial, with power and control over funds and key resources concentrated intensely in the hands of Soeharto. By contrast, Thailand had a much more pluralistic power structure by the 1980s. In Malaysia too, there has been far less concentration of power in the hands of Mahathir, despite a growing tendency towards cronyism there. The more deeply we probe, the more significant local conditions appear to have been.

Thailand experienced rapid growth and impressive industrial upgrading between 1987 and 1996. Different paradigmatic approaches have tried to explain how Thailand could achieve economic success in spite of the fact that political corruption has been pervasive. The critical issues raised in these debates include the nature of clientelism, as well as the economic effects of rent-seeking activities. These arguments, however, seem to neglect the role of economic agents and the importance of their business capabilities.

Akira Suehiro explores these aspects more carefully through an empirical study of a specific industry as well as a particularly prominent Sino-Thai business group. Suehiro takes the telecommunications industry and the Shinawatra Group as case studies, exploring significant elements that have contributed to the rapid growth of local business groups in this industry. He argues that political connections alone cannot fully account for the group's growth. Under the new economic circumstances of liberalization and competition, management reforms became increasingly significant for local groups, compared with traditional modes of political patronage. In addition, new styles of management involving professionals have become more important than those traditionally characteristic of family-run businesses.

During the Asian economic boom of 1987–97, Thailand's Charoen Pokphand agribusiness group began to rapidly expand and diversify its businesses. The group made massive investments abroad, becoming known as China's largest foreign investor. CP's businesses range from farming to motorcycle manufacturing, banking, telecommunications, oil refining and toy manufacture.

The Chearavanont family, which controlled both ownership and management of the group, aimed to become a 'Chinese *chaebol*', after the giant family-owned conglomerates of South Korea. However, well before the Asian crash of 1997, CP had already begun to suffer substantially from centralized family management, secretive accounting, and over-dependence on connections (or *guanxi*) – rather than other business fundamentals – to stake out positions in new industries. Paul Handley's chapter shows that while they were quick to grab opportunities, the group failed to adapt adequately to unfamiliar competitive environments and managerial challenges.

Sakkarin Niyomsilpa poses several broad questions in his chapter: Is the bureaucracy still the dominant force in Thai society? How has the Thai political economy changed and how important are rents in it? He tries to answer these questions by focusing on the political economy of telecommunications liberalization in Thailand. Sakkarin argues that Thailand has moved away from the 'bureaucratic polity' towards a more pluralistic socio-political system in which a broadly based 'liberalization coalition' has emerged. As bureaucrats have lost political supremacy over telecommunications policy, their control over and access to rents has given way to the liberalization coalition promoting the privatization programme that gained momentum from the early 1990s.

Rent concessions have played an important part in the growth of the new telecommunications business oligopolies in Thailand. At the same time, however, high-level political connections by big business groups, such as the CP group, were also leveraged to secure the award of exclusive new project contracts in the telecommunications sector. However, Sakkarin contends that there were signs that rents would decline in importance as liberalization gained momentum and business groups became more professional. The chapter examines three telecommunications privatization cases to understand the competition between pro-reform and anti-reform coalitions, and the politics of rents associated with these cases.

Ethnic Chinese business networks in regional and comparative context

While most of the pieces in this collection focus on business at the national or sub-national levels, this must be complemented by analysis of ethnic Chinese business networks at the regional level, especially as compared with their Japanese counterparts. While the importance of regional production networks in East Asia has now become widely recognized (Katzenstein and Shiraishi 1997; Hatch and Yamamura 1996), the much-vaunted apparent nimbleness and flexibility of ethnic Chinese producers lends itself to overestimation of their significance regionally (e.g. Peng 2000).

Kit Machado argues that many contemporary assessments greatly exaggerate the integrative power of ethnic Chinese business networks in East Asia. Instead, he argues, Japanese transnational manufacturing production networks have been more central to economic integration in East Asia. Much ethnic Chinese business activity is either not part of such networks, or plays a subordinate role in Japanese TNC-centred production networks. The latter remains overwhelmingly the most important force for economic integration in East Asia.

Conclusion

Of late, the dominant strands of discourse on overseas Chinese capitalism have become more nuanced and sophisticated. Recognition of flaws, contradictions and possible dysfunctionality has also grown, greatly accelerated by the onset of the East Asian debacle. But just as this volume rejects the all too easy essentialism of the earlier celebration of Asian (read Confucian) values, it also rejects the converse – the ready denunciation of the same, extended to cronyism, corporate governance failures and other alleged sins of the region. Instead, this volume points to the rich variety of ethnic Chinese business experiences in the region, not only over time, but also with context, size, market share, activity and so on. Suehiro, for instance, reminds us that new Thai Prime Minister Thaksin did not choose to control his telecommunications-based empire through family proxies, unlike other Sino-Thai firms of comparable size in similar businesses.

The complex and nuanced picture of ethnic Chinese business activity, organization, culture, norms and practices in the region continues to change in response to new circumstances and challenges as it has over time in the past. While the easy stereotypes are not completely without basis, they are invariably overdrawn and grossly exaggerated. Such attractively simplistic caricatures often do a disservice to ethnic Chinese in the region by lending them to racial stereotyping and easy demonization. But for those seriously interested in understanding social, including business, realities, they reinforce misleading essentialist fetishization that interferes with more serious and profound analysis.

Note

1   The Singapore authorities generously funded a research institute dedicated to the study of the subject, with a view to introducing some version thereof into the school curricula as an alternative to Western moral and religious education.

References

Brown, Rajeswary Ampalavanar (2000) *Chinese Big Business and the Wealth of Asian Nations*. London: Palgrave.

Chan Chee Khoon and Chee Heng Leng (eds) (1984) *Designer Genes: I.Q., Ideology and Biology*. Kuala Lumpur: INSAN.

Gomez, Edmund Terence (1999) *Chinese Business in Malaysia: Accumulation, Accommodation, and Ascendance*. Richmond, Surrey: Curzon Press, and Honolulu: University of Hawaii Press.

Gomez, Edmund Terence and Michael Hsin-Huang Hsiao (eds) (2001) *Chinese Business in Southeast Asia: Contesting Cultural Explanations, Researching Entrepreneurship*. Richmond, Surrey: Curzon Press.

Hatch, Walter and Kozo Yamamura (1996) *Asia in Japan's Embrace: Building a Regional Production Alliance*. Cambridge: Cambridge University Press.

Katzenstein, Peter J. and Takashi Shiraishi (eds) (1997) *Network Power: Japan and Asia*. Ithaca, NY: Cornell University Press.

Lim, Linda Y.C. (2000) 'Southeast Asian Chinese Business: Past Success, Recent Crisis and Future Evolution'. *Journal of Asian Business*, 16(1): 1-14.

Loh Wei Leng (2002) 'The Colonial State And Business: The Policy Environment in Malaya in the Inter-War Years'. *Journal of Southeast Asian Studies*, 33(2): 243–56.

Peng, Dajin (2000) 'The Changing Nature of East Asia as an Economic Region'. *Pacific Affairs*, 73(2), Summer: 171–91.

Post, Peter (2002) 'The Kwik Hoo Tong Trading Society of Semarang, Java: A Chinese Business Network in Late Colonial Asia'. *Journal of Southeast Asian Studies*, 33(2): 279–96.

Tan, Eugene Kheng-Boon (2000) 'Success Amidst Prejudice: *Guanxi* Networks in Chinese Businesses in Indonesia and Malaysia'. *Journal of Asian Business*, 16(1): 65–83.

Trocki, Carl A. (2002). 'Opium and the Beginnings of Chinese Capitalism in Southeast Asia'. *Journal of Southeast Asian Studies*, 33(2): 297–314.

Visscher, Sikko (2002) 'Actors and Arenas, Elections and Competition: The 1958 Election of the Singapore Chinese Chamber of Commerce'. *Journal of Southeast Asian Studies*, 33(2): 315–32.

Yeung, Henry Wai-Chung (1999). 'Under Siege? Economic Globalization and Chinese Business in Southeast Asia'. *Economy and Society*, 28(1): 1–29.

Yeung, Henry Wai-Chung and Kris Olds (eds) (2000) *Globalization of Chinese Business Firms*. London: Macmillan.

2 Chinese capitalism in Southeast Asia

Jomo K. S.

Chinese culture and capitalism

Not too long ago, it was the vogue to assert that Chinese culture was inimical to capitalism. Although such arguments predominated until the 1970s, the most influential one can be traced to Weber's argument about the ostensibly obstructionist role of Chinese religion in blocking the emergence of capitalism in China. Conversely, he stressed the importance of the Calvinist Protestant ethic for the emergence and early rise of capitalism in Western Europe. While certain cultural attributes are undoubtedly more conducive than others for certain economic relations associated with capitalism, one would be well advised to treat such grand claims with some caution and scepticism.

Weber argues that ascetic Calvinism – a branch of Protestantism – was key to the emergence of modern capitalism in Northwest Europe. He apparently did not find in Chinese religion this worldly orientation he considered favourable to capitalist pursuits. Citing Chinese-language sources, Tan (1994: 43) persuasively argues that the Chinese certainly did not lack the values considered necessary for capitalism by Weber such as diligence and frugality. If the problem did not rest with these Chinese values, Weberians attribute it to the ostensible absence of rationality, which is sometimes defined tautologically, i.e. if capitalism did not develop, it could not have been rational.

Understanding of the failure of capitalism to emerge earlier in China has to be sought in historical analysis of Chinese political economy and related institutions. The value orientation of ethnic Chinese who pioneered the expansion of capitalism, albeit primarily in commerce, in the very different conditions obtaining in much of Southeast Asia is best understood in this context. At the risk of stating the obvious, it appears that it is the combination of culture and conditions that has been favourable to Chinese capital accumulation in Southeast Asia, as elsewhere.

Hill Gates (1996) has advanced considerable evidence of thriving market exchanges in China for well over a millennium, primarily characterized by petty or simple commodity production, and not just involving agricultural produce. In fact, there is considerable evidence of developed Chinese market relations going back several millennia, with the introduction of coins in the pre-Christian period and paper money almost a millennium ago. The presence of money – the universal commodity – generally implies the emergence of more complex and sophisticated trade, going well beyond the limitations of barter exchange.

Almost as if permanently suspended in the ideal world of neo-classical economics, with perfect competition among many small enterprises, historical conditions in China – including cultural norms, practices and institutions – seem to have conspired to block enterprise-level accumulation, expansion and concentration. Debates about causation continue without resolution, with contending parties variously attributing primacy for this 'blockage' or 'low-level equilibrium' to the failure to achieve secure property rights, intellectual 'enlightenment', technological dynamism, economic transformation or various permutations of the preceding.

Shieh's (1992) study of Taiwan highlights the role of widespread and popular 'petty bourgeois' aspirations – especially of men – on the 'boss island'. This resulted in the proliferation of small and medium size enterprises (SMEs), and the much smaller role of large firms, especially conglomerates, as compared to both Japan and South Korea. Some of this can be attributed to the ruling Guomindang government's fear and discouragement of the potential political influence and power of large private firms, especially if controlled by 'native' Taiwanese (Fields 1995). However, other evidence from Hong Kong and elsewhere suggests that competitiveness on the basis of flexibility and other attributes of such small firms has been a feature of Chinese manufacturing success. With a few notable exceptions (consider, for example, the relatively small number of internationally-known Chinese firm brand-names), Chinese firms seem to have been left far behind in attaining the economies of scale and scope associated with the success of large firms.

Fukuyama (1995) is probably right that the trust that others may have in their respective states is not to be found among most ethnic Chinese, both in China as well as within the diaspora, albeit for different reasons. However, many – noting the ideological strength of 'rugged individualism' in American society – doubt his characterization as accurate for contemporary American society, and more recently, even for the Japanese, although for other reasons. However, even if he is right, this does not mean that trust (*xinyong*) has been absent or unimportant for economic relations in Chinese societies. This is perhaps even more important among vulnerable – e.g. minority – Chinese seeking to survive or thrive in hostile conditions, where they may have little confidence in, or worse, actually be wary of, or even fear the state, and hence cannot rely on it to enforce contracts, for instance.

Instead, it appears that the widespread lack of confidence in governments among Chinese capitalists has often encouraged them to adapt and transform co-operative mutual aid institutions. This has been true in most of Southeast Asia, where they constitute economically powerful, but politically vulnerable minorities. But arguably, this has also been the case in China, Taiwan, Hong Kong or Singapore where they constitute majorities, but perceive the state to be unsupportive of private business interests for various reasons. Generally, such institutions originally developed for survival in hostile alien conditions. Such institutions have usually been facilitative or supportive of accumulation, credit and investment without state support (e.g. in ensuring the rule of law or for enforcing contracts), or worse still, in the face of government uncertainty or even official hostility.

From an economic perspective then, according to Tan Chee Beng (1994: 32), trust (*xinyong*) refers to a 'person's reliability in economic relations', or 'an individual's or a firm's reputation, reliability, credit rating' (DeGlopper 1972: 304). Such trust operates in the social milieu of networks of inter-personal relationships (*guanxi*) involving different degrees of intimacy of relationships (*ganqing*) or mutual obligations among relatives or friends (*renqing*). Thus, business expansion does not only involve capital accumulation as conventionally understood, but also the sponsorship, patronage and cultivation of networks ensuring better and easier access to more influence, information, human resources, credit, markets, etc.

In the days of 'frontier capitalism', leadership of 'secret societies' offered control over labour resources. Later, community leadership, including patronage of Chinese schools, ensured the availability of schooled human resources independently of the colonial state. More recently, such leadership has mainly been important for those primarily catering to ethnic Chinese markets, whereas political influence can often be bought and turned to profitable advantage (Gomez and Jomo 1997). Hence, the extension of one's social standing and influence in the community offers economic advantage, which some now include under the rubric of social or cultural capital, though it would of course be vulgar to reduce all human behaviour to such functionalist interpretation.

Trust and such relationships are crucial for doing business without written contracts, whether involving verbal or even implied but unspecified contracts, or in the extension of credit without collateral. While the risk element seems to be significantly higher in such circumstances, this may not be seen as such for business transactions that do not expect the state or some other authority to enforce contracts or commitments. Arguably, such expectations have not been historically widespread among the politically excluded ethnic Chinese in colonial and post-colonial Southeast Asia. Such arrangements obviously avoid or reduce many transactions costs, and may imply some or even considerable flexibility, e.g. if debt repayment is presumed to be contingent on the success of the harvest.

Yet, the very vulnerability and tentativeness of such institutions – which some would characterize, arguably caricature, as reflecting insecure property rights – must surely take its toll. For instance, this would be manifest in a greater tendency for short-termism or a strong preference for asset liquidity, which, in turn, constrains the nature of enterprise investment and organizational development, affecting its willingness to make large, lumpy investments or to invest in research and development significantly beyond 'shop floor' or workplace innovation from experience or 'learning by doing', for example.

We therefore turn to a consideration of the norms, customs and institutions associated with the Chinese, particularly in the Southeast Asian diaspora, for new insights. Such norms, customs and institutions may well have enhanced –

but also limited – the business enterprise of ethnic Chinese in the region (for an excellent survey from which I have drawn heavily for this chapter, see Tan Chee Beng 1994). These are believed to have contributed to the strengths, as well as constraints, of Chinese business networks – often, but not necessarily built on kinship, real or imagined – improving access to information, credit, markets, labour and security.

As noted earlier, experience and related skills developed with exposure to the extensive development of market exchanges involving money in China (Yang 1952) implied a certain widespread degree of commercial experience and economic sophistication (Freedman 1959). Even peasant farmers at least had contact with the itinerant traders associated with periodic rural markets and more permanent, albeit somewhat seasonal, urban markets in China (Skinner 1964, 1965a, 1965b). Hence, though most Chinese who sought their fortunes in Southeast Asia came from poor peasant families in Southeast China, they were nonetheless better exposed than most autochthonous residents of Southeast Asia who had much less relevant experience. The former were thus better able to take advantage of the new commercial opportunities accompanying trade expansion from the fifteenth century, and later associated with European commerce and colonial expansion in the region.

The strong motivation of the voluntary – as opposed to the forced – emigrant should also be considered. Such emigrants have generally been prepared to put up with much more hardship and to face considerably greater risk (not just in an economic sense) than others. One would therefore expect them to work and strive harder to succeed. Tan Chee Beng (1994: 36) also suggests that 'competition for achievement is well-established' as 'an important feature of Chinese culture which emphasizes ancestor worship'. He approvingly cites Hsu (1949), who argues that while there is no competition between those of different status, 'there can and is bound to be competition' among those of equal status.

Tan emphasizes the apparent willingness of ethnic Chinese to forgo current comforts in favour of subsequent generations. Two values are involved here, namely thrift and the willingness to invest in education with the expectation of achievement and upward mobility for their children, presumably also bolstered by the supposedly Confucian emphasis on education and meritocratic norms. But unlike the Confucian norm, it is wealth, rather than learning, which is ascribed greater status among most ethnic Chinese in much of Southeast Asia, probably because unlike the old Confucian mandarinate, the contemporary scholar in Southeast Asia lacks political influence, except for those who work with ruling regimes. Nevertheless, official discrimination in Malaysia against ethnic Chinese in terms of access to education and employment by the state has probably only served to strengthen the resolve of most ethnic Chinese to advance academically despite the additional obstacles, if only in recognizing this as the main means for upward occupational and social mobility in this age.

Tan (1994: 39) also emphasizes the early business-oriented socialization of children, especially in the small family-based enterprises where children have often been expected to begin 'helping out' from an early age. Such socialization is apparently also significant for the relatively large modern firms that now dominate much of Southeast Asia, especially if they remain under family control, even if they are not entirely run by family members. Immediate family members, relatives and other employees are expected to share their knowledge and skills with the children of the patriarch. They are then expected to augment their capabilities with good education before returning to resume their apprenticeship in the firm (or sometimes in a strategically connected firm) and eventually succeeding the patriarch.

Maurice Freedman (1965) has emphasized the clearer business ideological orientation of ethnic Chinese, for example, in conducting different aspects of relationships with kin or friends. In her study of urban Singapore in the 1980s, Tania Li (1989) contrasts the ethnic Chinese willingness to get kin, friends and neighbours involved in commercial relationships with the apparent ethnic Malay reluctance to do so. Apparently, the kinship or other relationship of affinity has been effectively deployed among Chinese to enforce implied contracts, whereas such relationships often account for non-Chinese reneging on such commitments (Tan 1994).

Ethnic Chinese can be credited with developing much of the extensive commercial and related credit networks in Southeast Asia which soon linked production for exchange, especially export, in the interior and rural hinterlands with the international import-export trade. Only the latter was likely to be dominated by European colonial interests. While some of these trade and credit relations encouraged new production by Chinese, they often involved indigenous producers already involved in such production or who were ready to adapt to the new demands of the emerging markets. T'ien Ju K'ang (1953) provides a rich account of the close multi-layered relationship between credit and commerce in rural Sarawak involving Chinese farmers supplying firms in Singapore. Chia (1987) offers a useful account of the credit-commerce nexus involving Malay peasants and Chinese merchants in the Kelantanese interior.

Although modern banking and finance systems have been a relatively recent and, arguably, Western innovation in China and Southeast Asia, credit arrangements have a long history in China, including rural China (Yang 1952). Tan Chee Beng (1994: 28) identifies three main types of *hui*, variously translated as credit society, loan society, co-operative loan society, mutual aid club, rotating credit association. They have generally involved rotation by prior agreement (*lunhui*), by chance, e.g. by casting dice or drawing lots (*yaohui*), and by auction, i.e. according to the offer to pay the highest interest rate. Such arrangements are said to have been successfully adapted to raise capital for investment in Southeast Asia and elsewhere. Wu (1974: 566) has described how Chinese in Papua New Guinea used such institutions to develop 'extremely active and complicated financial networks'. He shows how multiple involvements (as organizer as well as subscriber), sometimes even involving proxies, can significantly enhance access to credit in complex, often interlocking, and hence vulnerable (to default) arrangements.

Ethnic Chinese in Southeast Asia are said to have evolved business strategies and management methods in response to the conditions in which they have found themselves, drawing considerably on inherited institutions, past practices and other cultural resources. Many observers have noted the seeming Chinese inability to develop and sustain large enterprises over time, resulting in the protracted persistence over more than a millennium of the family-based enterprise. Apparently, the family has been a successful basis for enterprise organization among ethnic Chinese, providing some flexibility in the deployment of human resources besides effectively pooling limited financial and other resources for accumulation and development. In recent decades, ethnic Chinese firms have displayed considerable growth potential, apparently due to their superior flexibility and other adaptive capabilities. But the apparent inability to transcend the family basis appears to have limited enterprise development and handicapped the growth of ethnic Chinese businesses over time (hence, for example, the preoccupation with inter-generational problems of various kinds), limiting the firms' scope as well as scale.

Considering the conditions in which they operate and the business strategies adopted, it should come as no surprise that many ethnic Chinese enterprises are engaged in what has been deemed 'cronyism', once praised as networking or social capital (for the most developed version of this argument in the Southeast Asian context, see Unger 1998). Hence, they do not appear to behave like the 'rational' profit-maximizing firms of neo-classical microeconomic theory, only engaged in 'arm's length' economic transactions with scant regard for underlying social relationships. Instead, Limlingan (1986: 159–60) claims that, not unlike the Japanese, the Chinese in Southeast Asia have been concerned with developing long-term economic relationships as well as capturing market share with a 'low margin/high volume strategy'.

Thus, Tan (1994: 39) insists that 'contrary to the indigenous people's stereotype, Chinese businessmen are guided by business ethics'. In contrast, 'only when one moves outside the field of people one knows well, where social sanctions are less binding, does short-term maximization at the potential expense of business reputation occur' (Silin 1972: 352). While this suggests some sanctions against short-termism, it also implies that greater social and cultural distance – e.g. in dealing with those from other ethnic or linguistic groups or with others on an intermittent basis – is likely to encourage more ruthless and short-termist behaviour.

Confusion over Confucianism

In the 1950s and 1960s, it was common to read or hear that the poverty of the Chinese masses and the backwardness of the Chinese economically were due to their cultural inheritance, norms and values, and often, more specifically, to their Confucian heritage. Two problems arose from such claims. There has been considerable dispute about whether the features (norms, values, etc.) associated with Confucianism were correctly attributed. Serious scholars of Chinese beliefs have long been agreed that the rich and complex variety of Chinese beliefs, including what is said to be Chinese religion, cannot be reduced to Confucianism, influenced as it is by Daoism and various other religious, philosophical and other creeds.

Even those who claim that Confucianism has been the single most important influence in Chinese thought for centuries readily acknowledge that there is no single Confucianism. Instead, there are said to be contending schools of Confucianism, as well as state ideologies claimed or deemed to be Confucianist, especially by the ideologists of the mandarinate, who have obviously been privileged by the social hierarchy associated with official or state Confucianism. While such official Confucianism must obviously have had much influence among the public, and must also have been strongly reflected in court and other official texts recorded for posterity, it is useful to distinguish this from the undoubtedly Confucian-influenced norms, values and belief systems associated with the Chinese.

Official Confucianism, it has often been noted, privileged the mandarinate, usually followed by the landed gentry, from which it was often drawn, and the farmers who sustained the entire social and economic edifice. For obvious reasons, military power too had to be given its due, with the traders and other urban elements displaced from the countryside taking up the rear. How such a 'Confucian' hierarchy can be said to have been conducive to the recent vigorous ascendance of Chinese capitalism remains a mystery. (This lowly status of the urban bourgeoisie was also true of the Japanese and other caste hierarchies, but obviously did not block the rise of Japanese capitalism with the Meiji restoration.)

Interestingly, the single most important Chinese intellectual movement in the twentieth century, and, arguably, in Chinese history was the May Fourth Movement of 1919, which denounced Confucianism as the greatest obstacle to the progress of the Chinese people and to the modernization of Chinese society. While there is much sympathy for this reaction to official Confucianism as the ideology of the state, it has been suggested that this led to throwing the baby out with the bath water. In the 1980s and 1990s, with growing recognition of the East Asian economic miracle, there was a corresponding appreciation that there was much in Confucianist teaching, norms and values to commend itself, especially if rescued from the self-serving mandarinate. With a sympathetic audience in the current liberal post-modernist intellectual clime in the West, some neo-Confucianist scholars have successfully sought to represent Confucianism as a progressive ideology for all times, for example, by conveniently obscuring its strongly patriarchal tenets.

Chinese business organization

Generally speaking, smaller Chinese enterprises are more likely to rely on more formally organized mutual aid associations, usually based on family, clan, village, province or area of origin or dialect group. Such relations and associations serve as a basis for mutual trust through which participants and members share information, make business connections, recruit employees, secure credit and so on at relatively low cost. Violation of such trust affects one's honour and reputation, and leads to social ostracization, which may not only adversely affect the individual concerned, but also his family, partners and so on, who are hence likely to exert pressure to conform. Such social sanctions are less costly but more effective than prosecution or litigation.

Conventional economic theory since Gary Becker's doctoral dissertation in the mid-1950s has asserted that discrimination against – and conversely, preferential treatment for – a particular group, say along ethnic lines, is costly, and therefore unlikely to be sustained over time. Discriminatory or preferential treatment, it is assumed, enables those who do not discriminate to buy or sell on more favourably competitive terms than others who discriminate. Clearly, such theory does not help explain the cohesiveness and other bases for entrepreneurial minority ethnic groups.

This singular emphasis on such costs from the perspective of conventional economic theory ignores the possible benefits of such discriminatory treatment. This static perspective also ignores the medium and long-term implications of such preferential treatment, e.g. in reducing transaction, transition and other costs associated with doing business in an uncertain and changing environment characterized by failures of the market (e.g. information asymmetries) as well as the state (e.g. poor legal framework). In such situations, informal arrangements become the bases for many lasting and often complex business relationships. Such arrangements are also generally less demanding, costly or time-consuming, thus facilitating business development in conditions of greater uncertainty and allowing more flexibility in doing business, besides reducing many business expenses.

Such informal arrangements thus facilitate efficient and flexible information transmission, supply of goods, credit and other financial arrangements. Since these arrangements are not based on national legal frameworks, they not only facilitate business relationships within national boundaries but also trans-border arrangements. Trust replaces the law, as mutual confidence replaces legally binding contracts in ensuring that commitments will be fulfilled.

The reliability of such inter-personal relations built on trust is especially crucial for effective transactions across legal systems or where the legal institutions are inadequate, or markets poorly developed. With a weak legal framework, transparency (e.g. disclosure requirements) and hence accountability may be inadequate, while contract law may be ambiguous or very difficult, time-consuming or costly to enforce. Information asymmetries are only one of several important sources of failure in commodity, labour as well as various financial markets.

As in much of the rest of the world, the family unit is the basis for many, if not most new ethnic Chinese business enterprises. However, extended kinship relations – whether 'real' or 'fictive' – seem to be the bases of more lasting and varied business relations among Chinese than most other ethnic groups, morally reinforced by numerous cultural norms and ethical values. Such ostensible kinship preference is easily perceived as ethnic preferences or discrimination by excluded 'outsiders', which has led to widespread resentment against ethnic Chinese businessmen and their apparent business practices by other 'excluded' ethnic and usually economically less successful cultural groups in Southeast Asia and elsewhere. Where such excluded ethnic majorities have been politically dominant, this has invariably led to various forms and degrees of Chinese political exclusion, raising the costs of doing business generally, and the costs of 'buying' political influence in particular, contributing to various rent-seeking arrangements and institutions.

In most family-run enterprises, agency problems, costs and risks are reduced, if not altogether eliminated, with the highly centralized nature of authority and decision-making, and the appointment of subordinate family members to key managerial positions. Business decisions are often informed if not influenced, but rarely determined by family and kinship considerations. While decision-making may well be quite rational from the perspective of the decision maker, the nature of the information and considerations likely to be employed suggest that 'intuition' as well as long-standing commitments and relations figure much more than in 'modern' corporate decision-making. Lack of transparency and limited outside access to privileged information have tended to mystify such decision-making considerations and contributed to the mystique of Chinese business.

The sources of strength of family enterprises are also the sources of weakness, i.e. the characteristics are double-edged. While agency problems may well be reduced, highly centralized decision-making by the family/business head and his closest aides can be problematic, if not disastrous. The desire for retaining direct family control could also limit the scope for expansion, though this does not seem to have been an important constraint on the emergence and expansion of very diversified Chinese family-controlled conglomerates.

The enigma of Chinese capital in Southeast Asia

Western anthropologists, sociologists and others used to explain East Asian, and particularly Chinese poverty in terms of Confucian and other ostensibly regressive values. By the 1980s, however, the situation had been reversed with an almost naive celebration of the ostensibly Confucian basis for the Japanese miracle and the rapid growth of the East Asian economies (Morishima 1982). The official rediscovery of Confucianism in Singapore since the 1980s has been government-sponsored and initiated by the Western-educated, suggesting that the contribution of culture there has hardly been traditional.

Confucianism has supposedly provided an important advantage over other cultural traditions because of its putative emphasis on diligence, loyalty and respect for authority. Such enthusiasm has, of course, been manifest in analyses of East Asian industrialization, especially since the Confucian credentials of the four 'first-tier' East Asian NIEs are not doubted. In any case, Confucianism has existed for millennia, which does not explain rapid industrialization in recent decades.

Some writers have gone further to attribute Thai, Malaysian and Indonesian economic performance to their respective Chinese minorities (e.g. Yoshihara 1988). Conversely, they blame Filipino underdevelopment on official repression of its ethnic Chinese minority (e.g. Yoshihara 1995), which makes it difficult to explain Malaysian and to a lesser extent Indonesian rapid growth until the mid-1990s.

Confucianism is often also invoked to explain the authoritarian nature of many East Asian newly industrializing economy (NIE) regimes. East Asians, it is suggested, are less resentful and more appreciative of such authoritarian regimes, especially if they are organized on a meritocratic basis. Most authoritarian East Asian regimes have sought and gained legitimacy by invoking external threats (North Korea in the case of the South, the communist-ruled mainland in the case of Taiwan and the surrounding Muslim Malay region in the case of Singapore). This has been complemented by achieving rapid growth and by ensuring socio-economic gains for most of the population through relatively egalitarian reforms and public expenditure.

The relative cultural homogeneity of Japan and the first-tier East Asian NIEs has probably facilitated supposed national consensus behind accelerated industrialization. These often simplistic cultural claims, however, do not seem to have stood up very well to counter-arguments. The East Asian NIEs are hardly culturally homogeneous, let alone simply Confucian. (Daoism and Buddhism have been influential, while the Western cultural impact has also been very significant, especially in Hong Kong and Singapore, while Christianity is the fastest growing religion in Korea today.) Regional conflict in South Korea is very significant. In the case of Taiwan, much of the island's political elite has comprised of refugees from the mainland and their descendants – which is important for understanding the main divide in Taiwanese politics since the 1950s. Until July 1997, Hong Kong was run by a British colonial elite and includes a significant ethnic Indian merchant community. Although Singapore is three-quarters Chinese, there have been significant tensions with the other ethnic minorities, especially Muslim Malays, who comprise 14 per cent of the population on an island surrounded by primarily Malay neighbours. Nevertheless, the virtual absence of serious ethnic troubles in the Northeast Asian NIEs stands in sharp contrast to the more ethnically divided societies of Southeast Asia such as Malaysia and Indonesia.

Some (e.g. Jesudason 1989; Bowie 1991; Yoshihara 1988, 1995) even argue that ethnic discrimination against Chinese has been responsible for the nature of much development policy and the problems of growth and industrialization in much of Southeast Asia. Ethnic redistribution goals have influenced the nature and quality of state interventions and the role of the public sector in much of Southeast Asia. Such priorities have, in turn, undermined the ability of Southeast Asian states (in Malaysia, Indonesia and the Philippines) to assume the kind of leading developmental role assumed by other newly industrializing country (NIC) states. It is argued that the politically dominant indigenous ethnic elites have emphasized inter-ethnic economic redistribution at the expense of other priorities. Consequently, alternative policy agendas more conducive to late industrialization efforts have been thwarted. There is certainly much merit in this argument, especially in its subtler versions, as there is little doubt that ethnic mobilization and concerns dominate politics and policy making in some Southeast Asian states.

A crucial question is whether or not there is or has been a capable and strong enough national bourgeoisie in the Southeast Asian context – even if only mainly from among the ranks of the Chinese businessmen – to have been able to effectively advance late industrialization. There are several reasons why the existence of such potential is doubted, beginning with the consequences of European colonialism. Unlike Japanese colonialism in South Korea and Taiwan, European colonial policies in Southeast Asia are believed to have strengthened the development of comprador or dependent elements of the primarily ethnic Chinese bourgeoisie. Hence, such interests have been integrated earlier on into international economic circuits as well as with foreign capital, at the expense of other business interests who might have been more inclined to undertake or support nationalist economic projects.

No strong post-colonial bourgeoisies clearly committed to nationalistic agendas have emerged beyond those who call for greater protection against transnational capital. Hence, not surprisingly, while import-substituting industrialization was being officially encouraged, the success of Chinese businessmen in Thailand, in Indonesia in the 1950s and in Malaysia in the 1960s caused non-Chinese – mainly ethnically 'indigenous' political elite – resentment against the Chinese to grow in these societies. Consequently, there were corresponding increases in official anti-Chinese discrimination in Thailand in the 1930s and 1950s, in Indonesia from the 1950s and in Malaysia especially after 1969. Ethnic Chinese business investments in the region, especially in Malaysia and Indonesia, over the last three decades suggest a greater inclination to invest in protected import-substituting manufacturing, finance, real property and other speculative, but fast (short-termist), high-yielding activities. Internationally competitive, export-oriented industrial production has generally only developed with state support and other advantages, e.g. 'natural protection' for resource-based industries. This pattern may well reflect rational responses to the investment environment, as shaped by state intervention and prevailing economic and political considerations.

Business uncertainty has been accentuated in much of the region by the presence of hostile, alien or simply unsupportive or unreliable states. Whether colonial, nationalist, ethnically discriminatory, communist party-led or simply predatory, most governments in the region can hardly be said to be the first preference of most investors. Hence, it appears that a distinct idiom of Chinese capitalism has developed in response to perceived, if not real hostility by the governments in Malaysia and Indonesia. Even in Thailand, which was never formally colonized by any European power, and where Buddhism is said to have allowed a greater degree of Chinese assimilation into the host society, it has been argued that anti-Chinese sentiment has been significant, especially during the early 1950s.

In combination with Islam, anti-Chinese sentiment in the Malay world is considered to be especially potent, as in Indonesia, Malaysia and Brunei, though it is far from unknown in the Christian Philippines (Yoshihara 1995). This was officially institutionalized with the *Benteng* (fortress) policy in Indonesia in the early 1950s (Robison 1986). The promulgation of the New Economic Policy (NEP) in Malaysia from 1971 has had the declared intention of achieving economic parity between the politically dominant Malays and the commercially ubiquitous Chinese. This policy priority is expressed in terms of the NEP goal of 'restructuring society to eliminate the identification of race with economic function' between the indigenes (*Bumiputeras*) and the non-indigenes (non-*Bumiputeras*) (Jesudason 1989: 71).

Ethnic Chinese businessmen in any Southeast Asian economy are far from homogeneous. In Malaysia, for instance, an economic cum political spectrum of Chinese capitalists has developed historically. At one end, there were the usually English-educated, often Straits-born Chinese – some of whom (the *Babas*) were quite alienated from Han Chinese culture and language – presumed to be collaborating with and subservient to foreign, especially British, interests producing for export. The dominance of British imports was ensured through policies of Imperial (later in the early post-colonial period, Commonwealth) Preference. At the other end were the small Chinese-educated businessmen manufacturing for the domestic market despite harassment by the colonial state. Of course, most Chinese capitalists were not neatly positioned at either pole or extremity, but rather, lay – inconveniently, for the purposes of such analysis – somewhere in between, in what undoubtedly involved more than two dimensions.

'Chinese' capital seems more ascendant in Thailand, even though ethnic Chinese only command a demographic majority in Singapore, where the state's strategy for growth and industrialization seems to have privileged foreign, especially technologically dynamic, capital. Yet, Chinese capital accumulation is proceeding rapidly in the rest of the region, despite the apparently hostile Muslim Malay-dominated states of Indonesia, Malaysia and Brunei. Some Chinese have undoubtedly bought themselves political influence and lucrative business or rentier opportunities in these states (the Indonesian *cukongs* or the Malaysian *Babas*). However, the vast majority probably resent, and hence tend to evade and bypass the state if possible, and have consequently developed a distinctive 'overseas or Southeast Asian Chinese' business idiom heavily reliant on informal credit, contracts and networks based on personal trust and kinship, real as well as contrived.

However, despite the important differences in context among, say, China, Taiwan, Hong Kong, Singapore and possibly Thailand on the one hand, and Muslim Malay Southeast Asia on the other, relations between capital and the state in both situations are generally less than collusive – although individual rentiers might be otherwise privileged (e.g. see Gomez 1999). Hence, such relations in the rest of the East Asian region are quite different from those obtaining in the Northeast Asian economies of Japan and South Korea, especially in terms of the absence of strong corporatist arrangements. Where the state is less sympathetic or even hostile, this idiom has taken on some characteristics of what might colourfully be described as insurgent or guerrilla capitalism based on institutions rooted in culture and community sanction, rather than systems of law and regulation enforced by the state.

Yet, some of the very features of this Chinese capitalism, which have enabled it to thrive in hostile or adverse circumstances, have also limited the development of such business enterprises. Business uncertainty stemming from such insecurity tends to encourage short-termism; such short-termism is generally inimical to the long-term commitment required for most productive investments, especially in heavy industry, high technology, research and development, as well as investments in marketing such as brand-name promotion. Such insecurity also tends to encourage the 'hedging of bets', e.g. by not 'putting all one's eggs in one (national) basket', thus inadvertently encouraging 'foot-looseness' and 'capital flight'.

In such circumstances, economic liberalization may actually open up new opportunities for capital outflows, thus eventually contributing to capital flight in particularly adverse circumstances. Hence, it is not surprising that Indonesian and other Southeast Asian Chinese buy real estate and otherwise invest in Singapore and elsewhere, not because of particularly favourable rates of return, but with a view to 'balancing one's investment portfolio'. There are other – not insurmountable – problems as well, including the well-known problems of family businesses, especially when they grow large, such as the failure of businesses to be organized meritocratically, and other problems posed by second and third-generation family business leaders.

Bibliography

Alatas, Syed Hussein (1972) 'The Weber Thesis and Southeast Asia', in *Modernization and Social Change: Studies in Modernization, Religion, Social Change and Development in Southeast Asia*. London: Angus and Robertson.

Bowie, Alisdair (1991) *Crossing the Industrial Divide: State, Society, and the Politics of Economic Transformation in Malaysia*. New York: Columbia University Press.

Buss, Andreas (1986) 'Max Weber's Heritage and Modern Southeast Asian Thinking on Development', in Bruce Matthews and Judith Nagata (eds) *Religion, Values and Development in Southeast Asia*. Singapore: Institute of Southeast Asian Studies.

Butcher, John and Howard Dick (eds) (1993) *The Rise and Fall of Revenue Farming: Business Elites and the Emergence of the Modern State in Southeast Asia*. London: Macmillan.

Chia Oai Peng (1987) 'Trust and Credit among Chinese Businessmen in Kelantan'. *Southeast Asian Business*, 14, Summer: 28–31.

Chia Oai Peng (1991) 'The Chinese in Kuala Krai: A Study of Commerce and Social Life in a Malaysian Town'. PhD thesis, University of Malaya, Kuala Lumpur.

Chun, Allen J. (1989) 'Pariah Capitalism and the Overseas Chinese of Southeast China: Problems in the Definition of the Problem'. *Ethnic and Racial Studies*, 12(2): 233–56.

DeGlopper, Donald R. (1972) 'Doing business in Lukang', in W.E. Willmott (ed.) *Economic Organization in Chinese Society*. Stanford, CA: Stanford University Press.

Fields, Karl (1995) *Enterprise and the State in Korea and Taiwan*. Ithaca: Cornell University Press.

Freedman, Maurice (1959) 'The Handling of Money: A Note on the Background to the Economic Sophistication of Overseas Chinese'. *Man*, 89, April: 64–5.

Freedman, Maurice (1965) *Lineage Organisation in South-eastern China*. London: Athlone Press.

Fukuyama, Francis (1995) *Trust*. New York: Free Press.

Gates, Hill (1996) *China's Motor: A Thousand Years of Petty Capitalism*. Ithaca and London: Cornell University Press.

Goldberg, Michael A. (1985) *The Chinese Connection: Getting Plugged in to Pacific Rim Real Estate, Trade and Capital Markets*. Vancouver, BC: University of British Columbia Press.

Gomez, Edmund Terence (1999) *Chinese Business in Malaysia: Accumulation, Accommodation, and Ascendance*. Honolulu: University of Hawaii Press (copublished, Surrey: Curzon Press).

Gomez, E.T. and Jomo K.S. (1997) *Malaysia's Political Economy*. Cambridge: Cambridge University Press (1999, second edition).

Hamilton, Gary (ed.) (1991) *Business Networks and Economic Development in East and Southeast Asia*. Hong Kong: Centre of Asian Studies, University of Hong Kong.

Jackson, James C. (1968) *Planters and Speculators: Chinese and European Agricultural Enterprise in Malaya, 1786–1921*. Kuala Lumpur: University of Malaya Press.

Jesudason, James V. (1989) *Ethnicity and the Economy: The State, Chinese Business and Multinationals in Malaysia*. Singapore: Oxford University Press.

Kao, John (1993) 'The World-wide Web of Chinese Business'. *Harvard Business Review*, March–April: 24–37.

Khoo Kay Kim (1988) 'Chinese Economic Activities in Malaya: A Historical Perspective', in Manning Nash (ed.) *Economic Performance in Malaysia*. New York: Professors World Peace Academy.

King, Ambrose Yeo-chi (1991) 'Kuan-hsi and Network Building: A Sociological Interpretation'. *Daedalus*, 120(2), Spring: 63–84.

Li, Tania M. (1989) *The Malays in Singapore*. Singapore: Oxford University Press.

Lim, Linda Y.C. (1983) 'Chinese Economic Activity in Southeast Asia: An Introductory Review', in Linda Y.C. Lim and L.A. Peter Gosling (eds) *The Chinese in Southeast Asia: Ethnicity and Economic Activity*, vol. 1. Singapore: Maruzen Asia.

Limlingan, Victor Simpao (1986) *The Overseas Chinese in ASEAN: Business Strategies and Management Practices*. Manila: Vita Development Corporation.

Mackie, Jamie (1991) 'Towkays and Tycoons: The Chinese in Indonesian Economic Life in the 1920s and 1980s'. *Indonesia*, Special Issue on 'The Role of the Indonesian Chinese in Shaping Modern Indonesia Life', pp. 83–96.

Morishima Michio (1982) *Why Has Japan 'Succeeded'?: Western Technology and the Japanese Ethos*. Cambridge: Cambridge University Press.

Redding, S. Gordon (1990) *The Spirit of Chinese Capitalism*. Berlin: de Gruyter.

Robison, Richard (1986) *Indonesia and the Rise of Capital*. Sydney: Allen and Unwin.

Shieh, G.S. (1992) *'Boss' Island: The Subcontracting Network and Micro-Entrepreneurship in Taiwan's Development*. New York: Peter Lang.

Silin, Robert H. (1972) 'Marketing and Credit in a Hong Kong Wholesale Market', in W.E. Willmott (ed.) *Economic Organization in Chinese Society*. Stanford, CA: Stanford University Press.

Simoniya, N.A. (1961) *Overseas Chinese in Southeast Asia: A Russian Study*. Ithaca, NY: Southeast Asia Program, Cornell University.

Skinner, G. William (1957) *Chinese Society in Thailand: An Analytical History*. Ithaca, NY: Cornell University Press.

Skinner, G. William (1958) *Leadership and Power in the Chinese Community of Thailand*. Ithaca, NY: Cornell University Press.

Skinner, G. William (1964) 'Marketing and Social Structure in Rural China – Part 1'. *Journal of Asian Studies*, 24 (1): 3–43.

Skinner, G. William (1965a) 'Marketing and Social Structure in Rural China – Part 2'. *Journal of Asian Studies*, 24 (2): 195–228.

Skinner, G. William (1965b) 'Marketing and Social Structure in Rural China – Part 3'. *Journal of Asian Studies*, 24 (3): 363–99.

Song Ong Siang (1984) *One Hundred Years' History of the Chinese in Singapore*. London: John Murray, 1923; reprint, Singapore: Oxford University Press.

Suryadinata, Leo (1988) 'Chinese Economic Elites in Indonesia: A Preliminary Study', in Jennifer Cushman and Wang Gungwu (eds) *Changing Identities of the Southeast Asian Chinese Since World War II*. Hong Kong: Hong Kong University Press.

Tai Hung-chao (ed.) (1989) *Confucianism and Economic Development: An Oriental Alternative?* Washington, DC: Washington Institute for Values in Public Policy.

Tan Chee Beng (1994) 'Culture and Economic Performance with Special Reference to the Chinese in Southeast Asia', in Teresita Ang See and Go Bon Juan (eds) *The Ethnic Chinese: Proceedings of the International Conference on 'Changing Identities and Relations in Southeast Asia'*. Manila: Kaisa Para Sa Kaunlaran.

Tan, Mely G. (1987) 'The Role of Ethnic Chinese Minority in Development: The Indonesian Case'. *Southeast Asian Studies*, 25(3): 367–71.

T'ien Ju K'ang (1953) *The Chinese of Sarawak: A Study of Social Structure*. LSE Monographs on Social Anthropology, no. 14, London.

Trocki, Carl (1996) 'Boundaries and Transgressions: Chinese Enterprise in Eighteenth and Nineteenth-century Southeast Asia', in Aihwa Ong and Donald Nonini (eds) *Ungrounded Empires: The Cultural Politics of Modern Chinese Transnationalism*. London: Routledge.

Unger, Danny (1998) *Building Social Capital in Thailand: Fibers, Finance, and Infrastructure*. Cambridge: Cambridge University Press.

Vaughan, J. D. (1971) *The Manners and Customs of the Chinese of the Straits Settlements*. Singapore, 1879; reprint, Kuala Lumpur: Oxford University Press.

Wang Gungwu (1991a) 'Among Non-Chinese', *Daedalus*, 120(2), Spring: 135–58.

Wang Gungwu (1991b) 'Little Dragons on the Confucian Periphery', in Wang Gungwu (ed.) *China and the Overseas Chinese*. Singapore: Times Academic Press.

Weber, Max (1951a) *The Religion of China: Confucianism and Taoism*, translated by Hans Gerth, edited with an introduction by C. K. Yang. New York: Free Press.

Weber, Max (1951b) *The Protestant Ethic and the Spirit of Capitalism*, translated by Talcott Parsons. New York: Charles Scribner and Sons.

Wickberg, Edgar (1965) *The Chinese in Philippine Life, 1850–1898*. New Haven: Yale University Press.

Wolf, Margery (1970) 'Child Training and the Chinese Family', in Maurice Freedman (ed.) *Family and Kinship in Chinese Society*. Stanford, CA: Stanford University Press.

Wu, David Y. H. (1974) 'To Kill Three Birds with One Stone: The Rotating Credit Associations of the Papua New Guinea Chinese'. *American Ethnologist*, 1(3): 565–84.

Wu, David Y. H. (1977) 'Ethnicity and Adaptation: Overseas Chinese Entrepreneurship in Papua New Guinea'. *Southeast Asian Journal of Social Science*, 5(1–2): 85–95.

Wu, David Y. H. (1982) *The Chinese in Papua New Guinea: 1880–1980*. Hong Kong: Chinese University Press.

Yang Lien-sheng (1952) *Money and Credit in China: A Short History*. Cambridge, MA: Harvard University Press.

Yoshihara Kunio (1987) 'The Problem of Continuity in Chinese Businesses in Southeast Asia'. *Southeast Asian Studies*, 25(3): 112–29.

Yoshihara Kunio (1988) *The Rise of Ersatz Capitalism in Southeast Asia*. Singapore: Oxford University Press.

Yoshihara Kunio (1995) *The Nation and Economic Growth: The Philippines and Thailand*. Kuala Lumpur: Oxford University Press.

3 The politics of 'seeing Chinese' and the evolution of a Chinese idiom of business

Alex G. Bardsley

Part I: How capital is (de)classified as Chinese

Before the financial crisis of 1997, the rapid development of several Southeast Asian economies (Singapore, Thailand, Malaysia, Indonesia), coming in the wake of East Asian 'successes' (Korea, Taiwan, Hong Kong), had started a hunt for the keys to this success. The crisis, in turn, has generated interest in the causes of economic collapse in several Southeast Asian countries as well as South Korea. Of the many common factors among the Southeast Asian cases, one stands out as apparently particular to the region: the prominence of people of Chinese descent in business. Although comprising a (sometimes tiny) minority in every Southeast Asian country except Singapore, ethnic Chinese are said to own and control a disproportionate amount of private domestic capital in each of the rapidly developing economies, and several of the others as well. When this observation is added to the Chinese character of two of the three East Asian NIEs and the acceleration of growth in China itself, it looks like a tempting line of investigation. Laying aside the question of how ethnic Chinese business might have contributed to the growth to be explained, much of the literature to date addresses a question that is as old as European colonialism in Southeast Asia:[1] 'why do the Chinese dominate business?'

A difficult question,[2] but what is important for our purposes is that it is impossible to answer in the terms in which it is posed. In investigating the problems and progress of the recent literature on overseas Chinese business, we will approach the question, 'why do the Chinese dominate business?', not as a question to be answered but more as a problem to be solved. The question conceals a number of other terms that need to be teased out and examined. We will find that the original terms in which the question is posed obscure both the relations of Chinese business to the broader political and economic environments, and the organising principles of the phenomenon 'Chinese business' itself. These organising principles comprise a kind of 'social know-how',[3] which is formulated, transferred and expressed in 'Chinese' terms, but which is not essentially Chinese.

The import of seeing 'Chinese'

The terms of the question, 'why do the Chinese dominate business?', beg another question, 'who are the (overseas) Chinese?'. This second question has produced many descriptive responses, and a number of tentative definitions,[4] but the root of the question has yet to be addressed: precisely what kind of category is 'the Chinese'? It is, on the one hand, a generic label for an ill-defined group, but since, as Weber remarks (1968: 395), 'the concept of the "ethnic" group...dissolves if we define our terms exactly', what the term denotes depends more on the argument being made than on any real-world referent. To illustrate, let us examine what 'the Chinese' does and does not define, and how the category operates.

For one thing, 'Chinese' does not define nationality, at least not with reference to people of Chinese descent in the ASEAN countries today. In every one of these countries except Brunei,[5] almost all the residents of Chinese descent are citizens.[6] As citizens, they are variously Thai, Malaysian and so forth. Thus, if the level of analysis is national-political, and 'Chineseness' is introduced, it has to be introduced on the left, as it were: Chinese (or Sino-) Indonesians, not Indonesian Chinese. While states might have their own definitions of 'Chinese', these do not apply consistently across the region or across time.

Once upon a time, 'the Chinese' defined a race, unproblematically. Race was a supposedly biological category, and as such, was totalisingly ascriptive. Nowadays, 'race' has, with a few troubling exceptions, been replaced by 'ethnicity', and it is usually in ethnic terms that 'the Chinese' are defined, though not without caveat. Yoshihara, for example, states that 'the Chinese in this book [!] come close to the people who are called "ethnic Chinese" ' (Yoshihara 1988: 37). After some elaboration, he concludes:

> The Chinese thus include three groups. One comprises immigrants from China who speak Chinese [*sic*]; another those who were born in Southeast Asia and speak Chinese; and the third, possibly the largest, consists of people who were born in Southeast Asia (sometimes in China) and do not speak Chinese, but who may have Chinese values (or the values of their Chinese *fathers*, which are substantively different from those of the indigenous population) and/or personal ties with the first two groups, which they may use to advantage in business.
>
> (Yoshihara 1988: 39, emphasis mine)

Were this a definition, it would be a remarkably inclusive one. Leaving aside the conflation of many Chinese languages into one, we may nevertheless easily imagine a Southeast Asian who speaks a Chinese language but is not a 'Chinese', or a Southeast Asian 'who may have Chinese values...or personal ties' to 'Chinese' but is not a 'Chinese' herself. And what about Southeast Asians with 'Chinese' mothers, but non-'Chinese' fathers?[7] Yoshihara's is not a definition, however, but a 'practical guide', and the guideposts are markers or signs of 'Chineseness', signs whose meanings are ambiguous, situational and contingent. We still do not know what Chinese ethnicity is, but we are told how to recognise it.

There are a couple of neat efforts at deconstructing 'Chineseness': Kasian Tejapira's 'Pigtail' (1992), and a paper by Vivienne Wee (1988). The gist of their arguments is that 'Chinese' is a historically constructed identity; that the agent that initially defines 'Chinese' is external; and that the mechanism of definition is political. Historically, among emigrants from China, narrower identities had a greater pull. These identities, sort of sub-ethnicities, were similarly contingent, and their naming is significant. Individually, their names (e.g. Hokkien, Teochew) referred to locations in China, specifically to territorially-defined political units of various sizes, and by extension to the people who came from them and the languages ('real' ones this time) those people spoke.[8] The lack of consensus among scholars about how to term these identities collectively (speech groups, dialect groups – see Skinner 1957: 35) points to their uncertain location in tacitly national frames of reference.

To inquire into the persistence or disappearance of these sub-ethnic identities would take us far afield.[9] The point is to problematise the ascriptive and categorical characters of the term 'Chinese'. Let us imagine, for a moment, that the waves of colonialism had washed over south China after 1842, creating British Guangdong, French Fujian, etc., and then receded, leaving independent states behind. 'Cantonese' might then be a nationality at home, and an ethnicity elsewhere, while 'Chinese' might be analogous to 'European' – that is, an abstract idea, detached from any ascriptive ethnic identity (or threatening political entity). Why then does 'Chinese' seem so natural? Why does a term that should be abstract and descriptive (Chinese 'style' capitalism, like European 'style' colonialism) tend to reify into something essential and ascriptive?

I would suggest that this way of seeing homogeneous, eternal 'Chinese' was originally a European, especially Dutch and British conceit, a conception born of the wider world-view and the mercantile organisation and orientation of the great trading companies – and not from 'European culture' as such (see Anderson 1991: 167–8, on Chinees and sangley). In the 1600s, the English and Dutch East India Companies roamed the world as mercantilist teams, competing on a proto-national basis with, among others, the Spaniards and the Portuguese (who had previously divided the world between themselves, with the blessing of the Pope – thus giving the Iberian project an unbounded religious legitimation). To the northern Europeans, 'the Chinese' were another 'team'.

Whatever the supposed motivational force of the Protestant ethic, Protestantism was having a systematic effect on the organisation of societies in northern Europe. It contributed to the erosion of ascribed, stratified status (the estates) by alternatively legitimating achieved status. While the estates in Europe would ultimately be replaced by a less rigid system of classes, this new evaluative framework placed a premium on vertical, ascriptive differentiation between peoples, and by extension, races. The trick of colonialism was to make race the 'legitimate' basis of a hierarchical, 'caste' system (see Wertheim 1964: 73–5). Wertheim argues:

But without a certain degree of acceptance of mutual roles and a measure of internalisation of the values imposed by the dominant group, the social structure could not last even for one day. A society held together only by force is a rare phenomenon indeed. The secret of any domination is a partial imposition of one's own value system upon the members of the dominated groups.

(Wertheim 1964: 68–9)

This sounds rather like Gramscian hegemony (Gramsci 1971: 12). Thus, both evaluative frameworks, ascriptive status (expressed in racialism) and achieved status (implied in capitalism), were contained in colonialism, creating tension in the colonial system. European attitudes towards Chinese economic activity were strikingly ambivalent. Though European profits often depended on Chinese economic activity, colonial rulers' anxieties focused on 'the Chinese' as the most 'capitalist', and hence, most upwardly mobile subject group: Chinese business may have threatened European interests, but it certainly threatened white status.

Still, our concern here is not so much where this way of seeing 'Chinese' came from, but how it operates analytically. The problem lies not with abstractions as such – where they describe patterns, processes, relations or structures – but that some abstractions (the Chinese, the state, capital) are treated as actors, and monolithic ones at that. Ruth McVey makes this point:

Generally, studies dealing with economic transformations are peopled with abstractions...whose struggles determine the outcomes. In the presence of such titans the endeavours of mere humans seem the dithering of ants.... [M]uch of the argument...has turned on...questions about the doers rather than the done.

(McVey 1992: 8)

In some cases, it is the state that appears as 'a monolithic and decisive entity' (McVey 1992: 14) – its internal conflicts and its unintended effects disregarded – while in others, the Chinese and capital play similar roles.

The question, 'why do the Chinese dominate business?', simply cannot address these concerns. Without, I hope, being too mechanical, we can restate the first half easily enough as, 'how does Chinese (style) business...', but the second half threatens to become an absurdity: '...dominate capital'! The issue here is one of ownership and control, and it is usually handled within the framework of political economy.

Controlling ownership and owning control

While works in a political-economic vein tend to focus on capital, capitalism and the state, we should note that even among these, the category 'Chinese' frequently intrudes. Yoshihara (1988: 37) and Robison (1986: 271) devote separate chapters to 'Chinese capital' and 'Chinese-owned capital' respectively. Suehiro

(1992: 39–40) plays down the Chineseness of capital, but still uses the ethnic character of 'dominant capitalist groups' to distinguish Chinese from European and Thai *sakdina* groups. Hewison (1989: 72), for his part, endeavours to resist intrusion by ethnic or cultural theories into his argument, but still notes that, under the first Phibun regime, 'the ethnic Chinese remained economically dominant'.[10] With the exception of Yoshihara, however, these are all single country studies, in which specific governments enacted and expressed specific (if variable) definitions of 'Chinese': and so 'Chinese' enters the analysis through state policy, rather than as a category a priori. 'Chinese' then, again except for Yoshihara, may denote, historically and nationally, specific political classifications of fractions of capital.[11]

While some theories of capital emphasise capitalists expressing their common interests as a class in conflict with other classes, other approaches to political economy divide capital into fractions, usually by sector, industry or even size, on the grounds that these fractions will have competing interests, and that this competition will be expressed politically as well.[12] Commonly, however, capital is also divided according to the (supposed) political loyalties of its owners, with the expectation (or fear) that these loyalties will somehow be expressed economically. To the extent that economies and markets are separated by political boundaries, these distinctions are seen to have real consequences. The concern, most aggressively argued by dependency theorists, that foreign firms will repatriate their profits, subordinate local capital and suborn local political elites is an example of this.[13] The discursive distinction between foreign and domestic capital is a powerful one, even if the interplay between 'interests' and 'loyalties' remains poorly thought out. Deciding into which category 'Chinese' capital falls, however, is not easy.

This is a point of contention in the literature that evokes some forceful assertions. Suehiro reasons:

> However, although the dominant domestic capitalist groups of Thailand have always been ethnic Chinese, they have mostly been locally born, hold Thai nationality, and use the Thai language; younger business leaders have been educated entirely in Thai schools. Unlike the pre-war period, most Chinese business leaders hold their economic stake within the country. For these reasons, I do not define these capitalists as alien but include them as 'domestic' or 'Thai' businessmen.[14]
>
> (Suehiro 1992: 39–40)

McVey asserts:

> In this connection we need to remember that the region's Chinese are a settled minority and function as domestic capitalists. Hence, Southeast Asia's capitalism is not affected systematically by the ethnicity of its business class. Certainly the international character of the overseas Chinese diaspora gives

a particular fluidity to Southeast Asian Chinese business organisations and capital placement, but this does not constitute a fundamental difference...
(McVey 1992: 18)

Hamilton (1996b: 331), on the other hand, declares: 'Chinese capitalism is *not* a domestic capitalism (i.e. the product of indigenous economic growth), but rather is integral to world capitalism itself.' Hamilton clearly means something quite different by 'domestic capitalism' (something 'authentically indigenous'?), and we may wonder how such a thing could *not* be integral to 'world capitalism', with all accumulation contained within the domestic market, thus a *separate* system? Or does he mean a (culturally) *different* system? We can see the sort of signs that fly around the term 'domestic': national identity of ownership, placement of investment, residence of ownership, 'function', and on the other side, 'indigenousness'.

The definitional blurring of Chinese capital, capitalists and capitalism is again a matter of optics. One distorting factor here, in addition to those examined earlier, is the conflation of nation with state (see Anderson 1990: 94–6). Regimes themselves are prone to identify both policy goals (which may express parochial interests), and the 'interests' of the state as an institution, with national interests, in order to borrow some of the nation's legitimacy. In a way, this is a natural process: the right to rule of most states today depends on their 'marriage' to a nation. What is interesting is how many scholars – particularly those concerned with policy or else inclined to view the state as a 'monolithic and decisive entity', as actor – see their subjects through the same state-centric, 'nation-state' optic.

As a result, although the national status of Chinese capital in the ASEAN countries should be uncontroversial, in some cases, it is not. Where the political loyalties of Chinese capital are suspect, as in Malaysia and Indonesia,[15] the domestic status of Chinese capital comes into question, and the questioning is often publicly expressed in nationalist rhetoric. Once the optic is corrected, however, it should become clear that Chinese capital has to be 'domesticated', not because it is alien in relation to the nation, but because, to the state, it is 'wild'.[16] State-owned and state-connected enterprises are common in Southeast Asia, partly in order to 'domesticate' and subordinate not just Chinese capital, but capital itself. Where non-state local capital is mostly Chinese-owned, two kinds of potential 'disloyalty' intersect, and are compounded by the competitive interests of state capital. Nowhere, even in Thailand or the Philippines, has a national bourgeoisie yet been able to politically express its interests as a class over those of government elites with consistent success: the 'wildness' of Chinese capital reflects these elites' anxiety that capital may not only escape subordination to the state, but may, in turn, subordinate the state to its interests.

Another factor contributing to the gap between a national definition of 'domestic' and a state-centred definition is the identification of the state with an alternative source of legitimacy: indigenism.[17] Indigenousness is a constructed political identity through which a group justifies its control over a territory by prior (and so primary) claim to possession of that territory. Prior possession is the basis of ownership most widely recognised as legitimate, while ownership is similarly the most widely recognised claim to legitimate control.[18] The trick lies in making this claim exclusive. One way of finessing the trick is the discursive conflation of ethnic identity with territory. Terms meaning 'sons of the soil' are not rare in post-colonial societies (see Horowitz 1985); pribumi in Indonesia and bumiputra in Malaysia have both served to wed an ascriptive identity to the land. To the extent that indigenism appropriates the two standard determinants of nationality, jus sanguinis and jus soli, and makes them interdependent, claims to citizenship and full participation in national sovereignty on the basis of jus soli alone are pre-empted: sovereignty 'belongs' to the rightful owners of the country.[19]

But indigenism, where it occurs, involves not just ownership and control of the country, but of the country's wealth as well. Wealth in capitalist Southeast Asia represents social prestige as well as economic power. In the context of competition between indigenous and non-indigenous groups, controlling wealth and the ownership of wealth are political concerns.[20] It is the success of some ethnic Chinese that challenges indigenous prestige. The legitimacy of Chinese ownership of wealth becomes questionable, and the language used to question it is similar to that once used by colonial administrations to describe the success of their non-European competitors.[21] Businesses, industries and whole economies are said to be 'in the hands of', 'controlled' or 'dominated' by Chinese. This language does a number of things. First, it erases the legitimacy of ownership. Second, it elides the workings of capitalism: a firm may be controlled through minority ownership, or the market for a particular product may be dominated through a commanding market share, but these processes are not the issue. What the language implies is power, not just the use or employment of capital, but total and possibly co-ordinated control: 'the Chinese' (as one) dominate (by means of unspecified, but nonetheless threatening) business, etc. Poorly documented statistics regarding the 'Chinese share' of national wealth are cited everywhere; statistics regarding the concentration of wealth within the Chinese community, on the one hand, or nationality without regard to ethnicity, on the other, are unavailable or unremarked.

What is disturbing, is the persistence of this discourse outside countries where indigenism is an issue, and its prevalence throughout the literature on Southeast Asian Chinese business. While it is quite possible that in some of the literature, the impulse is to question the legitimacy of capital ownership itself, and not Chinese ownership as such, the rhetorical effect is much the same: a monolithically conceived group is sinisterly linked to a monolithically conceived source of power and prestige. Why this is so is hard to say, except that McVey's 'titans' – in this case, the state, the Chinese, and capital, and as we shall see, culture – seem powerful enough to take over the studies of which they are the subjects.

Organising legitimacy

The contemporary Western faith in impersonal relations and administrative institutions obscures their normative character, to the point where the system they constitute appears as natural fact. A degree of common acceptance, however, is required to allow a social system to 'last even for one day' (Wertheim 1964:68). Acceptance involves recognition of the legitimacy of the framework in which social relations and behaviour are evaluated.[22] Systems of social evaluation reflect, legitimise and reproduce systems of social relations. They are the media in which political and economic power are organised and perpetuated.

European colonialism introduced new evaluative frameworks, along with new political and economic systems, to societies in Southeast Asia. These included the privileging of upward mobility implicit in capitalist activity, but also the racialist categorisation of peoples that restricted and channelled mobility. The colonial division of labour (which was reproduced in similar form in Siam)[23] directed immigrants from China into certain economic roles, among them wage labour and trading. Often unintentionally, this encouraged upward mobility within the limits of these roles. But systems of social evaluation and social relations that immigrants brought from China contributed to the formation of new institutions overseas in the colonial context and the post-colonial era. The question is what kind of institutions, and how they have developed.

Essentialist cultural explanations: the rise of ersatz Confucianism

The explicitly normative content of contemporary Chinese businessmen's own discourse on business behaviour has sent observers searching for a cultural explanation. This is partly because the observers do not recognise the normative aspects of political and economic systems themselves, and partly a matter of 'seeing Chinese'. The influence of social organisation on culture, as opposed to culture's impact on society, is underplayed. Hunting something 'authentically Chinese', they focus on socially-constructed identities they imagine to be primordial and unique: as McVey (1992:19) puts it, 'assigning a rigidity and consistency to cultures which they do not possess'. 'Following' Weber, they argue that culture motivates behaviour, and they point to Confucianism as the source of ethics in Chinese culture. Bits of the Confucian canon are cited, although ethnic Chinese business-men themselves use non-Confucian terms; and questions of how high Confucian values might have been transferred and mediated in their passage from the imperial state cult to contemporary business practices outside China are fudged with references to 'bourgeois Confucianism' and folk religious influences.[24] A host of observed social patterns (familialism, paternalism, personalism) are described as being derived from Confucian values, and thus, essentially Chinese. By seeking to embed ethnic Chinese businessmen and women in 'their' homogeneous, eternal culture, this line of argument detaches Chinese (style) business from the wider web of political and economic relations that condition it.

We have examined how the question 'why do the Chinese dominate business?' carries concealed political anxieties about loyalties to state, nation and ethnic group, as well as tensions regarding capitalism, power and the legitimate expression of interests. Such congeries of political issues pile up at the base of a signpost marked 'Chinese', though they have little to do with 'Chineseness' per se. Our task in the second part of this study will be to locate 'Chineseness', or at least a

Chinese idiom of business, by asking a very different question, 'how does Chinese (style) business employ capital?' Bearing the lessons of the first section in mind, we will ask how the Chinese business idiom in Southeast Asia works, how 'Chinese' it is, and perhaps how the idiom might serve as a model for business activity in other developing countries.

Part II: How a Chinese idiom of business evolved

In the first half of this study, we looked at the way the use of some concepts, among them, 'the Chinese', the state and capital, has clouded discussions of the role of ethnic Chinese in the developing economies of Southeast Asia, in part because of the political charge these concepts carry. These topics will be revisited in this section, but with a more historical eye, and with the intention of teasing out factors that inform what we will call a Chinese idiom of business. To the extent that this idiom constitutes a Chinese style of capitalism, it should be regarded as part and parcel of global capitalism, and not as an independent system. Similarly, local variation across Southeast Asia suggests the idea should not be accorded too much integrity. Finally, this idiom, as a social phenomenon, is subject to change over time. What will be described then is a pattern whose lineaments are marked by commonality across the region, difference from the encompassing system, and the shape of its historical trajectory. Clearly, in a study the length of this one, such a pattern can only be sketched.

The idiom of Southeast Asian Chinese business consists of the principles by which various factors of production are organised socially. That is, Chinese business mobilises resources – labour, capital, technology – in a system of communally accepted legitimacy.[25] The legitimacy of the system within the community is such that business has often not needed to rely on the state to the same degree that capitalism elsewhere has – either to regulate and legitimise the social relations of production, or to support the kind of formal financial institutions on which other styles of capitalism depend today.[26] This, however, is changing, and fast. As system trust in, and the prestige of, 'modern' administrative institutions increases, and as these institutions themselves develop in Southeast Asia, greater reliance is placed on them, and the particular idiom of Southeast Asian Chinese business becomes less distinctive.

Bringing the state in backwards

One common factor that has influenced the development of ethnic Chinese social systems historically and across Southeast Asia is the relations of these systems to the state, be it dynastic, colonial, or more recently, national. Government in south China under the Qing and in many of the European colonies was initially indirect. Even as rule became increasingly direct (generally around the turn of the twentieth century), it could still be described as indifferent, often ineffective, or even hostile to the interests of Chinese subjects or citizens. As a result, a number of institutional forms developed among ethnic Chinese social groups to handle political as well as other social functions that the state did not.

The state in imperial China did not penetrate deeply into society. The lowest unit of administration was at the district level. In south China under the Qing, an average district encompassed a great deal of territory and some 250,000 inhabitants (Ng 1992: 7). The district magistrate had little in the way of staff, and by law, had to come from another province. Even if he was Chinese and not Manchu, it was unlikely he spoke the local language. The imperial state provided few services, discouraged civil lawsuits, yet was 'most reluctant to encourage the formation of village-wide and other intermediate organisations between the family and the bureaucracy' (Ng 1992: 8), other than lineage groups. These, sometimes headed by local gentry, or having members of the gentry as patrons, not only served as the basic political unit of indirect rule in rural areas, but also took on functions the state did not, religious, educational and even military (Ng 1992: 5). Associations other than lineage groups organised themselves as fictive lineages to allay imperial suspicion.[27] The coastal cities, on the other hand, were filled with migrant workers who, separated from the rural gentry and the lineage system, organised themselves into associations that performed similar functions, usually centred around temples dedicated to the patron deities of their birthplaces, or sometimes to deities associated with a trade or occupation.[28] Here, at the periphery of the empire and at the increasingly open gates to foreign trade, merchants had the wealth to fund these organisations and, increasingly, the prestige to lead them, and to function as representatives of the various social groups in their relations with officialdom.[29]

These community-based, quasi-political entities were reproduced in immigrant enclaves in cities across Southeast Asia. The elaboration and strengthening of colonial (and Chakri)[30] bureaucratic administration were a gradual process, and initially governments in the region were content to administer Chinese populations through community leaders. Often, these were businessmen, who, in the course of their activities, had more frequent contacts with Europeans. Their appointment as 'Kapitan China' added to their prestige and political power. On the other hand, the Chinese gentry (with their ascriptive, aristocratic status) were absent from the overseas setting, and with them, the system that maintained a stable social hierarchy in rural China. State elites were European or native instead and except in Siam before Rama VI,[31] ethnic Chinese were generally barred from rising in the service of the state. Thus, while the possibility of upward mobility was greater for Chinese in Southeast Asia than in China, the route of advancement was largely restricted to business-related activities.

The main political benefit of the state to Chinese society in Southeast Asia was order, not law.[32] The legal system in Qing China was draconian and undependable. In Southeast Asia, the law was foreign. Proceedings, depending on the court, were conducted in European or local languages. European legal concepts were alien to China but not always as alien as European law might be to other Southeast Asians[33] – and their application was likely to be biased in favour of non-Chinese parties.[34] Trust in legal systems in general, and foreign legal systems in particular, remained low among immigrants from China. Intra-communal disputes and regulatory matters were instead handled within ethnic Chinese society, through various associations or with the intercession of a prestigious individual. Reliance on these mechanisms reconfirmed trust in the system.

As the state increased in capacity and expanded its functions in the Netherlands Indies, British Malaya, French Indochina and Siam,[35] governments extended control over Chinese organisations. Associations were ordered to register legally, often with restrictions on the activities they were permitted to engage in, or else, be banned. 'Respectable' organisations were encouraged: those perceived to have ties to labour, 'organised crime', or China-oriented politics, were suppressed.[36] The powerful *kongsi*[37] that ran tax farms and other government concessions were replaced with state monopolies. In most places, Chinese chambers of commerce became the association of associations, and their chairmen the most important representatives of the Chinese community before the state. Their position as mediators between the state and the Chinese communities, however, could damage their legitimacy in the community in periods of stressful relations with the government. The Kapitans China that the chamber chairmen replaced had lost their legitimacy, partly because of their recognition by the state. The chairman's status, by contrast, remained a function of Chinese social relations.

The arrivals of nationalism and socialism in Southeast Asia had a two-stage effect. First, the erosion of regional-linguistic distinctions and loyalties in favour of the new national identity, coupled with the exacerbation of political divisions reflecting politics in China, reordered the basis of Chinese community leaders' legitimacy. It also prompted the colonial and Siamese states to treat Chinese political activity with greater suspicion and hostility, further alienating Chinese society from local government. More importantly, however, the second-stage spread of nationalism among native elites[38] foreshadowed the uneasy relationship of Chinese communities with the independent states-to-be. Chinese prosperity depended on the colonial economic order, and Chinese political loyalties were seen to be tied to China. Even when collaboration with the colonial government and/or native elites was rewarded (Thailand, Malaya), the position of ethnic Chinese in independent Southeast Asian societies after the Second World War was often that of quasi-foreigners. The instability, unpredictability, or incapability of the new national states, whether real or perceived, slowed the development of greater trust in government among ethnic Chinese, just when these governments' efforts to consolidate their national identities amplified their anxiety about Chinese, both citizens and resident aliens.

The other side of the tael

Chinese socio-economic organisation followed a similar trajectory of adaptation and resistance to the encompassing economic system in Southeast Asia. Economic activity in rural south China was largely self-regulated,[39] but institutionally atomised: market networks were encouraged, but business-related organisations other than lineage groups were not. Chinese business activity in colonial Southeast Asia was often pioneering, relegated to sectors, niches, and peripheral areas not occupied by Europeans or reserved for natives. European business practices themselves were alien, and in their scope and use of capital, hard to emulate. European banks were difficult to use; European and more recently American and Japanese capital markets were located in the metropoles, and local capital markets are still developing. The economic vacuum left by colonial disengagement following the Second World War allowed business expansion, but large-scale enterprise has generally required co-operation with the government or foreign capital. Chinese business practices have evolved, either to manage dependence on impersonal institutions, or to do without them, with more confident reliance on them representing a recent trend.

The rice-centred peasant economy of the regions of south China from which most emigrants to Southeast Asia were drawn, was not greatly different from those of the most heavily populated areas of the Red River delta in Tonkin, central Java, or Luzon, except that the quality of land was poorer. Because of the age, size and bureaucratic structure of the Chinese imperial state, and the age and complexity of the economy over which it presided, however, Chinese peasants were accustomed to a greater degree of impersonality in exchange relations than their Southeast Asian counterparts. Laws, including those pertaining to land ownership and tenancy, however inequitable and inconsistent their implementation, were impersonal in conception. The circulation of bureaucratic officials, and their placement outside their home districts, minimised personal ties with those under their jurisdiction, and kept some social distance between the state apparatus and the populace. More importantly, the Chinese economy had been longer and more thoroughly monetised than those of its southern neighbours (Freedman 1959). Money is itself impersonal, and tends to override other determinants of status and value. While it is clear that money, in reducing the uncertainty of barter exchange by permitting comparison of different items of exchange according to a universal standard, enables the expansion of trade on a more impersonal and generalised basis, it is important to note that the primary mechanism of circulation in unmonetised economies is not barter, but obligation. Credit and debt precede money. Yet, as with trade, money enables the generalisation and depersonalisation of credit relations as well. Without reliable legal guarantees, however, the risk of impersonal exchange relations remains high, and other normative standards and personalistic practices must be incorporated to reduce this risk.[40] Economic culture in south China under the Qing forms an intermediate case between the particularistic practices of Southeast Asian peasants and the rational legal ideal of Western capitalism.[41]

The component of personalism in this culture was not of the atomised, individualistic type Western legal-rationalism imagines to be its polar opposite. Lineage groups were not only the privileged social institution of south China, they were the most important locus of identity and loyalty, short of immediate family, as well. Lineages often covered whole villages,[42] combining the principles of kinship and locality in one congruent unit. Intra-lineage exchange was internally regulated, and guaranteed by group loyalty, while the 'shadow' of the lineage stood behind participants in inter-lineage relations (marriage, trade, or feud). The ascriptive identity of lineage provided the norms and mechanisms through which exchange relations were mediated in rural south China. The lineage's size and cohesiveness enabled the expansion of particularistic ties on a broader basis than a narrower or looser familialism could have.[43]

The associations that replaced lineage groups in the lives of migrant workers in the cities of south China played a similar role. Although these were voluntary associations, the normative appeal of the particularistic principles of locality and kinship were invoked, through the worship of deities associated with one's birthplace, and through the rituals of brotherhood practised by 'secret societies'. These last were as likely to represent organised labour as organised 'crime'. While hierarchical in structure, they were less fixedly so than the lineage groups, in which one's position was tied to age and the seniority of one's branch of the lineage. The voluntary character of membership in an association made contractual relations imaginable; the achieved character of one's rank within it made upward mobility conceivable.

Immigrant labour from China started to arrive in the ports of Southeast Asia in a wholesale and generalised fashion in the second half of the nineteenth century.[44] Prior to that, large groups of labour were transported in bulk lots for enterprises engaged in primary production by Chinese business organisations called *kongsi*. Initially, these were huge partnerships, outgrowths of the voluntary associations and 'secret societies' of China's coastal cities, in which shares were purchased with capital or with the promise to provide labour. The *kongsi* were occupied in mining or large-scale cash-cropping of pepper and gambier, usually away from heavily populated areas, and the cost of transporting labour to site and providing supplies (not just necessities, but extras, including opium), tended to transform labour's shares in the enterprise into long-term indentured servitude (Chun 1988). It is an exaggeration to characterise the *kongsi* as 'democratic brotherhoods' of labour (Trocki 1991: 43), although the ideal of pooling resources and rewards among many participants echoed the broad corporate loyalty of south Chinese lineage groups and the a-legal contractual character of Chinese urban voluntary associations.

Some of the initial capital for these ventures may have come from merchants and prospective customers in China. In time, however, the *kongsi* were bought out or taken over by ethnic Chinese merchants in Southeast Asia with ties to European capital.[45] Wage and indentured labour became the rule,[46] and workers saved to gain the security of self-employment, much as peasants prefer owning land to tenancy.[47] In Java, Malaya, Siam and Indochina, rich merchants organised a different style of *kongsi* to bid for and operate state-licensed monopolies in the form of government concessions and tax farms, including the great opium farms.[48] This type of *kongsi* was more of a syndicate, organised in a patron–client network of families, often headed by the family of a Chinese merchant who might double as government-appointed Chinese 'officer' and simultaneously as secret society leader (the *kongsi* were largely responsible themselves for the enforcement of their monopolies: see Rush 1991; and Salmon 1991). Around the turn of the century, these syndicates were replaced by state-run monopolies (régies), and dissolved.[49]

The loss of the tax farms and the dissolution of the syndicates slowed large-scale capital accumulation by Chinese businesses, before their expansion and the emergence of Chinese-owned banks concurrent with the withdrawal of Western firms during the depression of the 1930s and the Second World War. Lack of easy access to and trust in formal financial institutions made capital for investment by Chinese entrepreneurs scarce. Some 'credit-worthy' Chinese established relations with Western banks and firms, and stood as guarantors for loans to other Chinese businesses, but comprador credit was expensive, and the need for personal ties to the comprador channelled credit to only a few top businessmen. Chinese business practices, however, encouraged the flow of credit, through elite urban firms (e.g. import-export companies), down across networks of smaller firms. The emphasis on business liquidity, especially in trade, and on putting resources to profitable use, often as credit, also helped pool capital and direct it to effective employment through the networks.[50] Networking facilitated exchange and lowered business costs, without sacrificing too much of the flexibility of market-mediated inter-firm relations. Long-term ties among individual firms reduced the costs of individual transactions. Maintaining a multiplicity of ties to regular suppliers and customers avoided too exclusive a dependence on any other firm, and undermined the formation of monopolies and monopsonies. Networking also spread risk across the market, as a poorly performing firm that failed to service its debt would receive less credit on stricter terms, while some of its business would flow to more reliable firms. The small size of individual units, along with access to credit through networks, promoted ease of entry into sectors where start-up costs, especially the amount of capital required, were relatively low. The nature of credit relations was such that capital accumulated as a portion of profits was passed back up through the networks to service debt with at least implicit interest. But the concentration of capital was slowed by the number of firms taking their cuts along the way, and the cost of credit remained higher than for Western firms.[51]

The often temporary demise or withdrawal of better-capitalised and -integrated Western firms from many sectors of the Southeast Asian economies following the Depression and the Second World War created vacuums into which Chinese businesses expanded. In Siam in particular, Chinese-owned banks, many of which started as adjuncts to trading and manufacturing firms, emerged as the hubs of constellations of related businesses.[52] Social upheaval in Indonesia, Indochina, and to a lesser extent, Malaya, the return of European capital to the region, especially to Singapore, and American financial support of Filipino capital, together slowed Chinese business expansion. Moreover, in Thailand, Indonesia and the Philippines, Chinese businesses were confronted with newly inter-ventionist, 'economic nationalist' states. The choice was to do business with the government (or political elites) and hope that the rents acquired through political connections offset the costs of these connections, or do business at a potentially severe disadvantage. Firms that 'co-operated' were better able to expand, diversify and ultimately form conglomerates. The patrimonial style of rule in the newly independent nations and Thailand slowed the movement towards Western rational legal norms among ethnic Chinese as well as in the surrounding societies.

Trust in Chinese systems of social relations contributed to the development of practices enabling Chinese businesses to operate with less reliance on Western-style financial institutions or formal political-legal institutions. Because of these practices, Chinese 'business groups have been able to escape (or limit) subordination to political power holders' (McVey 1991: 15) at some cost,[53] and, I believe, manage their dependence on foreign capital as well. More recently, however, Chinese business groups have been adopting more Western methods and invoking the norms that underlie them. The apparent superiority and worldwide prestige of Western style legal rational institutions encouraged greater trust in their operations. The more business-friendly policies of Southeast Asian states, and importantly, the growth of local capital markets makes adapting to Western standards and corporate forms more feasible.[54] The prestige and familiarity of the old system accounts for a certain amount of inertia in its convergence toward Western practices, especially where the system provides tactical advantages in developing markets, including China. But as the calculus of risk and opportunity changes, Western corporate forms are becoming more attractive, both as the dominant style in world capitalism, and for their ability to handle a multiplicity of distant and impersonal exchanges, as long as the required legal guarantees are in place.

Firming up the system

Unlike many studies of the subject, we have taken the system of Chinese business relations in a broad sense, rather than management practices at the level of individual firms, as the central characteristic of a Chinese idiom of business. Most of the characteristics observed at the level of the firm in other studies, including familialism, personalism, and paternalism, are present in greater or lesser fashion in *small* firms, especially sole proprietorships, everywhere,[55] and are readily discernible in the political cultures of much of Southeast Asia as well. Far from being peculiarly Chinese, the distinctive feature of these characteristics is their relative unimportance (but not absence), and their devalorisation in favour of rational legal norms in transnational corporations, with which Chinese businesses are implicitly compared. It is the comparison with TNCs, rather than with American mom-and-pop firms, that makes analysis at the network level appropriate, and it is here that the distinctive aspects of a Chinese business idiom can be located. The apparent rigidity and authoritarian style at the level of the small firm, for example, translates into autonomy and flexibility within a network. Networks co-ordinate business activity beyond the capability of small firms loose in an atomised market, without sacrificing the flexibility often lost in large, integrated firms.

The expansion of Chinese-owned firms is requiring the adaptation of more impersonal management practices, with older methods and norms gradually being subordinated to them. Chinese-controlled conglomerates are likely to reproduce old networks as webs of subcontracting relations more reminiscent of Japanese business style than American (although American companies are also 'slimming down' and contracting out more functionally specific parts of their businesses). Local political cultures continue to encourage personalism, especially in business-government relations, but this kind of business culture is also exemplified by conglomerates such as Fiat in Italy, where ethnicity is not a factor, but the incomplete hegemony of impersonal, rational legal norms is.[56] In this light, Redding's comparison of 'Chinese conglomerates in the West to "a guerrilla army that suddenly finds itself on a parade ground" ' (in *The Economist* 1993: 33–4) appears sensationalist and inaccurate: conglomerates are already a Westernised form, and their business cultures are not as incompatible as he implies. They all play golf nowadays.

'They' are elites, from government as well as business. As a sign of development, the golf course reveals more than most models. The image of Southeast Asians meeting on the links all across the region to cut deals among themselves and with their Taiwanese, Japanese, American and European guests, suggests how personal relations and personalistic norms still enable transactions in an increasingly impersonal business environment. At the same time, business on the golf course demonstrates a whole-hearted appropriation of a game of foreign origins. The prestige of golf, like the prestige of capitalism, permits the translation of the game across cultural differences and national frontiers. The same golf course, however, also points to the sacrifices commonly made in adopting, or adapting to, a new system: a good number of poor *kampung* dwellers have been abruptly dispossessed and relocated to free up land for elite playgrounds, their claims to the land, whether on traditional or contemporary legal grounds, carrying little weight.

The story of development in Southeast Asia, then, is largely the story of the expansion of capitalism. The role of ethnic Chinese has been as agents and translators of the terms by which the new system of production and exchange is organised, first as 'responsive' wage labour, then most importantly in commerce,[57] and latterly, as producers of goods and services. Government intentions have not brought about the success of (some) Chinese business, whatever the multifarious impact of the state on economic relations. The 'accident' of the role of Chinese immigrants as intermediaries between local societies and larger markets is not reproducible by policy, nor is the particular idiom of Chinese business imitable, except to the degree it generally reflects a pattern of reconciling capitalist and non-capitalist norms. Hostility towards Chinese 'domination' reflects the social disruption caused by the expansion of capitalism. What has been, and what ought to be, sacrificed in the process of capitalist development are the proper concerns of policy-making.

Notes

1   Or at least, the second, post-Iberian wave: see below.
2   The enormity of the question demands a certain strategy – a cross-disciplinary approach – which is fraught with tactical difficulties. Important among these is the problem of formulating and sustaining an analytically consistent argument. S.G. Redding calls for a 'collaboration across disciplines' (Hamilton 1991a: 30), but his 'occasional tentative venturing into economics, psychology or history' (Redding 1990: 5), not to mention religion, produces somewhat disappointing results (see Redding 1990: chaps. 2–6). The fault lies in appealing to what amounts to outside authority, without translating the 'evidence' into terms that may be interrogated as part of the analysis (cf. Benedict Anderson 1978: 232–3). This tactical error also manifests itself in the sudden invocations of Confucian ideology which are endemic in the literature on overseas Chinese business.
3   The argument will be that this social know-how operates as a factor of production. But what kind of resource it is – human, technological, even infrastructural – is less clear.
4   Hamilton bluntly (and tautologically) defines overseas Chinese as 'all Chinese who do not live within the People's Republic of China' (1996b: 330). This does not address ethnic identity at all, and historically China claimed many non-residents as subjects or citizens by jus sanguinis.
5   Limlingan (1986: 240–1) reports that some 90 per cent of Chinese in Brunei do not have citizenship, but 'were merely issued certificates of identity'. For subjects of the Sultan, citizenship is, perhaps, theoretically unnecessary.
6   On the provision of false identity cards ('effectively citizenship') to Chinese entering Burma, see *The New York Times*, 29 March 1994.
7   Sometimes they become king of Siam. Then, there are those of Chinese descent who are 'Chinese' only when they lie: see Anderson 1988.
8   The exception is called Hakka (Mandarin: *kejia*, 'guest families'). An old migratory group, the Hakka have internalised their 'difference' to the point of calling themselves by a name others obviously gave them. *Sanjiang ren*, by the way, referred to 'people of the three *jiang*': Jiangxi, Jiangsu and Zhejiang. Jiangsu and Zhejiang are provinces on the coast of China north of Fujian (whence *Hokkien*), lying more or less to the north and south of Shanghai. Jiangxi is the province to the west (inland) of Fujian, north of Guangdong, and east of Hunan. The term seems to have been used loosely for northerners, along with *Waijiang ren*, 'people beyond the Yangzi' (see Cheng 1985: 22).
9   See Supang (1991) on sub-divisions among Chaozhou (Teochew) in Thailand; see Cheng (1985) for similar sub-divisions among Hokkien in Singapore (note that the largest groups are the ones that divide); Cheng also contains maps showing the residential distribution of various regional-linguistic groups into separate neighbourhoods. Wee (1988) shows that historically, southern Chinese are not as purely 'Han' (taken to be the main Chinese ethnicity) as they are purported to be. The locals did not all migrate (say, to what is now Thailand or Indochina) in the face of Han southward expansion; over time, through intermarriage and name-changing, some became 'Chinese'.
10   The point is that he says *ethnic* Chinese. It is precisely at this period (mid-twentieth century) that many Chinese in Siam were foreign nationals (some acquired status as European rather than Chinese nationals). Previously, Chinese in Siam were subjects of the king, with nationality not yet an issue. From the late 1940s, most who were not born Thai citizens sought to be naturalised.
11   Most studies pay insufficient attention to the historical importance of the role of ethnic Chinese as wage labour. Where ethnic Chinese labour was relatively expensive because of scarcity or alternative opportunities, as in Java and Cochin-China, European employers encountered serious difficulties in getting locals to fill the part (see Elson 1986; also Ingleson 1983). The subject has received some attention in relation to Siam (e.g. Skinner 1957), where at one point the almost exclusive use of Chinese labour made wages the highest in Southeast Asia, but even here the elite-centred analyses are more inclined to focus on 'pariah capital' than on the possibility of 'pariah labour'.
12   This raises the question of how to theorise conglomerates in, say, the Philippines, which through diversification internalise inter-sectoral conflicts of interest, and compete on the basis of corporate interests and corporate (often family) loyalties alone.
13   Market divisions need not be as 'deep' as they are at the national level to produce a similar effect. It is common in the US to find state and local governments vying to attract or retain corporate

investment in their jurisdictions. The determining factor is less market imperfections than the territorial scope of the political unit. Interestingly, competition of this sort seems to have less legitimacy at the local level than at the national one.

14 What happens when some of these businesses go transnational (e.g. Charoen Pokphand: see Handley, this volume)? Does their national identity come back into doubt?

15 In New Order Indonesia, some Chinese capitalists might have been considered loyal to the *regime*, but this loyalty is precisely personal, and not (yet, at least) institutional.

16 '[T]he mobility of diaspora Chinese…manifests a wildness, danger, and unpredictability that challenges and undermines modern imperial regimes of truth and power' (Ong and Nonini 1997: 19).

17 Indigenism is important in Malaysia, Indonesia and Brunei; has been important in Thailand and the Philippines; and may be important in Vietnam, with the entry of foreign capital – into a country where capitalism is foreign and already the most successful local businessmen are 'Chinese'. Former *hoa* boat people who have done well abroad and are now returning to invest in Vietnam (so much for their disloyalty) are probably less threatening with their new American passports, that is, as long as they remain clearly foreign (and provided the Vietnamese government recognises their new citizenship: see 'Identity Crisis', *FEER*, 5 May 1994: 32).

18 The common legitimacy of ownership acknowledges, in a way, the hegemony of capitalist norms. The assertion of collective ownership, however, whether on an ethnic, class, or national basis, cuts across the grain of capitalism, which may explain why capitalism and nationalism are sometimes uneasy bedfellows.

19 If, as I have suggested above, the idea of ethnicity and the possibility of competition among categorically defined groups evolved from the contradiction between ascriptive and achieved status systems, it makes sense that ethnic competition should be expressed in terms of prestige as well as power. Horowitz (1985), and Jesudason (1989) following him, call these 'group worth' and 'group capacity', but I think they err in searching for a psychological, rather than social or political, explanation for the first in particular, rendering their argument ahistorical. The promise of prestige through group identification is required to legitimise, and thus sustain, intragroup co-operation as well as intergroup competition. But the promise in turn requires outsiders: status is, after all, a matter of comparison.

20 The almost universal spread of 'development' as a legitimating ideology and policy has amplified the political importance of capital. Regimes that can claim the right to rule through the success of their developmental policies – and this applies to all the ASEAN countries except for Burma – are better able to resist other demands, for political liberalisation especially. Although development is not concerned with group identity per se, the operations of prestige are apparent here as well in the rhetoric of achievement and competition, principally between nations, but between regions within them as well.

21 See, for example, Rush 1990: 203, Williams 1961. French commentators could be particularly vehement: 'stranglehold' is one of Dennery's (1931) favourite words, and he invests 'Celestial' with a vicious irony. See also a collection of citations in Skinner 1957: 160–1; and the report of the Philippine Commission, cited in Amyot 1973: 72. The Chakri dynasty in Siam was comparatively unworried before the accession of Rama VI in 1910 (Skinner 1957: 161–5).

22 Within the framework, however, the interpretation of norms is liable to contestation. See James Scott's critical discussion of 'hegemony' in Scott 1985: chapter 8.

23 See Skinner 1957: chapter 3; and Wyatt 1984: 217–19. As in the European colonies, one reason for employing Chinese was to keep native peasants on their farms and in their place.

24 For example, in Berger's introductory essay in Berger and Hsiao (1988: 7). Redding's efforts to make the connection do more to point out the flaws in the argument than to support it. His reference to 'the Confucian teaching deeply embedded in the school system' (Redding 1990: 45) exaggerates the availability of education – there was no 'system' – in south China under the Qing. (And what little Confucianism was taught in Chinese community schools in Southeast Asia was of dubious orthodoxy and held little popular appeal. On the Tiong Hoa Hwee Koan's (Zhonghua Huiguan) 'failure' to instil Confucianism among ethnic Chinese in Java and Confucianism's unpopularity as a subject in THHK schools, see Williams 1960.) According to Ng, 'only about five

to ten percent of *males*…had a sound grasp of the classics, [and] it is estimated that perhaps 30–45 percent of them possessed *some* ability to read and write' (Ng Chin-Keong 1992: 12–13, emphases mine). On the other hand, the plethora of European and American missionary schools that spread along the coast of China after the first Opium War could have as easily instilled the 'real' Protestant ethic in their students. (Missionary schools sprang up in varying concentrations across Southeast Asia as well.) Furthermore, young men who received any kind of education would have been better able to find opportunities in China and less inclined to emigrate. An historically more plausible vector for the dissemination of Confucian values would be public dramatic performances and professional story-telling. As with *wayang* in parts of Southeast Asia, such performances enacted or recounted popularly well-known stories, many with origins in elite literary works. But much elite literature in China was originally critical of the status quo (usually at a particular historical moment: allegory and historical displacement were favourite techniques for cloaking the criticism and avoiding reprisal), even before popular storytellers put their own spin on them.

25 Communal acceptance does not indicate complete consensus even within the community, but that the hegemonic norms of the system are to some degree understood and tolerated by its participants.

26 This is not to say that local capital has not been intimately tied to colonial, dynastic and national states in Southeast Asia, but that these relations have come about through state initiative (often coercive) or in response to opportunities to capture particular advantages through the state (e.g. tax farms).

27 Ng 1992: 8. And also to draw on the legitimacy of the privileged model for their members.

28 The religious centre of these associations points again to their normative character, as well as to their need for an appeal to some form of legitimation in addition to the (absent) family.

29 Ng 1992: 18–20. Even before British gunboats broke down the door, society in south China was undergoing dramatic change. Huge population growth and the gradual weakening of the Qing state were two factors in this. Of interest also is the entry through south China of large amounts of Mexican silver from the galleon trade in Manila, certainly stimulating the local economy and perhaps leading to inflation, followed by the termination of that trade in 1815.

30 The Siamese bureaucracy was expanded and rationalised under European, and especially British, 'guidance'. See Wyatt 1984: 210.

31 And elsewhere before the Europeans arrived.

32 Though the rhetorical marriage of law'n'order may not be an exclusively Anglo-American peculiarity, it serves nicely in English language contexts to gloss over the not-so-legitimate aspects of maintaining order. The Dutch were more concerned with 'quiet' than law: *rust en orde* was their watchword.

33 Property law, for example, and particularly law relating to land ownership and tenancy, was fairly elaborate in south China. Ownership of land could be divided between ownership of the subsoil, the topsoil, and current usufruct (tenancy or sub-tenancy). Land being relatively scarcer in south China than in most of Southeast Asia, a more impersonal yet exclusive (i.e. *alienable* and *private*) notion of property rights has evolved in south China, one more congenial to market relations. To even the most unsophisticated Chinese peasant abroad, European laws and norms regarding property might seem somewhat familiar.

34 Rulings in favour of 'indigenous' parties over Chinese reflected European ambivalence towards the presence of Chinese in the colonies, but also the often-unspoken ambiguity of Europeans' own position there – of which European anxieties about Chinese were partly a projection.

35 The incapacities of the Spanish colonial state in the Philippines contributed to its demise, while the subsequent hybrid American-Filipino state emphasised politics over administration, with a disregard for the latter compounded by a certain degree of American metropolitan indifference.

36 Although bias was sometimes shown in favour of one China-oriented political group or another, usually the most conservative.

37 See the discussion of *kongsi* as organisation below.

38 Partly through the example of Chinese nationalism.

39 That is, trade, crafts, and most primary production. As noted, land ownership and tenancy laws were elaborate, because the imperial state's primary economic concern was food, especially rice, production, and the taxes derived from it. Another exception was the government's monopoly of the salt trade.

40 As they are, to a lesser extent, in Western corporate business practice.

41 My characterisation of Southeast Asian peasants' economic culture does not apply to the traders of Malacca, Makassar and the Javanese *pasisir*, nor does it explain why Arab, Mon, Minangkabau and other trading groups have not been as obviously successful in business as some Chinese immigrants.

42 Ng 1992: 5. See also Amyot 1973: chapter 3. Both Ng and Amyot focus mainly on Hokkien people in Fujian: extending generalisations about Hokkien practices to the other peoples of south China is less well grounded.

43 The prevalence and influence of practices such as primogeniture versus partible inheritance, and patrilocal marriage, on the cohesiveness of south Chinese lineages would make an interesting study, especially if compared with the looser version of the north, thereby undermining homogeneous and Confucianist imaginings of Chinese culture.

44 In Malaya and Singapore earliest, in Siam 'after the 1860s' (Skinner 1957: 53), in Java around the 1880s (in time for an economic downturn).

45 Trocki 1991: chapter 2. Although this style of organisation may have disappeared in Southeast Asia, it has recently reappeared in rural China:

> For the most part, China's rural industries are, in the words of Ronald McKinnon, a Stanford economist, 'a form of corporate organisation that hasn't been created before'. Most of the rural industries, technically known as 'township and village enterprises' (TVEs), are controlled by units of local government: counties, townships or villages. Managers are answerable to local officials and to the householders who have started the business or invested in it (plenty of overlap, usually). Some of the TVEs' profits go into local infrastructure like roads and schools, some are retained for investment, some are paid out to individual households as dividends
>
> (*The Economist*, 28 November 1992: 12)

The 'TVEs' may well be lineage-based in some cases, but they incorporate local government instead of replacing it.

46 It is the familiarity with money, along with the idea of contracts, that made wage labour more easily conceivable for Chinese immigrants than other Southeast Asians. Chinese labour preferred Chinese employers in part because of distrust in legal guarantees and the prospect of access to more particularistic sanctions. Communal sanctions were also available to Chinese employers, but one key to the attractiveness of Chinese labour to employers both Chinese and European was that Southeast Asians were inclined to demand payment in advance: historically, their labour had been a scarce factor of production. On the difficulty of European employers in getting locals to fill the part of wage labour, see Elson 1986 and Ingleson 1983.

47 On peasants' standards of security and distaste for tenancy, see Scott 1976: 35–40.

48 On tax-farming in Java, see Rush 1990; for Malaya, Trocki 1991; for Siam, Skinner 1957: 118. Rush makes some references to opium farms and the régie in Indochina. On the Philippines, see Wickberg 1965: 113–19.

49 The size and degree of vertical integration of the *kongsi* syndicates demonstrates the capacity of Chinese business to organise on a large scale where risk and competition are reduced by government intervention – which is easier to explain than the success of more loosely connected networks in the face of competition *from* government.

50 See, for example, Limlingan 1986. His emphasis on accounting practices, however, is probably overdrawn. Quite sophisticated procedures were known in China: cf. Gardella 1992.

51 A study of credit relations in rural Southeast Asia before the Second World War would probably discover that, in places like Cochin-China and Luzon, interest charged to peasants by Chinese merchants was still lower than interest on loans from local native and *mestizo* landlords. The landlords were able, and wanted, to acquire more land: it was in their interest to drown smallholders in debt and then foreclose. It was also in their interest to extract as much as they could from their tenants – once the colonial state appeared to protect their position over society beyond its traditional basis, and gave them the legal tools to exploit. Acquisition of land by Chinese, on the other hand, was restricted in most of Southeast Asia, and the desire to maintain long-term relations with farmers who were both producers and consumers moderated credit and exchange between trader and

peasant. Additionally, it was the late colonial demand for payment of taxes in cash that most exacerbated peasant debt. Rural traders mostly offered credit in goods against the next harvest, and cash had scarcity value. See Scott 1976, and Ngo 1973.

52   Suehiro 1989 and 1992; also see Hewison 1989; and Skinner 1957 and 1958.

53   *Economic* subordination, that is.

54   Stock markets are also making corporate ownership and control more fluid, but perhaps no less vexed an issue.

55   See Ho 1992; and *The Economist*, 2 April 1994: 63. Family control is common among large American corporations as well, including a third of the Fortune 500.

56   Indeed, Chinese business idiom bears some resemblance to a (northern) Italian one. Cf. *The Economist*, 9 April 1994: 76.

57   Political anxiety about business is not just about wealth as such, but about the movement of wealth. Commerce is often seen not as producing wealth or enabling the production of wealth, but as removing wealth beyond the reach of a social or political jurisdiction, and any claims the community might make on it: out of the village, by villagers; out of the country, by the state. Even within a community, the liquidity of wealth on which commerce relies makes commercial activity harder to observe, regulate and tax than agriculture or manufacturing, which involve relatively fixed assets.

Bibliography

Abeyasekere, Susan (1990) *Jakarta A History*. Singapore: Oxford University Press.

Amyot, Jacques (1973) *The Manila Chinese*. Quezon City: Institute of Philippine Culture.

Anderson, Benedict (1978) 'Studies of the Thai State: the State of Thai Studies', in Eliezer B. Ayal (ed.) *The Study of Thailand*. Akron, OH: Ohio University Center for International Studies.

Anderson, Benedict (1988) 'Cacique Democracy in the Philippines: Origins and Dreams'. *New Left Review*, 169.

Anderson, Benedict (1990) *Language and Power*. Ithaca: Cornell University Press.

Anderson, Benedict (1991) *Imagined Communities: Reflections on the Origin and Spread of Nationalism*, revised and extended edition. New York: Verso.

Anek Laothamatas (1992) *Business Associations and the New Political Economy of Thailand*. Boulder, CO: Westview Press.

Barton, Clifton A. (1983) 'Trust and Credit: Some Observations Regarding Business Strategies of Overseas Chinese Traders in South Vietnam', in vol. 1, L. Lim and P. Gosling (eds) *The Chinese in Southeast Asia*, 2 vols. Singapore: Maruzen Asia.

Berger, Peter L. and Hsin-huang Michael Hsiao (eds) (1988) *In Search of an East Asian Development Model*. New Brunswick, NJ: Transaction Books.

Blim, Michael (1996) 'Cultures and the Problems of Capitalisms'. *Critique of Anthropology*, 16(1).

Blussé, Leonard (1981) 'Batavia, 1619–1740: The Rise and Fall of a Chinese Colonial Town'. *Journal of Southeast Asian Studies*, 12(1).

'Botan', (Supha Sirisingha) (1977) *Letters from Thailand*, Susan Morell (trans.). Bangkok: D.K. Book House.

Business Week (1993) 'Asia's Wealth', 29 November.

Cator, W.J. (1936) *The Economic Position of the Chinese in the Netherlands Indies*. Oxford: Basil Blackwell.

Cheng Lim-keak (1985) *Social Change and the Chinese in Singapore: a Socio-Economic Geography with Special Reference to Bang Structure*. Singapore: Singapore University Press.

Chia Oai Peng (1987) 'Trust and Credit among Chinese Businessmen in Kelantan. *Southeast Asian Business*, 14.

Chun, Allen J. (1988) 'Toward a Political Economy of the Sojourning Experience: the Chinese in 19th Century Malaya', Working Paper no. 93. Singapore: National University of Singapore.

Clad, James (1989) *Behind the Myth: Business, Money and Power in Southeast Asia.* London: Unwin Hyman Ltd.

Clammer, John R. (1981) 'French Studies on the Chinese in Indochina'. *Journal of Southeast Asian Studies*, 12(1) (March).

Cohen, Margot (1997a) 'The Outsiders'. *Far Eastern Economic Review*, March 13.

Cohen, Margot (1997b) 'Under the Volcano'. *Far Eastern Economic Review*, March 13.

Cushman, J. W. and Wang Gungwu (eds) (1988) *Changing Identities of the Southeast Asian Chinese since World War II.* Hong Kong: Hong Kong University Press.

Day, Clive (1972) *The Policy and Administration of the Dutch in Java.* Kuala Lumpur: Oxford University Press.

Dennery, Etienne (1931) *Asia's Teeming Millions: and its Problems for the West.* John Peile (trans.). London: Jonathan Cape.

Dirlik, Arif (1997) 'Critical Reflections on "Chinese Capitalism" as Paradigm'. *Identities*, 3(3).

Dobbin, Christine (1996) *Asian Entrepreneurial Minorities: Conjoint Communities in the Making of the World-Economy 1570–1940.* Richmond, Surrey: Curzon Press Ltd.

The Economist (1992) 'Survey of China', 28 November.

The Economist (1993) 'China's diaspora turns homeward', 27 November.

The Economist (1994a) 'Family Values', 2 April.

The Economist (1994b) 'New work order', 9 April.

Elson, R.E. (1986) '"Free Labor" in Nineteenth-century Java'. *Modern Asian Studies*, 20 (1).

Freedman, Maurice (1959) 'The Handling of Money: A Note on the Background to the Economic Sophistication of Overseas Chinese'. *Man*, 89.

Furnivall, J.S. (1956) *Colonial Policy and Practice.* New York: New York University Press.

Gardella, Robert (1992) 'Squaring Accounts: Commercial Bookkeeping Methods and Capitalist Rationalism in Late Qing and Republican China'. *Journal of Asian Studies*, 51(2) (May).

Godley, M.R. (1989) 'Reflections on China's Changing Overseas Chinese Policy'. *Solidarity* [Manila], 123, July–September: 108–12.

Golay, Frank, Ralph Aspach, Ruth Pfanner, and Eliezer Ayall (eds) (1969) *Underdevelopment and Economic Nationalism in Southeast Asia.* Ithaca: Cornell University Press.

Gosling, Peter (1983) 'Chinese Crop Dealers in Malaysia and Thailand: the Myth of the Merciless Monopsonistic Middleman', in vol. 1, L. Lim and P. Gosling (eds) *The Chinese in Southeast Asia*, 2 vols. Singapore: Maruzen Asia.

Gramsci, Antonio (1971) *Selections from the Prison Notebooks of Antonio Gramsci*, Q. Hoare and G.N. Smith (eds and trans.). New York: International Publishers.

Greenhalgh, Susan (1994) 'De-Orientalizing the Chinese family firm'. *American Ethnologist*, 21(4).

Hamilton, Gary (ed.) (1991a) *Business Networks and Economic Development in East and Southeast Asia.* Hong Kong: University of Hong Kong Centre of Asian Studies.

Hamilton, Gary (1991b) 'The Organizational Foundations of Western and Chinese Commerce; a Historical and Comparative Analysis', in G. Hamilton (ed.) *Business Networks and Economic Development in East and Southeast Asia.* Hong Kong: University of Hong Kong Centre of Asian Studies.

Hamilton, Gary (1996a) 'Competition and Organization: A Reexamination of Chinese Business Practices'. *Journal of Asian Business*, 12(1).

Hamilton, Gary (1996b) 'Overseas Chinese Capitalism', in Tu Wei-ming (ed.) *Confucian Traditions in East Asian Modernity: Moral Education and Economic Culture in Japan and the Four Mini-Dragons*. Cambridge, MA: Harvard University Press.

Hawes, Gary, and Hong Liu (1993) 'Explaining the Dynamics of the Southeast Asian Political Economy'. *World Politics*, 45(4) (July).

Hewison, Kevin (1989) *Bankers and Bureaucrats: Capital and the Role of the State in Thailand*. New Haven: Yale University Southeast Asian Studies.

Ho Kwon Ping (1992) 'Business in Transition'. *Journal of Southeast Asia Business*, 8(2).

Horowitz, Donald L. (1985) *Ethnic Groups in Conflict*. Berkeley: University of California Press.

Hu Yao-Su (1995) 'The International Transferability of the Firm's Advantages'. *California Management Review*, 37(4).

Hutchcroft, Paul D. (1991) 'Oligarchs and Cronies in the Philippine State: The Politics of Patrimonial Plunder'. *World Politics*, 43(3) (April).

Indonesia, special edition (1991) 'The Role of the Indonesian Chinese in Shaping Indonesian Life'. Ithaca: Cornell Southeast Asia Program.

Ingleson, John (1983) 'Life and Work in Colonial Cities: Harbour Workers in Java in the 1910s and 1920s'. *Modern Asian Studies*, 17 (3).

Jesudason, James V. (1989) *Ethnicity and the Economy: the State, Chinese Business and Multinationals in Malaysia*. Singapore: Oxford University Press.

Jomo K.S. (1986) *A Question of Class: Capital, the State and Uneven Development in Malaya*. Singapore: Oxford University Press.

Kasian Tejapira (1992) 'Pigtail: a Pre-History of Chineseness in Siam'. *Sojourn*, 7(1) (February).

Lam, Danny Kin-kong and Ian Lee (1992) 'Guerrilla Capitalism and the Limits of Statist Theory: Comparing the Chinese NICs', in Cal Clark and Steve Chan (eds) *The Evolving Pacific Basin and the Global Political Economy*. Boulder, CO: Lynne Rienner.

Lasserre, Philippe (1988) 'Corporate Strategic Management and the Overseas Chinese Groups'. *Asia Pacific Journal of Management*, 5(2) (January).

Leff, Nathaniel H. (1978) 'Industrial Organization and Entrepreneurship in the Developing Countries: the Economic Groups'. *Economic Development and Cultural Change*, 26(4) (July).

Li, Peter S. (1993) 'Chinese Investment and Business in Canada: Ethnic Entrepreneurship Reconsidered'. *Pacific Affairs*, 66(2).

Lim, Linda (1983a) 'Chinese Business, Multinationals and the State: Manufacturing for Export in Malaysia and Singapore', in vol. 1, L. Lim and P. Gosling (eds) *The Chinese in Southeast Asia*, 2 vols. Singapore: Maruzen Asia.

Lim, Linda (1983b) 'Chinese Economic Activity in Southeast Asia: an introductory review', in vol. 1, L. Lim and P. Gosling (eds) *The Chinese in Southeast Asia*, 2 vols. Singapore: Maruzen Asia.

Lim, Linda (1992) 'The Emergence of a Chinese Economic Zone in Asia?'. *Journal of Southeast Asia Business*, 8(1).

Lim, Linda Y.C. (1996) 'The Evolution of Southeast Asian Business Systems', *Journal of Asian Business*, 12(1).

Lim, Linda and Peter Gosling (eds) (1983) *The Chinese in Southeast Asia*, 2 vols. Singapore: Maruzen Asia.

Limlingan, Victor (1986) *The Overseas Chinese in ASEAN: Business Strategies and Management Practices*. Manila: De La Salle University Press.

Lubeck, Paul M. (1992) 'Malaysian Industrialization, Ethnic Divisions, and the NIC Model: the Limits to Replication', in R.P. Applebaum and J. Henderson (eds) *States and Development in the Asian Pacific Rim*. London: Sage Publications.

Mackie, Jamie (1989) 'Chinese Businessmen and the Rise of Southeast Asian Capitalism'. *Solidarity*, 123.

Mackie, Jamie (1992a) 'Changing Patterns of Chinese Big Business in Southeast Asia', in R. McVey (ed.) *Southeast Asian Capitalists*. Ithaca: Cornell University Southeast Asia Program.

Mackie, J.A.C. (1992b) 'Overseas Chinese Entrepreneurship'. *Asian-Pacific Economic Literature*, (May).

McVey, Ruth (1992) 'The Materialization of the Southeast Asian Entrepreneur', in R. McVey (ed.) *Southeast Asian Capitalists*. Ithaca: Cornell University Southeast Asia Program.

Menkhoff, Thomas (1990) 'Towards an Understanding of Chinese Entrepreneurship in Southeast Asia: Small Trading Firms in Singapore', Working Paper no. 138. Bielefeld, Germany: University of Bielefeld.

Menkhoff, Thomas (1991) 'Trust and Chinese Economic Behavior in Singapore', Working Paper no. 155. Bielefeld, Germany: University of Bielefeld.

Ng Chin-keong (1992) 'The Cultural Horizon of South China's Emigrants in the Nineteenth Century: Change and Persistence', in Yong Mun Cheong (ed.) *Asian Traditions and Modernization*. Singapore: Times Academic Press.

Ng, Lilian (1992) 'Keeping the Family in Business'. *Singapore Business*, (December).

Ngo Vinh Long (1973) *Before the Revolution: the Vietnamese Peasants under the French*. Cambridge, MA: MIT Press.

Omohundro, John T. (1983) 'Social Networks and Business Success for the Philippine Chinese', in L. Lim and P. Gosling (eds) *The Chinese in Southeast Asia*, vol. 1. Singapore: Maruzen Asia.

Ong, Aihwa and Donald Nonini (eds) (1997) *Ungrounded Empires: the Cultural Politics of Modern Chinese Transnationalism*. New York: Routledge.

Panglaykim, J., and I. Palmer (1970) 'Study of Entrepreneurship in Developing Countries: the Development of One Chinese Concern in Indonesia'. *Journal of Southeast Asian Studies*, 1(4).

Pasuk Phongpaichit and Sungsidh Piriyarangsan (1994) *Corruption and Democracy in Thailand*. Bangkok: The Political Economy Centre, Chulalongkorn University.

Pramoedya Ananta Toer (1960) *Hoa Kiau di Indonesia*. Djakarta: Bintang Press.

Redding, S.G. (1990) *The Spirit of Chinese Capitalism*. New York: Walter de Gruyter.

Redding, S.G. (1991) 'Weak Organizations and Strong Linkages: Managerial Ideology and Chinese Family Business Networks', in G. Hamilton (ed.) *Business Networks and Economic Development in East and Southeast Asia*. Hong Kong: University of Hong Kong Centre of Asian Studies.

Reid, Anthony (ed.) (1996) *Sojourners and Settlers: Histories of Southeast Asia and the Chinese*. St Leonards, NSW: Allen & Unwin.

Robison, Richard (1986) *Indonesia: the Rise of Capital*. Winchester, MA: Allen & Unwin.

Rotter, Andrew J. (1987) *The Path to Vietnam: Origins of the American Commitment to Southeast Asia*. Ithaca: Cornell University Press.

Rush, James (1990) *Opium to Java*. Ithaca: Cornell University Press.

Rush, James (1991) 'Placing the Chinese in Java on the Eve of the Twentieth Century', in *Indonesia*, special edition.

Salmon, Claudine (1991) 'A Critical View of the Opium Farmers as Reflected in a Syair by Boen Sing Hoo (Semarang, 1889)', in *Indonesia*, special edition.

Scott, James C. (1976) *The Moral Economy of the Peasant*. New Haven: Yale University Press.

Scott, James C. (1985) *Weapons of the Weak*. New Haven: Yale University Press.

The Siauw Giap (1966) 'Group Conflict in a Plural Society'. *Revue du Sud-est Asiatique*, 1–2. Bruxelles: Université Libre de Bruxelles.

Skinner, G. William (1957) *Chinese Society in Thailand: an Analytic History*. Ithaca: Cornell University Press.

Skinner, G. William (1958) *Leadership and Power in the Chinese Community of Thailand*. Ithaca: Cornell University Press.

Somers-Heidhues, Mary F. (1974) *Southeast Asia's Chinese Minorities*. Hawthorn, Victoria: Longman Australia Pty. Ltd.

Spence, Jonathan (1990) *The Search for Modern China*. New York: W.W. Norton and Co.

Suehiro, Akira (1989) *Capital Accumulation in Thailand, 1855–1985*. Tokyo: UNESCO Centre for East Asian Cultural Studies.

Suehiro, Akira (1992) 'Capitalist Development in Postwar Thailand: Commercial Bankers, Industrial Elite, and Agribusiness Groups', in R. McVey (ed.) *Southeast Asian Capitalists*. Ithaca: Cornell University Southeast Asia Program.

Supang Chantavanich (1991) 'The Origins of the Chaozhou Chinese in Thailand'. *Asian Review*, 5.

Suryadinata, Leo (ed.) (1989) *The Ethnic Chinese in the ASEAN States: Bibliographical Essays*. Singapore: ISEAS.

Suryadinata, Leo (1989) 'National Integration and the Chinese of Southeast Asia'. *Solidarity*, 123.

Tan Chee Beng (1989) 'People of Chinese Descent and China: Attitudes and Identity'. *Solidarity*, 123.

Tan Chee Beng (1992) 'Culture and Economic Performance: the Chinese in Southeast Asia'. *China Currents*, 3(1–2).

Taufik Abdullah (1997) 'Ketika SARA Menjadi Konflik Sosial'. *Kompas*, March 15.

Tong Chee Kiong (1989) 'Centripetal Authority, Differential Networks: the Social Organization of Chinese Firms in Singapore', Working Paper no. 99. Singapore: National University of Singapore. (Also reprinted in G. Hamilton (ed.) *Business Networks and Economic Development in East and Southeast Asia*. Hong Kong: University of Hong Kong Centre of Asian Studies.)

Trocki, Carl (1991) *Opium and Empire*. Ithaca: Cornell University Press.

Wang Gungwu (1990) 'The Culture of Chinese Merchants', Working Paper no. 57. Toronto: University of Toronto-York University Joint Centre for Asia-Pacific Studies.

Weber, Max (1968) *Economy and Society*, G. Roth and C. Wittich (eds). New York: Bedminster Press.

Wee, Vivienne (1988) 'What Does "Chinese" Mean? An Exploratory Essay', Working Paper no. 90. Singapore: National University of Singapore.

Wertheim, W.F. (1964) *East–West Parallels*. The Hague: W. van Hoeve Ltd.

Whyte, Martin King (1996) 'The Chinese Family and Economic Development: Obstacle or Engine?'. *Economic Development and Cultural Change*, 45(1).

Wickberg, Edgar (1965) *The Chinese in Philippine Life, 1850–1898*. New Haven: Yale University Press.

Williams, Lea E. (1960) *Overseas Chinese Nationalism*. Glencoe, IL: The Free Press.

Williams, Lea E. (1961) 'The Ethical Program and the Chinese of Indonesia'. *Journal of Southeast Asian History*, 2(2).

Willmott, Donald E. (1961) *The National Status of the Chinese in Indonesia, 1900–1958*. Ithaca: Cornell Modern Indonesia Project.

Willmott, William E. (1967) *The Chinese of Cambodia*. Vancouver: University of British Columbia.

Wong Siu-lin (1991) 'Chinese Entrepreneurs and Business Trust', in G. Hamilton (ed.) *Business Networks and Economic Development in East and Southeast Asia*. Hong Kong: University of Hong Kong Centre of Asian Studies.

Wyatt, David K. (1984) *Thailand: A Short History*. New Haven: Yale University Press.

Yao Souchou (1987) 'The Fetish of Relationships: Chinese Business Transactions in Singapore'. *Sojourn*, 2(1).

Yoshihara Kunio (1988) *The Rise of Ersatz Capitalism in Southeast Asia*. New York: Oxford University Press.

4 The cultural limits of 'Confucian capitalism'

Power and the invention of the family among Chinese traders in Sarawak[1]

Yao Souchou

It is ironic that at a time when culture has become for anthropologists 'a deeply compromised idea' (Clifford 1988: 12), a spectacular flowering of culturalist explanation is taking place in the management and social science literature devoted to the construction of 'Chinese capitalism' as a new economic paradigm. The momentum is undoubtedly provided by the economic growth in East Asia, particularly South China and South-East Asia, where capital, labour and business talent of the Chinese populations play an important part. It has been argued that the rise of Chinese capitalism is an integral part of the dynamics of global capitalism (Dirlik 1997), and that the discourse that grounds it is an outcome of the attempt by East Asian states like Singapore to inscribe an alternative 'Asian modernity' (Ong 1997). Yet right from the beginning when Herman Kahn (1979) first linked Confucianism with East Asian economic performance, the argument has always carried a faint Orientalist agenda. The discourse of Confucian or Chinese capitalism celebrates an essentialized 'perfect East' – culturally intact and industrially vibrant, economically competitive and politically stable, all the things that the 'West' seems to have lost. Consistent with the Orientalist strategy so cogently described by Said (1978), the discourse must make the wondrous working of Chinese business understandable and hopefully imitable. It is here that the deployment of 'Chinese culture' becomes crucial. For it is the major feature of the discourse of Confucian capitalism which reduces the intricate ordering of power and social relations into some ghostly notion of 'Confucian ethics'. The process thus transforms 'Confucian ethics' into a timeless essence of 'Chinese cultural heritage', something immune from the contingencies of history and practice, and which peoples of Chinese descent, wherever they are, find socially and psychically pertinent.

Among the so-called 'Confucian values', it is the high regard for the family which has been singled out as 'Chinese culture' proper, and as the key cultural resource contributing to the economic success of East Asian societies. In the minds of the political leadership in Singapore, the family is 'the building block of society' and the ideal of consensus and harmony, and by metaphoric extension, the principle for the organisation of the state (Koh 1993). The prosperity of Singapore – and East Asia generally, former ambassador to the United States, Professor Tommy Koh argues – is built upon a reciprocal relationship between the state and the individual, each with its own responsibilities of power and loyalty, fair government and social submission, within the larger framework of 'national consensus and teamwork' (Koh 1993: 7). The discursive strategy of Singapore implicates a dramatic construction of 'East Asian values' for the legitimation of state power and communal obedience.

If the East Asian economic model is tinged with an Orientalist shading, so is the Chinese family firm, which has become – for many social scientists, including those of Chinese descent – the perfect realisation of the culture and business efficiency argument. Wong, for example, emphasises the centrality of the family in Chinese business through the model of 'Chinese economic familism', characterised by 'nepotism, paternalism and family ownership' (Wong 1985: 1). But it is in business management circles that we find a more ebullient recital of the virtues of the Chinese family firm. Take, for example, the enthusiastic endorsement of Gordon Redding:

> [The family business] remains in essence a family fortress, and at the same time an instrument for the accumulation of wealth by a very specific group of people. It is guarded against incursions from outside, and its workings are not publicly known. It is usually run nepotistically, with benevolent paternalism throughout. Much of its effectiveness derives from intense managerial dedication, much of its efficiency from creating a working environment which matches the expectations of employees from the same culture. It is, in a very real sense, *a cultural artefact.*
>
> (Redding 1990: 3; emphasis added)

Much can be written about whether Chinese family business is indeed so efficient, its management indeed so benevolent and paternalistic that it 'matches the expectations of employees' (Redding 1990: 3). We may ask, for example, in what sense features like paternalism in Chinese business can be considered a part of the 'Confucianism' of old, rather than something closely linked to the political and industrial relations environment of the particular society. Leung has sharply contested the new Confucianism thesis by summarising the empirical findings from various studies:

> ...East Asia has not always been harmonious, even in Japan...; Korean workers do not appear to react to factory work in a manner significantly different from workers in other parts of the world...; and directly opposite to the picture painted by Khan, Chinese employees in Hong Kong and Taiwan have difficulties in identifying with their organisations...
>
> (Leung 1994: 27)

The valorisation of the family and 'Confucian ethics' in the narrative of Confucian capitalism, I argue, suppresses crucial issues of power, cultural invention, and the possibility of resistance in Chinese business organisation. Indeed, understanding the significance of Chinese familism cannot be settled outside the processes of social mediation, as anthropologists would say, taking place in specific conditions of social and economic relations and cultural imagining.

The critique of Confucian capitalism must begin by relentlessly confronting the question of social mediation and cultural invention which locates 'Chinese culture' in a specific empirical situation. A remarkable undertaking that attempts to do this is Susan Greenhalgh's 'De-Orientalizing the Chinese Family Firm' (1994). Focusing on the political conditions of post-colonial Taiwan, Greenhalgh brilliantly shows that the prevalent family firm in Taiwan, rather than being an outcome of Chinese cultural influence, can be traced back to the land reform of 1949–53, which forced landed families to reinvest in small urban industries. As most of these industries were established from 'acquired' property, rather than 'inherited' ancestral estates, the individual owners are able to exercise economic domination and personal control over all those in the work organisation, where daughters-in-law and unmarried sons are especially disadvantaged.

'De-Orientalizing the Chinese Family Firm' is a timely project which interrogates the cultural fetishism of the Confucian capitalism thesis. In this chapter, I hope to contribute to this critical enterprise; I do this, however, by taking a somewhat different analytical path. Instead of stressing the political and historical conditions which moved the Chinese to set up family businesses, what concerns me is the significance of the Chinese family – its cultural ideas and relationships – as it is played out in daily life in the shop. My approach is therefore ethnographic. I focus particularly on the daily routine in the family business in which 'Chinese culture' and its fragments are constantly evoked and reinvented. The appearance of paternalism in Chinese family business, I emphasise, arises not from the inner prompting of 'Chinese cultural habits'. Rather such cultural features come into being through the strategic manoeuvres of management to install controlling power in the workplace. In this deployment, Chinese cultural ideas about the family are seized upon and elaborated in order to make them an appropriate resource for organising management control. For in the outpost town of Karjan too, culture is, as they say, a contested terrain. In the attempt to institute a 'benevolent paternalism' in the family business, 'Chinese culture', transformed and renegotiated, also charts the very possibility of resistance.

The setting: doing business in Karjan

Karjan is a remote township of some 1,500 people located in the north-east interior of Sarawak, two days' journey by boat from the state capital, Kuching. The Education Department runs a boarding school there for children from the nearby native communities; about 600 students and some 25 teachers add to the total population during the school term. Since it was first established by the Brooke government in 1884, Karjan bazaar has developed over time into an important service point at the far end of the Rejang trading system that stretches from Kuching to Sibu, Kanowit, Kapit and the interior (Chew 1990). Local produce like rubber, pepper, coffee, cocoa, fish and game, and jungle goods like ilipe nuts and rattan, as well as woven mats and basket-ware, are traded there before being transported down river to wholesalers in Sibu and Kuching. For the native people in the nearby longhouse communities, Karjan is also the place where the 'praise and blame' of government administration – school, medical care and agricultural assistance on the one hand, and political control, government licences and tax collection on the other – are being organised. Since 1973, a full District Office, with some 22 administrative staff and development officers, has been located in the town. The District Office is the centre of the government presence; it oversees the administration of land tenure, agricultural development, public health, education and law and order (the District Officer also acts as the local magistrate). In addition, the DO handles the development fund and the salaries of government servants, including some 250 schoolteachers working in the nearby longhouse communities; money from these sources is spent on food, clothes, fuel, fertilisers, agricultural equipment and daily necessities, providing one of the main supports for local businesses.

Apart from the District Office, Karjan's main landmark is undoubtedly the Chinese shophouses. When one travels up the Rejang from Sibu and Kapit to Karjan, after a long journey through brown muddy banks and swamp land, the row of well constructed shop buildings, freshly painted and adorned with bright colourful signs in Chinese, English and Malay, is a welcoming sight. The shops are well stocked with clothes, plastic wares, stationery, canned foods, beer and soft drinks. Other than the shophouses, Chinese traders also operate the marine engine shops and petrol pumps at the waterfront as well as the twice daily express boat services between Karjan and Kapit.

The fifteen odd shops in Karjan sit in a straight row facing south towards the boat landing. These are the newer shops. Previously, traders lived and worked in ramshackle wooden sheds at the present site, before the government completed the new lots in December 1978. Running adjacent to the new shops are the so-called temporary lots, rows of 28 wooden shacks, most of which were burnt down by a fire in August 1995. Some of these shops have been moved to the new rows of shops behind the original lots away from the river. Here are found a variety of small shops, mostly owned by Malays and Kayans – the predominant native people in the Upper Rejang – and a few Chinese. Most of these are coffee shops offering simple food like boiled noodles and cakes; others sell soap powder, matches, dry batteries, mosquito coils, cooking oil and other sundry goods.

Family in business: business in family

So the main shops in the Karjan bazaar really form the economic centre of the town; and here of the fifteen shops thirteen are owned by ethnic Chinese. In these shops, the centrality of the family is so obvious that it is hard at first to take it seriously. Consistent with the model of the Chinese family firm, the manager is also the owner. Living and working with him is his wife, who seems to be everywhere at once: she helps in the shop by serving the customers or sitting at the cashier's counter and generally watching over the comings and goings, all the time attending to her domestic duties. If she is young enough, she will have a baby in tow who learns to walk in the shop, watched by its proud parents and admiring customers, followed about by its eager mother with a feeding bowl. The shop, we might say, *is* the family. For all family activities take place within it: in the shop, the *towkay* and his wife work and play, teach and socialise with their children, love and fight, and dream about better times and more prosperous places. In the shop too, the children grow up learning the best and the worst from their parents, and live their young years through a 'Chinese upbringing' before they are, usually at the age of 12 or 13 years, sent away for a high school education in Kapit, the nearest town down river, about an hour away by boat. The main shophouses in Karjan bazaar are typically two-storey linked houses, with the shop on the ground floor and living quarters upstairs. As the boys grow older, at the age of 9 or 10, they are gently pushed out from the upstairs to the 'real world' of the shop-front. Here they play, do their homework, carry out little business errands, and when night comes, sleep like the shop assistants (*huo ji*) on canvas beds laid out on the floor after closing time.

The shop is thus a social world in which family life and business are closely intertwined. In the flux of daily life, it is difficult to see where one begins and the other ends. For doing business in Karjan, as I have described elsewhere (Yao 1997), has always involved 'the family' – in seeking capital, credit and other forms of support from wealthier kinsmen in larger towns down river, or in seeking a wife who can share the burdens of economic ambition in this remote place in the jungle. Going back to the issue raised by Greenhalgh, in purely economic terms, the marital choice of a hardworking wife is crucial for saving labour costs and thus in contributing to capital accumulation, especially in the early years of business. At the same time, the wife's subservient position in the family will be affected by the nature of her marital relationship, and at times, her complicity in the discharging of patriarchal authority. All this, however, deserves a more detailed treatment at another time.

Meanwhile, I turn to examine the Chinese family firm in terms of what I call the 'socialisation of business'. I use the term to refer to the cultural authorisation of business as the only worthwhile endeavour that promises a social and economic future, so that all the strategic processes – mode of authority, management decisions and cultural ethos – towards this end are assembled as the 'edifice of normalcy' in daily life. In Karjan, the socialisation of business in this sense tends to transform the running of a shop into the very *raison d'être* of living in Karjan. Doing business takes on a special meaning as the only worthwhile undertaking for any man of ambition in that remote township in the jungle.

The source of this signification can be traced to the social and physical conditions in which trade is carried out along the Upper Rejang (Chew 1990; Yao 1997). Of the river hawkers who traded along the Rejang in the late nineteenth century, Daniel Chew writes:

> The experiences of the pioneers were similar in many respects: they invariably had to cope with physical hazards, ranging from accidents to murder and robbery; long boat journeys were inevitable; and contact with the natives to

effect economic exchanges was essential; most traders relaxed by indulging in gambling, drinking, and opium smoking.

(Chew 1990: 77)

But for all their endurance and heroic endeavour, social isolation and uncertain economic rewards haunted the Chinese traders. Chew continues:

> A few of the pioneers would have returned prosperous to their native villages, others would have stayed on in Sarawak. For the majority...who chose trading as an occupation, their dream of amassing riches...remained unfulfilled. They would have spent most of their days in Sarawak struggling against adversity and, having no choice, were forced to remain behind in Sarawak in remote riverine bazaars, or up-river in their atap-thatched boats.

(Chew 1990: 77)

Social deprivation aside, the remote geography of the area has always determined the returns to trading in the Upper Rejang. Setting up business here implies, relative to larger towns down river, smaller capital requirements and a reasonable profit by being near the source of native produce. The overall conditions of pioneering trade, while shaping the opportunity structure itself, also flood over to general perceptions about life along the Rejang, giving business activities in Karjan special meaning and discursive possibility. Indeed, in daily life among Chinese traders, the history of riverine trade and Karjan's geographical isolation are constantly being reinterpreted in a way which keeps alive the 'romance of Chinese capitalism', fuelling the self-construction of Chinese traders as men endowed with inner virtues of hard work, endurance, and business talent, for which Chinese everywhere are renowned (Yao 1997).

The 'use' of culture in family business

My concern here has been to highlight the specific meaning of economic activity in Karjan. Business may be about making money, but there is also much that is beyond the simple rule of profit and loss, of extracting maximum returns from each considered input of capital and labour. The 'fluid forms that property and wealth take', anthropologist George Marcus (1990: 339) reminds us, '...although seeming to fit squarely into our category of the economic, actually encompass a good deal of the cultural discourses and characteristics of the owners'. To understand the way business is organised in and perceived by Chinese society requires therefore a 'breach between economic and cultural analysis' (Marcus 1990: 331). With this in mind, it becomes evident that the history of pioneering trade, the geographical location of Karjan, and the self-imagining of Chinese traders deeply influence one another. The result, somewhat inevitably perhaps, is to give business enterprise in Karjan a certain existential aura which comes to envelop the way the Chinese trader thinks about his business and the way it should be run. This has serious implications.

For one thing, quite apart from the aim of making a profit, owning a shop in Karjan takes on a sense of urgency as the only way to 'compensate' for the social and material deprivation of life in the jungle. For all the financial risk and uncertain return, having your own business, as many informants express, offers an opportunity to turn one's life around. To run a shop even in a place like Karjan is to be your own man, the sole arbiter of one's destiny. What is important about this 'social investment' is the way it so dramatically constitutes the moral imperative of the family and the business organised around it. Family business comes to be ordained as a perfect fusion of economic and cultural project, a fusion that carves a sanctuary from the 'wind and dust of life', as the Chinese would say. Setting up a shop simply gathers family members around in a common enterprise under a 'culturally prescribed' paternal authority in the person of the owner.

In this context, it is interesting to turn to some of the vast literature on immigrant enterprises. Light and Bonacich (1988) in their study of Korean immigrant entrepreneurs in Los Angeles, have shown the way in which the family has provided the most obvious resources for building economic security in a new environment of defined opportunity structure and often social hostility. Echoing this finding, Waldinger (1990) has suggested that the strong moral climate surrounding the family among immigrant enterprises in the United States has, in fact, a significant social – and pragmatic – underpinning. Small business, he argues (1990: 414), relies on family members simply because 'unlike strangers, the characteristics of kin are known and familiar; hence, their behaviour is more likely to be predictable, if not reliable; and furthermore, trust may already be inherent in the family relationship'.

Much of the literature on the Chinese family firm similarly emphasises the role of the family in 'facilitating' management, control and ownership – indeed, the successful stories – of family business. But the numerous studies have been, in the main, less illuminating of the dysfunctional aspects of familial relationships, and the powerful ideological embeddedness and the structural relations in the family firm which make possible management control and the extraction of surpluses from family and related workers. These silences, as Susan Greenhalgh has pointed out, are largely moved by Orientalised perceptions of the way the Chinese family firm works. But these perceptions also derive much currency from the wider discourse of Chinese/Confucian capitalism as constructed by states in East Asia – Singapore, Taiwan and China – and by academics of Chinese descent in the region and the United States (Dirlik 1997). Much of the argument about the social and economic feasibility of 'Chinese economic familism' (Wong 1985: 58) can be seen within this context. However, if culture – in this case, the high regard for familial unity and co-operation – is indeed so 'useful', then the very notion of its functional dynamics demands an analytical reckoning.

My thinking through of the mutual entanglement of cultural values, social aspirations and economic conditions in Karjan would question the notion of 'Chinese culture' as something that is invariably drawn from Confucianism. Indeed, Confucianism is far distant from the mundane realities of the Chinese shops in the Sarawak town. The ethos of the family and its uncertain impingement on people's behaviour can be more realistically ascertained without appealing to the abstractive 'Confucian heritage', but through examining the nature of social relations and management practices: the way they are made and articulated. What I am concerned with here is the methodological fallacy of detaching 'culture' from practice, from the site of its production and reproduction. 'Culture' is always historically, socially and spatially located. In this context, in regards to Chinese family business, two questions can be raised. These are: first, how does family enterprise help to (re)produce the familial relationships and values that come to ground it? And second, how does the structure of family business provide the platform from which the ideology and power relations of the (Chinese) family can be launched?

The first question can be dealt with briefly. For Chinese traders in Karjan, as much as for new immigrants in the United States, small family business literally keeps the family together. The central values of familial relationships and unity are anxiously talked about and (re)produced in the shops as a way of negotiating the challenges of living in a new land. For Korean immigrant entrepreneurs in the United States, as Light and Bonacich (1988) have shown, modest grocery shops provide a measure of reprieve before they – or more likely their children – must venture out to explore educational and employment opportunities in the wider society. Among immigrant entrepreneurs generally, family business is always invested with crucial redemptive possibilities in both the social and economic realms. In other words, the 'meaning' of family business lies not only in its financial future, but also in creating, if only temporarily, a self-sustaining economic and social 'home' in what appears to be a sea of indifference and, at times, hostility. The conditions facing Chinese traders in Belga are, of course, different. Nonetheless for them too, family shops are sanctified places in which they can plan their economic destiny and organise the rewards and pleasures of life. Installation of the family – its values and structural relationships – in business is a socially and economically compelling project.

Invention of the family

The second question is more central to our discussion and deserves lengthier treatment. The trading stores in Karjan, as I have described, achieve a seamless blending of family life and business so that the cultural ethos of one and the calculative intent of the other are constantly evoked to be one and the same thing. The result is a subtle moral discourse which ties business success and family continuity into a single crucial undertaking. In the Chinese traders' thinking, there can be no business success without the family, and family happiness has no meaning without economic success. To give an example of the prevalent ethos, the most common gossip about business failure in Karjan finds the reason in a person's lack of focus (*zhuan xin*) or single-mindedness, such as when a person gives in to reckless business expansion almost out of the excitement of the moment. There are many tales of a Tsok or a Lee who dissipated his money by being 'over-ambitious'. These tales warn against the folly of economic adventurism to which one is all too easily tempted to succumb in a place like Karjan, and thus bring the family to ruin. From business failure to ruin of the family, the moral narrative authorises a turning inwards to the domestic sphere so that family interest provides the final arbitration for what is worthwhile and what is not. However, the other side of the equation is also true. Just as family interests temper business success, the mode of business organisation and management decision has to be validated by considering the way they affect 'family matters' (*jia shi*).

This ideological predilection for the family can be understood, I suggest, without turning to the idea of 'Confucian heritage' itself. In the social and geographical conditions of Karjan, the narrative of business venture – the social importance of its success and the moral implications of its failure – legitimises the family as the existential pivot of life in the jungle. By locating the family centrally in business, the narrative rewrites a new moral language about the social and cultural priority of the family. And in daily life, what this moral language speaks of is not the monumental weight of 'Confucianism', but a more pragmatic concern of how to make a living and keep the family together in Karjan. As one informant puts it:

> We are all uneducated 'rough people' (*cu ren*), all we know is make some small business (*xiao shen yi*) in order to survive. In a small place like Karjan, you cannot be too ambitious. It is enough if you earn [enough to have] 'a bowl of rice a day'. That is what most of us think. As long as there is enough to keep the family together, we are doing well.

Nonetheless, the modest tone of the informant belies the significant redemptive potential with which many Chinese traders think about their life and work in Karjan. Burdened with an existential purpose, the central ideas and practices of the family are simply too important to be left alone. They have to be subjected to continuous innovation and reinvention in the business organisation, providing the family firm with its central principle of management authority and control. What I call the invention of the family has to be seen in this context, as one of selective objectification of associated cultural ideas and practices. Nicholas Thomas writes of the nature of social – in his case, colonial – encounters:

> There is no abstract sense in which certain features of a society or culture are important and will therefore be prominent in objectification of that society or culture; rather, the process of choosing emblematic activities, dispositions, or material artefacts is indissociable from [the nature of]... particular encounters.
>
> (Thomas 1992: 213–14)

Similarly, it is through a grounded and strategic process, rather than the magical transmission of cultural heritage from that past, that the signification of the 'Chinese family' is inscribed in Karjan.

'Chinese family' and the *huo ji* system

In the daily life of the shop, what all this leads to is the selective deployment of the family, driving, at times, a tortuous interpretation of its cultural ideas and practices. Putting it simply, what the deployment aims at is to recast the moral significance of the family beyond the immediate kinsmen to include outsiders, in order to install an affectivity of power in a wider set of social relationships.

Even with their small operations, Chinese shops in Karjan often need to employ workers from outside the immediate family. This occurs when children are too young or are attending school, when the wife is too busy attending to her domestic duties, or simply when business is expanding beyond what the husband and wife can cope with. These workers are normally recruited from among poor relatives in Kapit or Kanowit, who send their young sons to Karjan to earn a 'rice bowl' and to learn about business by serving as an apprentice or a shop assistant (*huo ji*). In the way a shop owner usually puts it, taking on the young man is a favour to the young man's poor parents, out of obligation among kinsmen, however distant they are.

Right from the beginning, it is impressed upon the young man that he is a member of the family which employs him. His father's parting words, before leaving him and boarding the river ferry home, affirm that the *towkay* is to legitimately take on the parental role. The young man learns to respect the *towkay*'s authority, and turns to him for help when necessary. By all appearances, the *huo ji* is indeed a part of the *towkay*'s family. He eats at the same table with the family, sleeps on a canvas bed laid out after the shop closes, often next to the older children, and shares the intimate ups and downs of life in the shop. At festival time, he receives presents and *hong bao* (red packets of 'good luck money') before taking leave to visit his own family. These formalities, harmlessly normal as they are, nonetheless chart a path of moral import onto which a *huo ji* is imperceptibly drawn.

On one level, there is no doubt that the *huo ji* system forms an intrinsic part of the social economy of the family shop. The idea of a *huo ji* or shop assistant may suggest the peripheral role of a person still learning the trade, but as he becomes more familiar with his work, his duties in the daily running of the shop are anything but peripheral. He opens the shop first thing in the morning, receives goods arriving by the river ferry, serves customers and packs their orders in tidy parcels, generally working from 7:30 in the morning when the shop opens, until 9:00 in the evening when it closes. He works seven days a week, and takes no holidays except during Chinese New Year or occasionally other major festivals. He attends to the shop at all hours; when a customer knocks on the door at whatever hour asking for aspirin, or when a late drinking party comes by way past midnight to replenish its supply of Guinness stout or Chinese *samsu* (local liquor), he gets up from his sleep to supply the goods through the door.

For such work, the young man is paid a subsistence wage of 150–250 ringgit a month, though he is provided with food and accommodation even if only a simple canvas bed on the shop floor. In any case, since there is really nothing to spend his money on in Karjan aside from beer and small gambling parties of *mah-jong* or poker with friends, the young *huo ji* is often able to save and send money home. No doubt moved by parental expectation, most of the apprentices I interviewed said that they will try their best to serve the full term as agreed between their parents and the *towkay*, before better opportunities call them back to their home town, or more frequently, to the logging camps up-river.

The *huo ji*, however, is not slow to see through the language of kinship and recognise the reality of his position. While he enjoys the benefits and comforts of being a part of the *towkay*'s family, the iron grip of obligation and discipline also come to circumscribe his life. One young shop assistant said in an interview:

> Every time I ask for a raise, only ten dollars a month more [than my present wage], my uncle always says I had better talk with my father, and my father told him not to give me more money as I may pick up a bad habit like smoking. So he always says whatever he does is for my own good, and I have to be patient. Everything [between us] has to be brought to my father.

The informant Ngiu Ah Khew, aged 18, came from a poor farming family in Kapit. After finishing primary school, he could not find work and found himself washing cars and guarding them in the car park near the shops. His career as a *jaga kereta* (literally, car watcher) was short-lived when he started mixing with bad company from street gangs and got himself arrested by the police. His father, impatient with Young Ngiu's wandering ways, finally sent him to Karjan to work in Chop Hock Guan, one of the largest provision shops in town, the owner of which, Chong Yew Tong, is also Tapu Hakka like Ngiu's family. The young man calls Chong 'uncle' as a sign of respect, but also in accordance with the convention of claiming kinship by tracing their descent from ancestors from the same village in China.

When I met Ngiu in 1994, he had already been working for his 'uncle' for two years. He went about his work quietly, perhaps taking heed of his father's words and not wanting to disappoint his parents or his employer. But it was also clear that he was restless. He often told me that he had 'endured enough' (*shou guo le*) of the hard – and for a young man, boring – life in Karjan. He did not want to go back to his family in Kapit, however. What he wanted was to get a job in one of the logging camps which, as they finish their devastating work down-river, are gradually moving up to the forest in the Seven Division near Karjan. In July that year, he found a job as a store keeper in one such camp, at the wage of 850 ringgit, more than five times what he was earning at the time. After his departure, Old Chong often expressed disappointment that Ngiu had not stayed longer as he had plans for his young nephew, perhaps to make him an assistant manager one day since his own son was still in school and might go on to university. As it is, he said, Young Ngiu will never learn 'the way of commerce' (*zuo shen yi*), and when the logging is finished he will have to move on in search of another job.

There is nothing that more fatally misreads the mood and inner ambition of Young Ngiu than this validation of doing business (*zuo shen yi*) as an all-encompassing social purpose. The 'misunderstanding' between them was not only a matter of differences in age and perceptions of job mobility in the remote interior; it also had much to do with the older man's fetishistic appraisal of the importance of 'doing business' (*zuo shen yi*). Thus preoccupied, it is hard for Old Chong to see a world beyond the security of the family shop and to understand the impatience of a young man whose street-wise ways have made it hard for him to endure the daily grind of a tedious job. For Young Ngiu, a job in the logging camp promised freedom, excitement and better pay. Above all, as he quite rightly pointed out, he hoped later on to move from being a store-man to receiving training in operating a chain-saw and lifting crane, skills more practical and transferable than that of serving in a shop.

Kan dian, visual power and the family

The *huo ji* system therefore crucially depends on an artful reworking of the conventionally prescribed Chinese family values of obligation, gratitude and consensus. By bringing outsiders into the circuit of the family, the strategy hopes to broaden the catchment of people whose labour and resources can be harnessed. The 'Chinese family' has to be reinvented simply because there is no a priori and secure cultural rule which can be unproblematically put to such use. In this case, what renders unstable the sanctification of the 'family' is the changing opportunity structure in Karjan brought about by the ever rapacious logging camps. To recognise this reality is to open one's eyes to a different world – with its promises of a new social horizon and employment opportunities – outside the family shop. For Young Ngiu, his contesting reading of the 'Chinese family' is no dramatic gesture of sudden revelation, but a discovery of its ideological sham as he reflects on his own interests and daily life in the shop.

Once we look at it this way, the deployment of the 'Chinese family' in Karjan, as elsewhere, is no longer a straightforward affair which singularly fosters management efficiency and business profitability, as it is often argued. What the *huo ji* system demonstrates is the problematic nature and uncertain outcome of any imposition of the Chinese family model on the workplace. It is this sensitivity to the empirical situation which can help us to sort out the issue of the functional significance – or its opposite – of the Chinese family in economic enterprise. In what follows, I would like to further draw out the intricate problems of the 'use of the Chinese family' by looking at the responses of another worker of different position in – and thus different power relationship to – the management.

In Chop Hock Guan, besides the young apprentice Ngiu and the owner Chong, the other worker is Liek How Seng, a man in his early forties who has been in the shop for almost five years. He is usually referred to as *tou shou*, or foreman, who is, as the title signifies, responsible for running the shop in consultation with the owner. In a similar fashion to Ngiu, he was 'rescued' from unemployment, and in his case, bankruptcy, when his small dealership in marine engines in Kapit went under. He got to know Old Chong when he was a salesman visiting Karjan regularly as a representative of the Japanese Yanmar brand outboard motor. In 1987, Liek accepted the position in Chop Hock Guan at a salary of 650 ringgit a month, leaving his wife and children with his mother in Kapit.

For Old Chong, the employment of Liek was intended to relieve him of duties in the shop in order to take on a business venture he had been planning for years. This was to set up a purchasing agency in the nearby longhouse of Kenyah people, buying and storing fish and wild game carcasses in a refrigerator before sending them down river to Sibu and Kuching. In the 1980s, before the heavy felling of timber along the river destroyed much of the game in the area, this had been a lucrative business making substantial profits for some of the Karjan shops. In any case, the arrangement required Old Chong to travel up-river, and to be away from Karjan for three or four days at a time. During such periods, the running of the shop was left to Liek, assisted by Young Ngiu, under the 'delegated authority' of Old Chong's wife and their young son, 14-year-old San Peng. It is in this situation at the shop, in the absence of the *towkay*, that the practice of *kan dian* or 'watching the shop' has evolved.

The notion of *kan dian* conjures up the image of a shop owner – or his wife or elder son – sitting by the counter perhaps next to the cash register, looking over the shop, receiving customers and salesmen, and generally helping the workers when they are busy. In daily life, when two older men meet in the bazaar or in the coffee shop, the term may appear in an exchange something like this:

A: Old Wong, how are you? I heard your son came back. You should *shou san* [retire; or literally, 'retreat to the mountain'] and let the young people take over.

B: Well, the world now belongs to the young people. I can help them a bit by *kan dian* [watching the shop]; it is up to him. We old ones are useless now.

In the language of ritual modesty, the exchange suggests, with a candid casualness, that *kan dian* is something 'useless old men' do to pass the time, and to help out the son, who having inherited the business, is now in charge. In one way, *kan dian* is indeed so informal. As one shop owner explained:

Really it is just about keeping an eye on things. One of us [in the family] always has to be there [in the shop], to watch over things. Sometimes the *huo ji* may not be trusted, or still lacks experience [at work]. So you need someone who can greet the customers and suppliers. It is like telling people there is someone in charge, and [the shop is] is not in the hands of outsiders.

Yet, the casualness of the practice, and the easy way it is talked about, belies the social affectivity of the practice. Indeed, *kan dian* is about signifying the fact of economic ownership and management control through the physical presence and visual power of the proprietor. As he casts his gaze over the place that has been his life and work, *kan dian* has a strong sense of surveillance, of monitoring all that is taking place. The gaze is perhaps the more effective precisely because it is without a specific target, but distributed over the shop, taking note of what is taking place, making sure that things are done in a certain way. There is no doubt that *kan dian* is meant to be effective, capable of rectifying any mistake or what is seen as recalcitrant behaviour in the workplace. The practice is taken very seriously by the *towkay*. When he plans to be away, there is discussion in the family about who will take his place, perhaps the wife, or the elder son, or even the aged parent. The idea is that some member of the family will be there among the 'outsiders' working in the shop. *Kan dian* operates, in short, by announcing the signification of power and its associated structural relationship as unmistakably originating from the *towkay* and his family.

Kan dian, visual power and resistance

What *kan dian* aims to achieve in the context of the shop, in another sense, is no less than establishing systematic differences between family members and outsiders, employer and employees, business interests and workers' aspirations. We have already seen something of this in the case of the young *huo ji* Ngiu. *Kan dian* is also an innocuous affirmation of differences, but through the forceful visual presence of the 'family' in the workplace. All this takes place, we have to remember, in the pervasive ethos of 'bringing workers into the fold of the family'. Indeed the treatment of *tou shou* Liek in the shop is no less elegiac than what Young Ngiu experienced. Both Young Ngiu and Chong's children will call Liek to the table when the meal is ready, as a sign of respect. There is evident rapport between the *towkay* and his *tou shou*, with whom he discusses various matters concerning the shop; and when the *towkay* visits Kapit, he often brings a present or some simple token of personal greeting to Liek's wife and mother living there. But how do these and other gestures of 'familism' gel with a practice clearly aimed at installing control over and discrimination against 'outsiders'?

When asked about the nature of the practice, and why Chong's wife or his young son always have to be around when the *towkay* is away, both Young Ngiu and *tou shou* Liek are likely to reply something to the effect that *kan dian* is simply what the *towkay* has to do: he has to look after the shop in the way he sees fit. But in truth, while they appear to accept many management practices, even rationalising them from the *towkay*'s perspective, there are moments that betray the appearance of easy compliance.

To illustrate, when asked why *kan dian* is necessary, Old Chong explained why some workers could not be trusted, and related several past incidents in which a *huo ji* was found taking money from the cash register, or goods from the shop for his own use or to resell. For these reasons, certain preventive measures are developed. For example, when a worker is leaving the shop for a holiday, or when he resigns from the job, the *towkay* checks his bag. Instead of asking to have the bag opened and be shown its contents, he quickly dips his hand into it, and finding nothing, quickly withdraws the hand. This somewhat ineffectual searching is carried out moments after the voicing of good wishes and reminders to the younger workers to be filial and kind to their parents. Checking the bag thus has some of the character of a parting ritual, like pay packets, bonuses and personal greetings. For the worker concerned, however, this is clearly an accusatory gesture, implying dishonesty and deceit on his part. So checking the bag is done swiftly to avoid an embarrassing silence. And as I watched this happen the day of Young Ngiu's departure, Old Chong could barely look him in the face or meet the cold fury in his eyes.

So, the workers' outward compliance and apparent observance of the ethos of the 'family' cannot be made to suggest a lack of insight into their position *vis-à-vis* the management. Just as the quiet outrage during the parting ritual is there for those who have eyes to see it, the subversive response to the practice of *kan dian* is also staged for an appropriate audience at the right moment. Resistance would be a useful term here if we consider the connotations of strategic intention in conscious and more or less organised actions, as used by James Scott in his *Weapons of the Weak* (1985). Perhaps more appropriate to my ethnography is the notion of resistance that takes place imperceptibly in the course of daily life as developed by de Certeau (1984). Undertaken by ordinary people (e.g. shoppers and window-gazers in a mall), this kind of resistance is not expressed through heroic gestures, and people are not always conscious of the political implications nor the precise target of their action. (Wearing a T-shirt in highly regulated Singapore with the caption 'Singapore – a fine city: parking fine, littering fine, etc.' is a good example.) What takes place in Chop Hock Guan are similarly undramatic gestures which by their very ordinariness pose a meaningful response to management power and control.

The results are revealing, if at times somewhat comical. Normally when the shop is busy, and when the workers immerse themselves in work, they are quite oblivious to the monitoring presence of the *towkay*. But when business is slow, with no customers around, they will begin to feel the presence of watchful eyes. At such moments, there is no question of relaxing and they must find something to do: dust the shelves, clean and polish the shop counter, go through the accounts, or whatever. A moment of reprieve comes during the temporary absence of the *towkay* when he is away, perhaps talking with a salesman in the coffee shop. But when the *towkay* returns and steps into the shop, they quickly put down the newspaper or stop their gossiping and return to the chores they have left.

Resistance and the workers looking back

To understand the effectiveness of *kan dian*, it is useful to refer to the insights of Foucault (1979), who alerts us to the significance of this kind of visual power in the monitoring of social behaviour in society. When Foucault talks about 'biopolitics', he has in mind the repressive project of the modern state achieved through the management of population, through the constituting of productive bodies. This 'bio-power', he suggests, is concerned with developing and enforcing rules and rituals that increase the surveillance and thus control of the population. To achieve this surveillance, the instrumentality of power and control must install visuality and 'seeing' so that power is cast on, and distributed over, docile bodies in society (1979: 135).

It is not too much of a theoretical anomaly to consider this form of 'visual power' of the modern state in examining what takes place in a Chinese family business. *Kan dian* similarly 'watches' and 'controls'. What it aims to achieve is compliance among workers. Certainly, as many workers confess, being 'watched' by the boss is unnerving. It is no less so when *kan dian* is carried out by the wife or the young son when Old Chong is away. As immediate members of the family, they 'represent' the fact of economic ownership and management authority in the organisation of the shop. There is, however, a certain contradiction here. For reasons of gender and age, and in a patriarchal culture which never invests too much authority in either of them, both Chong's wife and young son simply find it hard to live up to the role they are asked to take on. In spite of the continuous family discussion about the importance of 'watching over the shop', especially when Chong is planning to be away, the problem of delegated authority is never completely resolved. Not infrequently, such discussion leads to quarrels between Chong and his wife. As she once complained somewhat dramatically, 'the Old Man does not know how we suffer (*shou qi*) in the shop'.

What Chong's wife did, in fact, was to tell the other side of the story about the practice of managerial monitoring. If the *towkay* is single-minded about the need to mark the 'family interest' in the shop, he is also somewhat blind to – or unwilling to acknowledge – the difficulties facing his wife and young son who take over when he is away. When the wife talked about the experience of *shou qi*, or being mistreated or bullied, she harked back to her experience of not being taken seriously, and having to see her authority being openly defied by the workers. For the simple fact is that *kan dian* by anyone less than the *towkay* allows significant laxity in workers' performance, and thus the possibility of 'looking back', of resistance itself.

A notably more relaxed atmosphere prevails in the shop when Old Chong is away. Both Young Ngiu and foreman Liek begin to slow down their pace of work, and even evade some of their responsibilities. They read newspapers with grave concentration, making customers wait. When a salesman comes, Liek may leave the shop and spend a long time with the salesman in a coffee shop, discussing replenishment of stock or whatever. This occurs under the watchful eyes of the *towkay*'s wife or his young son, who have left their usual duties and are now conspicuously present in the shopfront. Such recalcitrant behaviour, however, is rarely witnessed when Old Chong is present. To the workers, his substantive authority comes from his age, and more importantly his long years of experience and deep knowledge of the various aspects of the business. He commands respect too, one suspects, because he has the power to dismiss any worker from his employment. Such authority and power of sanction are simply not available to Chong's wife and their young son. In the context of such uneven distribution of authority, it is not surprising that both Young Ngiu and Liek find it convenient to negotiate their discontent in the presence of the wife and young son, who become direct targets of the employees' discontent.

In this context too, one particular behaviour seems even more successful in generating a degree of 'resistance': the deployment of gossip. Gossip generally, through the telling of elaborate tales and even lies about a person, can be a crucial means of transacting a strategically bounded meaning and social position (Goffman 1962; Gilsenan 1976). Indeed, when exchanged between people who share the same grievances, gossip enables the powerless to regain initiative in a relationship through creating and recreating 'stories' and targeting them at the specific object of complaint. When his boss is away from the shop, Liek becomes quite free in telling stories he claims to have heard about Old Chong in Kapit or Sibu, stories about his business incompetence in being cheated in a deal or being charged a higher than market price for certain goods. Almost as a deliberate attempt to hurt, gossiping about Old Chong is also carried out in front of his wife and son. Since they lack the authority to prevent or rebut such 'stories', the experience is humiliating: it is this which Chong's wife complains of. I recorded one remark foreman Liek made to a visitor in front of the *towkay*'s wife:

> Well, Old Bald Head [Chong is exceedingly bald] is so stingy he won't even buy Ah Lam [salesman of Gold Fish mosquito coil] a cup of coffee when he has come all the way from Sibu. So they [the salesmen] do not have a good impression of him. He has no face before them, and he doesn't even know it... [laughter].

To give another example, once when Old Chong was away and did not return in time to issue the monthly wages, his wife took on the task. As is normal practice, she deducted any cash advances and put each employee's wages in a used envelope, then distributed the pay packets to the workers. When Liek received his packet, feeling bitter perhaps because he realised that his pay that month would be meagre after having taking a substantial advance to give to his wife, he picked up his money sullenly. Avoiding Chong's wife's eyes, and turning to his friends who had come to take him for an evening out, Liek said with a sigh '*niu tou qian*' or literally 'an ox's money', implying that his wages were a poor return for having worked like a ox. The statement was clearly for the *towkay*'s wife's ears. By turning to those present in the shop, he also sought their sympathy and support for his dissatisfaction.

The woman's face, hot and flushed, registered the hurt that she felt. One wonders about the psychological impact on her and her teenage son of hearing Old Chong being talked about in such an offensive manner. The 14-year-old San Peng was generally expected to be in the shop when he came back from school in Kapit. Though he always obeyed, he obviously did not enjoy being there. When he was called away from our English lessons in the coffee shop, he became depressed and could hardly contain his anger. He felt uneasy, he told me, sitting in the shop 'pretending to help and serve the customers when I did not know the price of merchandise', and hearing his father being talked about by the workers 'deeply embarrassed' him.

Conclusion

The resistance of the workers sharply demonstrates the uncertain outcome of management practices like *kan dian*. The invention of the family, so central to Chinese business organisation, is exposed by its weakness which workers eagerly exploit. My discussion of the intricate processes and consequences of the cultural invention of the family in Chinese business serves to give a more complex assessment of the culture and economic behaviour arguments in the literature. The anthropological approach I have adopted is intended to restore the dynamic sense of constructiveness and location in the notion of culture, a dynamic sense that has been undermined by the Confucian capitalism thesis. However, methodological caution is perhaps necessary here. The critical evaluation of culture is not to see it as simply an ideological tool without its own specific mode of operation and effectiveness. The temptation of this critique is to do away with culture altogether, so that management decisions in Chinese business become purely pragmatic adaptive responses to given socio-economic conditions. Note, for instance, the following explanation of culture and economic behaviour among Overseas Chinese in Southeast Asia:

> It is precisely because individuals are spontaneous, unpredictable and multi-dimensional, and it is because no assumption can be made about the existence and operation of guiding laws, of chains of cause and effect, of pre-programmed traits and of recursive structures, that there are no set behavioural, institutional and moral patterns. ...What is of far greater interest and significance is the rotation of multidimensional actions, institutions and values, and the manner in which, and the ends to which, they are directed by individuals, and the motivation and purposes for which individuals create unidimensional presentations.
>
> (Hodder 1996: 11)

Here behaviour is primarily a matter of directing means to an end, in which culture and values no longer have a place. This crude materialist humanism, I suggest, is the direct result of the critical erasure of culture. In contrast, I maintain that 'culture', constructed and ideologised as it is, mediates 'doing business' (*zuo shen yi*) by investing it with a social and existential meaning. The anxious validation of business as a social and economic project is, as we have seen, anything but a 'cultural delusion'. In Karjan, as in many similar situations in which new immigrants find themselves, family business offers a viable organisational form through which to exploit a given economic opportunity. Yet the family business has a significance far beyond the economic: it is also the site where values and key relationships of the family are reproduced and vitalised.

The point then is not to see these two 'objectives' as separate – as a product of strategic adaptation, on the one hand, and as a result of ideological illusion, on the other. Neither 'objective' is sufficient in itself to give a complete sense of the economic urgency of and existential investment in family business as a major project among 'Overseas Chinese'. Instead the cultural meaning of business and the strategic 'use' of the family work in dialectical conjunction, mutually reinforcing and giving life to each other. The operation of the Chinese family business is largely dependent on this dual exploitation of economic opportunity and of 'culture' as an ideological resource.

Looking at the deployment of culture in this way, it is no longer possible to go back to an essentialized notion derived from historical texts. If the validation of the family is indeed a Confucian trait, what gives it its social relevance and psychic force is not so much the magical working of 'Confucian heritage' but the socially mediated and historically constituted sense of cultural values in contemporary society, in which Chinese family business is located. One may, with good reason, question whether the notion of 'Confucianism' is at all useful in explaining the complex happenings taking place in Chinese shops in a place like Karjan. To put the question another way: is it Confucianism or another more contingent process of making and remaking 'cultural values' that helps to make sense of management practices and workers' responses? My ethnographic approach focusing on day-to-day events and interactions precisely is meant to redress the failure of an abstract notion of 'Confucianism' in its exegetic task. Furthermore, it is the ethnographic engagement with the workers, the *towkay* and his family in the shop which should provide a deep experience of the highly contentious nature of culture and its reinvention. For both the workers and the *towkay*, family values and relations are 'real' only because they have made them so in their lives in Karjan. In its strategic elaboration by the owner Old Chong and the recalcitrant conduct of Young Ngiu and foreman Liek, the 'Chinese family' is much more, and much less, than what Confucianism textually prescribes. In the social, economic and geographical conditions of Karjan, the Chinese family is a viable institution operating – to use a psychoanalytical phrase – as an imaginary.

The limits of the Chinese/Confucian capitalism thesis therefore lie beyond its fetishised evaluation of 'culture'. More than that, they come about through the violent rupture of the dialectical unity that binds economic purpose and existential intent, management decision and cultural invention, into a single undivided project. From this point of view, it is important to see the management processes I have described not only as something concerning the efficiency of work performance. 'Bringing workers into the fold of the family' and 'watching the store' (*kan dian*) are also crucial practices which embellish, fabricate and particularise the vague notion of 'Chinese family'. What these practices show is the highly unstable field of values and relations in which Chinese family business operates: it is this situation which enables the workers, even as the owner attempts to install his pervasive influence in the workplace, to act out their resistance to management control.

Note

1 This study is based on stretches of fieldwork between February 1992 and October 1995. A preliminary survey of Karjan was carried out in August 1987 on a grant from the Institute of South-East Asian Studies, Singapore, as a part of the Community Network Programme. I am indebted to Jayal Langub, Dr Peter Kedit and L.K. Lee for their assistance and friendship. The revision of this paper has greatly benefited from the valuable comments of Donald Nonini and Jomo K. S.

   Names of persons and places have been changed to protect the anonymity of informants. All values are in Malaysian ringgit. In July 1996, the exchange rate of the ringgit to the US dollar was M$2.505 to US$1. (The recent financial crisis has made exchange rates too volatile for practical comparison using more current values – ed.)

Bibliography

Chew, Daniel (1990) *Chinese Pioneers on the Sarawak Frontier, 1841–1941.* Singapore: Oxford University Press.

Clifford, James (1988) *The Predicament of Culture: Twentieth-Century Ethnography, Literature, and Art.* Cambridge, MA: Harvard University Press.

de Certeau, Michel (1984) *The Practice of Everyday Life*, Steven Rendall (trans.). Berkeley: University of California Press.

Dirlik, Arif (1997) 'Critical Reflections on "Chinese Capitalism" as Paradigm'. *Identities: Global Studies in Culture and Power*, 3(3), January.

Foucault, Michel (1979) *Discipline and Punish.* Harmondsworth, England: Penguin.

Gilsenan, Michael (1976) 'Lying, Honor, and Contradiction', in Bruce Kapferer (ed.) *Transaction and Meaning – Direction in the Anthropology of Exchange and Symbolic Behaviour.* Philadelphia: ISHI.

Goffman, E. (1962) 'On Cooling and Marking Out', in A. Rose (ed.) *Human Behaviour and Social Processes.* London: Routledge and Kegan Paul.

Greenhalgh, Susan (1994) 'De-Orientalizing the Chinese Family Firm'. *American Ethnologist*, 21(6).

Hodder, Rupert (1996) *Merchant Princes of the East – Cultural Delusions, Economic Success and the Overseas Chinese in Southeast Asia.* Chichester, England: John Wiley.

Kahn, Herman (1979) *World Economic Development: 1979 and Beyond.* New York: Morrow Quill.

Koh, Tommy (1993) '10 Values That Help East Asia's Economic Progress, Prosperity'. *The Straits Times*, December 14.

Leung Hon-chou (1994) 'Confucianism and Beyond: Culture and Society in East Asian Development', in Richard Harvey Brown (ed.) *Culture, Politics, and Economic Growth: Experience of East Asia.* Williamsburg, VA: Department of Anthropology, College of William and Mary.

Light, Ivan and Edna Bonacich (1988) *Immigrant Entrepreneurs – Koreans in Los Angeles 1965–1982.* Berkeley: University of California Press.

Marcus, George (1990) 'Once More into the Breach between Economic and Cultural Analysis', in Roger Friedland and A. F. Robertson (eds) *Beyond the Marketplace: Rethinking Economy and Society.* New York: Aldine de Gruyter.

Ong, Aihwa (1997) '"A Momentary Glow of Fraternity": Narratives of Chinese Nationalism and Capitalism'. *Identities: Global Studies in Culture and Power*, 3(3), January.

Redding, S. G. (1990) *The Spirit of Chinese Capitalism.* Berlin and New York: W. de Gruyter.

Said, Edward W. (1978) *Orientalism.* London: Routledge.

Scott, James C. (1985) *Weapons of the Weak: Everyday Forms of Peasant Resistance.* New Haven: Yale University Press.

Thomas, Nicholas (1992) 'The Inversion of Tradition'. *American Ethnologist*, 19(2).

Waldinger, Roger (1990) 'Immigrant Enterprise in the United States', in Sharon Zukin and Paul DiMaggio (eds) *Structures of Capital.* Cambridge: Cambridge University Press.

Wong, Siu-lun (1985) 'The Chinese Family Firm: A Model'. *The British Journal of Sociology*, 36(1).

Yao Souchou (1997) 'The Romance of Asian Capitalism: Geography, Desire and Chinese Business', in Mark T. Berger and Douglas A. Borer (eds) *The Rise of Asia: Critical Visions of the Pacific Century.* London: Routledge.

5 All are flexible, but some are more flexible than others

Small-scale Chinese businesses in Malaysia

Donald M. Nonini

> ...[S]tudies dealing with economic transformation are peopled with abstractions –
> capital, labour, world systems, development strategies, hard and soft states – whose
> struggles determine the outcome. In the presence of these titans the endeavours of
> mere humans seem the dithering of ants; we may forget they are behind the
> abstractions.
>
> (McVey 1992: 8)

In this chapter, I present findings about small-scale Chinese businesses in Malaysia
based on several years' intermittent ethnographic research among Chinese in
one urban setting in Peninsular Malaysia. Because I write as an anthropologist, I
give special privilege to the voices of my informants, although it is also my
obligation to contextualize their voices within the everyday political and
economic settings in which they live. The voices of those persons engaged in the
work of small-scale Chinese businesses do not speak uniformly, but make
conflicting and overlapping claims from many perspectives, arising from their
differing positions in the structures of inequality in class, gender, age, and national
origin found in Malaysia. Moreover, in some instances, informants speak but
few words are said, because they are silenced and censored by those more powerful
than they.

My conclusions are based on intensive ethnographic research in one setting,
and they are, strictly speaking, limited to it. Nonetheless, I suspect that they are
more broadly generalizable to Chinese small-scale businesses elsewhere in
Malaysia, and perhaps to settings where small-scale Chinese businesses operate
in other ASEAN nation-states. But their generalization is not my main objective.
Instead, I am more interested in demonstrating through an extended case study
one important way – ethnography – through which the processes that connect
diasporic Chinese commercial discourses and practices to the constraints set by
'the economy', can be investigated. I seek to show, for example, how Chinese
business practices redefine what is, from an economist's perspective, 'competition',
'the market', 'monopoly', and so forth. By examining these processes in one
specific setting, I hope to generate transposable methodological concepts and
insights applicable to other diasporic Chinese business circumstances.

In this chapter, I make two assumptions – the first theoretical, the second historical – which should be made explicit. The theoretical assumption is that there is no such thing as such as 'Chinese small-scale business' that manifests the same definitive characteristics in all times and places. Thus, for example, claims such as 'all Chinese businessmen do such-and-such e.g. use particularistic relationships (*guanxi*) or depend on "credit" (*xinyong*) etc.', are immediately suspect because they make essentializing claims, instead of investigating the variability of Chinese commercial practices and the contexts within which these take place. Nor are there, say, universal 'Chinese' family characteristics associated with Chinese business organization. Across the different spaces of ASEAN nation-states (and beyond), Chinese business practices and Chinese business families alike show vast variability depending on different contexts of enterprise size, the structuring of market competition, the politics of ethnic rivalry, the degree of modernization of the national economy, and so on. In regional and national settings, these contexts are multifarious and often radically different from one another. Methodologically, it is perhaps most important to inquire into the relationships Chinese businesses have not only with one another, but also with other institutions and actors in the economy – large-scale corporations, government regulators, customers, suppliers, and various publics, both Chinese and non-Chinese, with whom they interact. In contrast, when essentializing statements are made about 'all Chinese businessmen' we must then ask: what are the rhetorical-political contexts within which such claims are being presented – what is at stake for those who engage in such persuading moves? Do they seek, for example, to glorify Chinese familial values and a purported 'Chinese culture'? Or emphasize cultural (and potential commercial) ties with the 'fatherland' of China? Or, in contrast, to excoriate Chinese as vicious and 'clannish' competitors *vis-à-vis* non-Chinese?

My historical assumption, made for the purposes of presentation, is that the Malaysian economy, like other economies in the ASEAN states, displays a 'modern' institutional hybridity. The Malaysian economy has over the last fifty years, and particularly over the last thirty years, manifested (what I reluctantly call) 'modern-ization', due to the presence of transnational corporations in Malaysia, post-war innovations in institutional and legal structures (e.g. large-scale corporate organizations, the emergence of public limited companies and stock exchanges), and the dissemination of new communication and transport technologies (computers, satellite communication, air travel, miniaturization, etc.) within and beyond the ASEAN region. As a result of these changes, over the last several decades the Malaysian economy has simultaneously become more regionally integrated with other ASEAN and indeed other Asian economies (regionaliza-tion has occurred) and also become more 'modern' in that it displays *dominant* organizational and technical features similar to those present in capitalist economies outside of, as well as within, Asia. Over the same time, these 'modern' capitalist features have come to connect up with, rather than displace, pre-existing forms of commercial organization, including Chinese small-scale businesses –

and the presence of these features has transformed, rather than eliminated, the latter.[1] As a consequence, the Malaysian economy shows a hybridity, not a uniform 'modernity', of organizational and institutional structures and practices, and it is within this hybridity that small-scale Chinese businesses are integrated. Such hybridity is the source of the 'flexibility' to which I refer below. Market rigidities have been and continue to be important in Malaysia; yet flexibility marks the ways which pre-existing forms such as Chinese family businesses fit into, and are in turn transformed by, the modern hybrid economy.

In what follows, I make the following points. First, subcontracting for small Chinese businesses in Malaysia is the crucial social and economic arrangement through which they are articulated with both the larger institutions of Malaysian capitalism – with transnational corporations, national-level domestic firms, joint venture enterprises (involving private and semi-statutory government investments) – and with one another. Second, *guanxi* ('relationship' or 'connection' – a set of putative predispositions toward trust and mutual assistance between two persons who stand in certain social positions *vis-à-vis* each other) is one conventional way, but not the only way, that Chinese in Malaysia conceive of the human interactions that now characterize subcontracting. *Guanxi* discourse is a euphemized form of speech about practices associated with subcontracting that mystifies more than it negates the differentials in power and the potential for exploitation between parties that characterize most subcontracting arrangements. Third, I confirm 'what everybody knows', that, like elsewhere, small-scale Chinese businesses I have studied in an urban Malaysian setting are constructed around family connections, but I also argue that there are crucial power differentials within Chinese family-owned businesses along the lines of gender, age, and class, which allow for the 'exploitative capacity' that the flexibility inherent to subcontracting requires. These power differentials, however, in turn generate a 'petty accumulation trap' that constitutes a self-limiting contradiction to this form of petty 'capital': the equal division of inherited family property among males required by Chinese patriarchal power comes up squarely against, and founders upon, the low levels of capitalization of the family business. Neither this power differential nor the petty accumulation trap it generates are attended to in the current prevailing literature that has, until recently, emphasized the triumphal emergence of the Chinese family version of the new 'Asian capitalism'. Fourth, transnational practices among small-scale Chinese business families are both intimately tied to, and estranged from, state capital and state policies due to the interaction of economic constraints with the cultural politics of ethnicity and citizenship in Malaysia. On one hand, small-scale Chinese businesses depend via subcontracting on the export-oriented industrial enterprises promoted by state investment policies and often operated by state-private joint ventures; at the same time, on the other hand, Chinese small-scale business families are opting out of this dependence through 'transnational traversals' that allow them to enter other markets beyond Malaysia in the Asia Pacific (Nonini 1997). But before I go into these points in detail, I will discuss my methods briefly.

A note on method: the history of research and the starting point

The materials for this chapter were collected over several years' intermittent ethnographic research in and near a market town in the Penang region of Peninsular Malaysia during 1978–80, 1985, then 1991–2. Although my research required the collection of quantitative commercial census data in 1979–80, this essay draws primarily on ethnographic qualitative interviews conducted in 1978–80, and again in 1985, 1991 and 1992, among small-scale Chinese business informants. In particular, my research has focused on the truck or lorry transport industry of this market town – on its organization and history as a field for the cultural production of discourses and practices of diaspora Chinese business activity in Malaysia. In addition to interviews with informants as to their business activities, I also engaged in participant observation at the offices and homes of families and individuals engaged in truck transport, even to the extent of going on several long-distance truck trips with drivers from the market town to larger cities in central Peninsular Malaysia, including Kuala Lumpur.

I draw on this earlier research (Nonini 1983a, 1983b, 1987) for part of the findings reported here. On my return to this market town in 1991 and 1992, I interviewed informants who had participated in the town's truck transport industry from 1978–85 – some still were participants, others had changed occupations or business lines. My research in and near the town since the early 1990s has focused on Chinese male labourers, many of whom I originally met in my earlier fieldwork when they were truck drivers. Those labourers who were truck drivers or attendants have provided me with further insights from the other side, as it were, of the class divide between capitalists and employees. Moreover, I have maintained contact with informants from the earlier fieldwork who were then in other lines of business, and have continued in business or retired, to obtain a broader sense of the regularities of Chinese business activity.

My earlier interest in the truck transport industry, therefore, has been the point of departure in a research project now of several years' standing. Over the years since 1978, I have noticed changes both within the town's truck transport industry and, more broadly, its Chinese business circles. In my recent fieldwork, I have maintained my earlier ties to families and persons engaged in truck transport activities to investigate, with their assistance, other areas of local economic life; this is an advantage which long acquaintance with persons in a specific social setting brings. Most of my informants are now middle-aged friends who have concerns about the succession of generations within their own families, who have confronted major life-passage changes – marriages, births, deaths. They have, moreover, examined the course of their own lives and have come to view themselves as successes or failures, as the case may be. In my recent visits in the 1990s, they have reflected with me about our shared experiences and knowledge of the past which we revisited together for historical insights and reflection.

Ethnographic research has inherent limits. For instance, given the high degree of social segregation between men and women among urban Chinese, it is perhaps inevitable that a very large proportion of my informants are middle-aged or older men, and in this sense, this essay may, to some extent, privilege their voices. Yet, wherever possible, I have sought out additional voices other than theirs, although at times they have neither appreciated nor understood why I might want to do so.

Subcontracting and *guanxi*

The *guanxi* of the overseas Chinese family business provides a perfect complement to high-tech Western firms that lack the necessary economic and political connections to navigate a treacherous foreign business environment.

(Weidenbaum and Hughes 1996: 57)

Zhisizhibi, baizhanbaisheng (if you know your competitor as you know yourself, one hundred wars yield one hundred victories);

Hairenzhixin bu ke you, fangrenzhixin bu ke wu (you can't seek to harm someone, but you can't not seek to protect yourself from him)

(Proverbs cited by Malaysian Chinese merchants)

In Malaysia, the principal mechanism of flexibility connecting large- and medium-scale enterprises and small-scale Chinese businesses has been the subcontracting arrangement. It is best viewed not only as a mode of business organization, but also as a form of labour control, particularly the control of the labour power of young working women and, to a far lesser extent, men (Ong 1991). Historically, subcontracting arrangements in Malaysia as elsewhere in Asia long predate the recent transformations of ASEAN capitalism; I would argue, however, that these culturally specific arrangements have been harnessed in new ways, with new potentials, in an era of flexibility. In Malaysia, post-war innovations in transport and communication (telephones, road systems, efficient internal-combustion vehicles), and cheap energy sources from the 1950s and 1960s have since been complemented by electronic and other changes (use of faxes, computerization, miniaturization, etc.) to make possible the specific combination of decentralized operation with centralized control that makes outsourcing and thus subcontracting feasible over vast spaces within the increasingly short time horizons required for enterprise profitability. Small- and medium-scale Chinese firms have become principal players in the new subcontracting arrangements because of the flexibilities they have in their practices of labour control over contingent, part-time, and unpaid labourers. Deploying these forms of labour, small Chinese subcontractors can constitute new labour forces and set diverse production processes in motion readily in response to market demand, yet quickly shift their capital and their labour forces to new lines of production when the market changes.

For example, as I interviewed truck transport *towkays* (businessmen) from 1978–80, then again in later years, they told me of the various subcontracting arrangements they had with other enterprises. They solicited the patronage of managers of large-scale Japanese, Malaysian joint-venture, and American and European corporate manufacturers and distributors in the Kuala Lumpur region to carry their freight for them to markets elsewhere in Malaysia or in Singapore. These corporations thus outsourced the transport of their goods to consignees throughout the peninsula to these small- and medium-scale transport companies.

'Flexibility', of course, does not mean the same for all parties: all are flexible, but some are more flexible than others, and those with greater capital, on the whole, set the terms for doing business. Although it was obvious that the capacity to outsource truck transport work conferred great flexibility and discretion on corporate factory managers, truck transport company proprietors often viewed this flexibility rather differently: as arbitrary and whimsical. But, in an extraordinarily competitive market, and facing the high fixed costs of operating their trucks, transporters sought the business of a limited number of large corporate consigners, felt they had little choice other than to accept such arrangements if offered them, and even worked arduously to maintain them. Several of my informants spoke of these corporations as *tukushengyi*[2] 'businesses of the original storehouse', or, more simply translated, 'monopolists', who stipulated what charges they would accept from transporters, and it was 'take it or leave it'. For their part, truck *towkays* complained continually about being at the beck and call of factory managers, who would, say, consign three truck loads of freight to them one week, but only one load to them the next.

The flexibility of subcontracting exercised by truck *towkays* was, instead, implemented in other directions – toward or against those with less capital and hence less power. These men dealt directly with corporate consigners, yet many of the consignees for the imported and manufactured goods from the Kuala Lumpur region were petty retailers and wholesalers located in the small cities and towns of the northern states. Truck *towkays* told me that there was little profit to be gained by having one of their partially loaded large six- or ten-wheel trucks driven for an entire day to make such small deliveries – say two or three boxes of televisions in this town, then two dozen rice-cookers in that one, fifty kilometres further upland. Instead, they made standing arrangements with other local transport *towkays* whose trucks were smaller and whose geographical scope was confined to the northern region, to take on such petty freight for delivery in return for a 'cut' of the transport charges received from Kuala Lumpur consigners. Here too, larger truck owners succeeded in offloading the costs of 'flexibility' arising from the fluctuations in their business volumes onto others less well endowed with capital. In this way, smaller operators were able to get in on the action when they subcontracted out with the former to carry part of the freight, but hardly under price conditions of their own choosing. Indeed, it was precisely from such subcontracting arrangements that the market town of my research had gained a regional reputation as a point for freight transhipment, and – when smuggled goods such as drugs were involved – regional notoriety as well.

The costs of 'flexibility' were, however, passed on by both medium- and small-scale truck *towkays* to others even further down the line. Drivers, also Chinese men, complained to me that their 'bosses', *laoban* (in this case the transport *towkays*) at times pushed them to exhaustion by pressing them to start one long-distance trip as soon as the previous one was completed when there was an excess of freight awaiting immediate transport; at other times, when there was no freight to haul, empty trucks were parked at the company depot, and drivers earned no wages, being paid with piecework per-trip wages. Piecework wages in the truck transport industry, as elsewhere where subcontracting arrangements prevail, turn the drivers into the pettiest, and least powerful, 'subcontractors' in the industry. It is not surprising that, under these circumstances, I found that there were endemic contestations between *laoban* and drivers over the latters' 'disputatiousness' and attempts to make illicit 'rice-eating money' (say, by stealing fuel money) to supplement their wages (Nonini 1999). I return to this below when I discuss the family basis of small-scale Chinese businesses.

What about *guanxi*, that supposed cultural ingredient of Chinese business success so vaunted by business-school pundits such as Weidenbaum and Hughes (1996)? Businessmen often explained to me that their conduct – the deals they made, the commercial opportunities they found, and so on – arose from the 'individual relationships', *geren guanxi*, they had with others. Such rationalizations were given as if they were self-evident: two men who are 'old friends' do each other business favours in Kuala Lumpur or Penang because they attended the same secondary school in the town where I did research; another merchant obtains confidential commercial information from Thailand because he, like his alters in Haadyai, is Teochew and descended from migrants from the same district in Guangdong province in China. But such rationalizations are far from self-explanatory; instead, they beg for explanation.

The transport *towkays* who were my informants spoke of *guanxi* as highly unevenly distributed among the players in the industry. Transport *towkays* who dealt directly with factory managers and 'storekeepers' spoke to me more often of the onus of the cost of 'entertainment' (*yingchou*) which they were expected to provide the latter with, than of any *guanxi* they had with them. They spoke of 'entertainment' as the special favours they owed the latter as representatives of 'monopolists' in return for being provided freight to carry, at charges set by fiat – take it or leave it. Nor did truck drivers often speak to me of *guanxi* in character-izing their relations with their *towkay* bosses, except in a few exceptional instances. For the most part, *guanxi* was spoken of as only characterizing relations between transport *towkays*, particularly when one was in a subcontracting relationship to another.

Now, this brings up an important point: that *guanxi* implicates a way of speaking between persons who identify themselves as Chinese. Moreover, since *guanxi* is relational, it makes sense that what one person says about his relationship to another (having *guanxi* or not) to a third person may well not be the same that the first says to the second face-to-face. In discussing *guanxi*, it is also helpful to distinguish *guanxi* bases, *guanxi* discourses, and *guanxi* practices (Yang 1994; Tong n.d.). A *guanxi* base is some attribute shared by two or more individuals said to lead to familiarity – it may be a shared experience within a larger institution, or merely an imputed affinity. Both possibilities are circumscribed by the affix *tong*, 'same' or 'common': *tongxiang*, 'persons from the same native place', *tongxue*, 'classmates', *tongshi*, 'co-workers' or 'colleagues', etc. (Yang 1994: 111). A *guanxi* base does not guarantee a *guanxi* relationship between two persons, but it makes it possible. Clearly, a *guanxi* base can only be defined by *guanxi* discourse, but the latter extends far beyond the former.

If it takes at least two Chinese to engage in *guanxi*, this is because one of the distinctive features of *guanxi* discourses is that these explicitly form a kind of 'knowledge' by Chinese about Chinese, which may be more or less systematized. *Guanxi* discourse is not so much the reporting of social fact or representation but 'a social fact in and of itself, whose history, conditions of formation, and specific contours provide information not only on its referent, *guanxi* practices, but also on the large social forces that produced the discourse and gave it prominence' (Yang 1994: 6–7). *Guanxi* practices, although constituted through *guanxi* discourse, are by no means reducible to it. The distinction between *guanxi* discourse and *guanxi* practices comes out most clearly when certain practices reflect unspoken, but often quite elaborate, aspects of strategy – the timing of gifts, the calculation of their value, the hidden messages in language, and much more (Hsing 1997).

The example of subcontracting in the truck transport industry which I have discussed here should put a definitive end to the idea that Chinese business practices can, in any seriously informative sense, be reducible to explanations based on *guanxi*, *ganqing* ('feeling'), *xinyong* ('credit'), and similar terms in the Chinese business lexicon of relationships. As the example shows, there are many people with whom small Chinese businessmen interact, but whom they say they have no *guanxi* with – whom they seek to take asymmetrical legitimate advantage of, or at least, whom they try not to be taken advantage of or abused by. It is worth asking: what are the tactics structuring these antagonistic practices, the forms of violence they encode, and their limits? Such practices are articulated in circumspect anecdotes, proverbs, and gossip which scholars who extol the virtues of *guanxi* rarely attend to. For instance, a merchant in Malaysia with whom I developed close ties once described the existence of 'trolling-for-money companies' (*laoqian gongsi*). These were companies that merchants established with the sole aim of cheating someone else, and which the proprietors then allowed to go out of existence and become bankrupt. He gave as an example a friend who had cheated a Malay-owned company of several hundred thousand Malaysian ringgit worth of goods extended to his company on credit, and had then disappeared. When asked about this, he answered, 'The trick is to cheat the international companies or Malay-owned companies, and not the ones owned by Chinese around here'. So much for *xinyong*!

Yet, even where two people do have *guanxi* arising from some *guanxi* basis, their invocation of their *guanxi* may euphemize relations of domination and exploitation (Nonini and Ong 1997: 22). It is this ambivalence that the two proverbs I cited above point to – that even with the best relations, engaging in business is like engaging in war and, despite appearances, one must be wary of others and of their capacity to harm one. For the transport *towkay* owning a large fleet of trucks that carry merchandise from Kuala Lumpur, what does *guanxi* with a less wealthy *towkay* – to whom he occasionally subcontracts out the transport of a few items of transhipped freight – mean, when the latter has a half dozen competitors with whom the former could also do business? Perhaps such *guanxi* is important to the former *towkay* but, chances are, not nearly as much as it is to the latter, who depends on him to provide most of the freight the latters' trucks carry.

Business families, power asymmetries, and the petty accumulation trap

> [The Chinese family business] is particularly well adapted to its socio-cultural milieu...It is also peculiarly effective and a significant contributor to the list of causes of the East Asia miracle.
>
> (Redding 1990: 4)

> Mr. Teh,[3] a friend, and I visited his friend's house in Kampong...We sat watching while, congregated in the front room before the family altar, his friend's wife and three children hurriedly packed name-brand sports wear into fold-out boxes for a European-owned clothing manufacturer sited in a nearby industrial estate, on a piecework basis – so many boxes packed per ringgit. The youngest child could not have been more than six or seven years old.
>
> (Nonini, fieldnote, 1991)

Small-scale Chinese businesses in urban Malaysia are, indeed, centred on 'family'. For instance, in a 1980 commercial census of the downtown area of the market town in which I carried out research, I discovered that of the 1,242 businesses I surveyed, the median number of non-family employees was zero, and the seventy-fifth percentile number of non-family employees was only three (Nonini 1983a). I seriously doubt that there has been much change in these figures since the early 1980s.

And, of course, Chinese businessmen talked to me about 'family' constantly, as the rationale for much of what they did – there is, in fact, a dominant self-conscious discourse of familism. When I asked businessmen why they worked so hard to make money, almost invariably they replied with some version of, 'It's for my family' (*wei wo de jialiren*) or 'It's for my children' (*wei wo de haizi*).

For deeper insights, however, it is necessary to examine the 'accumulation strategies' of Chinese business families, within which the dominant familistic discourse is embedded. In order to do this, we need to ask at least two questions. One is: accumulation of what? Briefly, accumulation of 'capital', but here by this I imply not only economic 'capital' but, following Bourdieu (1986), a variety of 'capitals' – economic, cultural, symbolic, educational, social, and linguistic – which can be characterized as resources that are mutually convertible and can be converted into personal power and thereby define one's life chances or social trajectory (Postone, LiPuma and Calhoun 1993: 4–5).[4] Thus, for example, the cultural capital of a university degree can be converted, under specific conditions, into economic capital (wealth) and social capital (prestige), and eligibility for legal citizenship (see Nonini 1997). Economic capital is focal – like the axis of a wheel – for Chinese strategies of accumulation, in that it is ultimately convertible into all other forms of capital, whereas the converse is by no means assured.

I would like to historicize Bourdieu's concept of 'capitals' by proposing that, under the conditions of intensified 'time-space compression' associated with late capitalism (Harvey 1989), both the velocity of conversion and the capacities for convertibility between capitals have accelerated, while conversions of capital now overcome even greater extents of space than previously. This has promoted the proliferation not only of small-scale Chinese transnational family businesses (about which more below) but also of Chinese transnational practices of all kinds – in pursuit of different kinds of capital – over the last two decades.

A second question, equally difficult, is: accumulation by whom? By 'Chinese' of course, but that is insufficiently specific. A closer approximation might be: accumulation by Chinese 'families'. It is tempting to accept this answer because of the existence, as I noted above, of the dominant discourse of familism in which all business practices are rationalized on behalf of 'family', but the temptation should be resisted. When Chinese businessmen have told me they engage in business as they do 'for my family', I do not doubt the subjectively real status of such statements, but I observe that whatever else such statements do rhetorically, they also euphemize the unspoken-of tactics of elder male domination: the rationale for the accumulation of economic (and other forms of) capital by older men, and for their control over the lives of other family members, lies in their hard effort and self-sacrifice, their *keku nailao*, 'working hard to overcome difficulty', 'for the family', 'for the children'. This self-interested claim brackets out the exploitation and disciplining of younger female and male family members and non-family employees which lie at the heart of the 'family's' accumulation strategy. 'Family' refers to a discursive construct as much as to a group of people, and as a construct, has its uses within the rhetoric of male domination.[5] That is, the discourse of 'family' operates within the sphere of the practices by which patriarchal power is deployed in 'families'. Moreover, positions of power within families are constructed, not only by familistic discourses among Chinese, but also by state and capitalist regimes of labour regulation that discipline gendered and aged bodies differentially (Ong 1990, 1991).

Nonetheless, despite variations, there is a prevalent structure of power within Chinese business families in Malaysia. It is necessary to distinguish what people call 'the family' or in business circles, 'the house', *jia*, from the patriline embedded in the 'family'/'house'. The 'family'/'house' consists of a married couple and their children (and possibly other kinfolk, including adoptive children) who share both a common consumption budget and a regime of work centred on the family business, while the patriline is made up of two or more generations of males connected through patrilineal descent, within which 'family' wealth, including economic capital, is more or less exclusively transmitted – fathers and sons, brothers, etc. This patriline, *zu*, is named as such only, to my knowledge, as a part of rituals held in Chinese 'clan' or same-surname halls in Malaysia; it also implicitly – in the form of the tablets of a husband's patrilineal ancestors – is the focus of worship at many families' household altars, on the 'birthdate' of the husband's father, and on the first and fifteenth days of the Chinese lunar calendar. Since modern electronic media influences stigmatize exclusive male inheritance, Chinese patrilines as such keep a low profile. Nonetheless, the dominant strategy of accumulation within diasporic Chinese families tends to occur far more often than not through decisions taken by the senior active male of a family's patriline, and these decisions are buttressed by a hegemonic discourse of 'filial' deference, *xiao*, which disciplines women, younger men, and non-family members alike within Chinese business families. Beyond this dominant strategy, there are various individual and usually covert strategies on the part of family members, particularly women, who seek to subvert it, since in almost all instances they do not stand to inherit property, or to influence major family business decisions. Moreover, in polygynous families, there may also be strategies of accumulation set by mothers on behalf of themselves and their sons over and against other wives and their children. The dominant strategy of accumulation operates as effectively as it does due to several causes. Male rights and the patriline are supported both by Malaysian law and by the culturally specific Chinese discourse of 'filial' deference. Equally important, the patriline of fathers and sons forms a potentially strong coalition, based on shared material interests as well as on enduring, diffuse emotional ties of trust which are simultaneously effective in struggles against others within families, and sufficiently flexible to operate, when necessary, across the broad spaces associated with subcontracting arrangements.

The dominant strategy of accumulation fits the requirements demanded by, and takes advantage of opportunities offered by, the flexibilities of mobile capitalism which have emerged since the 1970s, in several ways. First, this strategy leads to the formation of independent small- and medium-scale industrial and trade enterprises managed by family members, with the oldest male of the patriline in charge. The scale of these enterprises remains at the lower end due to a scarcity of economic capital. Second (and this is what makes transnational operation of these enterprises possible) men in a family's patriline can be spatially distant from each other while they co-ordinate actions as managers of branches of the business, in order to take advantage of the lower costs of labour in certain places rather than others, and to open and expand market share across regions, either within nation-states, or beyond them, in the Asia Pacific. I found in my (1983b) study of the spatially dispersed Chinese truck transport industry within Malaysia that the vast majority of successful and long-lasting transport companies were managed by either a father and his sons (each typically in charge of a branch office), or by two or more adult brothers (each managing a different branch), and that partnerships among non-relatives, while they existed, showed little longevity. Third, by maintaining a strict association between being a family member, especially an adult male, and profit-sharing, these enterprises have a cultural mechanism for sustaining extremely high levels of exploitation of non-family employees, with resultant rapid labour turnover, which in turn facilitates the flexibility that characterizes subcontracting arrangements – that is, the flexibility that those with economic capital possess *vis-à-vis* those with less, or no capital. The consequences of exploitation of non-family employees I discuss below. Such exploitation is connected to the labour-intensive industrial production and services these enterprises provide as subcontractors for large-scale corporate capital, as well as to low profit margins within highly competitive lines of business, and is made possible by familistic discourses and disciplines – it is 'one big family' and the supervising male family member is like an 'elder brother' – as well as by state regulation. Fourth, such flexible exploitation is not limited to non-family employees but also extends to women of the family, particularly if they are young and unmarried, who engage in unwaged clerical, accounting, and petty supervisory labour within the family enterprise, or work outside it and remit part of their wages as subsidies to it.

Yet, these conditions represent a petty accumulation trap into which the enterprise falls – a trap that causes it to dissolve. This trap has several variants. One is that there may be no heir deemed suitable by patriarchal discourse: a man may have only grown daughters. Another is that even if there are one or more sons, none may be viewed as suitable by temperament or talent to managing the family enterprise. Both risks may be overcome by either adopting-in sons or promoting a son-in-law to the ranks of management and ownership, although this is no sure response. Small-scale family businesses do go out of operation due to such factors.

But a third variant of the trap is the most deadly, because least avoidable. There is a strong rule, which animates the contentious practices associated with the inheritance of family property, that there must be an equal division among the unannounced heirs – the younger men of the patriline – of the economic capital of the enterprise. Yet the discourse of equal inheritance subverts the pragmatics of prolonged co-operative and co-ordinated management among these men, while it in fact (if not in law) excludes women either entirely (the sisters of these men) or in part (their wives). After the death or retirement of the patriarch, few or none of the adults working in the family enterprise have a vested interest in its continuation, with the exception of a brother groomed to 'carry on' the business; brothers frequently seek to divide family wealth for their own (new) family strategies of accumulation. Women – whether sisters or wives of brothers – have even less reason to commit themselves to working in the family enterprise. The most likely outcome is the dissolution of the family enterprise through the division of its liquid capital and fixed property.

However, certain practices within contemporary flexible capitalism may impede the dissolution – but these serve primarily the interests of patriline males. First, when, as noted above, the operation of a business requires that its goods or services span long distances (and in some cases cross national borders), the spatial dispersion of fathers and grown children, or of two or more adult brothers, may paradoxically work to maintain good relations between male rivals for family property and authority. When each brother manages a branch, or when one remains in the home locale while another goes outstation, absence and shared profit-taking indeed may make the heart grow fonder. As I noted above, longer-lived transport companies with operations extending across regions of the peninsula illustrate this well. When such distancing is combined with a complementary division of labour in managing, e.g. with one brother responsible for overseeing production, another for sales in foreign markets, a third for purchasing raw materials as inputs, then the life of the enterprise can be prolonged. In this situation, all (men, that is) stand to lose much if the enterprise fails. Certainly, this meshes well with a general feature of contemporary capitalism in Malaysia as elsewhere – centralization of control combined with decentralization of operation across variegated spaces. On the other hand, male relatives do, on occasion, embezzle or steal from the accounts of the family business – and I have recorded several accounts of such conflicts among men in the owning families of truck transport firms. Moreover, there is rarely an equal division of power among men engaged in different tasks in the business; some men told me that they bridled under the authority of their brothers in family businesses, but, over the short term, could do little about it.

Second, the senior male of the patriline may attempt, over time, to convert the family's economic capital into other forms of capital by subsidizing the acquisition by his sons and/or daughters of educational capital, that is, a university degree or certificate representing a marketable skill. This may allow one or two sons to carry on the family enterprise and buy out the shares of the others, while the latter move out into the professions or technocratic/managerial employment by large corporations or bureaucratic states, or start their own businesses. My informants have provided me with many such examples. This option promotes flexible capitalism by extending the reach of the family business across regional, and sometimes national, spaces. Sons or, exceptionally, daughters are placed – or place themselves – in university settings abroad and so acquire technical knowledge and saleable credentials, while participating in what I have called the 'traversal' of 'middling' Chinese transnationalism – a transnational exploration of new national spaces either for future residence for family members, investment of family wealth, or for new markets (Nonini 1997).

As I observed above, the competitive and continually shifting pressures to reorganize work and shift factors of production which are characteristic of subcontracting arrangements often lead the patriarchs and male managers of small-scale family businesses to 'flexibly' impose onerous working conditions and unstable hours on non-family employees and to inflict verbal or even physical abuse on them. These oppressive manoeuvres tend to backfire and to undermine the profitability and longevity of small Chinese businesses. Non-family members who become managers (as does happen) suffer from the personal abuse, low salaries and long hours demanded of them by family males – but then quit the business to set themselves up as competitors with their previous employer, at times 'stealing away' his customers when they leave. This is evident in the stories told me of how several truck transport companies were started by angry and disgruntled ex-employees. Similarly, other employees engage in theft, sabotage, and other forms of 'everyday resistance' (Scott 1990) that have real costs to the bottom lines of small-scale Chinese businesses.[6] Truck drivers told me of their pursuit of 'rice-eating money' gained illicitly through theft of cargo or fuel money – a pursuit that drivers saw as most morally justified when their truck transport *laoban* was treating them particularly abusively. The high labour turnover that results also leads to the need for costly and constant training of new employees (Jomo: personal communication). Both outcomes can lead to profit losses and threaten the continuity of the family business over time.

Patriarchal power and the system of subcontracting associated with flexibility among small-scale Chinese businesses thus go hand in hand, but in complex ways that, in the case of small-scale Chinese family businesses, simultaneously reinforce and undermine their existence, given that the vast majority are undercapitalized. It is thus the class-specific quandaries associated with a 'petty bourgeois' condition that, above all else, account for the instability and transitory quality of small-scale Chinese enterprises. Only the large- and medium-scale Chinese family businesses can over time escape the petty accumulation trap, although even among extraordinarily wealthy Chinese mercantile families, this is by no means assured, as the occasional spectacular failure of, say, a William Soeryadjaya of Indonesia, indicates.

Transnationalism: intersections of cultural politics of ethnicity and the contradictions of state-led economic growth

> Only Malay transport companies are allowed to carry containerized cargo. The large company in…[a nearby town] that has the right to do this is called Probumi. Throughout the country, there are only five companies which have the exclusive right to carry such containerized cargo – two in Penang, two in Klang, and one in Johore Bharu. Well you know that large-scale factories now pack their goods in these containers, so they only call on those companies to carry them to ships at port, where the containers are then transferred to ships. There is discrimination against we Chinese because we are not allowed to carry such containers. Indeed, aren't I, who was born in Malaysia, as much a *bumiputra* as any Malay?
>
> (Mr Lim, a truck transport *towkay*, 1991)

These were angry words. I cite them not by way of judgement – nor am I claiming that they are accurate – but only to illustrate one Chinese rhetoric that reflects the intersection between the effects of state-induced capitalist growth in Malaysia and the cultural politics of ethnicity. What I want to point out is that these and similar words constitute an orientation among small-scale Chinese businessmen which encourages their transnational practices. For example, in the instance of Mr Lim, they were spoken in the course of a conversation in which he informed me that three of his four grown sons currently resided in Australia – two being physicians there, a third a computer specialist for an American company there. (Predictably, one son, his eldest, now co-managed his truck transport business in Malaysia.) Within the context of our conversation then, Lim's argument took a classic form of *reductio ad absurdum*. Interpreted freely, it would go something like this: Look where my birth in Malaysia and my effort of a lifetime as a hardworking transporter has got me – the government still discriminates against me because I am Chinese, and fixes the rising market in containerized cargo transport on behalf of another ethnic group. Over the long run, I can't compete no matter what I do. I give up. It may be too late for me (and my eldest son), but at least part of my family can and has opted out, and successfully at that - out of Malaysia.

These are, as I said, contentious words, and no doubt would have called down on Mr Lim a spirited critique by advocates of government policy had they been uttered in public. I am not defending his words. All the same, they are broadly representative of a very large proportion of small-scale Chinese businessmen. The larger arguments and conflicts into which his words enter constitute a discursively-formed cultural politics which activates the imaginations of a very large number of Chinese businessmen in thinking about the past, the future, and their place (or non-place) in Malaysian society. As such, his rhetoric is not something that I judge on this occasion to be right or wrong, but rather wish only to consider in terms of what it reveals about an attitude, orientation, or perspective on life.

I have extensively discussed elsewhere the larger cultural politics of ethnicity and class in Malaysia which promotes transnational practices among Malaysian Chinese (Nonini 1997, 1999), and I have referred above to certain conditions characterizing subcontracting, flexible capitalism, and small-scale family business operation which conduce to transnational relocations by Chinese business families. These promote the tactics of transnational traversals (Nonini 1997).

In one sense, Mr Lim's anger was curious. As of 1991, he lived a comfortable life, and was moderately well to do, even by Malaysian standards. He and his transport company were successful: he owned several trucks which carried manufactured freight throughout the peninsula. He was well-regarded by other *towkay*s in the transport industry. Certainly, he had high social standing due to the fact that three of his four sons had received university educations and were highly successful professionals. Nor could Mr Lim have been entirely ignorant of the dynamics of that grand social experiment, the New Economic Policy, nor of the fact that it has been state-induced and state-driven economic growth that, in a real sense, accounts for much of Malaysia's current prosperity – although I never discussed these topics as such with him. Surely, he knew that his own commercial fortunes were very much tied to factories, industries, and export-oriented industrialization – all promoted by far-seeing government policies and programmes that were, in the last analysis, implemented in the interest of Malaysian society as a whole and all Malaysians?

I cannot answer these questions about Mr. Lim, much less on his behalf. But I do have an alternative sympathetic understanding of Mr Lim's situation, similar to that of many other small-scale Chinese businessmen, which I can, for better or worse, relate. Irrespective of Mr Lim's abstract attitudes or knowledge about the NEP or state-induced economic growth, he and countless other Chinese men know that they occupy a position of subordination relative to more powerful institutions within the Malaysian economy. These institutions – transnational corporations, government agencies, joint-venture firms, banks – have set the harsh conditions and constraints under which the new flexible capitalism, and Mr Lim's own little piece of its action operate. As my discussion of subcontracting in the case of the truck transport industry demonstrates, small-scale truck transporters are at the receiving end of monopoly corporate price-setting and government regulation and, at times, official harassment. Relative to these dominant institutions, they are undercapitalized – e.g. they can only modestly, if at all, invest in modernizing innovations required by competition in rising markets. The flexibility possessed by transnational corporations generates 'down the line' an extraordinarily competitive commercial milieu among small-scale truck transporters in which, as one of the proverbs quoted above about business as a kind of warfare suggests, all are engaged in warfare against all. In short, to be colloquial, Mr Lim is one of the 'little guys', and I believe that much of the resentment conveyed in his words above arises from his sense of being relatively powerless in the face of these powerful institutional forces – however abstractly beneficial they may be for him and other small-scale Chinese entrepreneurs 'in general' and 'in the long run'.

But Mr Lim, as the patriarch of a small business firm, does have certain resources to deploy. One such is the mobility of the human beings and resources he dominates within his family and its business. Although he cannot significantly change the constellation of everyday economic and political forces that constrain his day-to-day commercial milieu, he can choose which such constellations of such national forces he and other family members will be subject to.

His and his family members' potential mobility thus represents a kind of power which is necessarily conferred by the same broader, global forces that reproduce contemporary capitalism in Malaysia as elsewhere in the Asia Pacific – the high demand for technical, managerial, and financial expertise and training, technical innovations in air travel, in electronic communication, the rapidly changing market conditions that operate not only in Malaysia, but elsewhere, and so on (Nonini and Ong 1997). As to the high-velocity movements of capital, human beings, commodities, ideas, technologies, financial arrangements and media images, and as to the institutionalized processes of conversion of economic capital into educational, social, cultural and other forms of non-economic capital, and of their reconversion back into mobile economic capital: these movements and processes are the linchpins and essential ingredients of contemporary capitalism in the Asia Pacific. The accumulation strategy adopted by Mr Lim was thus similar to countless other small-scale Chinese capitalists: send younger family members abroad for technical expertise, and – if conditions outside Malaysia are more advantageous – have them relocate there, and indeed, perhaps relocate there oneself.

At the same time, however, it would be incorrect to see Mr Lim as simply having opted out of Malaysia. After all, in 1991, he still resided in Malaysia and, despite being almost seventy years of age, still operated his truck transport business – and when I last saw him in 1991 he was still loading cargo into the back of one of his trucks. And what could be a more land-locked form of business? Instead, Mr Lim's strategy, like that of many other small-scale business people, is, as another of my informants put it, one of 'walking on either of two roads', not only one. That is, as the patriarch of a family enterprise in the broadest sense, Mr Lim is engaged in a truly transnational practice: he is in different ways simultaneously in Malaysia and elsewhere (in his case, Australia). I can relate numerous similar examples of cross-national positioning or 'traversal': Chinese men and women who have embodied stakes, in effect, not only in Malaysia, but in Singapore, Thailand, Hong Kong, Australia, New Zealand, Taiwan, Canada, the United States, and other nation-states in the Asia Pacific.

I do not intend to idealize the efforts of Chinese patriarchs like Mr Lim who deploy the dominant strategies of accumulation of Chinese families. After all, patriarchal power exacts a high price from those who are subordinate in Chinese families and their enterprises – women, children, unrelated employees, at the very least. But I do want to conclude by pointing out that the power that mobility under flexible capitalism confers on Chinese businessmen, and often on those persons subordinate to them in families as well, is very real, and not about to disappear soon.

This is something that both social theory and political policy alike have yet to adequately come to terms with. It is about time that they do so.

Acknowledgements

The first version of this chapter was prepared for the conference, 'Chinese Business in Southeast Asia', convened by Professor Jomo K.S. (Institute for Advanced Study and Faculty of Economics and Administration, University of Malaya), and held at the University of Malaya, Kuala Lumpur, Malaysia, 23–25 June 1997. I have benefited greatly from the incisive and thoughtful comments of Prof. Jomo K.S., and of Prof. Yao Souchou (Anthropology, University of Sydney), the conference commentator for my paper, and I cannot express sufficiently my gratitude to them. I also received constructive suggestions from other participants at the conference. Support for the research discussed here was provided by a National Science Foundation Dissertation Grant (1978–80), an SSRC/ACLS Advanced Research Grant in Chinese Studies (1985), and an SSRC Advanced Research Grant in Southeast Asian Studies (1992), for all of which I am grateful.

Notes

1 For a comparable analysis of the mechanisms by which modern capitalist relations graft onto, but do not entirely displace, pre-existing forms of production, see Dupré and Rey 1978.
2 In this chapter Chinese words (with the exception of personal names) are given in Mandarin pinyin transcription. Fieldwork interviews were conducted primarily in Mandarin Chinese, with Penang Hokkien also spoken in the 1991–2 interviews.
3 All personal names used in this essay are pseudonyms.
4 Here I agree with Calhoun that one of Bourdieu's

> key original insights are that there are immaterial forms of capital – cultural, symbolic, and social – as well as a material or economic form and that with varying levels of difficulty it is possible to convert one of these forms into another.
>
> (Calhoun 1993: 69)

5 The same may be said to be true for the term 'Chinese', another term within the rhetoric of domination. I thank Jomo K.S. for pointing this out to me.
6 For another example, see the chapter by Yao Souchou, this volume.

Bibliography

Bourdieu, Pierre (1986) 'The Forms of Capital', in J.G. Richardson (ed.) *Handbook of Theory and Research for the Sociology of Education.* New York: Greenwood.

Calhoun, Craig (1993) 'Habitus, Field, and Capital: The Question of Historical Specificity', in C. Calhoun, E. LiPuma and M. Postone (eds) *Bourdieu: Critical Perspectives.* Chicago: University of Chicago.

Dupré, Georges and Pierre Philippe Rey (1978) 'Reflections on the Relevance of a Theory of the History of Exchange', in David Seddon (ed.) *Relations of Production: Marxist Approaches to Economic Anthropology.* London: Frank Cass.

Harvey, David (1989) *The Condition of Postmodernity.* Oxford: Basil Blackwell.

Hsing, You-t'ien (1997) 'Building *Guanxi* Across the Straits: Taiwanese Capital and Local Chinese Bureaucrats', in A. Ong and D.M. Nonini (eds) *Ungrounded Empires: The Cultural Politics of Modern Chinese Transnationalism.* New York: Routledge.

McVey, Ruth (1992) 'The Materialization of the Southeast Asian Entrepreneur', in R. McVey (ed.) *Southeast Asian Capitalists.* Ithaca, NY: Southeast Asia Program, Cornell University.

Nonini, Donald M. (1983a) 'The Chinese Community of a West Malaysian Market Town: A Study in Political Economy'. PhD thesis, Dept. of Anthropology, Stanford University, Stanford: Stanford University.

Nonini, Donald M. (1983b) 'The Chinese Truck Transport "Industry" of a Peninsular Malaysian Market Town', in L.Y.C. Lim and L.A.P. Gosling (eds) *The Chinese in Southeast Asia, Volume I: Ethnicity and Economic Activity.* Singapore: Maruzen Asia.

Nonini, Donald M. (1987) 'Some Reflections on "Entrepreneurship" and the Chinese Community of a West Malaysian Market Town'. *Ethnos,* 52 (3–4): 350–67.

Nonini, Donald M. (1997) 'Shifting Identities, Positioned Imaginaries: Transnational Traversals and Reversals by Malaysian Chinese', in A. Ong and D.M. Nonini (eds) *Ungrounded Empires: The Cultural Politics of Modern Chinese Transnationalism.* New York: Routledge.

Nonini, Donald M. (1999) 'The Dialectics of "Disputatiousness" and "Rice-eating Money": Class Confrontation and Gendered Imaginaries among Chinese Men in Peninsular Malaysia'. *American Ethnologist,* 26 (1): 47–68.

Nonini, D.M. and A. Ong (1997) 'Introduction: Chinese Transnationalism as an Alternative Modernity', in A. Ong and D.M. Nonini (eds) *Ungrounded Empires: The Cultural Politics of Modern Chinese Transnationalism*. New York: Routledge.

Ong, Aihwa (1990) 'State vs Islam: Malay Families, Women's Bodies and the Body Politic in Malaysia'. *American Ethnologist*, 17 (2): 258–76.

Ong, Aihwa (1991) 'The Gender and Labor Politics of Postmodernity'. *Annual Review of Anthropology*, 20: 279–309.

Postone, M., E. LiPuma and C. Calhoun (1993) 'Introduction: Bourdieu and Social Theory', in C. Calhoun, E. LiPuma and M. Postone (eds) *Bourdieu: Critical Perspectives*. Chicago: University of Chicago.

Redding, S. Gordon (1990) *The Spirit of Chinese Capitalism*. Berlin: Walter de Gruyter.

Scott, James C. (1990) *Domination and the Arts of Resistance: Hidden Transcripts*. New Haven: Yale University Press.

Tong, Chee-Kiong (n.d.) 'The Dynamics of *Guanxi*, *Xinyong* and Chinese Business Networks'. Paper presented at conference, 'The Transnationalization of Overseas Chinese Capitalism: Networks, Nation-States, and Imagined Communities', National University of Singapore, Singapore, 8–12 August 1994.

Weidenbaum, M. and S. Hughes (1996) *The Bamboo Curtain: How Expatriate Chinese Entrepreneurs are Creating A New Economic Superpower in Asia*. New York: The Free Press.

Yang, Mayfair Mei-hui (1994) *Gifts, Favors, and Banquets: The Art of Social Relationships in China*. Ithaca, NY: Cornell University Press.

6 The leading Chinese–Filipino business families in post-Marcos Philippines

Temario C. Rivera

Large-scale capital accumulation in the Philippines took root in three major processes resulting in the emergence of at least three identifiable key fractions of big capitalists. By the late nineteenth century, in response to world market demands, an indigenous landowning, agricultural export-oriented class developed and constituted the first major fraction of the capitalist class. Comprising the most powerful segment of this class were the sugar landowners and sugar mill operators, mostly Chinese *mestizos,* from whose ranks would come many of the dominant local and national politicians in the country.[1] The second major fraction of the local capitalist class emerged from accessing choice government franchises and licences to extract natural resources, particularly lucrative logging and mining concessions, and also special loans, either from existing government financial institutions or from special government-controlled funds such as the postwar Japanese reparations fund. A third major bloc of the local capitalist class developed from local trading and commercial activities by individuals who initially had no access to land and had weak or little access to state resources. Many of the capitalists comprising this fraction were originally ethnic Chinese who suffered from discriminatory laws and policies during both the colonial and post-colonial period. By the twilight of Spanish colonial rule in the nineteenth century, foreign capital and firms had also started to build a significant presence in Manila and the country's key ports, further pushing the process of capital accumulation to new heights.

The country's emerging capitalist classes further intensified the process of capital accumulation through their direct access and to use of state resources in their capacity as elected politicians in key local and national positions of power. Historically, the big landed classes in export agriculture proved to be the most organized and accomplished practitioners of combining landed power with state power to advance both their economic and political interests.[2] Other class fractions indirectly accessed the use of state power and resources by nurturing close relationships with powerful political leaders through generous electoral campaign contributions, or by providing choice company positions to influential political personalities and generous gifts to power brokers. Due to legal impediments and racial discrimination in the past, the ethnic Chinese business families have traditionally resorted to more indirect ways of accessing state power and resources, but they have nonetheless shown remarkable skills in producing results in this manner.

This chapter examines the growth and development of the leading Chinese–Filipino business families in the Philippines, particularly its most powerful segment represented by six families: those of Alfonso Yuchengco, Lucio Tan, John Gokongwei, Jr, George Ty, Henry Sy and Andrew Gotianun. Combining business sophistication and political skills in dealing with heightened competition from both local and foreign players, these leading Chinese business families have positioned themselves extremely well in key sectors of the economy. In a situation where these families have to contend with long established non-Chinese Filipino business groups and overcome more difficult barriers in accessing state power and resources, the leading Chinese–Filipino business families have not only shown increased economic prominence, but also remarkable political resilience and increasing political influence.

The ethnic Chinese in the Philippine economy: an overview

The ethnic Chinese in the Philippines have played an important role in the development of the economy since colonial times. Long before the Spanish conquest of the country, Chinese merchants carried on trading activities with native communities along the China coast. During most of the Spanish colonial era, the Chinese controlled trading and commercial activities, serving as retailers, artisans, and providers of food for various Spanish settlements in the country (Wickberg 1965; Wong 1999).

During the American colonial era, the Chinese continued to control a significant portion of the retail trade and internal commerce of the country. Callis describes the extent of Chinese control of the economy during this period:

> Chinese predominated in the retail trade with US$25 million investment; they owned 75 per cent of the 2,500 rice mills that are scattered throughout the islands. They controlled 10 per cent of the capital invested in the lumber industry. Their influence in banking was not negligible. The total resources of the China Banking Corporation in Manila was US$27 million in 1937, representing mainly the capital of Chinese residents…it has been estimated that total Chinese investments in the Philippines reached US$100 million, which would have given them second place among foreign nations doing business in the islands to the Americans.
>
> (Callis 1942: 21)

As the oldest and largest immigrant minority in the Philippines, the Chinese population was estimated at about 600,000 in 1975, or about 1 per cent of the country's population (McCarthy 1975: 348). Today, the ethnic Chinese in the Philippines comprise about 1.5 per cent of the country's population (Ang See 1990). In 1975, Marcos issued a new citizenship law that drastically liberalized the naturalization process, enabling thousands of ethnic Chinese residents to become full-fledged citizens.

The ethnic Chinese who went into import substitution manufacturing during the 1950s and 1960s were primarily traders and merchants. In 1954, the government passed the Retail Trade Nationalization Act that further pushed Chinese traders and retailers into manufacturing. By restricting retail trade to Filipino citizens, the new policy led many Chinese entrepreneurs who could not get Filipino citizenship under the existing tedious and expensive naturalization laws to shift from retailing to manufacturing and wholesale trading (Palanca 1977).

To track down the position of the Chinese–Filipino entrepreneurs in the postwar economy, three studies are compared: 1) the pioneering work of Yoshihara Kunio (1985), which used 1968 data for the top 250 manufacturing firms; 2) the present author's study (Rivera 1994) of the top 120 private domestic manufacturing firms, using data for 1950–86; and 3) a study by Ellen H. Palanca (1995) on the economic position of Chinese–Filipinos among the top 1,000 corporations in 1990.

Yoshihara's study showed that 32 per cent of the top manufacturing firms in 1965 were owned by Chinese–Filipinos and were mostly in manufacturing sectors such as tobacco, paper and paper products, metal fabrication, soap and cosmetics, and rubber. My research reveals that the Chinese–Filipinos owned 45 per cent of the top 120 manufacturing firms by 1986. My study, however, did not include foreign manufacturing firms in the country. This same study stresses that the Chinese–Filipinos dominated three manufacturing sectors: tobacco and cigarettes, textiles, and rubber footwear. The Chinese–Filipino firms also controlled a significant share of the processing of coconut products, flour, food products, and the steel industry. Finally, the study by Palanca indicates that Chinese–Filipinos owned 35 per cent of the top 1,000 corporations in 1990.

The study by Palanca further demonstrated that the share of Chinese–Filipino owned firms in the top 1,000 corporations based on sales, income, assets, liabilities, and equities was smaller compared to the Filipino non-Chinese and foreign firms. One possible explanation provided by Palanca for the relatively smaller size of the Chinese business groups lies in the Chinese preference for setting up conglomerates of businesses rather than expanding one business.

The leading Chinese–Filipino business families

The six leading Chinese–Filipino business families included in this study – those of Lucio Tan, John Gokongwei, Jr, Alfonso Yuchengco, George Ty, Henry Sy and Andrew Gotianun – nearly all represent 'new money' rather than 'old wealth'.[3] Among the six families, only the Yuchengco clan can solidly trace its wealth to relatively well established economic activities started before the Second World War. Thus, the Yuchengco family's longest existing core financial firm, the Malayan Insurance Company (non-life), can be considered as a successor of China Insurance and Surety Co., established in 1930 by Ernesto Tiaoqui Yuchengco (*Businessworld* 1994: 117). In contrast, the Gokongwei and Sy families established their flagship firms only in the 1950s while the three other *taipan* families (Ty, Tan and Gotianun) established theirs only in the 1960s. While the Gotianun and Gokongwei families may indeed trace their business lineages to Pedro Gotiaco (Go Bon Tiao, 1856–1921), a relative by extension who was a wealthy business-man by the early twentieth century, their core business companies only took root and flourished after the Second World War.[4]

Four of the six leading Chinese–Filipino business families started their business operations in financial and commercial activities but two families, Tan and Gokongwei, initially gained their wealth through manufacturing activities. Tan's core company is Fortune Tobacco, which manufactures cigarettes, while Gokongwei's business empire was built on food processing, the manufacture of commercial glucose and corn starch, through Universal Corn Products (later renamed Universal Robina Corporation) (Wong 1992).

Three of the families (Yuchengco, Ty and Gotianun) built their conglomerates on resources accumulated through banking and financial operations. The Yuchengco family's wealth was rooted in its insurance business started in the 1930s and which continues today through its Malayan Insurance Group of Companies. George S.K. Ty established Metrobank in 1962 and nurtured its growth as the country's premier private commercial bank. Although George Ty's father (Norberto Ty) was one of the country's leading entrepreneurs in the textile and flour industry, George is reputed to have built Metrobank largely on his own efforts (Flores 1999). In the case of the Gotianun family, its wealth was generated through a combination of real estate development (Fil-Invest Develop-ment Corporation) started in the 1960s and banking operations in the 1970s up to the early 1980s (Family Savings Bank and Insular Bank of Asia and America). Finally, the Sy family started its mega-retailing operations with the establishment of the first ShoeMart store in 1958, although a much smaller shoe store had been opened by the family as early as 1945.

Like most of the Chinese big business groups in Southeast Asia (notably Thailand, Malaysia, and Indonesia), the Chinese–Filipino conglomerates continue to be essentially 'family firms', meaning that 'ultimate control is exercised by one man or one family, rather than joint-stock companies with widely dispersed shareholders'. But as Mackie also correctly goes on to note, in the case of the Southeast Asian Chinese big business, their status as family firms 'has not prevented their growth into giant conglomerates' (Mackie 1992: 162). Of the six families in the study, the Yuchengco flagship companies show the most dispersed shareholdings. In two of its core companies, the Rizal Commercial Banking Corporation (RCBC) and the House of Investments, the Yuchengco family controls only 25 per cent and 48 per cent respectively of the equity shares. However, the Yuchengco family retains full control over Malayan Insurance Co., the country's top non-life insurance firm. The family of Lucio Tan appears to have the tightest control over its core and affiliated companies and the least public stock offerings. In the case of Tan, however, the absence of updated data about his companies makes it difficult to provide precise figures.

Through public stock offerings, the core companies of the other families have also increased the share of non-family stock, but without posing any danger to continued effective control of the lead firms by the families concerned. The families' effective control over their lead companies, despite public stock offerings, is shown by the following data: the Sy family controls 85 per cent of SM Prime Holdings, Inc. (SM Prime Holdings, Inc. 1994); the Gokongwei family controls 83 per cent of JG Summit Holdings, Inc. and 75 per cent of Universal Robina; the Ty family owns 78 per cent of Metrobank, its flagship bank; and the Gotianun family controls 70 per cent of Filinvest Land Corporation and 80 per cent of East West Bank. Thus, while almost all of the *taipan* families have engaged in capital expansion through public stock offerings, such capital enhancement activities have not resulted in the separation of ownership from control of the lead firms by the families.

Nonetheless, it is quite significant that in the face of increasing competition and the pressure for capital expansion, almost all leading Chinese–Filipino business families, notably those of Gokongwei, Sy, Yuchengco, and Gotianun, have offered stock options in the open market. In this context, a recent case study of Chinese–Filipino firms of varying sizes shows that the owner-managers 'appear strongly committed to owner management as the preferred mode of enterprise management', even as the entrepreneurs themselves 'have adopted control systems and practices similar to those used in modern large-scale enterprises' (Roman *et al.* 1996: 115). The same study points out that the adoption of more modern management systems and practices by Chinese–Filipino business firms can be explained by at least four factors:

> exposure to Western management practices through formal business education; growth in the size and complexity of the firm; strains on the system of family management resulting from increases in the number of family members in later generations and the weakening of family ties among them; and the dilution of family-owned interests due to diversification and continued expansion.
>
> (Roman *et al.* 1996: 115)

It is also significant to note that all of the families whose initial wealth was not generated through banking and financial activities eventually ended up owning a bank or participating as a major stockholder of well-established banks. In 1977, Lucio Tan acquired ownership of an existing bank, the General Bank and Trust Company, formerly owned by the Yujuico family, and incorporated it as Allied Bank in the same year. Moreover, Lucio Tan took control of the country's leading government bank, the Philippine National Bank (PNB), when he acquired 67 per cent of the bank's shares in 1999 in the aftermath of the government's privatization program. The Sy family is the majority owner of Banco de Oro, a commercial bank, and also has substantial shares in China Banking Corporation (14 per cent), the Philippine National Bank, and the Far East Bank and Trust Co. (7 per cent). On the other hand, the Gokongwei family up until 1999 was a leading stockholder in two key commercial banks, the Far East Bank and Trust Co. (19 per cent), and the Philippine Commercial and International Bank (PCIB) (24 per cent).[5] Awash with cash with the high-profit sale of his shares in Far East Bank and PCIB, the Gokongwei family has been aggressively looking for a bank to take over. They could just also build up their existing wholly-owned Robinson's Savings Bank. Meanwhile, the Gotianun family, which sold its Family Savings Bank and its 30 per cent equity share of Insular Bank of Asia and America in 1984, put up a new family-controlled bank, East West Bank, in 1994. In 1999, George Ty of Metrobank also expanded his banking empire with the acquisition of two more banks, Asian Bank and Global Business Bank.

Of the top ten private commercial banks in 1993, the Chinese–Filipino families were in control of four (Metropolitan Bank, Allied Bank, Equitable Banking and China Banking), with Ty's Metrobank ranked the highest in percentage share of gross revenues, net income and total assets. Another study also estimates that nine Chinese–Filipino-owned banks controlled 38.43 per cent of the total assets of private domestic commercial banks in 1993 (Juan 1993). By 1999, a major realignment of the ownership of private commercial banks took place, with Equitable Banking merging with Philippine Commercial and International Bank; Ty's Metrobank acquiring Asian Bank and Global Business Bank; and Lucio Tan assuming majority control of the privatized Philippine National Bank. All of these changes further enhanced the control by Chinese–Filipino business families of the private commercial banking sector.

All of the six families have rapidly diversified their business operations. Each family has a flagship firm engaged in banking and finance and real estate development. The Yuchengco group of companies is the most diversified, and with the biggest number of companies engaged in agro-business operations. The Malayan Insurance Co., owned by the Yuchengco family, is the biggest non-life insurance business firm. In manufacturing activities, the Gokongwei and Tan group of companies lead the rest. Gokongwei's food processing firms (Universal Robina and Consolidated Food Corp) are among the country's biggest and the family has also expanded into the airline business (Cebu Pacific Air), property development (Robinsons Land Corporation) and telecommunications (Digital Telecom Philippines, Inc.). Lucio Tan's cigarette company, Fortune Tobacco, controls the largest market share in the country. Under both the Aquino (1986–92) and the Ramos (1992–8) administrations, however, Tan's tobacco manufacturing operations had been the target of multi-billion peso tax-evasion suits filed by the government, which Tan has succeeded in fending off so far through protracted court litigation, resulting in some decisions in his favour. Tan had also challenged the long-established monopoly of the beer industry enjoyed by the country's top food and drinks conglomerate, San Miguel Corporation, by putting up his own beer company, Asia Brewery, Inc. Moreover, Tan also acquired majority control in the early 1990s of the country's erstwhile flagship airline, the Philippine Airlines (PAL), thus further expanding his industrial empire.

An important indicator of the capacity of the *taipan* families to develop competitive niches in the regional and global economy is the degree of their international linkages. By this indicator, the Yuchengco group of companies shows the most extensive linkages with foreign investors, particularly with Japanese corporations such as Sanwa Bank, Nomura International, Fuji Xerox Corp., Tokyo Marine and Fire Insurance, Daiwa House, and Matsushita Electrical Inc. Through its car assembly operations, George Ty has also forged important linkages with Toyota Motors and other Japanese corporations such as Mitsui and Co. With Ty as the major Filipino partner, Toyota Motor Philippines is the country's leading firm in the manufacture and assembly of motor vehicles. Moreover, through its flagship bank, Metrobank, Ty has also established bank branch offices in China and Taiwan as well as in Guam, New York and Hong Kong (*Philippine Daily Inquirer* 1994b). In May 2000, both Ty and Tan were finally granted official licences to operate commercial banks in China, with Metrobank seeking to establish its first branch in Shanghai, while Tan already had built a 36-story Bank Center in Fujian Province, which also houses his Xiamen Commercial Bank (Flores 2000). For the Gokongwei family, its overseas expansion is seen in the 23 per cent equity held by its flagship holding company, JG Summit Holdings Inc., in Singapore-based affiliate United Industrial Corporation. The Sy family has Hong Kong-based Dao Heng Bank as a partner with a 13 per cent equity in the family-controlled Banco de Oro (Batino 2001).

The Gokongwei group of companies has extensive joint ventures and licensing agreements in branded consumer foods, with foreign partners such as United Biscuits of the UK, Hunt-Wesson Foods of the US, Nissin Foods of Japan, and Tootsie Roll, Inc. of the US. It also markets Keebler biscuits, Hunt's pork and beans and tomato sauces, Nissin's Ramen noodles and Tootsie Roll candies (JG Summit Holdings, Inc. 1994: 11). Moreover, through its snack food arm, Universal Robina Corp., the Gokongwei family also operates five food subsidiaries in China, two in Malaysia and one each in Thailand and Singapore (Torrijos 2001). Through a partnership with Marubeni Corporation of Japan, the Gokongwei group is also poised to construct an 11.6 billion peso petrochemical plant in Luzon (*Philippine Daily Inquirer* 1994a). The Gokongwei and Gotianun families have also expanded into sugar milling, an industry traditionally controlled by the old sugar elite families. The Gokongwei group of companies established the Universal Robina Sugar Milling Corp. and the Cagayan Robina Sugar Milling Co., while the Gotianuns put up the Davao Sugar Central Co. Finally, the Sy family continues to diversify its business operations by linking up with the Keppel group of Singapore in taking over the country's largest ship repair facility, Philseco. The Sy's flagship company, ShoeMart, continues to lord it over the country's department and variety stores retailing business, accounting for almost half the total assets of all firms in this line of business.

In real estate development, Andrew Gotianun's family-owned firm, Filinvest, ranks second only to the long-established Ayala Land. The increasing clout of the Gotianun's real estate firm was amply demonstrated in 1993, when Filinvest bested Ayala Land in the bidding for a hotly contested piece of real estate, the Alabang stock farm area. Gotianun was also a key player in the Metro Pacific Corporation Salim group-led consortium that won the bidding in 1995 for the prized 117-hectare Fort Bonifacio land project. Among the prominent Chinese–Filipino groups that were part of this winning consortium were Allied Bank of Lucio Tan and the China Banking Corporation of the Dee-Yuchengco-Sy families. In this bidding contest, Ayala Land proved to be a poor second.

Elite linkages and access to state power

It is important to understand an important dimension of the success of ethnic entrepreneurs such as the Chinese–Filipino families – how they are able to adjust to and eventually turn to their advantage the vicissitudes of politics and state policies. This is particularly important for minority ethnic entrepreneurs, whose access to state power and resources has traditionally been more difficult and more costly compared to their well-established local counterparts. In this chapter, only one aspect of this complex problem is discussed, that of the local elite linkages and partnerships that the leading Chinese–Filipino families have developed through the years in their business operations.

Following the career tracks of the six leading Chinese–Filipino entrepreneurs, those of George S.K. Ty and Alfonso Yuchengco show crucial linkages with key members of the Filipino elite in the early years of their business operations. In the establishment of Metrobank, Ty had as co-founders a formidable array of former leading public officials, which included the following: Pio Pedrosa, former finance secretary; Placido Mapa, Sr, former secretary of agriculture; and Emilio Abello, an influential businessman and former ambassador (Metrobank 1992: 4). Throughout the years, Ty has been able to rely on highly trained professionals to serve as the president of his flagship bank including Andres Castillo, former Central Bank governor, and Edgardo Espiritu and Placido Mapa, Jr, who both served as presidents of the Philippine National Bank.[6] In Metrobank's 1992 Board of Directors were also two former top public officials: Querube C. Makalintal, former chief justice of the Supreme Court, and Cesar E.A. Virata, former prime minister under Marcos, who served as the bank's senior consultant.

In the establishment and nurturing of his core companies, Alfonso Yuchengco also enjoyed the support of important Filipino partners. For his commercial bank, Rizal Commercial Banking Corporation, Yuchengco had the Antonino family as one of his original partners, whose patriarch was a logging magnate and one-time senator of the republic. For his flagship Malayan Insurance Company, Yuchengco had the influential former US ambassador and Foreign Affairs Secretary Carlos P. Romulo as chairman of the board from 1970–85 (Francisco 1994: 111). Moreover, the Yuchengco family has a prominent Filipino lawyer as a business partner, Leonardo Siguion-Reyna. During the Aquino administration, Yuchengco's economic and political clout was recognized with his appointment as ambassador to the People's Republic of China. As further proof of the family's ability to draw to its fold influential personalities, Yuchengco's holding company, the House of Investments, elected in 1994 former prime minister Cesar E.A. Virata as its chair. Showing his political durability, Yuchengco bagged another key diplomatic post under the Ramos administration with his appointment as ambassador to Japan.

Among the leading Chinese–Filipino entrepreneurs, Lucio Tan's business career has been marked by the greatest controversy. Acknowledged as one of the richest, if not the richest, man in the Philippines today, his critics argue that his rise to economic power was due primarily to his crony ties with Marcos, where he was supposedly the beneficiary of extensive tax, financing and regulatory concessions (Manapat 1991: 344–52). In the post-Marcos era, Tan hired as his top managers former well-placed military generals, further fanning speculations about his management strategies. Tan's flagship tobacco company, Fortune Tobacco, was headed by a retired general and former customs commissioner, Salvador Mison. Another retired general and former chief of the National Pollution Control Commission, Guillermo Pecache, served as president of Tan's Asia Brewery. A powerful bloc of political support for Tan lies in a grouping of about 27 legislators of the lower house of Congress, who represent the tobacco-producing provinces of the Ilocos region. Since the 1960s, Tan's tobacco and cigarette business has served as the major buyer of the tobacco products of the Ilocos region, an economic and political capital that Tan has cultivated well in his struggles with government and his other detractors. Acknowledged as one of the key financiers of the Estrada presidential campaign in 1998, Tan enjoyed special ties with the deposed president and was believed to be behind some key presidential appointments. Under the Estrada administration, the longstanding multi-billion peso tax evasion cases filed against Tan reached a dead end with the collusive passive stance of the government lawyers assigned to his case. Under the same administration, Tan's Philippine Airlines (PAL) was also the beneficiary of some highly contentious policies that for some time favoured PAL, involving disputes over flying rights with other international airlines. Moreover, Tan was also accused of using his special ties with the Estrada administration to facilitate his takeover of the Philippine National Bank even while his interests were suspect because of the substantial indebtedness of PAL to the same bank. But demonstrating once again the political dexterity and deviousness that has marked his highly controversial career as a businessman, Tan also initiated an immediate rapprochement with the new Macapagal-Arroyo administration in its first weeks of power, in Tan's capacity as the new president of the highly influential Federation of Chinese–Filipino Chambers of Commerce.[7]

For the Gotianun family, the key Filipino partner was D.M. Consunji, who is related by affinity through the marriage of a Gotianun son with a Consunji daughter. Consunji founded a leading engineering and construction firm that served as a natural link to the real estate development business of the Gotianuns. In the case of John Gokongwei and Henry Sy, working with prominent Filipino business partners came later when their core business firms had already got off the ground. For Gokongwei, the major business partner has been no less than one of the old rich families, the Lopezes. Admitting to 'a close relationship with Mr Lopez', Gokongwei joined hands with Eugenio Lopez, Jr in 1987 to buy from the government the majority stocks in Philippine Commercial International Bank (PCIB) (Wong 1992: 4). In 1993, these two families got together once again to build a 215-megawatt power plant under a build-operate-transfer agreement with government. Finally, the Sy family had as their partner in their core trading firm, ShoeMart, a relatively unknown businessman named Senen Mendiola, who continues to be a top official of the Sy group of companies. However, in 1994, the Sy family took in former Social Security System administrator and governor of the Central Bank, Jose L. Cuisia, Jr, as vice-chairman of SM Holdings.

The new generation of leaders

With most of the top Chinese–Filipino business leaders in their seventies, the issue of succession and leadership increasingly looms large. What makes this issue compelling for the Chinese–Filipino business families is a style of leadership which combines increasing reliance on professional managers while at the same time ensuring that key decisions are ultimately made by the family core members.[8] However, the appropriateness of this style of leadership is being increasingly challenged by the rapid diversification and expansion of the conglomerates owned by the Chinese–Filipino business leaders, as well as by the rapid changes brought about by the far more competitive and liberal domestic and foreign markets. The demise of the founding business patriarchs will also put to test the integrity and coherence of family ownership due to potential problems of inheritance and the division of family wealth. Moreover, the increasing decentralization of political power and authority in the country and the emergence of more centres of power-brokering in local government units will also require more sophisticated skills in accessing and cultivating necessary political connections. Finally, the new generation of leaders will have to live and operate in a business environment deeply embedded in and activated by international capital, commodity and knowledge circuits.

To the credit of the current Chinese–Filipino business families, they have largely succeeded in training a new generation of well-educated leaders. For instance, John Gokongwei's son Lance, now in his thirties, is a graduate of the University of Pennsylvania and serves as a senior vice-president of the family conglomerate. All of the four children (one daughter, three sons) of Henry Sy are college graduates (Assumption and De La Salle University), with degrees in business management or engineering, and they now serve in various management positions. Sy's eldest child, Teresita, is the president of ShoeMart and Banco de Oro. Alfonso Yuchengco (the most senior of the business patriarchs) has two of his children actively involved in the management of his vast conglomerate. Helen Y. Dee, the eldest daughter of Alfonso, has an MBA and serves as president of her family's leading non-life insurance firm, while Alfonso III, the youngest son, has a degree from De La Salle University and takes charge of running the family's House of Investments, Inc. The Gotianun family also boasts of a second-generation set of leaders with advanced degrees from various American universities. Jonathan Gotianun has an MBA from Northwestern University, while Michael Gotianun has a business administration degree from the University of San Francisco. Lourdes Josephine G. Yap, the daughter, finished an MBA from the University of Chicago while her husband, Joseph Yap, who now serves as a vice-president in the family business, has an MBA from Harvard. The university education and graduate degrees acquired by the successor generation of the Chinese–Filipino business families have not only equipped them with state-of-the-art knowledge in business management practices and techniques, but also provided them with the international linkages and contacts for their business operations. In a deeper sense, this formal training in major national and international institutions is crucial because of the sense of self-confidence developed in the successor generation.

Conclusion

Considering the cultural and institutional biases that they have had to contend with, the leading Chinese–Filipino business families have shown remarkable business and political skills that have enabled them to operate effectively. Undoubtedly, one outstanding feature of their economic success has been their skilful cultivation of partnerships and social linkages with key members of the indigenous elite. In a regime of greater economic liberalization and political stability, the Chinese–Filipino business families, particularly its most powerful groups, are well positioned to lead the competition. By combining essentially family-based control of their diversified economic activities with the recruitment of tested professionals for management functions, the leading Chinese–Filipino families have maintained a leading and significant presence in almost every sector of the economy. Their traditional leadership and management practices are being challenged by a far more competitive and liberal business environment and a decentralizing political system, but they also have at least two distinct assets that could further enhance their advantageous economic and political positions in the country, i.e. a well-educated successor generation and their network of linkages with overseas Chinese capital.

Notes

1 The Chinese *mestizos* were children of mixed marriages between the ethnic Chinese and the local people. Due to the confluence of particular political and economic conditions during the nineteenth century under Spanish colonial rule, the Chinese *mestizos* adopted Filipino ways and practices and came to be considered and accepted as Filipinos by the local population. See Wickberg (1964: 62–100).
2 A classic exemplar of the Chinese *mestizo*, sugar planter family that rose to national elite prominence from its provincial origins is that of the Lopez family of Iloilo province. See McCoy (1993: 429–536).
3 Here, I adopt Jamie Mackie's distinction between 'old wealth' and 'new wealth'. By old wealth, Mackie refers to 'family firms that were well established before World War II…or are today second generation firms'. In contrast, he uses the term 'new wealth' to refer to firms 'which have come to prominence over the last twenty or thirty years'. See Mackie (1992).
4 For the possible lineages of the Gotianun and Gokongwei families to Pedro Gotiaco, see Hedman and Sidel (2000: 65–87).
5 The Far East Bank and Trust Company was absorbed by the Ayala family-controlled Bank of the Philippine Islands (BPI) in 1999 while PCI Bank merged in the same year with Equitable Bank, controlled by the Chinese–Filipino Go family.

6 During the short-lived Estrada Administration (1998–2001), Espiritu served as its first Secretary of Finance.
7 The Federation of Chinese–Filipino Chambers of Commerce is a powerful anchor of economic power and political influence for the Chinese business community. While the leading Chinese–Filipino business families have enough clout to negotiate their own interests and not be too dependent on the Federation, most of the smaller and medium-scale Chinese–Filipino business enterprises have traditionally channelled and negotiated their corporate and community interests through the Federation.
8 For a discussion of the ownership and management structure of the leading Chinese–Filipino business families, see Koike (1995: 35–71).

References

Allied Banking Corporation Annual Report, various years.
Batino, Clarissa S. (2001) 'UBS Affiliate to Acquire 16.96% of Banco de Oro'. *Philippine Daily Inquirer*, 16 April. Available http://www.Inq7.net/bus/2001/apr16/bus_8-1.htm.
Businessworld (1994) 'Philippines, Inc.: Who Owns the Philippines?' (seventh Anniversary Report). Makati: Businessworld, Philippines, Inc.
Businessworld Top 1000 Corporations, various years.
Callis, Helmut G. (1942) *Foreign Capital in Southeast Asia*. New York: Institute of Pacific Relations.
Flores, Wilson Y. Lee (1999) 'Who'll Be the No. 1 Banker in 2000?'. *Philippine Daily Inquirer*, 20 December.
Flores, Wilson Y. Lee (2000) 'Ty Was First but Tan Was Right Behind Him', *Philippine Daily Inquirer*, 22 May.
Francisco, Rosmarie V. (1994) 'Yuchengco: Silent Billionaire No Longer' (seventh Anniversary Report). Makati: Businessworld, Philippines, Inc.
Hedman, Eva-Lotta E. and John T. Sidel (2000) *Philippine Politics and Society in the Twentieth Century: Colonial Legacies, Post-colonial Trajectories*. London and New York: Routledge.
Hutchcroft, Paul D. (1998) *Booty Capitalism: The Politics of Banking in the Philippines*. Ithaca: Cornell University Press.
JG Summit Holdings, Inc. (1994) 'Annual Report'.
Juan, Go-Bon (1993) 'Ethnic Chinese in Philippine Banking'. *China Currents*, 4(4): 21–4.
Koike, Kenji (1995) 'Changing Ownership and Management Structure of Taipans Compared with the Ayala Group', in Temario C. Rivera and Kenji Koike (eds) *The Chinese–Filipino Business Families Under the Ramos Government*. Joint Research Program Series No. 114, Institute of Developing Economies, Tokyo.
McCarthy, Charles J. (1976) 'The Chinese in the Philippines: Today and Tomorrow'. *Fookien Times*, Manila.
McCoy, Alfred W. (1993) 'Rent-Seeking Families and the Philippine State: A History of the Lopez Family', in Alfred W. McCoy (ed.) *An Anarchy of Families: State and Family in the Philippines*. Madison: University of Wisconsin Center for Southeast Asian Studies.
Mackie, Jamie (1992) 'Changing Patterns of Chinese Big Business in Southeast Asia', in Ruth McVey (ed.) *Southeast Asian Capitalists*. Ithaca: Cornell Southeast Asia Program.
Manapat, Ricardo (1991) *Some are Smarter than Others: The History of Marcos' Crony Capitalism*. New York: Aletheia Publications.
Metrobank (various years) 'Annual Report'.
Palanca, Ellen H. (1977) 'The Economic Position of the Chinese in the Philippines'. *Philippine Studies*, 25: 80–94.

Palanca, Ellen H. (1995) 'An Analysis of the 1990 Top Corporations in the Philippines: Economic Position and Activities of the Ethnic Chinese, Filipino and Foreign Groups'. *Chinese Studies Journal*, 5: 47–84.

Philippine Daily Inquirer (1994a) 'Marubeni to Invest in Big Industrial Projects in RP', 1 March.

Philippine Daily Inquirer (1994b) 'Metrobank Eyes $1-B Capital in '95, Plans Asian Expansion', 20 December.

Rivera, Temario C. (1994) *Landlords and Capitalists: Class, Family and State in Philippine Manufacturing*. Quezon City: University of the Philippines Press.

Rivera, Temario C. and Kenji Koike (eds) (1995) *The Chinese–Filipino Business Families Under the Ramos Government*. Joint Research Program Series No. 114, Institute of Developing Economies, Tokyo.

Roman, Emerlinda, E.S. Echanis, E.P. Pineda and Ma. T.M. Sicat (1996) *Management Control in Chinese–Filipino Business Enterprises*. Quezon City: University of the Philippines Press.

Securities and Exchange Commission (SEC) (various years) *General Information Sheets*, various companies.

See, Teresita Ang (1990) *The Chinese in the Philippines: Problems and Perspectives*. Manila: Kaisa Para sa Kaunlaran Inc.

SM Prime Holdings, Inc. (1994) 'Prospectus Relating to an Offer of Common Shares of Stocks', *Makati*, 6 June.

Torrijos, Elena R. (2001) 'JG Summit to Expand Overseas', *Philippine Daily Inquirer*, 20 April. Available http://www.inq7.net/bus/2001/apr20/bus_4-1.htm.

Wickberg, Edgar (1964) 'The Chinese Mestizo in Philippine History'. *Journal of Southeast Asian History*, 5(1), March.

Wickberg, Edgar (1965) *The Chinese in Philippine Life, 1850–1898*. New Haven: Yale University Press.

Wong Kwok-Chu (1999) *The Chinese in the Philippine Economy, 1898–1941*. Quezon City: Ateneo de Manila University Press.

Wong, Ramon H.K. (1992) 'Filipino-Chinese Business Tycoon: John Gokongwei, Jr', *Forbes Zibenjia*, September (translated English version of the article).

Yoshihara Kunio (1985) *Philippine Industrialization: Foreign and Domestic Capital*. Quezon City: Ateneo de Manila University Press.

7 Pre-1997 Sino-Indonesian conglomerates, compared with those of other ASEAN countries

Jamie Mackie

Explanations of the remarkable increases in wealth of Southeast Asia's Chinese minorities in the decades prior to the 1997–8 financial crisis have generally put more emphasis on what they have in common than on the differences between them.They tend to look for the secret of their success by the well-tried technique of identifying common elements in their socio-cultural heritage or methods of business organization as the main source of clues to their outstanding commercial skills.That is understandable, since many features of their Chinese cultural heritage are still found in all the ASEAN countries[1] to some degree, often distinguishing local Chinese sharply from the indigenous communities amongst whom they live, hence it is likely to provide part of the answers given to this question. But significant differences between the region's various Chinese minorities are also discernible, arising out of their diverse experiences. Many of these have made Southeast Asian Chinese far less uniformly 'Chinese' in their characteristics and much more 'Southeast Asian' in the 1990s than they were sixty years earlier.

These differences deserve closer attention than they usually receive. One of the principal aims of this chapter is to urge that we look at them at least as closely as the similarities, for we will see more deeply into the socio-economic dynamics of particular Chinese communities by exploring their distinctive characteristics, economic roles and business trajectories in depth and across time. Above all, we should be suspicious of articles on 'the Overseas Chinese' by instant experts on the subject who conclude from a hasty glance at their reliance on *guanxi* and their widespread commercial networks that all 23 million or so Southeast Asian Chinese are essentially similar and might constitute the nucleus of an 'Overseas Commonwealth' of like-minded Chinese entrepreneurs.[2] Attention will be directed here to the so-called 'conglomerates' in Indonesia, better called 'business groups', in comparison with those that have emerged in the other ASEAN countries in order to show the influence of the local context in each country that makes them so different from one another.

There are two methodological reasons why this approach is useful. First, if we focus solely on what these institutions have in common as if it were the significant causal factor responsible for their success – let's just call it 'factor X' for the moment to avoid prejudging the issue, or else 'factors X, Y, Z, P, Q' etc. so as to accommodate multi-factorial explanations – it becomes dangerously easy to slide towards an overemphasis on racial or cultural elements as the key factors, in effect on their 'Chineseness', or the values and cultural predispositions deriving from something like their so-called 'Confucian tradition'.[3] Those factors cannot of course be ignored in any investigation into this subject, but they do not provide the whole answer to the puzzle here. Confucian values (if that term can usefully be applied at all in this sphere) have not proved to be a necessary and sufficient condition for commercial progress among either the Chinese in China or ethnic Chinese overseas in all times and places; in fact, at times they have been regarded as an obstacle to economic development rather than a spur to it.

That mode of reasoning can be called 'the essentialist fallacy' – i.e. the belief that the clue to explaining a phenomenon such as this is to identify some crucial factor, like a Platonic 'essence', that all Chinese share, or some set of personal qualities they tend to embody more abundantly than other races or cultures. We should be wary about any such resort to racial characteristics in matters like this (or even cultural ones), in any part of the world, since they rarely correlate at all neatly with any other social characteristic. Instead, they distract attention from the need to look more widely and deeply at a variety of other elements that may be relevant to the explanations we are seeking. Moreover, the essentialist approach to social analysis of any kind is badly flawed methodologically and is best avoided altogether.

Second, a strong reason for looking into the differences between various groups of Southeast Asian Chinese as well as their similarities is that it draws our attention to the importance of the local context. Where local circumstances have been favourable, the various Southeast Asian Chinese minorities have generally prospered remarkably, as in Thailand between the late 1950s and 1996, or Singapore (where they form a 77 per cent majority and their situation is radically different from elsewhere in ASEAN). Where the local context has not been favourable, as in Burma since 1960 or in Indonesia in the late Sukarno years, their Chinese social or cultural heritage has not in itself been sufficient to make them prosperous. In China itself, the local context was highly unfavourable to private business enterprise under the later Ch'ing dynasty and throughout most of the Mao Zedong era. Only in the more favourable circumstances applying under Deng Xiaoping has the situation changed. As soon as we look into the circumstances in which Southeast Asian Chinese have flourished or struggled throughout various parts of the region over the last 200 years it is quickly apparent that local conditions have been crucially important. So it is more useful to explore differences of that kind and their relevance to the various economic roles played by ethnic Chinese in various times and places than to generalize grandly about their common Chinese cultural or social heritage. The latter is certainly not unimportant, but does not alone provide the clues we need to answer the key questions here.

In the case of the Indonesian Chinese, the distinctiveness of the local socio-economic and political context has been profoundly important in shaping the main characteristics of the big Sino-Indonesian conglomerates over the last thirty years, because of the highly patrimonial features of President Soeharto's 'New

Order' regime (Crouch 1979). That context has been very different from the more pluralist political context in Thailand or Malaysia or any other country in the region, as we shall see, although there are also similarities, of course. The reasons for those differences can more readily be understood by looking at the local socio-economic context in which the various ethnic Chinese business groups have been operating than by searching for some set of deep-seated commonalities amongst them. If we were able to look more closely at the characteristics of Chinese small-scale and medium enterprises also in all those countries, the results might be even more illuminating. But as it is not nearly as easy to get reliable data on the latter as on the big conglomerates in any part of the region, that aspect of the problem cannot be explored here.

Indonesia

In the mid-1990s, Indonesia had about ten very large conglomerates, each with an annual turnover in 1993 of more than US$1 billion. There were also about 40 or 50 that might be called second-rank, with turnovers above US$200 million, plus at least 200 smaller ones above US$50 million (Table 7.1). About 80 per cent of them, at all levels, appear to be owned by Sino-Indonesians, with the remainder of the top twenty dominated by members of the Soeharto family or a few indigenous businessmen closely connected to the Palace circle, hardly any of whom were independent of political connections.

Twenty years previously, there were just a few emerging private conglomerates. That word only came into common usage in the early 1980s. But with the rapid growth of the economy from 1986–7 on, especially in the boom years after deregulation of private banking and the shift to export-oriented industrialization which got under way in 1988–9, the conglomerates grew in size enormously and, to a lesser degree, in number. While they may have appeared superficially similar to those of Malaysia or Thailand in some respects, they differed significantly in others, the socio-political context in which they emerged having been especially different, both economically and politically, the trade and competition policy regimes in particular. Nearly all the Indonesian conglomerates came into prominence after 1968, hardly any having achieved significant size before Soeharto's New Order regime came to power in 1965–6, as several had done in Malaysia and Thailand. When one recalls that the New Order initially seemed likely to be hostile to the Chinese community, the military and Muslim groups behind it having previously been strongly anti-Chinese, it is remarkable that so many Chinese business enterprises have been able to flourish as they have since 1965–6.[4]

The explanation for that has to be sought in the way President Soeharto himself has made use of the unique set of relationships he established with Liem Sioe Liong, Bob Hasan and others closely associated with them as suppliers of unofficial funds, commonly known as *cukong*, for his various purposes, enabling him to avoid the financial constraints of the formal system from the earliest years of the New Order until now. It is hardly surprising that he ordered prompt and

Table 7.1 Major business groups in Indonesia, 1993

Group	Principal owner	Principal activities	Turn-over (Rp. mil.)	Ranking, 1993	No. of companies, 1993
Salim	Liem Sioe Liong	cement, finance, food, gro-ind., autos, etc.	18,000	1	450
Astra	Prasetya Mulya group and public	autos, plantations	5,890	2	205
Lippo	Mochtar Riady	finance, real estate	4,750	3	78
Sinar Mas	Eka Cipta Wijaya	agro-ind., pulp and paper, finance	4,200	4	150
Gudang Garam	Rachman Halim	kretek (cigarettes)	3,600	5	6
Bob Hasan	Bob Hasan, Sigit Harhojudanto	timber, plantations	3,400	6	92
Barito	Prajogo Pangestu	timber, petrochemicals	3,050	7	92
Bimantara	Bambang Trihatmojo	trade, real estate, chemicals	3,000	8	134
Argo Manunggal	The Ning King	textiles	2,940	9	54
Dharmala	Soehargo Gondokusumo	real estate, agro-ind., finance	2,530	10	151
Djarum	Budi Hartono	kretek	2,360	11	25
Ongko	Kaharuddin Ongko	real estate, finance	2,100	12	59
Panin	Mu'min Ali Gunawan	finance	2,080	13	43
Roda Mas	Tan Siong Kie	chemicals	2,000	14	41
Surya Raya	Soeryadjaya	property, plantations, trade	1,980	15	242
Jan Darmadi	Jan Darmadi	real estate	1,940	16	60
CCM/Befca	Murday Widyawimarta Poo	electronics	1,800	17	32
Humpuss	Hutomo Mandala Putra	trade, chemicals	1,750	18	11
Gadjah Tunggal	Sjamsul Nursalim	tyres, finance, real estate	1,650	19	49
Raja Garuda Mas	Sukanto Tanoto	pulp and rayon, finance	1,590	20	66
Gemala	Wanandi	chemicals, autos	1,550	21	78
Pembangunan Jaya	Ciputra and others	real estate	1,390	22	57
Metropolitan	Ciputra and others	real estate	1,200	23	57
Soedarpo	Soedarpo Sastrosatomo	shipping, trade, pharmaceuticals	1,200	23	35
Tahija	Julius Tahija	finance	1,200	23	39

Source: Adapted from Hill 1996: 111. Based on *Warta Ekonomi*, 24 April 1994 (and earlier), with assistance from Dr Thee Kian Wie.

stern action against anti-Chinese riots whenever they broke out, unlike the situation under Sukarno, when the authorities were often ambivalent or divided over how to respond to such outbreaks (Mackie 1976b). Nor is it surprising that most members of the Chinese community seem to have recognized that they had become far better off materially under his regime than they had been previously, hence that they had a strong vested interest in its survival.

The Indonesian socio-political context

The Sino-Indonesian minority is generally estimated to be approximately 3 per cent of the total population, hence about 6 million, a much smaller fraction of the total population than the Chinese in Malaysia (28 per cent, or 5.5 million) or Thailand (about 10 per cent, or 6 million, give or take perhaps a million or more), but considerably larger than in the Philippines (less than 1 million, about 1.5 per cent) (Mackie 1996: xxiii). As in most other parts of Southeast Asia, ethnic Chinese control the greater part of modern-sector economic activities (although they had hardly any part in the important mining or plantation sectors in Indonesia until the late 1980s) at both the large-scale and SME levels. The reasons for that are much the same as in other parts of Southeast Asia, although with minor differences which derive from diverse patterns of development established during the formative years of the late colonial era.

The Chinese communities scattered throughout Indonesia are probably more heterogeneous than those in Malaysia, Thailand or the Philippines on several scores. There is not the same degree of dominance of a single dialect-group – Hokkien, Teochiu, Hakka or Cantonese – as is observable elsewhere, but a fairly even spread among them all. There is a sharper division than elsewhere between the long-established *peranakan* communities, which have mostly lost their ability to use Chinese languages, and the *totok*, who are either immigrants or children of recent immigrants, Chinese-speaking and more oriented towards China, Hong Kong or Taiwan, and more entrepreneurial in their economic activities (Wang 1976). There are also sharper regional differences between, for example, Jakartan Chinese (the largest agglomeration, by far), Surabaya, Semarang and Bandung Chinese and the very different, more strongly *totok* Medan community, as well as between big-city Chinese and the many thousands scattered throughout hundreds of smaller towns and even a few rural areas.[5] Relations between the Chinese minorities and the host communities also vary a good deal across the country, reflecting the past history of minority-majority relations in different places. But very little is known about such matters.

Features of the Indonesian conglomerates

Until the 1970s, relatively few Sino-Indonesian large-scale enterprises existed; nearly all ethnic Chinese businessmen were engaged in small or medium firms. They were often predominant at the local level and in the main cities, but rarely able to expand sufficiently to become as large (relatively) as in neighbouring countries. The reasons for that state of affairs are clear enough. Relatively few Chinese enterprises had been able to grow to any great size during the Dutch colonial era, due to the constraints of Dutch economic policies. And only a handful had succeeded in achieving significant growth during the unsettled years 1945–65, when the economy was often in disarray and the opportunities for private-sector business were at times highly unfavourable, especially for people regarded as 'aliens'.[6] Even in the 1970s, as economic conditions began to improve and many Chinese businessmen started to seize the opportunities that were arising for them, there were still major constraints because the state sector of the economy was still very large and privileged, especially in access to state bank capital, while discriminatory restrictions on Chinese economic activity in certain sectors still posed severe problems for them. Only from the mid-1980s on did things begin to improve dramatically for them, as the state had to rely far more on the private sector as the main engine of growth to achieve the goals of its development plans.

The proliferation of large conglomerates, which became such a prominent feature of the business landscape, was one of the most striking features of socio-economic development in Soeharto's Indonesia. It was closely linked with the shift to a more deregulated and competitive economy, as well as the structural changes brought about by that, especially in the rapid growth of new sectors like the urban property market, construction and real estate development, shopping malls and retailing, banking and financial services, and so on. But it is debatable how far the conglomerates were the cause or an effect of growth.

None of the big Sino-Indonesian conglomerates could be described as 'old wealth', with origins that extend back to prominent families of the late colonial era, as can be found in Malaysia and Thailand (and the Philippines, to a lesser extent). The largest and most effective of the pre-war commercial empires, the Oei Tiong Ham Concern, survived only until 1961 (Yoshihara 1989). Hardly any of the top forty conglomerates of the 1990s were more than small-scale operations prior to 1965. Nearly all the rest have grown from modest beginnings to fabulous wealth since then, taking advantage of the expanding opportunities presented by the steady growth achieved under Soeharto's New Order. Liem Sioe Liong was by far the most outstanding of the owners, having built up close personal links with Soeharto when they were both in the early stages of their careers in Central Java during the 1945–9 independence struggle against the Dutch. Bob Hasan, the timber king, has been another with similar links from their Central Java days. But most of the others rose to prominence much later. The *nouveau riche* character of both the Chinese and indigenous families which make up the contemporary Indonesian elite is very striking, in both the best aspects of that phrase and the ugliest. While the same can be said about the elites of Malaysia, Singapore and Thailand in the 1990s (but to a lesser extent in the Philippines) it seemed much more striking in Indonesia because it was such a new and sudden growth.

Political connections have been crucial for nearly all large private enterprises in Indonesia, but far more so for the small handful of very large conglomerates than for second-ranking ones (which frequently have to buy off lower-level officials but rarely have access to the highest ones). The reasons for that derive mainly from the highly patrimonial character of the New Order political system rather than from any special feature of the Sino-Indonesian business community as such. Nearly all Sino-Indonesian businessmen (and the very few prominent women) would probably prefer the sort of relatively level playing field they see in Singapore, or even in Malaysia and Thailand, where there are fewer arbitrary exactions, but they have to settle for what they can get. It has become increasingly difficult to conduct business in Indonesia without becoming drawn into 'the system' of widespread patron–client relationships there from the highest levels of government to the provincial level and below.

The most notorious cases of political connections were those of Liem Sioe Liong, with his long and very close relationship with President Soeharto, extending back to the 1940s when both men were relatively unknown, and those of Bob Hasan which have also been of long standing but much more prominent over recent decades than they were initially. That did not mean that Liem was nothing more than an 'ersatz capitalist' as categorized by Yoshihara (1988), for he showed his commercial talents time and again after his rise to stardom began in the late 1960s.[7] (The very fact that a man of such limited education was able to make the transition from the small-scale commerce in which he started to cope so competently with large-scale enterprise is surely also testimony to that.) But the personal connection with Soeharto was undoubtedly immensely beneficial to him. Also prominent in the 1990s was Prajogo Pangestu, initially a little known Kalimantan timber merchant, who rocketed into the limelight in the 1980s, largely because of his close business ties with Mbak Tutut (Sitii Hardiyanti Hastuti) and other children of the President with whom he went into petrochemicals; but Prajogo does not appear to have had very cordial links to the President himself.

On the other hand, Eka Cipta Wijaya, head of the huge Sinar Mas–BII (Bank International Indonesia) conglomerate, who also ranked close to the top of the big league in the 1990s, was often described as a bit of a loner and a rough diamond, not noted for personal or business links with the Palace. He had a phase of close but not very satisfactory business association with Liem in the 1980s in the oil palm sector, his initial sphere of expertise before he moved into pulp and paper also. Ciputra, one of the pioneer property developers and construction industry giants in Jakarta, relied at first mainly on his good political links with the Jakarta municipal government under Ali Sadikin (who later fell out with the President) rather than with the Palace, although he later diversified in the latter direction through his political and business ties with Liem and others. Likewise, Mochtar Riady's Lippo group might earlier have been classed as one of the less blatantly 'political' ones before 1990, when he was primarily a banker running Liem's highly successful Bank Central Asia; but after he left to branch out on his own with Lippo Bank and an extensive real estate empire, as well as some high-profile investments in China, political connections began to matter more for him, so the cautious banker was transformed into a more buccaneering risk-taker.

Among the less clearly 'political' *taipan* (the term being relative, since no large enterprise can dispense with political connections of various kinds altogether, high or low; but some have tried to keep at a greater distance from the national political leadership than others), the most interesting case used to be William Soeryadjaya, founder of the Astra automotive enterprise, the second-largest conglomerate throughout the 1980s. Astra ran into severe financial difficulties in 1991–2 and was allowed to collapse (its core activities eventually being taken over by a consortium headed by Prajogo Pangestu and other big *taipans*) without getting any help from the authorities. William had been almost blatantly detached from the Palace circle over the previous fifteen years, having had his fingers badly burnt when an Astra show-room was attacked by rioters in 1974 because Ibu Tien, the President's wife, was said to be a part owner in the early days of the enterprise. It was widely rumoured that Astra would probably have received more help from the authorities in riding out its financial problems if William had taken more care to keep his links with the Palace in better repair; but he was left to go under. Another of the foremost (relatively) non-political *taipans* is Soehargo Gondokusumo, head of the fast-growing Dharmala Group, who rose from very humble origins in East Java in the 1940s (not unlike Liem Sioe Liong in his early years) to the top of the pile without relying heavily on any particular set of political connections, it seems. He made his start in cassava trading, then making cassava pellets for export to Europe, then moving into property development in Surabaya and Jakarta with signal success before diversifying into banking, financial services and other activities in the 1980s.

Likewise, the two large and highly successful *kretek* manufacturers, Gudang Garam and Djarum, tended to keep their distance from political patrons as far as possible in their earlier years, although always taking care to keep on the right side of the local authorities in Kediri and Kudus respectively through their financial contributions. But they later began to diversify modestly into other fields, which meant they must be prepared to pay a price for political protection to a greater degree than previously. In one sense, these two might be regarded as not strictly conglomerates at all, since their activities are heavily concentrated in their core business and not much diversified beyond that. That was probably due in part to the fact that the *kretek* industry was highly profitable, enjoying a huge nation-wide demand for its product, quite unique in Indonesia, for there was no foreign competition.[8]

How did the pattern of political connections in Indonesia compare with the sort of cronyism practised by Marcos in the Philippines in the 1970–80s? Not to the same extent at all, one might have replied prior to 1990, although far less confidently thereafter, as various scandals unfolded involving the President's children and their tie-ups with people like Liem, Bob Hasan and Prajogo. But whereas Marcos gave his half-dozen cronies wide powers over several of the country's key economic sectors (causing them ruinous damage in the process), out of an unrealistic aspiration to create something like the South Korean *chaebol*, Soeharto seemed to be confining the extent and depth of the highly privileged segment of the economy to a fairly modest and affordable level until his final years (although it later proved far worse than most observers realized at the time), while maintaining generally sound macro-economic policies which achieved high rates of economic growth overall. The objections to his form of cronyism arose more from its political implications than the economic. It generated a great deal of discontent with the New Order regime and the conglomerates more generally, and with the high economic status of the ethnic Chinese minority as a whole. And the great danger in that situation was that if brush fires broke out on any one of these fronts, as they did in 1998, they were likely to spread explosively to the others. That was one of the most disturbing aspects of the entire tangle of problems.

Changes among the top conglomerates

Outwardly, only minor changes occurred in the general character and rank-order of the top twenty or thirty conglomerates from the mid-1980s through to 1997. Many floated part of their equity on the Jakarta Stock Exchange from 1989 onwards (although never enough to endanger their family control over those enterprises), and started employing professional managers more frequently, thereby sharpening the line of distinction between ownership and management in what used to be essentially old-style family firms. But for many there was still a long way to go in that direction before family control was significantly reduced.

Only one of the three largest conglomerates of the 1980s, William Soeryadjaya's Astra Corporation, collapsed and had to be re-shaped under a consortium of big *taipans*; several others slipped down the ladder slightly, but none disappeared entirely.[9] The major new-comers in the 1990s were the business empires of Prajogo Pangestu and Mochtar Riady, plus those of President Soeharto's children, who built up by far the largest *pribumi* (indigenous, non-Chinese) conglomerates, with strong positions in many of the country's newest and potentially most lucrative areas of business. Bambang's Bimantara group was generally regarded as the most solid and effective of them, whereas the Humpuss group of Hutomo Mandala Putra ('Tommy') was a fast-growing hothouse plant, heavily reliant on special privileges, as also were the lavish infrastructure projects of Mbak Tutut (Sri Hardijanto Rukmana). Estimates of their net worth diverged greatly, some putting them in the top ten, others much lower. The depth of unpopularity aroused by that nepotism was one of the most damaging features of Soeharto's record, even worse than the corruption attributed to the big Sino-Indonesian groups, while the damage they did to the small group of relatively independent *pribumi* businessmen who were starting to emerge in the early 1980s was one of the most serious socio-economic disasters of the New Order.

Liem Sioe Liong's huge Salim group[10] had become much more dominant by the mid-1990s than a decade earlier, notably his vast Indofood, Indocement and Indomobile groups and Bank Central Asia. He was not adversely affected too much by the deregulation policies of the late 1980s and since, despite predictions to the contrary.[11] Until the mid-1980s, Liem had been only *primus inter pares* at the head of the largest set of Indonesian conglomerates, along with Soeryadjaya's Astra automobile empire; but after 1990 his group's pre-eminence was quite unrivalled, and quite unique in Southeast Asia. His steadily growing offshore investments were making him probably the largest and most influential of all Southeast Asian Chinese international investors, along with Charoen Pokphand of Thailand. Nothing comparable to the immense concentration of economic power within and around one group could be found in Malaysia, Thailand, Singapore or the Philippines. Whereas the Bangkok Bank group and the Kuok group were finding themselves pursued by rivals, and the overall structure of big business in those countries was becoming more pluralistic and competitive in some respects, the trend in Indonesia was almost in the opposite direction. The explanation for that state of affairs derived mainly from the uniquely patrimonial and personalized character of the Indonesian political system and the immense political and financial resources controlled by President Soeharto. That is one reason why questions about the future of 'the conglomerates' were so often mentioned among the most contentious issues on the political scene in Indonesia, as the problem of 'the post-Soeharto succession' loomed closer. In other parts of the region, the existence of similar business groups aroused nothing like such controversy.

Malaysia

The situation of Malaysian Chinese business groups, the largest of them in particular, had some similarities with that faced by their Indonesian counterparts, most notably through the emergence in the 1980–90s of a lot of so-called 'paper millionaires' and 'rent-seekers' exploiting political connections; but there were also several major differences, outlined below.[12] The business environment in Malaysia was highly distinctive, because of the depth of the racial division between Malays and Chinese and the importance of the New Economic Policy (NEP) during the years 1971–90 in deliberately engineering a major redistribution of wealth in favour of the *bumiputra*. But it was in general a much less capricious form of ethnic discrimination than in Indonesia, particularly at the lower levels, although government officials could often be troublesome there too. Above all, the rule of law had much greater strength in Malaysia, at least at the middle and lower levels, while the more open and competitive political system provides more avenues of protest against arbitrary harassment by officials than in Indonesia. Hence while it was certainly true that many owners of the larger Malaysian-Chinese groups played highly political games with national leaders, others seemed able to survive there adequately without doing so, to a far greater degree than was possible in Indonesia's more patrimonial system.

Other differences between the two countries worth highlighting here are, first, the general character of the Malaysian political system, then what I call the 'proportionality factor' (i.e. the much greater proportion of ethnic Chinese in Malaysia's population and their long-established roles in the economy and deeper networks with *bumiputra* at many levels), the greater influence of 'old wealth' among the Malaysian Chinese, the impact of the New Economic Policy (NEP) on the policy environment prior to 1990, and the different impacts of the stock exchanges in the two countries on their patterns of corporate wealth.

The pattern of business-government relations in the two countries differed greatly, in part because the nature of the two political systems has become profoundly different during the forty years since they obtained their independence. Both are similar in having some strongly authoritarian features (although of very different types). Malaysia was often described as an essentially one-party system in which United Malays National Organization (UMNO) rule could not be overturned at the polls and the opposition parties knew they could never hope to gain power; but it was also what Crouch has called a 'repressive-responsive' system in which the government has always had to take note of public opinion in order to win elections, which cannot simply be ignored or rigged too drastically.[13] As a prime minister of long standing Dr Mahathir accumulated a high degree of personal authority; he was never as insulated from popular pressures as President Soeharto, yet he wielded considerable power. Two big differences, however, are that Indonesia under Soeharto was structurally a much more authoritarian regime, with the military playing a dominant role, unlike anything seen elsewhere in ASEAN (at least until the admission of Burma), and the Indonesian president is vested with almost unlimited constitutional and political power, at the head of a highly autocratic, patrimonial regime. Conversely, parliament and the elections to it in Malaysia still had considerable influence upon the intra-UMNO and inter-party manoeuvring that the prime minister always had to give attention to, whereas these things were of secondary importance (at best) in the Indonesian political chess-game.

The differences between Malaysia and Indonesia on the matter of business– government relations could be described as matters of degree rather than of kind, for the powers in the hands of the prime minister over the allocation of public funds or large contracts to major corporate enterprises in Malaysia has also been considerable. Hence some of the relationships between the heads of big Malaysian business groups and key government leaders have had similarities with those in the Indonesian case, although on a very different scale. The political, legal and even constitutional constraints on the prime minister's ability to distribute largesse arbitrarily in return for services rendered were vastly stronger in Malaysia than Indonesia. The political system was more pluralistic there, and the socio-economic ethos about business-government relations there was more strongly influenced by the rules and conventions inherited from British democratic-capitalist institutions than was ever the case in Indonesia.

Next, the 'proportionality aspect' – i.e. the fact that ethnic Chinese make up almost one third of the population in Malaysia but barely one thirtieth in Indonesia – was another major difference influencing the development of minority– majority relations in both countries. The issues involved are too diffuse and complex to explore at length here, but can be summarized as follows. To put it very crudely, it would be patently impossible and economically ruinous to contemplate expelling or dispossessing the entire Chinese population of Malaysia. Yet in Indonesia such suggestions were often made by extremists. Hence, many in the Sino-Indonesian minority felt far more vulnerable to ethnic violence than most Chinese Malaysians now do.[14] Moreover, because so many Indonesian Chinese were 'new wealth', with many of the insecurities of the *nouveaux riches* everywhere, whereas various leading Malaysian Chinese families and their business firms were 'old wealth', with much deeper and broader roots in the wider com- munities they belong to, their social and political relations with the Malay leadership differed considerably from the comparable situation in Indonesia. Malaysian Chinese have been moving into the economic roles vacated by the British for more than forty years now, gradually and without much political drama, quite unlike the political and economic upheavals created by the sudden expulsion of the Dutch from Indonesia in 1957–8. They were never stamped as 'pariah capitalists' to anything like the same extent as the Indonesian Chinese, or forced into such deeply clientelistic relations with the political authorities at the national or regional levels.

The biggest difference between the Malaysian socio-political context and the Indonesian derives from the influence on the former of the New Economic Policy (NEP) of 1971–90, which was specifically intended to restructure the society in such a way as to achieve a less unequal distribution of wealth between Chinese and *bumiputra*. This kind of approach to 'the Chinese problem' in Indonesia was always rejected by President Soeharto, although voices have at times been raised in favour of it among fringe elements of the national elite. The nearest that Indonesia ever came to such a policy before 1998 was the introduction of specific regulations from time to time giving concessions to *pribumi* enterprises, none of them very effective in promoting a class of *pribumi* capitalists, far less effective than Malaysia achieved under the NEP.

Several points about the NEP are particularly relevant to our concerns here. One is that the burdens it created for the smaller Chinese enterprises appear to have been relatively heavier than those it caused for the largest enterprises, many of which were very successful in devising survival strategies that enabled them not merely to survive but to go on prospering throughout the NEP years. During the 1970s they benefited also from the fact that many British companies were divesting their Malaysian holdings, so that the Chinese share of corporate capital actually increased over that decade, as well as the Malay share. In the 1980s, the Chinese share continued to rise, although less rapidly, but there was a major shift in the character of the leading Chinese groups as two new trends came into play. One was the importance of their political connections with Malay political leaders or well-connected Malay business enterprises after Dr Mahathir became prime minister and Daim Zainuddin finance minister. The other was the emergence of a group of 'paper millionaires' (mainly Malay) whose wealth depended more on political links, stock market transactions and company takeovers than on traditional forms of productive enterprise like rubber plantations and tin mining. The 'old wealth' companies with major interests in those fields tended to fall behind in the 1980–90s as 'new money' tycoons with good political connections, both Malay and Chinese, came to the fore (Table 7.2). If that trend is compared with the use of political connections in Indonesia, however, the differences are very striking, for the Malaysian pattern is much more pluralistic and fluid, as is the political system.[15] Neither the Kuok brothers nor any of the other foremost *taipans* in Malaysia ever had anything like the same relationship with Dr Mahathir as Liem Sioe Liong and Bob Hasan had with President Soeharto and his family.

Of the 'new money' tycoons who emerged in the 1980s, the most outstanding of the Chinese were Khoo Kay Peng (MUI group) and Vincent Tan (Berjaya), plus Loy Hean Heong (MBf), Lim Thian Kit (Multipurpose Holding (MPH), ex-Kamunting), and several others. The complexity of the business and political links between these firms and their Malay partners, or UMNO business vehicles, have been well depicted by Gomez (1991, 1994) and Searle (1999). Both Searle and, to a lesser extent, Harold Crouch (1996), have argued that despite the rent-

Table 7.2 Malaysian business groups, 1995–6

Chinese 'old wealth'

a: 'Adaptable' groups
   OCBC/Lee family (Singapore-based)
   Perlis Plantations/Robert Kuok Hock Nien
   Genting Bhd./Lim Gih Tong
   Bolton Properties/Lim Thiam Leong
   Lion (Amalgamated Steel)/William Cheng Hem Jen
   Selangor Properties/T.K. Wen
   MBf Holdings Bhd./Loy Hean Heong
   Hong Leong/Quek Leng Chan
b: 'Static' groups
   KL Kepong/Lee Loy Seng
   Public Bank/Teh Hong Piow
   See Hoy Chan/Teo Soo Chiang
c: 'Declining' groups
   Landmark/Chong Kok Lim
   Oriental Holdings/Loh Boon Siew

Chinese 'new wealth'
   MUI/Khoo Kay Peng
   Berjaya/Vincent Tan Chee Yioun
   Kamunting/Lim Thian Kit

Malay newly emerging capitalists

a: UMNO-based
   Renong group/Daim Zainuddin and Halim Saad (i.e. Fleet group, Hatibudi Sdn. Bhd.,
     Halimtan Sdn. Bhd., KUBB)
   Peremba Bhd./Daim Zainuddin
b: 'UMNO proxy capitalists-turned-businessmen'
   Daim Zainuddin (Fleet, Peremba etc.)
   Halim Saad (Renong)
   Wan Azmi Wan Hamzah (Arab-Malaysia Bank)
   Datuk Ahmed Sebi Abubakar (Sehasrat Sdn. Bhd.)
   Tajudin Ramli (Technological Resources)
c: 'Politicans-turned-businessmen'
   Abdul Ghafar Baba
   Datuk Harun Idris
   Datuk Syed Kechik
   Datuk Abdullah Ahmad

Sources: Adapted from Searle (1999) and Gomez (1999).

seeking proclivities of these enterprises, many of them were becoming 'real' capitalists, or effective businessmen, prior to the 1997–8 crisis, as also some of the new Malay groups emerging since the 1980s, even though it could not be said that they yet constituted anything like the kind of bourgeoisie that pioneered the growth of capitalism in the West in the nineteenth century. The basic fact is that in Malaysia, as in Indonesia, big business has developed recently within such a highly politicized environment that it would be unrealistic to assess it as if it did not represent 'real capitalism' just for that reason.

Finally, the influence of the Kuala Lumpur Stock Exchange (KLSE) on the development of big business in Malaysia deserves mention because it has been so much more prominent for considerably longer than its Indonesian counterpart, the Jakarta Stock Exchange (SEJ), and it illustrates how much more deeply institutionalized the structures of the capitalist economy are in Malaysia. Even before the KLSE split off, effectively if not formally, from the Singapore exchange in 1973, from which it had earlier developed, many Malaysian firms had been listed on the latter and had some experience of it as a source of capital from public savings, hence also of its effects in separating ownership and control of enterprises. The Jakarta Stock Exchange was almost moribund until the deregulation drive of 1988–9 brought it to life for the first time since independence. It then experienced relatively rapid growth, but as Table 7.3 reveals, the increase in the total capitalization of the KLSE has vastly exceeded that of the Jakarta exchange. By 1996 it represented more than three times the value of Malaysia's GDP, a high ratio for a developing country, whereas the Jakarta exchange was capitalized at only a little over a third of Indonesia's GDP.

Another institutional aspect of the socio–political environment relevant to all this is the broader importance of legal, administrative and commercial infrastructure in Malaysia, which has had a high degree of continuity ever since British colonial times and has become much more deeply rooted in the whole gamut of business practices in Malaysia than in Indonesia, where the multiple disruptions of 1945–65 caused immense damage which is still only partially repaired. The legal profession and courts function far more effectively than in Indonesia, as does the accounting profession. More broadly, the salaried and professional middle class is much stronger and larger (in proportion to the total population) in Malaysia and better able to defend the integrity of such institutions than the still-fragile new middle class in Indonesia's main cities (Crouch 1984, 1996). That greatly affects the business climate within which the conglomerates have had to operate.

Singapore

The business environment facing the big Chinese business groups in Singapore has been so utterly different from Indonesia's that comparisons are almost meaningless, unless taken to great lengths. The mere fact that Singapore is virtually

Table 7.3 Market capitalization of KLSE and SEJ, 1983–96

	KLSE		SEJ	
	Value (US$bn)	% of GDP	Value (US$bn)	% of GDP
1983	23	76	0.1	0.1
1989	58	152	3.6	3.7
1994	199	281	51	32
1996	268	302	74	37

Sources: 1983–94, Hill 1996: 111; 1996, *Asiaweek* 30 August 1996.

a Chinese city state, but minuscule in size (with a population less than 2 per cent of Indonesia's), highlights that point. But several other interesting and even surprising points of contrast are worth noting. One is that the dozen or so major privately-owned business groups in Singapore have been given very little direct encouragement or assistance by the Peoples Action Party (PAP) government over the last 35 years. The PAP has always operated at arm's-length from private (domestic) business there and maintains a more scrupulously fair 'level playing field' than any other ASEAN country. It has relied primarily on foreign capital and state enterprises to implement its development plans for the island; only since the 1980s has it begun to give much attention to developing private-sector investment in Singapore, and off-shore.

Another and related point is that the entrepreneurial talents of Singapore firms, particularly at the large-scale enterprise level, are commonly said to have atrophied badly over recent decades (although that has been far less true at the small and medium enterprise level and is not true of all the larger groups), due to limited opportunities to spread their wings, unlike the very different Indonesian (or Malaysian) situation. A third point is that the main fields of activity of the major business groups in Singapore have been in the banking and financial services sector, hotels and property development, retail trading and other tertiary services, but not much in manufacturing industries (where the state enterprises have been more prominent) – apart from foreign investment in electronics – because of the minuscule size of the market.

One other and especially interesting feature of the Singapore situation in recent years has been the increase in off-shore investment there by several of the largest Indonesian conglomerates, most notably the Salim group (now controlling a major segment of the cement industry there, as well as others) and, to a lesser extent the Riady, Wijaya and Gondokusumo families prior to 1997. As a major capital exporter itself, with the strongest commitment of all Southeast Asian countries to open markets and unrestricted international trade, Singapore is bound to draw in some such capital. Several other Indonesian large-scale enterprises (LSEs) also have quite large investments there, while minor household nest-eggs are said to be held there by many smaller fry (to an unknown and unknowable degree). Yet we should be careful not to exaggerate the extent of those capital flows by simply extrapolating from what the largest enterprises are doing as part of their broader off-shore investment strategies towards an assumption that all or most Southeast Asian Chinese firms, large and small, are involved in that sort of operation. According to informants in Jakarta most of the smaller fry have neither the capital to spare nor sufficient information about market conditions off-shore to dare incur the risks involved in international business.

Thailand

Business groups (BGs) were emerging as major players on the Thai economic scene by the 1970s – and a few of them had started to emerge about twenty years or more before then – as described by Krirkkiat and Yoshihara (1983), who depicted about twenty of them as they were in 1979 in one of the first writings on the subject in Southeast Asia. All but a small handful of these were still at the top of the ladder there in 1996 (although many crashed soon after) and only a few newcomers have made it into the top twenty since about 1980, to which I will return later. Yet the pattern of development of BGs in Thailand differs from that in Indonesia in several respects, especially in respect of the two countries' patterns of business–government relations.

One is that a sharper theoretical distinction could be drawn in the early years between 'finance capital' and 'industrial capital' or 'merchant capital' (Suehiro 1989; Hewison 1989) than we have seen anywhere else – although that distinction has become much more blurred in both theory and practice since the 1980s. The largest BGs were then the 'Big Four' banks, which were far more dominant than private banks were anywhere else in the region until quite recently – i.e. the Bangkok Bank, the Thai Farmers Bank (TFB), Bank Ayudhya and the Bangkok Mercantile Bank (BMB), owned or controlled respectively by the Sino-Thai Sophonpanich, Lamsam, Ratanarak and Tejapaibul families. A number of small banks also existed, owned by Sino-Thai families and several state-connected instrumentalities, but the former have nearly all been falling far behind the leaders since 1980. Because few alternative sources of capital were at first available to businessmen, neither large state-owned banks, as in Indonesia and Malaysia, nor foreign banks, those Thai banks exerted very great power over the rest of the private business sector between about 1960 and the 1980s. But that situation has changed radically over the last decade or so as other sources of capital have become available, most notably the Stock Exchange of Thailand (SET), which had previously been moribund but has grown rapidly as a source of private capital in recent years. The Bangkok Bank and TFB have been increasing their market share steadily over the last decade, creating in effect a Big Two rather than a Big Four, while the BMB has been slipping back (whereas thirty years ago it rivalled the Bangkok Bank for top place), apparently due to less successful investment strategies. All the big banks have become increasingly diversified beyond the banking and financial sectors, controlling substantial shareholdings in commercial, industrial and property enterprises, like most large BGs throughout the region.

Another distinctive feature of Thailand's BGs in the 1990s was the emergence of three spectacularly successful new players at the top of the business ladder; Charoen Pokphand (headed by Dhanin Chearavanont, son of the founder), the Shinawatra telecommunications empire and (until its recent collapse) the Bangkok Land property development and construction group, controlled by the Kanjanapas family. Nothing comparable to these highly entrepreneurial groups – very successful ones, apart from Bangkok Land – can be found anywhere else in Southeast Asia. Two of them are pioneering new forms of investment, well beyond the traditional spheres of Sino-Thai business, commodity exporting, banking-finance, domestic trade or manufacturing for the home market. Charoen Pokphand (CP), in particular, has become one of the most dynamic business enterprises in the region, for it was not much more than a successful seed and feed-grain merchant until the mid-1970s when Dhanin took over control from his father and struck out in new directions with dramatic success. Initially, it set up various off-shore branches, including one in Indonesia, coinciding with the success of the 'Green Revolution' there; then it started to open up branches throughout China from the early 1980s, long before the big surge of foreign capital into China gained momentum a decade later. CP is often said to be the largest single foreign investor in China, with more than US$1 billion invested there by the mid-1990s. It has also become a major player in Thailand's booming telecommunications sector, as well as in Burma, Laos and Vietnam. Thaksin Shinawatra is of interest for other reasons, having risen dramatically from being a relatively minor official handling communications equipment in the Police Department to head a fast-growing telecommunications conglomerate and move into the political arena also in the 1990s.

Political connections were crucially important for the owners of all these enterprises in their early years, as in most of Southeast Asia, but they seem to have become less so – or changed in character – since the 1970s when the old-style 'bureaucratic polity' collapsed, giving way to a more pluralistic form of government in which political parties began to play significant parts, albeit restricted ones, between 1976–88. The Bangkok Bank, for instance, relied heavily on its links with key military officers close to the top of the governmental structure from the 1950s until the overthrow of the Thanom-Praphat regime in 1973, but has since been careful to diversify its political connections across various political parties and government leaders.[16] Some of the big groups are more closely associated than others with particular parties, officials or government departments, but the pattern is much more varied now than it used to be. Since political parties have been playing a major part in the formation of governing coalitions under Chatichai Choonhavan (1988–91), Chuan Leekpai (1992–5), Barnharn Silpa-archa (1995–6) and Chaovalit (1996–7), the character of the political linkages created by the major business groups has changed utterly from the pre-1973 pattern. But it is harder, paradoxically, to discern any clear-cut pattern of affiliation between the large modern enterprises (*jao sua*) and the major parties than it is among the rural *jao pho*, or 'god-fathers', and some of the minor ones. Personalistic and patron-client relations still retain a great deal of influence there.

What this Thai pattern reveals, perhaps more clearly than the political connections observable in any other ASEAN country, is that while nearly all Southeast Asian Chinese businessmen utilize political connections where they can (as do most businessmen anywhere), it is the character of the political environment at any time or in any place – and the changes in those connections – that it is most crucial to understand. Simply to remark that they all seem to try to establish such connections is, in itself, to tell us very little.

Most of Thailand's top thirty or forty conglomerates were prominent for three or four decades before 1997, some even longer, although none of the largest pre-war groups remained prominent. Not only is there a high degree of continuity among the major groups but also a tendency towards greater concentration of ownership among the largest enterprises, to a greater degree than elsewhere.

State enterprises have played a much smaller part in Thailand's economy since the 1940s–50s than in any other ASEAN state, creating little competition for the private sector, hence for Sino-Thai businesses, large and small. Foreign enterprises have also been relatively unimportant, except as joint-venture partners, until the late 1980s, when a surge of foreign capital from the Northeast Asian NICs began to flow in. Broadly speaking, the large Sino-Thai firms have had a relatively unconstrained run since the end of the 1950s, without suffering the sort of discrimination against them of an economic nationalist kind that they were previously subject to. In that respect they have differed greatly not only from the Indonesian Chinese but also from others in the region.

The Philippines

In the Philippines, not only is the situation of the ethnic Chinese minority (Philippines Chinese as they are most commonly called) very different from elsewhere, but the development of the most eminent 'Six *Taipans*' and half a dozen slightly smaller business groups has been quite distinctive.[17] That minority is relatively small (although in the past a large Sino-*mestizo* element that inter-married with the Filipino elite generated a significant proportion of the latter, with some element of Chinese ancestry several generations back, such as Cory Aquino and Eduardo Cojuangco, now regarded as fully 'Filipino'), and estimates of their numbers have always varied wildly. Under US colonial rule the exclusion laws against alien immigration were applied strictly, although widely evaded, and it was very difficult for Chinese who were able to gain entry to obtain Philippines nationality until Marcos amended the law in 1975. Since then, the Philippines Chinese have flourished in their business activities, especially after the fall of Marcos in 1986. But they control a much smaller fraction of the modern economy there than they do elsewhere – around a third is a common estimate (Rivera 1995: 8–9) – and they have had to compete with a powerful class of 'indigenous' businessmen from the traditional landed elite, many of them of earlier Sino-*mestizo* origins, for which there is no counterpart in any other Southeast Asian country. They have been further handicapped over the last fifteen years by the fact that the Philippines economy suffered severe stagnation during most of the 1980s and only began to reach modest rates of growth under President Ramos between 1994–8. So the opportunities for rapid expansion, which have been abundant for thirty years or more in the other ASEAN countries, have been much more limited and recent there. Yet, the growth of the new Philippine Chinese business class under those conditions has been remarkable.

Of the 'Six *Taipans*' who suddenly emerged in the late 1980s, John Gokongwei Jr, Henry Sy, Alfonso Yuchengco, George Ty, Lucio Tan and Andrew Gotianun, only one could claim to be from an 'old wealth' family: Yuchengco, a respected community leader whose father set up Malayan Insurance in 1930. Gokongwei and Henry Sy started their business careers in the late 1950s but only came into prominence in the 1980s, mainly in the years since the fall of Marcos (although they had grown bigger during his time). Lucio Tan, who started with a small cigarette manufacturing business in the 1960s, became one of the notorious 'cronies' of Marcos, benefiting greatly from the favours he received in return, allegedly, for financial kickbacks to Marcos. He survived the post-Marcos backlash better than the other cronies and has since elevated his Allied Banking and other investments, including a controlling interest in Philippines Airlines, to a level where he is often said to be the wealthiest man in the country. George Ty, who has made Metrobank the top-ranking bank over the last decade, and Gotianun, a real estate giant, have both shot into the limelight since the fall of Marcos. They are an interesting and remarkable bunch, for they have become wealthy at a time when the Philippine economy was stagnating, yet they are now competing vigorously with the biggest indigenous (or Spanish-mestizo) groups such as the Ayala Corporation and San Miguel.

A second-ranking bunch of wealthy Chinese conglomerates, still well behind the previous six, which have also come into prominence in the last decade, includes those of Tan Yu (or Ty, a real estate developer who made big money in Taiwan and seems to thrive on living dangerously), Alfredo Ramos of National Bookstores (an unlikely source of great wealth, one might have thought, but with surprisingly strong international connections, including Robert Kuok of late) and other interests, William Gatchalian, the 'plastics king' and construction wizard, and Roberto Coyiuto, an insurance and real estate magnate (Rivera 1995; Palanca 1995). It is noteworthy that real estate and urban retailing are major sources of their wealth, as also of the top six, whereas manufacturing industry is relatively minor, except in the cases of Lucio Tan, Gokongwei and Gatchalian. Three of the six *taipans* made their money solely or largely from the banking-finance-insurance sector, controlling some of the largest private banks in the country (old Filipino elite families have long been well entrenched in the other major banks), or have later been buying into that sector since it was deregulated in the Aquino-Ramos era. None are heavily involved in sugar or other agribusiness sectors, the traditional staples of the country's economy, which have been in decline since Marcos wrecked them.

All the top six business groups are diversified to some degree, with property or finance holdings as well as their core businesses, Yuchengco's most of all, Lucio Tan's and Gotianun's the least (so far). In that respect, they are like their counterparts elsewhere in Southeast Asia. Their political links with either political leaders or elite-level Filipino families are quite varied (Rivera 1995: 20–2), reflecting the distinctive characteristics of the Philippines political system over recent decades, and marking them off from the other ASEAN countries, thus bringing us back yet again to the importance of the political context. Yuchengo and George Ty have former high-level officials on their boards while Gokongwei is closely linked with the Lopez family (both of them originating from Cebu), and Lucio Tan has had a range of political connections. But such contacts are very different from those we see in Indonesia or Malaysia.

Conclusion

What conclusions about Indonesia's conglomerates (or any others in the region) can we draw from the picture given here? The most obvious point is that political connections are very important to nearly all of them, more so than in any other ASEAN country except perhaps Malaysia (for some), because of the nature of the political system. I would not go as far as Yoshihara (1988), who regarded them all as 'ersatz capitalists' and mere rent-seekers, not 'real' capitalists, largely for that reason, although terms like that could justifiably be applied to some of them. But many of the Indonesian *taipans* have shown themselves to be very competent businessmen (and women, in a few cases), most notably Liem Sioe Liong, Eka Cipta Wijaya, Gondokusumo (of Dharmala Corporation) and the *kretek* kings, as well as many lesser figures, although they have also benefited greatly from their political connections. In Thailand, Singapore and the Philippines, too, many heads of the leading conglomerates of the 1990s must be ranked as a good deal more than mere rent-seekers, and even some of the Malaysian high-fliers also, although perhaps fewer of them. It is probable that some of the Indonesian conglomerates will run into political storms in the post-Soeharto era and not survive in their present shape, highlighting the importance of their political connections, but it is unpredictable how many will survive or which will collapse.

Are Indonesia's conglomerates significantly different from their counterparts elsewhere in other respects? Are they any more, or less, 'Chinese' than any others in the region because of the socio-economic circumstances in which they have emerged? It would be difficult to argue the case strongly either for or against that proposition, although the Sino-Indonesian minority in general has certainly been undergoing a process of desinification throughout the twentieth century that has in some respects been more marked than elsewhere (although in others perhaps less). One striking feature is that a disproportionate number of the big *taipans* in today's Indonesia are of *totok* background (i.e. first-generation new-comers to the country from China, or second) and Chinese-speaking, hence less Indonesianized than the *peranakan*, although it is impossible to tell if the proportion is higher than elsewhere. It could not be said that they are any less or more family-oriented in their business arrangements than other Southeast Asian Chinese, or more inclined towards modern professional management practices, since the patterns are mixed in all the ASEAN countries. Everywhere there has been an increasing tendency towards the use of professional managers but also to retain family ownership and control, even if part of the family firm or holding company may have been floated on the stock exchange. Because Indonesia lagged several decades behind Malaysia and Singapore in developing an effective stock exchange, as we have seen, the effects of that on corporate ownership structures have been short-lived so far, although gradually following down much the same path as other business groups in those countries.

The off-shore investments of a few major Indonesian conglomerates have attracted a lot of attention in recent years, Liem Sioe Liong's in particular. But it would be misleading to infer that this is a general or widespread tendency. Far more family firms in Malaysia and Singapore seem to have invested capital overseas than the Sino-Indonesian ones do, perhaps also those in the Philippines, if only as a nest-egg in case of emergencies. In Thailand the situation is harder to gauge; although Charoen Pokphand has long been famous for its off-shore investments, it is more striking that very few of the other big conglomerates there have yet established major interests abroad (apart from Hong Kong, in branch businesses and real estate) rather than how many. The pattern seems rather similar to Indonesia's.

Finally, a point of some importance is the extent to which the conglomerates in Indonesia or elsewhere contributed to the dramatic increase in exports of manufactured goods from the late 1980s on. It is commonly said in Jakarta that few of them were doing so to any great extent, except in the timber-plywood and petrochemicals industries. The manufactured exports that have been growing very rapidly in Indonesia were produced mainly by foreign capital (especially in footwear by Reebok, Nike *et al.*) and by small local firms, whereas the big conglomerates were oriented mainly to the expanding domestic market and reluctant to shift into less secure pastures. That may also be true of Malaysia, but certainly not of Thailand, again because of differences in their various trade regimes. It would be useful to have some international comparisons of the degree to which big business groups are active in the manufacturing sector in the various countries, as against tertiary services, particularly property development, and the effects of this (if any) on their business organization and practice. The Indonesian conglomerates seem to have been more widely involved in manufacturing than the Malaysian and Singapore ones are, although perhaps less so than the Thai groups. But because of the problems of measurement in this field, it is impossible at this time to make more than impressionistic judgements on this score.

Notes

1 By 'ASEAN countries' I am referring here only to the original five members, Indonesia, Malaysia, Singapore, Thailand and the Philippines, not Brunei (a special case, due to the overwhelming private wealth and political power of the Sultan and the fact that only one Chinese, a wealthy hotel owner, is remotely comparable to the conglomerate owners under discussion here) nor the former communist countries, and Burma, which are simply not at all comparable.

2 The estimated number cited here is taken from a table (not entirely reliable) in *The Economist*, 18 July 1992. On the 'Overseas Commonwealth' of Chinese, see a widely cited but rather contentious article by Kao (1993), Sender (1991).

3 The influence of the Confucian tradition on economic life in East Asia beyond China is well treated in Hofheinz and Calder (1982).

4 On the crisis facing the ethnic Chinese community in Indonesia in the mid-1960s and the violence they suffered earlier in that decade, see Coppel (1983) and Mackie (1976b).

5 Few comprehensive surveys of the Indonesian Chinese have appeared since Skinner (1963) and Coppel and Mackie (1976), apart from Suryadinata (1978); see the bibliography by Coppel in Mackie (ed.) (1976) for a comprehensive guide to the numerous earlier publications about them.

6 The civil status of ethnic Chinese, as either Indonesian nationals or aliens (Chinese nationals), was not fully resolved until the 1960s; it was a highly contentious issue until the 'dual nationality' issue

was clarified with China in 1961–2 (but not fully implemented until much later; some issues were still unresolved in the late 1980s); for details see Meili G. Tan (1991).

7 It is worth recalling that Liem had not achieved outstanding success in business during the decade or more before 1967 when he was merely one of many Chinese businessmen in Jakarta. For an excellent study of Liem's business strategies under the Soeharto regime, see Yuri Sato (1993).

8 There were four huge *kretek* firms throughout the 1970s–80s, but one of them, Bentoel, has since collapsed; the fourth, Sampoerna, used to be relatively small, concentrating on a special, high-quality, small-market brand of long standing. It has recently increased its market share greatly by vigorous marketing, while also diversifying into other activities under a new-generation head of the family firm.

9 William Soeryadjaya lost control of Astra in 1992 after his son's banking business, PT Summa International, became overextended and William intervened in a vain attempt to save it. No effort was made by the government or the central bank to help him overcome the crisis (unlike certain other banks with better connections), and he eventually had to sell out to a consortium of big *taipans* headed by Prajogo Pangestu.

10 While Liem Sioe Liong has maintained complete control over the whole of his vast group, reportedly over 400 companies and many divisions, minor shareholders in the Salim group also include the President's children and 'the Liem investors', Djuhar Sutanto, Ibrahim Rasjid, and Sudwikatmono, Soeharto's cousin (Yuri Sato 1993). The Salim group also has or has had big stakes in enterprises involving Prajogo Pangestu, the Sinar Mas group (Eka Cipta Wijaya), Ir Ciputra and others (Siregar and Widya 1989; Soetiyone 1989).

11 Because so many loopholes have been incorporated in the various deregulation packages announced since the mid-1980s, most of the special privileges and protective tariffs benefiting the Palace-linked *taipans* have been maintained. Deregulation has by no means created an entirely level playing field. For example, as one Chinese businessman put it to me: 'Why is Liem Sioe Liong able to get credit from the state banks at 8 per cent and I have to pay 15 or 20 per cent on the open market? He is being given a margin of over 7 per cent for nothing'.

12 On the Malaysian 'paper millionaires' see Heng (1992), Sieh (1992), Gomez (1991, 1994) and Searle (1999).

13 The best and most recent analysis of the Malaysian political system is Crouch (1996).

14 Apart from the May 1969 riots sparked by the election results of that month, few episodes of serious interracial violence have occurred in Malaysia. In Indonesia, by contrast, there were several major outbreaks in 1963 and 1965–7, all with complex socio-political dynamics underlying them (Mackie 1976). Calls to expel all Chinese from Indonesia were frequently made in 1966–7, although the Soeharto government rejected them and tried to damp down the tensions giving rise to them.

15 It is revealing to compare a 1985 list of nine top Malaysian businessmen cited by Heng Pek Koon (1992) with the 1994 list of 18 Malaysians mentioned amongst the 75 leading ASEAN business groups published in *Warta Ekonomi* (Jakarta) 28 February 1994: the 18 Malaysians, 15 of them Chinese, did not include four of the 'old wealth' groups named on Dr Heng's list, which had declined in standing, but a number of new names were prominent.

16 But not without setbacks, as when Marshall Sarit took over from Chin Sophonpanich's former patron in 1958, leading Chin to remove himself to Hong Kong until Sarit died.

17 'Philippines Chinese' is the name most commonly used, although the foremost writer on their status and identity, Teresita Ang See (1990), Ang See and Baviera (1992), has also used the term Chinese-Filipinos at times (a better analogy to the more appropriate form 'Sino-Thai' used in Thailand).

References

Ang See, Teresita (1990) *The Chinese in the Philippines. Problems and Perspectives.* Manila: Kaisa Para Sa Kaunlaran, Inc.

Ang See, Teresita and Aileen S.P. Baviera (1992) *China Across the Seas. The Chinese as Filipinos.* Manila: Philippine Association for Chinese Studies.

Coppel, Charles (1983) *Indonesia's Chinese in Crisis*. Kuala Lumpur: Oxford University Press, for ASAA.

Coppel, Charles and J.A.C. Mackie (1976) 'A Preliminary Survey', in J.A.C. Mackie (ed.) *The Chinese in Indonesia: Five Essays*. Melbourne: Thomas Nelson, for AIIA.

Crouch, Harold (1979) 'Patrimonialism and Military Rule in Indonesia'. *World Politics*, 31(4): 571–87.

Crouch, Harold (1984) *Domestic Political Structures and Regional Economic Cooperation*. Singapore: Institute for Southeast Asian Studies.

Crouch, Harold (1996) *Government and Politics in Malaysia*. Ithaca: Cornell University Press.

Gomez, Edmund Terence (1991) *Money Politics in the Barisan Nasional*. Kuala Lumpur: Forum.

Gomez, Edmund Terence (1994) *Political Business: Corporate Involvement of Malaysian Political Parties*. Townsville: James Cook University.

Gomez, Edmund Terence (1999) *Chinese Business in Malaysia: Accumulation, Accommodation, and Ascendance*. Honolulu: University of Hawaii Press (copublished with Curzon Press).

Heng Pek Koon (1992) 'The Chinese Business Elite in Malaysia', in Ruth McVey (ed.) *Southeast Asian Capitalists*. Ithaca: Cornell Southeast Asian Program Publications.

Hewison, K. (1989) *Bankers and Beaurocrats: Capital and the Role of the State in Thailand*. New Haven: Southeast Asian Studies, Monograph Series No. 34.

Hill, Hal (1996) *The Indonesian Economy Since 1966*. Cambridge: Cambridge University Press.

Hofheinz, Roy, Jr and Kent Calder (1982) *The East Asia Edge*. New York: Basic Books.

Kao, John (1993) 'The Worldwide Web of Chinese Business'. *Harvard Business Review*, March–April: 24–36.

Krirkkiat Phipatheritham and Yoshihara Kunio (1983) *Business Groups in Thailand*. Singapore: ISEAS.

Mackie, J.A.C. (ed.) (1976a) *The Chinese in Indonesia: Five Essays*. Melbourne: Thomas Nelson, for AIIA.

Mackie, J.A.C. (1976b) 'Anti-Chinese Outbreaks in Indonesia, 1959–1968', in J.A.C. Mackie (ed.) *The Chinese in Indonesia: Five Essays*. Melbourne: Thomas Nelson, for AIIA.

Mackie, J.A.C. (1996) 'Introduction', in Anthony Reid (ed.) *Sojourners and Settlers. Histories of Southeast Asia and the Chinese*. Sydney: Allen and Unwin, for ASAA Southeast Asia Publications Series.

Palanca, Ellen (1995) 'Chinese Business Families in the Philippines since the 1890s', in Rajesvary Ampelvanar Brown (ed.) *Chinese Business Enterprise in Asia*. London: Routledge.

Rivera, Temario (1995) 'The Chinese-Filipino Taipans and Industrial Reform in the Ramos Administration', in Temario C. Rivera and Kenji Koike (eds) *The Chinese-Filipino Business Families Under the Ramos Government*, Joint Research Program Series No. 114, Institute of Developing Economies, Tokyo.

Sato, Yuri (1993) 'The Salim Group in Indonesia: The Development and Behaviour of the Largest Conglomerate in Southeast Asia'. *The Developing Economies*, 31(4): 408–41.

Searle, Peter (1999) *The Riddle of Malaysian Capitalism: Rent-Seekers or Real Capitalists?* Honolulu: University of Hawaii Press (ASAA Southeast Asia Publications Series).

Sender, Henny (1991) 'Inside the Overseas Chinese Network'. *Institutional Investor*, August: 29–43.

Sieh Lee Mei Ling (1992) 'The Transformation of the Malaysian Business Groups', in Ruth McVey (ed.) *Southeast Asian Capitalists*. Ithaca: Cornell Southeast Asian Program Publications.

Siregar, S.E. and Widya, K.T. (1989) *Liem Sioe Liong: Dari Futching ke Mancanegara*. Jakarta: Panca Merdeka.

Skinner, G. William (1963) 'The Chinese Minority', in Ruth McVey (ed.) *Indonesia*. New Haven: HRAF.

Soetiyono, Eddy (1989) *Kisah Sukses Liem Sioe Liong*. Jakarta: Indomedia.

Suehiro, Akira (1989) *Capital Accumulation in Thailand, 1885–1985*. Tokyo: The Center for East Asian Cultural Studies.

Suryadinata, L. (1978) *…Pribumi Indonesians, the Chinese Minority and China.* Singapore: Heinemann Educational Books (Asia) Ltd.

Tan, Meili G. (1991) 'The Social and Cultural Dimensions of the Role of the Ethnic Chinese in Indonesian Society'. *Indonesia*, Special Issue on The Role of the Indonesian Chinese in Shaping Modern Indonesian Life, pp. 113–25. Ithaca: Cornell Southeast Asia Program.

Wang Gungwu (1976) 'Are Indonesian Chinese Unique? Some Observations', in Mackie, J.A.C. (ed.) *The Chinese in Indonesia: Five Essays*. Melbourne: Thomas Nelson, for AIIA.

Yoshihara Kunio (1988) *The Rise of Ersatz Capitalism in South-east Asia*. Singapore: Oxford University Press.

Yoshihara Kunio (ed.) (1989) *Oei Tiong Ham Concern: The First Business Empire in South-east Asia*. Kyoto: Centre for South-east Asia Studies.

8 Determinants of business capability in Thailand

Akira Suehiro

From 1988 through the mid-1990s, Thailand enjoyed an economic boom and experienced substantial changes in the sectoral composition of its GDP, as well as in the structure of trade and of its labour force. In line with many other efforts to account for Thailand's economic success, the World Bank's *The East Asian Miracle* (1993) focuses on three sets of policies which purport to explain the economic achievements of the so-called high performing Asian economies (HPAEs) over the past three decades. One, economic fundamentals (macro-economic stabilization, accumulation of high quality human capital, effective monetary policies, limiting price distortions, agricultural development, etc.). Two, good governance, institutional capability (an able bureaucracy, an adequate implementation and monitoring system, good physical and social infrastructure provision). Three, selective government intervention (export promotion, financial repression and selective promotion of industries).

Although the World Bank has acknowledged the significant contribution of directed credit and of government-organized 'contests' in Japan and South Korea, it has principally attributed the economic success of the HPAEs to economic fundamentals, especially government efforts to ensure macro-economic stability. Proponents of this view claim that the HPAEs achieved rapid economic growth and transformation by getting prices right, and that Thailand, for one, met these conditions. The Thai government and its monetary authority have long pursued policies aimed at ensuring macro-economic stability; the authorities have succeeded in managing both money supply and the foreign exchange rate without causing serious inflation (Warr 1993). Unlike South Korea, the Thai government seldom intervened selectively to promote particular industries (Christensen *et al.* 1997).

A second group of radical political economists has characterized the Thai experience as one of 'distorted' growth and 'dependent' development, and has mainly stressed the negative consequences of 'rent-seeking' activities. It has stressed two major factors: political patronage for privileged domestic business groups, such as Siam Cement and the Charoen Pokphand (CP) Group; and the massive infusion of foreign capital – led by Japanese multinational corporations (MNCs) – into 'growing' industries. By providing a variety of tax incentives to favoured groups, the Thai government effectively facilitated the dominance of the national economy by a few Thai business groups and giant multinational corporations (Suthy 1991). Such measures have limited competition among local firms and have resulted in an oligopolistic economic system characterized by widening income disparities and widespread political corruption. According to this argument, connections to the political elite have become the decisive element for both Thai and foreign investors in gaining concessions, licences and privileges from the government, and have encouraged 'rent-seeking' among them. For example, as Pasuk and Sungsidh (1994) argue, political corruption has increased with greater electoral democracy and the Thai economic boom from the late 1980s (see Table 8.1). However, this argument does not directly address the questions of why and how Thailand has achieved rapid economic growth and developed international competitiveness in some industries despite the widespread prevalence of 'rent-seeking' activities and political corruption (Mauro 1995).

To answer this question, a third group has stressed institutional factors, while acknowledging both the government role in ensuring macro-economic stability, as well as the widespread 'rent-seeking' in the Thai economy. Unlike the World Bank economists and the radical political economists, they focus on non-governmental institutional factors (Doner 1992) such as business associations, business networks and relations between the government and the private sector (Doner 1991; also see Doner and Ramsay 1997). For example, Doner and Ramsay argue that leading textile firms developed their businesses through cultivating close relations with political leaders, but that such clientelism did not result in an uncompetitive and inefficient market structure in the Thai textile industry. Rather, both rivalry among politicians and well-organized Sino-Thai businessmen have ensured a competitive market structure in the industry. Furthermore, successful lobbying by business associations and flexible but supportive industrial policies pursued by technocrats have helped transform Thai textiles from a domestic market-oriented industry into an internationally competitive one. In sum, 'rent-seeking' in the Thai textile industry did not just have negative effects, but positive ones as well, in the form of new institutional arrangements, or structures of rights more conducive to achieving rapid industrial growth and export competitiveness.

Table 8.1 Assets from leading politicians on grounds of corruption (unit: million baht, %)

Items	Sarit 1957–63	Thanom-Praphat 1964–73	Chatichai and ministers 1988–90	Chatichai alone 1988–90
Seized assets	604.0	600.0	1,900.0	284.0
Average per year	86.3	60.0	633.3	94.8
As % of capital expenditure in budget	6.1	1.0	1.1	0.2
As % of GDP	0.14	0.05	0.04	0.01

Source: Pasuk and Sungsidh (1994: 36).

I share this view of the 'competitive' character of 'rent-seeking' in Thailand, which is also consistent with Unger's (1998) argument on contestation within the Thai textile industry. However, like most others, Doner and Ramsay seem to pay little attention to another significant element, namely the capability of private firms to respond to government policies. Underestimating or overlooking firm capabilities is common in the development literature, which largely ignores firms' efforts to improve and innovate. The World Bank (1993) report highlighted, for the first time, the important role of institutional factors in the HPAEs' industrial development and acknowledged the contribution of effective bureaucracies, though generally stressing the desirability of market competition. It nevertheless neglected the role of private firms in contributing to industrial dynamism in these countries. Even the political economists who emphasize oligopolistic business dominance have overlooked the significance of the corporate reforms and restructuring efforts that Thai business groups have undertaken in recent years.

It is difficult to attribute Thai industrial development exclusively to any one factor such as government macro-economic policies, strong connections with political leaders or institutional arrangements. Rather, other factors, such as firm capability, should also be considered together with these other elements to explain why and how Thailand has developed internationally competitive industries and prominently upgraded its industrial structure between 1987 and 1996. All these factors, including corporate capability, have been important in the development of export-oriented industries, including agro-industry as well as textiles and garments (Suehiro and Nambara 1991). This has also been true of giant business undertakings such as the integrated petrochemicals project, integrated steel industry and automobile engine assembly (Suehiro and Higashi 2000: Chapter 3). I will examine what has taken place at the enterprise level in the telecommunications industry in Thailand from 1988 to 1994 from this perspective.

The tripod structure of capital in Thailand

Three major economic agents appear to have been responsible for the industrialization of the Thai economy (Suehiro 1989; Suehiro 2000: Chapter 7): one, Thai state-owned or public enterprises (TPEs); two, Thai private enterprises, mainly belonging to Thai business groups (TBGs); and three, foreign enterprises, composed mostly of multinational corporations (MNCs). Table 8.2 shows changes in the distribution of the top 100 firms in Thailand in terms of their total sales in 1979, 1985 and 1992.

Table 8.2 shows that Thai growth cannot be exclusively attributed to any particular enterprise category. Rather, all groups have been economically significant in terms of sales. In 1992, 19 TPEs accounted for 34 per cent of total sales, down from 41 per cent in 1985. Similarly, 29 MNCs had 25 per cent of total sales in 1992, dropping from 45 per cent in 1979. Interestingly, the number of TBGs in the top 100 category rose from 44 in 1979 to 52 in 1992. In other words, there has been a shift from TPEs and MNCs to TBGs in Thailand.

Table 8.2 Thailand: distribution of top 100 ranked firms in terms of total sales, classified by capital ownership, 1979, 1985 and 1992

By number of firms	1979	1985	1992			
Thai public enterprises	19	22	19			
Thai private enterprises	44	49	52			
Foreign enterprises	37	29	29			
Total	100	100	100			

By total sales	1979		1985		1992	
	(mil. baht)	*%*	*(mil. baht)*	*%*	*(mil. baht)*	*%*
Thai public enterprises	54,271	22.8	229,651	41.0	509,606	34.4
Thai private enterprises	75,979	31.9	185,740	33.2	605,626	40.8
Foreign enterprises	107,652	45.3	144,299	25.8	367,455	24.8
Total	237,902	100.0	559,690	100.0	1,482,687	100.0

Sources: 1) Private firms in 1979 and 1985: Pan SIam Communications Co., Ltd (1981) and International Business Research Co., Ltd (1987). For foreign enterprises in 1979, 1985 and 1992: Suehiro personal data base. For public enterprises in 1979 and 1985: Suehiro survey.
2) Private firms in 1992: Advanced Research Group Co., Ltd (1994). Public enterprises in 1992: Tara Siam Business Information Ltd (1995).

Notes
1 Including commercial banks and financial institutions. For banks, sales were replaced by 'total revenues'.
2 A foreign firm is one in which foreign investors own at least 30 per cent of registered capital.

While TPEs played a significant role in building oil refineries and developing the petrochemical industry, and MNCs rushed to Thailand to expand domestic market shares and to produce for export markets,[1] TBGs were certainly not left behind during the Thai 'economic boom'. On the contrary, TBGs advanced into 'growth sectors' such as export-oriented manufacturing, telecommunications, real estate, hotel services and modern retail businesses (Borisut and Chanphen 1994).[2] Hence, the origins, development and roles of TBGs cannot be overlooked in any meaningful discussion of the contemporary Thai economy (Pasuk and Baker 1994).

'Rent-seeking' and corporate capabilities

Since the end of the 1950s, the Thai government has adopted industrial promotion policies to accelerate industrial development. In 1959, the Board of Investment (BOI) was created to become the sole agent for the promotion of industrial development, empowered to select, protect and promote targeted industries. The BOI formulated guidelines and set conditions, such as the number of companies to be promoted, the production capacity desired, and the minimum registered capital. Only firms meeting these conditions enjoyed the incentives offered. Such BOI policies constituted 'selective intervention' and the degree of selectivity was to increase over time.

The leading business groups in Thailand also expanded the scale of their businesses with the help of such government promotion policies. The Sukree and Saha Union Groups in textiles, Siam Cement in construction materials, the Siam Motors Group (now the Siam Group) in automobiles, and the Charoen Pokphand (CP) and UNICORD Groups in agro-industry were able to rapidly expand their business ventures thanks to government incentives (Suehiro 1989: Chapter 7; Suehiro and Nambara 1991: Chapter 2). Besides the leading business groups, many other domestic firms received favourable treatment from the government when they started manufacturing production.

The development of the CP Group, which has become the largest agro-industry conglomerate in Southeast Asia, provides an interesting case (*Prachachat Thurakit* 12 February 1983; Than Setthakit 1993; Suehiro 1997). Chia Ekchor, the founder of the CP Group and a Teochiu Chinese, started his business by importing vegetable seeds and exporting eggs, and later extended his business to importing feed meal. When it started domestic production in the 1960s, CP was not one of the 'five big tigers' importing feed meal. With strong support from military leaders (the Sarit-Praphat clique) to protect their privileged position, the 'big five' established importers had organized a sort of cartel to monopolize the domestic market. As they were reluctant to expand into manufacturing because of the risks involved, outsiders such as CP quickly moved into manufacturing feed meal, for which the BOI offered tax incentives. After setting up its first feed meal plant in 1967, the CP Group rapidly expanded and extended its business lines from feed meal production into chicken breeding, poultry farming, and processing and exporting frozen chickens. Although they had no technical experience, they soon became the largest exporter of frozen chickens by introducing hybrid stock from a US-based MNC (Arbor Acre Inc.) and modern processing equipment (e.g. the individual-quick-freezing or IQF system) from Japanese trading companies (Suehiro and Nambara 1991: Chapter 2).

What elements contributed to the rapid expansion of the CP Group in the early years? CP could enjoy a privileged status in agro-industry owing to government tax incentives from 1969 until 1977. CP sought and secured protection from the BOI and other government agencies though its political connections were not as strong as those of the traditional feed meal importers (Suehiro 1997: 42–4). However, the CP Group's capability in effectively combining various innovative elements – such as foreign technology, financial support from domestic commercial banks, mobilizing farmers for poultry farming and development of new markets outside Thailand – soon transformed it into an internationally competitive business. By the second half of the 1970s, when CP established its vertical integration system in the broiler chicken industry, the 'five big tigers' importing feed meal had been almost completely shut out of the domestic market. The CP Group undertook drastic management reforms after 1984 under increasing pressure from local competitors such as the Laem Thong Sahakan, Saha Farm, CENTACO and BETAGRO Groups, all of whom had also enjoyed tax incentives from the government. CP was proud to be the first Thai agro-industrial group to introduce an American-style divisional-department system in its management structure and to list the group's companies on the stock market (interviews, September 1985 and October 1989).

More interesting developments in the complex relationship between 'rent-seeking' and corporate capabilities occurred under the Chatichai regime, when the government launched large-scale petrochemicals, integrated steel and telecommunications services projects. For instance, the Sahaviriya Group successfully secured a monopoly for its integrated steel plant project through its political connections with the Chatichai government.[3] Likewise, the CP Group was awarded a huge project to install three million telephone lines nationwide thanks to its close connections with the prime minister, influential ministries and directors of the Telephone Organization of Thailand (TOT) (interviews, March 1993).

However, fast-increasing demands associated with the rapid expansion of the national economy as well as other pressures for economic liberalization compelled the government to reduce its restrictive policies on the supply side and to give additional licences to others. In the case of steel, the BOI approved another two local groups – the NTS and SSP Groups – for hot-rolled steel plates, and the Siam Cement Group, with Shin Nippon Steel, for cold-rolled steel plates (Board of Investment 1995). In addition, competition intensified among domestic business groups, or between domestic business groups and MNCs, forcing firms to reform corporate management. For this reason, for example, on the occasion of its fortieth anniversary in December 1993, the Sahaviriya Group drastically reorganized its corporate structure and launched management reforms aimed at transforming the traditional family business into a more modern corporate organization.[4]

The rapid expansion and growth of specific business groups cannot be attributed to clientelism or collaboration with foreign firms alone. Rather, it seems worthwhile to look into how domestic private firms have advanced and developed by investigating such aspects as corporate capability, including the development of managerial skills, the introduction and improvement of imported technology on the shop floor, and the development of new markets. In this sense, the telecommunications industry provides a very good example of the relationship between 'rent-seeking' and 'entrepreneurial' activities in contemporary Thailand (Suehiro 1995; Tara Siam Business Information Ltd 1993; Sakkarin 1992).

Sampathan and the Thai telecommunications industry

The practice of *sampathan* – or granting concessions – has a long history in Thailand dating back at least to the mid-eighteenth century, when King Rama III introduced the tax farming system for the liquor and gambling businesses. The *sampathan* system was also practised in the tramway, river transportation, teak and tin mining industries during the reign of King Rama V. The king granted special privileges to a few ethnic Chinese or Western firms in exchange for fixed concession fees or targeted state revenues. With monopolistic status, the firms reaped tremendous rents for a specific period, say three years (for opium and liquor), or even for as long as fifteen years (e.g. teak concessions) (Suehiro 1989: Chapter 3). The granting of *sampathan* was usually conducted on the basis of bidding, but one should not exaggerate the competitive nature of the process. In those days, the determining factor was not the bidders' managerial skills, but rather the strength of their political connections with the king, influential members of the royal family and key officials.

Even after the Second World War, *sampathan* continued to be practiced for lucrative businesses such as liquor (Mekong whisky), lumber, rice exports, pig slaughtering and construction contracts. The 1950s and the 1960s saw the development of new yet similar mutually beneficial relationships between military leaders and ethnic Chinese businessmen in Thailand (Suehiro 1989: Chapter 5). When military rule collapsed in 1973, the growth of such practices was temporarily put on hold. The new government restricted policies that economically favoured specific business groups and tightened control over public works and utilities. However, the elected Chatichai government from 1988 introduced modern versions of *sampathan* for new projects like telecommunications services as it pursued both the retreat of the public sector (via enhancing deregulation) and the creation of business opportunities for newly-emerging businessmen-cum-politicians based on political parties.

Before the Chatichai administration, major telecommunications services were under the control of either one of two government agencies in the Ministry of Transportation and Communications, namely the Telephone Organization of Thailand (TOT) and the Communications Authority of Thailand (CAT). Other related services, such as wireless radio broadcasting, were controlled by either the military or the police. Since telecommunications requires huge investments, sometimes beyond the capacity of single private sector firms, and ostensibly involves national security considerations, including defense and the handling and control of highly sensitive and classified information, the government has been reluctant to allow the private sector to provide these services. When Boonchai, the chairman of the UCOM Group, asked the Prem government to permit UCOM to participate in a public phone service project, the TOT immediately rejected the application on the grounds of national interest (Boonchai 1991: 71).

After Chatichai Choonhawan became prime minister and appointed Montri Phongphanit minister of transportation and communications, the government first privatized telephone services, and then other telecommunications services, citing two major reasons. First, there had been widespread complaints about the inefficient services provided by TOT and CAT, and the slow TOT response to addressing these inadequacies. Second, the government lacked the financial resources to undertake the massive nationwide expansion programme to provide three million telephone lines under its Seventh Five Year Economic and Social Development Plan (1991–6) (Tara Siam Business Information Ltd 1993).

Privatizing telecommunications services occurred not only in Thailand, but also in Singapore, Malaysia and Indonesia (Ohkawa and Teshiba 1992). In Thailand, however, the government adopted the build-operate-transfer (B-O-T) method rather than full-scale privatization. In other words, the government granted monopolistic or privileged status to selected private firms in exchange for a fixed percentage of the profit or gross revenue from these services. Under the B-O-T scheme, upon expiry of the contract period, the concessionaire transfers all installed equipment and management rights to the government. The B-O-T concession scheme thus shares some common characteristics with the traditional *sampathan* system.

Table 8.3 provides a summary of all telecommunications industry concessions granted from 1986 to 1993. The case of telephone services allows us to examine the bidding process and the factors that determined the decision to grant a concession to a particular firm. As for the nationwide telephone service expansion project involving three million new lines (two million in metropolitan Bangkok and a million in the countryside), the government announced a new policy of granting the whole project to one or two private firms in 1989, calling for bids in early 1990. Five major groups offered proposals and made bids for the project: Telefonaktiebolaget LM Ericsson of Sweden with Furukawa Electrical of Japan; Alcatel CIT of France; NTT and NEC, with the Mitsui Bussan Group, all of Japan; NYNEX Network System of the US with the Tomen Group of Japan; and British Telecom (BT) of the UK with the CP Group of Thailand (*Bangkok Post* 14 September 1990) – i.e. most leading international firms in the telecommunications industry submitted bids for this huge project. After screening all the proposals, the government decided to award the contract to the BT–CP joint venture. Among the conditions set: 16 per cent of gross revenue from telephone services in metropolitan Bangkok and 22 per cent of gross revenue from public phone services in the countryside would be paid to the government for the next 25 years. Total investment was expected to reach as much as 150 billion baht (*The Nation,* 19 September 1990).

Between 13 September 1990, when the government announced its decision to award the project to the BT–CP joint venture, and the Cabinet meeting on 9 October, there was heated discussion among Cabinet members, political party leaders and top executives of the state enterprises concerned over the decision taken and the desirability of private firms undertaking a state enterprise's responsibility. While this debate was taking place, newspapers alleged the CP Group had given huge bribes to top officials, including the prime minister, and other key people in the bidding process. However, the government did not rescind its earlier decision to award the contract to the BT–CP joint venture, or even reconsider the conditions set (*The Nation,* 4 October 1990; 10 October 1990).

But in February 1991, the military seized power before being forced to give way to a technocratic reform interim government under Anand Panyarachun. Identifying the project as a case involving political corruption and violating contract law, the new government raised the contract price of the project. Negotiations between the CP Group and the new government were eventually reopened. On 12 August 1991, CP was forced to conclude a new contract with the Anand government with the following changed conditions. First, the project would be divided into two parts – one, for two million lines in metropolitan Bangkok, and the other for one million lines in the countryside – with CP giving up the latter. Second, the CP Group promised not to take part in any new

Table 8.3 Thailand: concessions to private firms in the telecommunications industry, 1986–93

Projects	Granted by	Concessionaire (operator)	Year	Period	Government share
Paging services	CAT	Pacific Telesis	1986	10	33% of gross revenue
	TOT	Shinawatra Paging (Shinawatra Group)	1989	15	25–40% of gross revenue
	TOT	Percom Service	1989	15	25–40% of gross revenue
	TOT	Hutchison Telecommunications	1990	15	25–46% of gross revenue
	TOT	Worldpage (UCOM Group)	1993	15	41% of gross revenue (min. 1.5 billion baht)
Data communications *via* satellite	PTD	Samart Telcoms (Samart Group)	1988	15	5% of gross revenue
	PTD	Compunet (BKK Group)	1988	15	5% of gross revenue
	TOT	Shinawatra Datacom (Shinawatra Group)	1989	10	15–20% of gross revenue
	TOT	Acumen (Jasmine Group)	1991	15	17–25% of gross revenue
	CAT	Thai Skycom	1992	15	23.5% of gross revenue (min. 0.8 billion baht)
Cellular mobile phones	TOT	Advanced Info (Shinawatra Group)	1990	20	15–30% of gross revenue (min. 13.1 billion baht)
	CAT	Total Access Communications (UCOM Group)	1990	15	12–25% of gross revenue (min. 9 billion baht)
	TOT	Fonepoint (Shinawatra, CP, UCOM)	1990	10	15% of gross revenue
Telephones (Bangkok)	TOT	TelecomAsia (CP Group)	1991	25	16% of gross revenue
Telephones (Countryside)	TOT	Thai Telephone and Telecom-munications (Loxley Group)	1992	25	43% of gross revenue
Satellite	MOTC	Shinawatra Satellite (Shinawatra Group)	1991	30	minimum 1,415 million baht
Trunked radio phones	CAT	United Communication Industry (UCOM Group)	1992	15	9–16% of service charge
	TOT	Radiophone (CP, Jasmine Groups)	1992	15	25–28% of gross revenue
Videotext	TOT	Lines Technology (CP Group)	1993	15	15–25% of gross revenue

Sources: Tara Siam Business Information Ltd (1993); *The Nation*, 1 March 1993; *Prachachat Thurakit*, 16–19 August 1992.

Notes
TOT – Telephone Organisation of Thailand; CAT – Communications Authority of Thailand; PTD – Postal and Telegram Department; MOTC – Ministry of Transportation and Communications.

telephone service project in the next 25 years. Third, in addition to the 16 per cent of gross revenue to be paid to the government, CP would have to pay another 70 billion baht from its profits. Fourth, the CP Group agreed to invest in the TOT's future equipment modernization programme (*The Nation*, 3 August 1991). The conditions of the new agreement were clearly much less advantageous to CP. Before the final decision was announced, BT decided to withdraw from the project, allegedly due to frequent government intervention. NYNEX Network System Inc., a subsidiary of the Bell Atlantic Group of the US, replaced BT to establish a new joint venture with CP, TelecomAsia Co. Ltd.

Following the retraction of the one million rural public phones project from CP, the government called for new bidders in October 1991. Four groups submitted offers: SG Telecom of Sweden with the Saen Thong rice exporter group of Thailand; B. Grimm and Siemens of Germany; the Shinawatra Group of Thailand with AT&T of the US; and the Loxley Group of Thailand with NTT of Japan (Phacharaphon 1992: 7). The Loxley-NTT partnership was awarded the contract on the condition that they pay 43 per cent of gross revenue to the government over the next 25 years. The final contract price cost the Loxley-NTT partnership an additional 11 per cent of gross revenue as compared to the previous bidding by the CP-BT Group (Tara Siam Business Information Ltd 1993: 80, 207).

Several interesting points about 'rent-seeking' in contemporary Thailand emerge from the case of the nationwide telephone lines project. First, there is no doubt that political connections were still the key means by which domestic business groups gained access to lucrative large-scale projects. However, even political connections cannot always guarantee privileged economic status indefinitely, nor does such privilege go unchallenged indefinitely, due to political change and increased transparency, through a more independent mass media – as Doner and Ramsay argue for the textile industry. Thailand's unique clientelism has unintentionally facilitated competitive 'rent-seeking' in Thailand.

Second, even though a domestic business group succeeds in obtaining a concession, actual rent capture remains uncertain due to changing conditions, which may increase competition, raise bidding costs and cause political uncertainty. In an unpredictable political environment, it is difficult for business interests to secure rents through alliances with particular political leaders. With greater competition, 'rent-seeking' has become more expensive; the costs of securing *sampathan* escalate to such an extent that domestic firms can no longer expect to make much from rents alone. Rentier firms must therefore innovate to enhance productivity and thus profitability by effectively utilizing their managerial skills.

Business groups and strategic alliances in the telecommunications industry

As the above case study of the telephone lines project suggests, three unique features in the Thai telecommunications industry are of relevance to our discussion

(Suehiro 1995: 33). First, the exceptionally rapid progress in telecommunications technology has required Thai business groups to co-operate with leading inter-national firms. Obtaining and maintaining technical arrangements with big-time international players in the industry has been essential for Thai business groups bidding for government projects. Second, the granting of concessions in the telecommunications industry has been under strict government control. Hence, foreign firms need influential local partners who have close ties with Cabinet members, TOT or CAT board members and the military or police. Third, the telecommunications industry entails huge investments of capital, including bribes. Hence, domestic entrepreneurs cannot advance in the field without the financial backing of commercial banks and financial syndicates inside and outside Thailand.

These factors partly account for why the B. Grimm-Siemens partnership could not win the one million rural public phone lines project despite the fact that B. Grimm has, for over 70 years, been known for efficient technical servicing of imported machinery in Thailand, and Siemens had promised full technical support to B. Grimm. In contrast, the Loxley Group – the core firm of the Lamsam family, one of the most prominent Sino-Thai business families – has maintained close relations with the military through past dealings in aircraft and military tanks. Through the Thai Farmers Bank owned by the same Lamsam family, the Loxley business empire could easily gain financial support for the phone project. Moreover, the Loxley Group has maintained good relations with a number of prominent foreign firms in the industry through business deals in computers and data communication services, including IBM of the US, NTT of Japan, Northern Telecom of Canada, the Hutchison Group of Hong Kong and the Pacific Network of Australia. The Loxley Group was therefore well placed with its political connections, financial backing and technological know-how (Suehiro 1995: 36–7; Phacharaphon 1992). A similar pattern may be found in the case of the CP Group, which achieved total control over the poultry industry in Thailand through such practices (known as *si-prasarn*, or 'four comrades'): 'harmonizing co-operation between the four groups – the government, financial institutions, local manufacturers, and farmers' (Christensen 1990: 170).

The leading business groups in the Thai telecommunications industry are shown in Table 8.4, and may be classified into three major groups by origin and development (see Somwan 1992: 88–112; Tara Siam Business Information Ltd 1993: 171–254; Suehiro 1995: 34–9). Groups in category A can trace their origins to the importation, distribution and repair of communications equipment, such as wireless radios and TV antennas, including those who have extended their businesses to telecommunications services, including data communications via satellite. The Samart Group (which started as manufacturers of TV antennas in 1975), the UCOM Group (the sole distributor of Motorola's communications equipment from 1980), and the IEC Group (distributor of various kinds of communications equipment) belong to this category. Category B includes groups whose business ventures originated from technical services for mini and personal computers (PCs). The Shinawatra Group, the Jasmine International Group and the Loxley Group fall into this category. Finally, category C includes groups that

Table 8.4 Thailand: major business groups in the telecommunications industry, 1994

Group	Year established	Name of company	Capital ownership	Partners	Business activity
Shinawatra Group (B)	1982	ICSI Limited Partnership	90%		Computer services
	1983	Shinawatra Computer & Communications	50%	Foreign investors (24%)	Computer services system integrator
	1985	International Broadcasting	55%		Cable TVs
	1986	Advanced Info Service	72%	UCOM Group (4%)	Mobile phone service
	1989	Shinawatra Datacom	34%	Singapore Telecom International (49%)	Data communications
	1990	Shinawatra Paging	40%	Singapore (60%)	Paging services
	1991	Shinawatra Satellite	75%	American International Assurance (10%)	Satellite
	1991	Shinawatra Directories	42%	AT&T	Directories services
	1991	SC Matchbox	75%		Advertising
	1993	Shinawatra International	100%		Investment
CP Group	1989	Fonepoint (Thailand) (Bangkok Feedmill)	27%	Shinawatra (36%)	Mobile phones
	1990	TelecomAsia Corp.	85%	UCOM group (27%) NYNEX Network Systems (15%)	Public phones (Bangkok)
	1991	Telecom Holding	100%		Investment in T
	1991	Radiophone (Telecom Holding)	60%	Jasmine group (40%)	Long distance transmission
	n.a.	Com-Link (Telecom Holding)	20%		Long distance trunked call facilities
	1992	China's satellite (Chia Tai International)	25%	China government	Satellite (1994)
	1993	Lines Technology (Telecom Holding)	90%		Electronic messaging system called 'Videotex'

Table 8.4 continued

Group	Year established	Name of company	Capital ownership	Partners	Business activity
Jasmine Group (B)	1982	Jasmine International	93%		Sale of computers
	1984	Siam Teltech	n.a.		Sale of communications equipment
	1988	Acumen	96%		Data communications
	1991	Radiophone (Jasmine International)	40%	CP group (60%)	Long distance transmission
	1992	Thai Telephone & (Telecom Holding)	20%	Loxley group (34%) NTT (20%): Japan	Public phones (countryside)
Samart Group (A)	1975	Samart Engineering	100%		TV antennas
	1986	Samart Telecoms	60%	OTC International (40%): Australia	Data communications
	1988	Samart Satcom (Samart Corp.)	80%	Shinawatra (20%)	Manufacture of parabolic antennas
	1989	Samart Corp.	100%		Investment of TI
	1992	Cambodia Samart Communication	n.a.	Cambodian Government	Mobile phones in Cambodia
	1980	United Communication Industry (UCI)	93%		Import of communications equipment
UCOM Group (A)	1989	Total Access Communication	56%	CP group (10%)	Mobile phone service
	1989	Fonepoint (Thailand)	27%	CP group (27%) Shinawatra (34%)	Paging
	1991	Worldpage	100%		Mobile phone
Loxley Group (B)	1990	Thai Skycom	40%	Thanayong (60%) NTT (20%)	Data communications
	1992	Thai Telephone & Telecommunication	34%	Jasmine (20%)	Public phones (countryside)
Srifueng-fung Bangkok Bank	1986	Compunet Corp.	30%	Cable & Wireless PLC (40%): UK	Data communications

Sources: Tara Siam Business Information Ltd (1993); *Khu Khaeng*, 23 February 1991; Sakkarin (1992)

Note: (A) (B) and (C) refer to business group categories based on origin and development.

never really had any previous business base in the telecommunications field, but 'strategically' extended and expanded their businesses into the telecommunications industry from the end of the 1980s because of the prospects of high growth and returns. This category includes several giant conglomerates like the CP Group, the Bangkok Bank Group and the Thanayong Group, leaders in agro-industry, banking and real estate, respectively.

Groups belonging to categories A and B may be said to have accumulated some technical know-how in communications and/or computer services, and to possess close ties with the military and police through past business deals. However, they are disadvantaged by a shortage of capital funds. But thanks to the unprecedented 'stock market boom' that Thailand experienced from the end of the 1980s, these groups could easily mobilize huge amounts of money from local investors expecting high returns from their stock investments.[5] On the other hand, foreign investors with keen interest in the Thai telecommunications industry organized international financial syndicates to provide investment funds. In these circumstances, new entrepreneurs in the telecommunications industry were able to achieve rapid growth in short periods of time.

Besides new entrepreneurs, existing conglomerates also diversified rapidly into the industry. Although they had advantages in terms of investment funds and political connections compared to groups in categories A and B, their major drawback has been not having a prior technological base in the industry. Therefore, they had to seek 'strategic alliances (*phanthamit thurakit*) with (potential) competitors' or with foreign players in the industry to secure technological co-operation (see Figure 8.1). Such alliances have generally gone well beyond traditional Chinese business networking by, for example, ignoring differences in clan, provincial or dialect group affiliations.[6]

For instance, the CP Group made investments in several affiliated firms of the UCOM Group to utilize the latter's accumulated technical know-how. For its part, UCOM saw in this a good opportunity to ask CP to let them use the satellites which CP had planned to put up in co-operation with the Chinese government and American firms. Likewise, in its attempts to compete with CP, the Shinawatra Group launched joint ventures with the Samart Group in data communication services via satellite. The Thanayong Group has also attempted to diversify its business from real estate to the more promising businesses of cable TV and satellite services. To achieve this, it approached the Loxley Group to utilize the Asia-wide networking of Loxley's Hong Kong-based partner, the Hutchison Group. These strategic alliances involve a new type of 'business behaviour', quite different from the business tie-ups of the past, which were principally based on family ties or other similar affiliations.

To conclude, in addition to factors such as political connections, corporate capability has also determined the performance of firms as well as the related emergence of new business groups. Different elements have interacted to spur rapid growth in the Thai telecommunications industry, giving rise to new business groups, as the case of the Shinawatra Group illustrates.

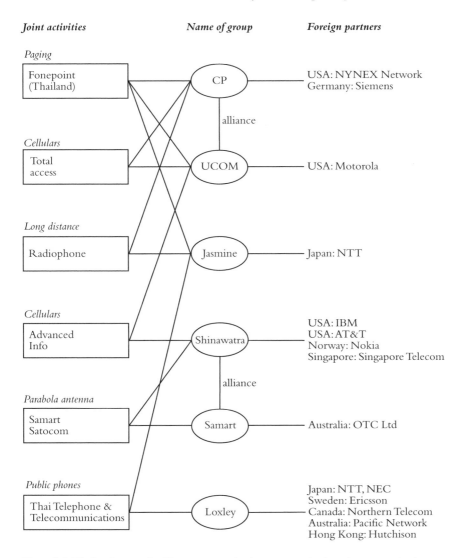

Figure 8.1 Thailand: strategic alliances among business groups in the telecommunications industry

The Shinawatra (SHIN) Group

The Shinawatra Group (renamed the SHIN Group) provides an interesting case study of a business group that has emerged with the telecommunications boom in Thailand. Led by Police Lt. Col. Dr Thaksin Shinawatra (elected prime minister in January 2001), the Shinawatra Group business empire has been built in the last decade and a half around the so-called 'two-C' industries – computers and communications. The growth trajectory of this group has been quite unique, and very different from the traditional family business groups. Hence, the mass media refer to Thaksin as the 'Knight of the Third Wave' (*Assawin Khlun Luk-thi-sam*) (Sorakon 1993: 132), meaning that he is representative of a new breed of businessmen involved in the third wave of the industrial revolution (computers and information industries) that Alvin Toffler identified. Moreover, quite coincidentally, the name suits Thaksin, who is a third-generation Sino-Thai of the Shinawatra family (Hakka Chinese with Sae Khu), who were pioneers in the silk industry and operate a wide range of business activities in Chiang Mai (Prani 1980; Praioo 1987; Thanawat 2000: 110–19).

Interestingly, there are two versions of Thaksin's success story. The first emphasizes his strong political connections and his family background style (Sakkarin 1992; Pasuk and Baker 1995; Rut 2001), while the second stresses the 'modern' or 'professional' (*phu chiawchan*) nature of his business (Sorakon 1993; Suehiro 1995). Born in July 1949, Thaksin started his 'apprenticeship' quite early. At seventeen, he was appointed manager of a tanning factory owned by his father. But the young Thaksin showed no interest in running it, leaving the family business and entering a preparatory school for the military academy. In 1973, Thaksin graduated from the police college of the military academy with highest honours, qualifying him for an overseas scholarship. Police Department scholarships took him to the US (Kentucky and Texas) twice, where he completed his Ph.D. in criminal justice in 1979. Upon his return to Thailand, Thaksin worked at the Data Processing Centre of the Police Department, which handles voluminous data on crimes, traffic accidents and car registrations. Becoming the director general of the Data Processing Centre two years later, he was chiefly responsible for the Herculean job of promoting a computerized on-line system in the Police Department. While still employed at the Police Department, he made his own business deals. For instance, he would purchase computers from IBM (Thailand) and rent them out to the State Railways, Chulalongkorn University and the Police Department itself.[7] To advance his private business interests, he established ICSI Ltd (Sorakon 1993: 21–6).

As shown in Table 8.5, Thaksin's business expanded rapidly from 1983. In 1983, he ventured into computer services; in 1985, paging systems; in 1986, cellular mobile phones; in 1989, cable TVs; and in 1990, data communication services via satellite. In only ten years, Thaksin, who retired from the Police Department in December 1987, incorporated or took over around 22 companies, and successfully built his business empire around both computer and communications services. At present, the Shinawatra (or SHIN) Group consists of five major sub-groups, largely categorized by the type of service offered (Shinawatra 1994): one, computer services; two, cable TV broadcasting; three, pager and cellular phone business, and data communication services via satellite; four, satellite operations; and five, overseas businesses. The Shinawatra Group had 56 per cent of Thailand's cellular phone market in 1993 (Advanced Info 1994). Total assets of all affiliated companies jumped from 5.8 billion to 35.2 billion baht, and combined profits from 276 million to 2,590 million baht between 1990 and 1993 (see Table 8.6). The *Far Eastern Economic Review* survey of the '200 Leading Companies in Asia' ranked the Shinawatra Group third in Thailand in 1993, following the Bangkok Bank and the CP Group (*Far Eastern Economic Review*, 6 January 1994).

Table 8.5 Development of the Shinawatra Group, 1982–93

Date	Business expansion
Dec. 1982	Thaksin Chinawat established ICSI Ltd to engage in computer distribution and services.
June 1983	Set up Shinawatra Computer Services & Investment Co., Ltd (SCSI). Rented computers to State Railways and Chulalongkorn University.
Feb. 1984	Changed name of SCSI to Shinawatra Computer Co., Ltd (SC).
June 1985	Started paging business in cooperation with Pacific Telesis Engineering Co., Ltd of USA – 'PAC-LINK'.
Sept. 1985	Established International Broadcasting Co., Ltd (IBC).
April 1986	Established Advanced Info Service Co., Ltd (ADVANC). Started mobile phone services.
Dec. 1987	Thaksin retired from Planning Division of the Police Department
March 1989	IBC obtained cable TV concession from CAT. IBC started broadcasting service from Sept. 1990.
March 1990	Established Shinawatra Datacom Co., Ltd (joint venture with Singapore Telecom). Started data communication business.
June 1990	Took over Digital Paging Services Co., Ltd, reorganized into Shinawatra Paging Co., Ltd. Started paging services.
Aug. 1990	Listed SC on the Security Exchange of Thailand.
Sept. 1990	ADVANC started mobile phone services (Cellular 900).
April 1991	Owned 42% of ATT Directories (Thailand) Co., Ltd. Started telephone directories business; firm reorganized as Shinawatra Directories Co., Ltd.
June 1991	Invested in Fonepoint (Thailand) Co., Ltd paging business.
Sept. 1991	SC reorganized into Shinawatra Computer & Communications Co. Ltd. From Jan. 1993, this firm became a public limited company.
Oct. 1991	Obtained paging service monopoly from the Ministry of Finance for the World Bank annual meetings in Bangkok.
Nov. 1991	Established Shinawatra Satellite Co. Ltd to launch and operate the first domestic satellite.
Jan. 1992	Bid for public phone services for countryside (one million lines) but defeated by the Loxley Group.
Sept. 1992	Shinawatra Datacom extended business to whole country.
Feb. 1993	Advanced into cable TVs in Cambodia. Established International Cambodian Broadcasting, a joint venture between Shinawatra (70%) and the Cambodian Government (30%) (dissolved in 1995).
March 1993	Bid for trunk radio phone jointly with the UCOM group.
June 1993	Advanced into communications services in Laos for 15 years. Joint venture between Shinawatra (70%) and the Laos Government (30%).
Oct. 1993	Alliance with the Samart group, with Shinawatra and the Samart group investing in each other.
Dec. 1993	Launched first 'THAICOM' satellite.
Dec. 1993	Owned 30% of Isla Communications Co. Ltd of the Philippines

Sources: Suehiro (1995: 52); news articles in *Phu Chatkan Raiwan*, *Khu Khaeng* and *The Nation*.

How can the rapid growth of Thaksin's business empire be accounted for? Sorakon (1993: 136–40) points out four major elements promoting and facilitating business growth. One, Thaksin's technical knowledge of and experience with computers. Two, the personal contacts he had established during his stay at the military academy (police college). Three, the personal contacts he developed during his stays in the United States. Four, his know-how of the complicated procedures for obtaining concessions from the government. Of these four elements, the know-how accumulated during his stint at the police department is said to have contributed greatly to his success in obtaining the concessions for pagers, mobile phones and cable TVs.

It is notable that Thaksin does not seem to have relied on his family assets and network either to begin or to expand his business. After all, his relatives include Suraphan Shinawatra, an elected representative of Chiang Mai province in parliament. The Shinawatra family had raked in large profits from silk manufacture and export, and from real estate ventures in Chiang Mai (Suehiro 1995: 47–9). On the other hand, Thaksin's uncle was deputy permanent secretary in the ministry of transport and communications in the mid-to-late 1980s before he retired, and his influence may have helped. But there is no evidence that Thaksin utilized these connections and resources. Also, his business activities and expansion have been quite different from traditional Chinese family businesses; the unique development of his business may be summarized as follows:

1 He aggressively recruited professionals and engineers to join his companies. These professionals and engineers included key people from CAT, TOT, National Statistical Office (NSO), IBM Thailand (Phu Chatkan Raiduan 1990; Phairo 1999) and Thai engineers who had worked in NASA, IBM, AT&T, Compression Lab Inc., Texas Instruments, Hughes Aircraft and other major firms in the US.[8] In recent years, the Shinawatra Group has contacted promising Thai students in engineering faculties at the University of Tokyo, the Tokyo Institute of Technology and the University of Osaka in Japan.[9] Unlike TelecomAsia of the CP Group, the boards of directors and other key positions in the Shinawatra Group are not filled by family members.

2 Rather than using assets and fortunes from existing family businesses, Thaksin has fully utilized the stock market and off-shore markets to raise investment funds for his computer and communications businesses during the stock boom. He has listed all his core companies on the stock market. Shinawatra Computer and Communications Public, established in 1983, was listed in 1990; Advance Info Services Public, established in 1986, was listed five years later. International Broadcasting Corp. Public, established in 1985, was listed in 1992, while Shinawatra Satellite Public, established in 1991, was listed in 1993 (Securities Exchange of Thailand 1992, 1993, 1994). With this set-up, the Shinawatra Group is not Thaksin's own personal or family business as is the case with other Sino-Thai family business groups.

3 Aside from its modern management style and ownership structure, the Shinawatra Group has established close relations with politicians and government officers. For instance, Thaksin invited two key persons – Phaibun Limpaphayom, the managing director of the TOT, and Bunkhlee Plangsiri, the managing director of the CAT – to serve on the board of Shinawatra Computer and Communications to cement relations with these government

agencies (Phairo 1999; SHIN Corporation PLC 2000). In 1993, he also set up an 18-member 'advisory group' which has included Chaloem Chankachon, the former director of metropolitan police, and other influential retirees from the Police Department, the Ministry of Environment, Technology and Science and other government enterprises (Shinawatra Computer and Communications PCL 1994). It is frequently suggested that Thaksin's bids for cable TV and satellite operations have succeeded due to his strong connections with bureaucrats and economic technocrats.

In October 1994, Thaksin decided to retire from active involvement in his businesses when he was invited to become foreign minister in the Chuan Leekphai government. At that time, he disclosed to the public that his private assets were worth 57.2 billion baht (US$2.23 billion) (Suehiro 1995:51; *Mathichon Supsapda*, 25 November 1994), reflecting his success as a businessman and how quickly Thaksin had amassed his wealth. Then, Thaksin became leader of the Palang Tham party and deputy prime minister in the Banharn government at the end of 1995 before resigning in 1996. He then set up his own political party, Thai Rak Thai, in July 1998, and finally he was appointed the twenty-third prime minister of Thailand after the general election in January 2001 (Rut 2001).

His successful entry and meteoric rise in the political arena has, in turn, been attributed to his business success and to the strong political connections and networks he has cultivated since his career in the Police Department. The Shinawatra Group, which is no longer considered Thaksin's own business empire, has continued to expand after Thaksin's retirement. This suggests that the growth of the Shinawatra Group has been due not only to his own talents and influence, but also to the well-organized capability of the professionals, including engineers, who run the companies in the group (Phairo 1999).

Reconsidering the 'economic boom' and 'business capability' in Thailand

Many economists who attach significance to the institutional elements promoting industrial development in developing countries only examine government policies and the role of economic technocrats. Their explanations are often wanting because they tend to neglect corporate behaviour and corporate capability, which I have emphasized. After all, if the responses of the domestic private sector to government policies are overlooked, it will be difficult to understand why and how the East Asian countries have industrialized.

Political connections are undoubtedly still important for understanding Thailand's industrialization. 'Political patronage' and 'rent-seeking' can be widely observed, not only in the regulated industries producing for the domestic market, but also in BOI-promoted export-oriented industries. As long as the Thai political system – characterized by patron–client relations – remains unchanged, private firms and business groups will continue to use political patronage for profitable investment and expansion.

How then do we explain the relationship between 'rent-seeking' and industrial development in contemporary Thailand? Generally speaking, 'rent-seeking' itself causes social waste rather than generating social surplus. In Thailand, however, it appears that such waste is more than offset by the long-term gains from government intervention. Also, the rent transfers involved in corruption may not involve much social waste. Government policies have encouraged successful entry into promoted industries and have not prevented the market structure from remaining quite competitive (Doner and Ramsay 1997). Keen competition increases 'rent-seeking' activity and associated social waste, but the perception of limited access would tend to have the opposite effect. Domestic firms have not only attempted to strengthen their connections and influence with government agencies, but have also promoted management reforms within their firms, as the cases of the CP and the Shinawatra Groups clearly show (Suehiro 2000: Chapter 9; Suehiro 2002: Chapters 2 and 7). Some domestic firms can utilize technological assets accumulated by MNCs through joint ventures and technological purchases – as observed in the case of the telecommunications industry. Even though domestic firms may not have the technical base or capability to develop new technology, they can cultivate international competitiveness by effectively combining favourable government policies and decisions, capital funds from banks and the stock market, as well as imported technology and managerial skills into successfully organized and very profitable business activities, which together have been the basis for Thailand's industrial dynamism.

Business capability seems to have become more significant and decisive, not only in the telecommunications industry, but also in other industries affected by government deregulation in the 1990s. These industries include cement, plate glass, liquor, auto-assembly, iron and steel, and petrochemicals. Deregulation, together with tariff reduction on imported products, has undermined the mono-polistic privileges of government-promoted firms, causing fierce competition between domestic and foreign firms as well as among domestic firms. In such circumstances, domestic firms have to pay much more attention to developing business capabilities and enhancing efficiency to improve their competitiveness. The capability to absorb, master and improve upon imported technology has also become more crucial for domestic manufacturers who enter 'growth' industries such as electronics, auto parts and plastics. Hence, in the future, political connections may become less crucial, as corporate capability becomes more critical in ensuring business success. This seems to be borne out by studies of Thai business groups who survived the 1997 economic crisis (see Suehiro 2001a, 2001b).

Notes

1   Looking at the latest survey by the author on the top 100 non-financial firms, manufacturing ones accounted for 55 firms in 1989, 51 firms in 1994 and 65 firms in 1997. Out of these firms, foreign manufacturers have increased their proportion against combined total sales from 33 per cent in 1989 (17 firms) to 38 per cent in 1994 (18 firms), and further to 58 per cent in 1997 (36 firms) due to the FDI boom (Suehiro 2000: 196).

2 Interesting case studies of domestic business groups are found in 'special issues' of *Phu Chatkan Raiduan* (*The Manager*, monthly, in Thai) and *Who's Who in Thailand* (monthly, in Thai).

3 Madam Prapha Wiriyaphraphaikit, the founder and chair of the Sahaviriya Group, served as a vice president of the Thailand-China Friendship Association, while (eventual prime minister) Chatichai Choonhawan occasionally served as president. The mass media reported that the Sahaviriya Group obtained privileged status in the integrated steel industry from the Chatichai government through personal connections.

4 Management reforms in the Sahaviriya Group in 1993 consisted of three major developments: one, reorganization of the diversified corporate activities into five divisional departments of steel, financing, real estate, engineering and overseas activities; two, Prapha, the founder, retired, and Suthy, the former governor of the Bank of Thailand and finance minister, was invited to be chairman of the group; three, more managerial power was given to the professional staff recruited from outside the owner-family members (Sahaviriya Group 1993). However, the Sahaviriya Group was forced to transfer their ownership of the Sahaviriya OA Group to their Taiwanese competitor, the Acer Group, after the economic crisis.

5 The government also promoted the listing of telecommunications companies in the stock market in the 1990s. As a result, most such companies became public limited companies (PLCs). See Suehiro (2001a).

6 This new word for 'strategic alliance' was introduced by local newspapers in the (*Phu Chatkan Raiwan*, 1–2 January 1994). This strategy is also observed in retail business (between Central Department Store and Robinson; and between the CP Group and the Mall Group) and the real estate business.

7 Since these state enterprises and government organizations had no budgetary resources to directly purchase computer equipment, Thaksin leased the equipment to them at his own risk.

8 Information obtained from the annual reports of Shinawatra Computer and Communications Public, International Broadcasting Corp. Public, Advanced Info Services Public, Shinawatra Satellite Public, etc.

9 Interviews with members of the Association of Thai Professionals of Japan (*Samakhom Nak-Wichachip Thai nai Jipun*) in December 1996.

References

Advanced Info Service Public Co., Ltd (1994) *1993 Annual Report*, Bangkok.

Advanced Research Group Co., Ltd (1994) *Thailand Company Information 1993–94*, Bangkok.

Bangkok Post (1990) 'B150,000 Phone Goes to Single Consortium', 14 September.

Board of Investment, Thailand (1995) 'Rai-ngan Phiset: Utsahakam Lek-kla' (Special Issue: Steel Industry). *Thailand Investment Promotion Journal*, August.

Borisut Kansinphila and Chanphen Wiwatsukhseri (1994) *Phlik-khamphi Bangkok Land and Land & House: Ton Tamrap Phatthana Thi-din* (Revealing Bangkok Land and Land & House: The Leading Land Developers). Bangkok: Matichon.

Boonchai (1991) 'Poet-tua Boonchai Bencharongkun: Boss Yak Telecom UCOM' (Disclosure of Mr Boonchai Bencharongkun's opinion: The Boss of the Big Telecom UCOM), *Transport and Communications* (in Thai), August–September: 69–79.

Christensen, Scott R. (1990) 'Coalitions and Collective Choice: The Politics of Institutional Change in Thai Agriculture'. Ph.D. dissertation, Madison: University of Wisconsin.

Christensen, Scott R., Ammar Siamwalla and Pakorn Vichyanond (1997) 'Institutional and Political Bases of Growth-Inducing Policies in Thailand', in Thailand Development Research Institute (TDRI) *Thailand's Boom and Bust*. Bangkok: TDRI.

Doner, Richard F. (1991) *Driving A Bargain: Automobile Industrialization and Japanese Firms in Southeast Asia*. Berkeley: University of California Press.

Doner, Richard F. (1992) 'Limits of State Strength: Toward an Institutionalist View of Economic Development'. *World Politics*, 44, April: 398–431.

Doner, Richard F. and Ansil Ramsay (1997) 'Competitive Clientelism and Economic Governance: The Case of Thailand', in Sylvia Maxfield and Ben Ross Schneider (eds) *Business and the State in Developing Countries*. Ithaca: Cornell University Press.

Far Eastern Economic Review (1994) 'Asia's Leading Companies', 6 January: 62–3.

International Business Research Co., Ltd (ed.) (1987) *Million Baht Business Information Thailand 1987*, Bangkok.

Khu Khaeng (1991) 'Aphi-maha Thurakit Daothiam' (Satellite as a Super Big Business), 23 February.

Mathichon Supsapda (1994) 15(744), 25 November.

Mauro, Paolo (1995) 'Corruption and Growth'. *The Quarterly Journal of Economics*, 110(3), August: 681–712.

Ohkawa Masashi and Masaki Teshiba (1992) 'Hattensuru Ajia no Telecom Sangyou (I), (II)' (Development of the Telecommunications Industry in Asia). *Nomura Ajia Jyouhou*, 22–29 September and 22–29 November.

Pan Siam Communications Co., Ltd (ed.) (1981) *Million Baht Business Information Thailand 1980–81*, Bangkok.

Pasuk Phongphaichit and Chris Baker (1996) *Thailand's Boom*. Chiang Mai: Silkworm.

Pasuk Phongphaichit and Sungsidh Piriyarangsan (1994) *Corruption and Democracy in Thailand*. Bangkok: Chulalongkorn Political Economy Centre.

Phacharaphon Changkaew (1992) 'Shinawatra Pata Loxley: Khrai Khaeng kraeng Khwa-kan' (Shinawatra Group Attacks the Loxley Group: Which Competitor Will Become Stronger). *Phu Chatkan Raiduan* 9(103), April: 110–52.

Phairo Loetwiram (1999) 'Bunkhlee Plangsiri: Phu-nam SHIN Corp' (Bunkhlee Plangsiri: Leader of the SHIN Corporation). *Phu Chatkan Raiduan*, 17(193), October: 43–62.

Phu Chatkan Raiduan (ed.) (1990) 'Somphop Amatayakun: Nai Sathanakan "Samong-lai" thi IBM' (Somphop Amatayakun: Brain Drain from IBM). *Phu Chatkan Raiduan*, 8(85), October: 107–32.

Phu Chatkan Raiwan (1994) 'Rai-ngan Phiset: Phanthamit Thurakit Yutthasat haeng Pi' (This Year is the Year of the Strategic Alliance) 1–2 January, Special Issue.

Prachachat Thurakit (1983) 'Chak Chia Tai Chung thung Charoen Pokphand' (From Chia Tai Chung to the Charoen Pokphand Company), 12 February.

Prachachat Thurakit (1992) 'Rai-chue Phu-rap Sampathan' (List of Concessionaires), 16–19 August.

Praioo Chananon (1987) *Nai-thun Phokha kap Kan Ko-tua lae Khayai-tua khong Rabop Thun-niyom nai Pak Nua khong Thai Pho.So, 2464–2523* (Merchants and the Expansion of the Capitalistic System in Northern Thailand, 1921–1980). Bangkok: Sangsan.

Prani Sirithon na Patthalung (1980) *Phu Bukboek haeng Chiangmai* (Pioneers in Chiang Mai). Bangkok: Ruangsin.

Rut Mantira (2001) *Thaksin Shinawatra: Nayokrattamontri Khon-thi 23* (Thaksin Shinawatra: The twenty-third Prime Minister of Thailand). Bangkok: Namphon.

Sahaviriya Group (ed.) (1994) *40th Anniversary of the Sahaviriya Group*. Bangkok: December.

Sakkarin Niyomsilpa (1992) 'From Monopoly to Regulated Competition: The Political Economy of Telecommunications Policy in Thailand'. PhD dissertation, Canberra: Australian National University.

Securities Exchange of Thailand (ed.) (1992) *Sarup Kho-sonthet Borisat Chot-thabian Borisat Rap-anuyat*. Bangkok: Securities Exchange of Thailand.

Securities Exchange of Thailand (ed.) (1993) *Sarup Kho-sonthet Borisat Chot-thabian Borisat Rap-anuyat*. Bangkok: Securities Exchange of Thailand.

Securities Exchange of Thailand (ed.) (1994) *Sarup Kho-sonthet Borisat Chot-thabian Borisat Rap-anuyat*. Bangkok: Securities Exchange of Thailand.

SHIN Corporation PLC (2000) *Rai-ngan Pracham Pi 2542 Baep 56/1* (SHIN Corporation Annual Report 1999, Form 56/1, March). Bangkok: Stock Exchange of Thailand.

Shinawatra Computer and Communications PLC (1994) *1993 Annual Report*. Bangkok.

Somwan Udomsriloet (1992) 'Kan Tham-thurakit Khluen nai Huang Awakat' (Communications Service Business in the Atmosphere). *Phu Chatkan Raiduan*, 9(106), July: 88–112.

Sorakon Adunyanon (1993) *Thaksin Chinawat:Assawin Khlun Luk-thi-sam* (Thaksin Shinawatra: The Knight of the Third Wave). Bangkok: Matichon.

Suehiro, Akira (1989) *Capital Accumulation in Thailand, 1855–1985*. Tokyo: Centre for East Asian Cultural Studies.

Suehiro, Akira (1995) 'Chinawat Gurupu: Tai no Jyohou Tsuushin Sangyou to Shinkou Zaibatsu' (The Shinawatra Group: The Telecommunications Industry and Newly Emerging Business Groups in Thailand). *Ajia Keizai*, 36(2), February: 25–60.

Suehiro, Akira (1997) 'Modern Family Business and Corporate Capability in Thailand: A Case Study of the CP Group'. *Japanese Yearbook on Business History*, 14, Tokyo: 31–57.

Suehiro, Akira (2000) *Kyattchi-appu-gata Kogyoka-ron: Ajia Keizai no Kiseki to Tenbo* (Catch-up Industrialization: The Trajectory and Prospects of the Asian Economies). Nagoya: Nagoya University Press.

Suehiro, Akira (2001a) 'Asian Corporate Governance: Disclosure-Based Screening System and Family Business Restructuring in Thailand', Institute of Social Science, University of Tokyo. *Shakai Kagaku Kenkyu*, 52(5), March: 55–97.

Suehiro, Akira (2001b) 'Family Business Gone Wrong?: Ownership Patterns and Corporate Performance in Thailand', Asian Development Bank Institute Working Paper No. 19, May.

Suehiro, Akira (ed.) (2002) *Tai no Seido Kaikaku to Kigyo Saihen: Kiki kara Saiken e* (Institutional Reform and Corporate Restructuring in Thailand: From Crisis to Recovery). Tokyo: Institute of Developing Economies.

Suehiro, Akira and Makoto Nambara (1991) *Tai no Zaibatsu: Famili Bizinesu to Keiei Kaikaku* (Zaibatsu Groups in Thailand: Family Business and Management Reforms), Tokyo: Doubunkan.

Suehiro, Akira and Shigeki Higashi (eds) (2000) *Tai no Keizai Seisaku: Seido, Soshiki, Akuta* (Economic Policy in Thailand: The Role of Institutions and Actors). Tokyo: Institute of Developing Economies.

Suthy Prasertsart (1991) 'The Global Context and the New Wave of Japanese Investment in Thailand', in Shoichi Yamaguchi (ed.) *Transfer of Japanese Technology and Management to the ASEAN Countries*. Tokyo: University of Tokyo Press.

Tara Siam Business Information Ltd (1993) *Thai Telecommunications Industry 1993/94*. Bangkok.

Tara Siam Business Information Ltd (1995) *Thai State Enterprises 1994/95*. Bangkok.

Than Setthakit (ed.) (1993) *CP:Thurakit Rai Phrom-thaen* (CP: Indefinite Business Expansion). Bangkok: Than Setthakit.

Thanawat Sap-phaibun (2000) *55 Trakun Dan Park 1* (Fifty-Five Distinguished Families, Volume 1). Bangkok: The Nation Multi Media Group.

The Nation (various dates).

The Nation (1991) 'Phone Deal Gives Govt. BT 70bn'. 3 August.

The Nation (1993) 'Telecom Gears for New Era'. 1 March.

Unger, Danny (1998) *Building Social Capital in Thailand: Fibers, Finance, and Infrastructure*. Cambridge, UK: Cambridge University Press.

Warr, Peter (ed.) (1993) *The Thai Economy in Transition*. Cambridge: Cambridge University Press.

World Bank (1993) *The East Asian Miracle: Economic Growth and Public Policy*. New York: Oxford University Press.

Interviews

CP Group directors, Bangkok, September 1985, October 1989.

News writers and businessmen in the telecommunications industry, Bangkok, March 1993.

Members of the Association of Thai Professional of Japan, December 1996.

9 De-mythologizing Charoen Pokphand

An interpretive picture of the CP Group's growth and diversification

Paul Handley

Introduction

There is a joke in Bangkok about the Charoen Pokphand or CP Group, which made the rounds after yet another government official – the Thai ambassador to Beijing – left government service to join the group. Thai civil service rankings are known as C levels. The lowest rank is C1, then C2, and so on up to C11. And after C11, people say, is CP. The joke is meant to suggest that CP's influence spreads through powerful civil servants, as well as other political leaders. Two recent true stories add to the popular image of how CP builds and exploits such connections.

In April 1997, a French journalist visiting the public relations office of the Charoen Pokphand group found them very busy with an uncommon task: to find several trained Thai elephants to export to China for a small, economically unimportant group that wanted them for a tourism attraction. The person in charge of doing this favour-begets-favour for the Chinese was the daughter of the former Thai Prime Minister, Banharn Silpa-archa.[1] Also in April 1997, with no warning or public deliberation, the government suddenly reversed a long-standing ban on cockfighting and its associated gambling. When asked why the sudden change, minister of the interior Snoh Tienthong said that the CP Group had asked him to remove the ban because there was money to be made in breeding fighting-cocks. Dhanin Chearavanont, chairman of CP, said promoting cockfight gambling would help build the commercial fighting-cock breeding industry (*The Nation*, 18 May 1997).

It would be an unfair characterization of the CP Group's more than 70 years of success to suggest that its expansion and diversification have depended primarily on the assiduous exploitation of political connections. Having started out in the business of developing and selling better seeds to farmers, the group's roots are in superior technology and efficient trading. Entrepreneurial and managerial talent, investment in research and development, and an understanding of consumer behaviour in growing economies helped CP expand to become a formidable agro-industry and food processing group. As a core aspect of its entrepreneurialism, however, one cannot overlook CP's emphasis on employing political or other connections – *guanxi*, as it is called in Chinese – to achieve business success. Undeniably, the reliance on political support, through exchanging favours with persons in positions of power, has forever been an important part of business everywhere. The practice simply reflects a lack of transparency and full competition in a free market capitalist economic system, and it will always be a means of seeking advantage over business competitors.

Nevertheless, what is interesting about the CP Group over the past decade, as an example of the evolution of Chinese family business and of patterns of growth and development in a large business conglomerate, is CP's seemingly increasing reliance on connections, rather than on generating competitive advantage internally from technological, managerial or marketing abilities. Combined with its rapid and supposedly successful diversification into new industries, and its achievements as one of the leading, most powerful foreign investors in China, CP's public image has fed into a myth of the group having incomparable strengths and talents. Those talents make CP, in much popular literature and contemporary journalism, a paragon within the uniquely successful networks of overseas Chinese business, and especially among the family-run ethnic Chinese conglomerates of South-East Asia. Based on its perceived strengths, CP is frequently portrayed as one of the principal organizations that will take the world's ethnic Chinese communities, and Asia, into global economic leadership in the next century.[2]

There are, however, many weaknesses to this myth, and they are connected to the deficiencies of the type of entrepreneurialism which has made CP famous: the ethnic-based networking, the *guanxi*, the family-based management, and so on. In fact, CP's expansion and diversification have been far less than successful. Among the competitors in many of its new businesses, it remains distinctly average, if not inferior; in a number of ventures, it has ended up losing substantial sums of money where management originally assumed easy profits. Seeming to believe its own image, CP has overemphasized growth, networks and connections, while ignoring important issues including the development of management skills and technical capabilities. In its rush to diversify as well, it has ignored opportunities to build on areas of its original success, like trading farm goods or food processing, which could serve to establish a global presence in commodities trading or the prepared foods industry.

CP's goal, according to statements by the chief executive, Dhanin Chearavanont, appears to be to climb quickly into the ranks of prominent global conglomerates, like those of South Korea and Japan, diversified over a myriad of businesses and industries (*Nation News Talk*, 1994 and 1996; *The Nation*, 13 August 1997). To achieve this, CP needs a platform from which to take off, and it has concluded that Thailand as a home base is not large enough, while China is – and that the best way to build that platform in China is through the creation and exploitation of political connections for competitive advantage (*International Herald Tribune*, 16 November 1995). If it can diversify in China, and build large economies of scale in any industry based on the huge Chinese market, CP believes that it will then be able to move further up the ranks of global conglomerates.

There are flaws to this approach. First is that CP is seen by neither country to be a 'national company' deserving of the kind of governmental support provided for a Mitsui, or Daewoo, or in the Thai case, Siam Cement; or in the Chinese case, a CITIC or China Resources. Second, given the group's focus on exploiting connections, CP's rapid and seemingly uncontrolled diversification is undertaken with apparent neglect to developing group abilities in management, technology and marketing. Due to this neglect, and to many traits commonly associated with overly conservative and traditional Chinese family-run businesses, CP continues to have difficulty making the leap from being a big Thailand-based conglomerate with impressive assets in China, to becoming an important regional and global player. Large investments expected to achieve great profits have performed badly, and many announced projects have never proceeded, thanks to poor planning, marketing and the lack of due diligence in management. Although there is nothing static about the group and its family management, it appears that their approach is an important limiting factor in CP's development, rather than the most important aspect of success.

History

With over 70 years in agribusiness in Southeast Asia, CP and the Chearavanont family are no overnight rags-to-riches success story. The group originally started with the Chaozhou dialect name Chia Tai, which is still used for many group names, both in the Chaozhou version and also the Mandarin pronunciation, Zheng Da. Currently CP is best known in China as Zheng Da Jituan. Another name frequently used in Chinese is Bu Feng, interpreted by one source as a transliteration of the Thai name, 'Pokphand'. The group was started and is firmly controlled by members of the Xie (or Chia, in Chaozhou dialect) family, originally from Hua Sua, Chenghai, near Shantou in Guangdong province. In Thailand, the family adopted the name Chearavanont, alternatively spelled Chiaravanond, Jiaravanon, and other similar versions.[3]

Early this century, the Chia family raised vegetables, and possibly seeds, for markets in the Shantou area. Following an exodus of local Chinese from Shantou to then-Siam, Chia Ekchor[4] went to Bangkok in 1921 to explore possibilities in the growing Chinese-run market gardens there. After that trip, Chia Ekchor and brother Chia Siew-whooy established Chia Tai Chuang (Zhengda Zhuang) in Bangkok's Samphatawongs district – the main ethnic Chinese district – importing seed grown on the family farm in Shantou for sale to market gardeners. Later, other farm goods and implements were added to the line. Between the 1920s and 1950s, Ekchor, Siew-whooy and family expanded their seed distribution throughout South-East Asia, and were apparently already quite substantial prior to the Second World War. They operated branches in southern and north-eastern Thailand, expanding into Malaya and Singapore, and reportedly also into Indochina.

Most of the family was involved in the business.[5] Ekchor and Siew-whooy each had twelve children, the first by two wives and the latter by three; Ekchor had four sons and Siew-whooy nine sons. Ekchor's sons (in Thai: Jaran, Montri, Sumet and Dhanin) were named in a way that suggests their father's strong

Chinese nationalism: each was named in the pattern (in Mandarin) Xie *X* Min, and the middle character of each, from the eldest brother to Dhanin, the youngest, spells out Zheng Da Zhong Guo, using the business group name in the first two characters but altogether meaning 'Great China'.

Ekchor spent the Second World War in Singapore and Malaya, and returned to Shantou after the war. There he further built the family farming and seed distribution business, while Chia Siew-whooy managed the family trading business in South-East Asia. According to Jaran, as cited in the *Thansetthakij* book (Suwannaban 1993), Chia Ekchor's success was rooted in part in a natural talent for developing new strains of seed and, later, livestock. After the Second World War, he is said to have built something of a name in Guangdong and even farther afield for popular and productive breeds of rice, geese, and flowers which he developed himself. The *Thansetthakij* account quotes Dhanin as saying that they were the largest seed distributor in South-East Asia. If true, exactly when this was achieved is not clear. In South-East Asia, Chia Tai was also agent for superior brands of Japanese-produced seeds, which the firm apparently struggled to have sold eventually under its own brand.

In 1950–1, the family business in Shantou was apparently nationalized by the communists. At the same time, apparently, Chia Ekchor was put in charge of a state-owned agricultural business. Speculation is that it was his own business that he continued to manage, until he left China for Hong Kong and later Singapore in 1958. Why he left China is not clear, but the timing coincides with the economic and political turbulence associated with the Great Leap Forward and other campaigns.

Chia Ekchor's first son, Jaran, came to manage the business in Thailand in the 1950s alongside Chia Siew-whooy and other family members. In that period, they began to expand into side businesses, creating compound animal feeds, raising chickens for eggs and then meat, and also investing in factories to make jute bags for grains and feeds. By the late 1950s, when Dhanin (b. 1939) was still a student, the group had already developed or acquired relatively high-yielding strains of chicken for egg-laying. But probably as important for their business development, was that Jaran had built up CP as one of the country's largest importers and distributors of fertilizer, a highly important commodity, both economically and politically (Pananond 1996).

The group's economic influence in Thailand grew. A photograph from 1953 demonstrates its prominence in post-war Bangkok: at a ceremony in Suan Amphorn, the royal gardens in the centre of Bangkok, CP is shown making a donation to the palace, while in the background there is a very large billboard advertising CP's 'rua bin' (flying boat) brand of seeds (Suwannaban 1993). By the end of the 1950s, CP held a seat on the board of the government's slaughterhouse monopoly, a lucrative position which put management on a level of power (and in contact) with top army and police generals. According to the *Thansetthakij* book, Dhanin, after his 1958 return from studies in China and Hong Kong, was given this position in 1960 (Suwannaban 1993). The group's economic strength was demonstrated by the ability to charter aircraft to fly chickens and eggs to Hong Kong when famine hit China beginning in 1959 (Suwannaban 1993). CP set up a large distribution operation in Hong Kong that not only supplied the colony, but also sold food into China.

The history of CP's move into the modern mass production of chickens, with high-yield American breeds of layers and broilers, is not completely clear. Most sources say that the group learned in the late 1950s or early 1960s that US chicken was cheaper than Thai, prompting CP to acquire US breeds to introduce into Thailand.[6] Whatever the case, the group began to take a more scientific approach in the 1960s, recruiting biological and agricultural researchers to support the development of new products. This included recruitment in Taiwan, where CP was also developing strong links. And by 1970–1, at the peak of the Vietnam war, CP established a formal joint venture with leading US poultry producer Arbor Acres, long a CP supplier, for marketing and technical co-operation.

In summary, CP's business development in its first four decades was rooted in steadily expanding areas of agribusiness. In addition to a large and successful trading network, the primary key to CP's success was superior technology, especially the better seeds and animal breeds developed by Chia Ekchor, or later acquired from more advanced foreign companies, including some in the US and Japan. From this base, the group expanded and added value through vertical and horizontal diversification in the 1950s and 1960s. In the 1960s and 1970s, the group continued to focus on feeds and poultry farming, and farm products distribution. Some chicken farming was apparently launched in Malaysia and Singapore, though not on as large a scale as in Thailand. At the same time, several attempts were made to enter manufacturing and other fields. Jaran's jute bag factories could be considered horizontal integration. Larger feed mills were also constructed.

One can see that, at least in Thailand, CP had become conscious by the 1950s of what would become an important strategy in the group's development: beyond offering better products, capturing superior market position would provide pricing power in the market. Strength in the marketplace not only gave CP a competitive edge, but the beginnings of important political leverage as well.

While the group's expansion in South-East Asia took place, it appears that CP continued to maintain trading ties with China. Though these may have degenerated after Chia Ekchor left Shantou in 1958, there is some suggestion that two-way trade with China continued in the 1960s. If that is true, then their links were never fully cut, and may have enhanced CP's 're-entry' into the Chinese market in the 1980s.

The most important move for the group in the 1970s was its major investments in Indonesia and then China in the integrated feed mill and poultry industry. The first investment was in Indonesia in 1971, with the establishment of PT Charoen Pokphand Indonesia. Over the next decade, CP became the leading poultry feed producer and chicken processor in Indonesia. In 1979, CP launched into China on the same basis.

Both moves were related to policy changes in each host country. As Soeharto's 'New Order' regime stabilized, Indonesia opened up poultry farming to corporate investors, rather than restricting it to individual farmers. In China, Deng Xiaoping's open door policy was launched. In addition, both countries offered huge untapped markets where per capita meat consumption was very low, and was expected to grow as it had in Thailand as the Thai economy developed. For CP, the growth of chicken consumption in Thailand validated the lesson of the US: that whatever the culture, as a society becomes more wealthy, its people eat more meat, and for price, taste and nutritional reasons chicken becomes an important part of their diet.

CP also learned the social and political value of its approach, originally based heavily on contract farming: it supplies farmers with chicks and all the inputs and buys the chickens for processing once they have grown to a certain size. Although contract farming did not really make farmers rich, because CP controlled all supply and pricing of inputs, as well as the output, it did provide them with a greater and more stable income. Such stability was highly valued by governments in Thailand, Indonesia and China.

To develop its business in Indonesia, CP sent Ekchor's third son, Sumet, who eventually took Indonesian citizenship and an Indonesian wife.[7] The business was launched with support from business groups close to President Soeharto, and some unconfirmed sources have said that CP provided the technical support for Soeharto relative Probosutedjo to start his own poultry business at the same time – a means of fending off accusations of monopoly-building without losing market control.

In China, according to one company official, CP was ready to invest as soon as the Deng policy was initiated. The official said that the group holds the very first foreign investment permits, numbered 0001, issued in both Shenzhen and Shantou. This suggests that the group had indeed maintained trade and investment contacts with China over a long period, and so could enter the newly-opened market with confidence. CP's first investments were in feed mills, together with the US's Continental Grains group, which provided advanced technology, against CP's willingness and *guanxi*.

In both countries, as the economies grew, so did chicken consumption, and CP was able to expand its feed mill and poultry businesses rapidly. In China today, CP has feed mills and poultry farm and processing operations in nearly every province. In Indonesia, expansion has not been as fast, and there is some suggestion that, at the end of the 1980s, CP was still viewed as an outsider that had uncomfortable pricing power in an important industry too far outside the control and influence of the Indonesian government. Though details are unclear, this apparently led to some political squeezing of the business by Indonesia-based competitors, discouraging CP from much further expansion in Indonesia. In the 1990s, CP seemed to de-emphasize its future in Indonesia, turning most efforts to China. Sumet left Jakarta, settling in Hong Kong to oversee China operations around 1989.

Equally important in CP's middle-period growth was the launch of chicken exports. This was only a small part of the business in Thailand until, in the early 1980s, the Thai government was able to force Japan to cut tariffs on chicken imported from Thailand to a level more in line with Japan's tariffs for US-sourced chicken. Thai exports – dominated by CP – of frozen, boned chicken to Japan rocketed, stealing away much of US sales. It was significant in Thailand as a diversification of exports into a new area of processed foods. Frozen chicken became a major Thai export category.

CP's diversification during this middle period built on its existing strengths in agribusiness. The group attempted to replicate its success in the chicken industry with farmed black tiger prawns, an industry started by others in Taiwan, but adopted by CP. The group plunged into developing prawn farms and support industries, including feed mills, research and development, and processing and export of prawns as a commodity rather than a luxury food item. CP soon became the world's leading farmer and exporter of farm prawns, again, as with chickens, cloning its integrated business organization in China, Indonesia and other countries.

The change in economies and trade patterns in Asia in the 1980s enhanced CP's growth in agribusiness and food processing. As Japan, Hong Kong, Singapore and Taiwan became more wealthy, their demand for raw and processed food imports grew. CP moved into many areas of processing and exporting, from raw fruits to prepared chicken and shrimp dinners, exporting to richer countries from Thailand, Indonesia, China and elsewhere. This began to give the group the appearance of a truly independent multinational, one which, like Japanese groups, can allocate production and trade to various sites regardless of respective national interests.

CP attempted to diversify away from agribusiness in the 1960s and 1970s, but only on a small scale. A joint venture in the 1960s with a half-Thai half-American named Campbell made the group importers and distributors of Ovaltine and of American refrigerators, among other items. For unexplained reasons this did not work out and the business was left to CP's partner. In the mid-late 1970s, CP linked up with several Japanese companies in joint ventures, the most significant of which was in paint trading, and then production, with Nippon Paint. But committed diversification away from agribusiness only truly began in the mid-1980s, after Dhanin Chearavanont took over as chief executive.

Family issues: who and what is CP today?

CP as a group originally consisted of the businesses Chia Ekchor and brother Chia Siew-whooy left to their families. According to one of Siew-whooy's sons working in the group, Wanlop Chearavanont, the business legacy was all considered part of one family group, 50 per cent owned by Ekchor's four sons and 50 per cent owned by Siew-whooy's nine sons. Wanlop insisted that any company not reflecting this arrangement on its board or in its share-holding structure cannot be considered part of the CP Group (*FEER*, 24 June 1993). The share-holding structure of CP Group Co., the group management company, partially follows this pattern. Dhanin and his three brothers comprise four of the nine board members; Wanlop and his brother Cherdchai account for two seats;

the rest are occupied by three key CP group managers. Of 23 individual share-holders, the first ten are Ekchor's four sons and six of Siew-whooy's sons.[8]

Confusion arises, however, from the rarity with which other group companies, clearly managed from CP offices by CP officials, share a similar share-holding arrangement. Many partially reflect it, and some only marginally so. One reason is that CP has never had a central holding company (CP Group Co. is mainly a management company, with some equity holdings in subsidiaries). Instead, the bulk of shares in hundreds of companies, from operating farms to larger industrial firms, to numerous shell companies themselves holding two or three others, are all held directly by the core individuals of CP group management and some of the Chearavanont family. Dhanin and Sumet, for instance, are often the main and direct shareholders of small, individual farms that are grouped only for management purposes (not ownership) under another company. In many such companies there is no obvious presence of any other brothers or cousins. Share-holdings are not consolidated through a pyramid structure that follows management structure. This appears to be changing in the mid-1990s, but only slowly.

An easy way, then, to identify CP would be to identify either or both Dhanin and Sumet, respectively CP Group Co.'s chairman and president, as significant shareholders in the firm, for it appears that anything they have become involved with they have included under the CP umbrella – the businesses are supervised from CP offices. Still, that does not satisfy Wanlop's definition of a CP company, that all of the two brothers' sons are represented among core shareholders. But there are few companies like this. If it was true in the past, the lack of such companies today might be explained by adjustments to share-holdings made by the individual heirs of Ekchor and Siew-whooy, through shares sold, rights issues not being taken up, and shares further passed on as inheritances. Public listing of agribusiness operations has likely distorted share-holdings further. An additional possibility, for which there is some evidence, is that individuals among Ekchor's and Siew-whooy's heirs started their own ventures which were then brought under the CP umbrella, but remained specific 'projects' of the brothers or cousins. The usefulness of this would be to give a picture of a united family, retaining close family bonds, while allowing individuals not involved in top level CP group management to run their own businesses.

Nevertheless, the incident which brought about the author's conversation with Wanlop appears to support the argument that what is CP is in fact what Dhanin and Sumet control, along with their top managers. The conversation occurred immediately following the 1993 fire at the Kader Industrial (Thailand) toy factory in which 188 workers were killed. Although the factory appeared to have CP links, specifically through Jaran and his son-in-law, Wanlop insisted it was not a CP group company, because it did not have the classic family ownership structure. At the time, CP also denied Kader Industrial (Thailand) was part of the group, claiming no connections at all. Subsequently, and after top CP officials denied any personal or group link to Kader, documents surfaced that demonstrated that control of 40 per cent of the Kader factory was held by Honbo Investments, a shell holding company in the hands of Dhanin, Sumet, and a core group of Dhanin's top lieutenants who manage all CP operations. Honbo held contractual responsibility for building and operating the factory. (Another 40 per cent was held by the joint-venture partner, the Kader Toys group of Hong Kong's wealthy Ting family, and 20 per cent by Taiwanese individuals contracted by CP to manage the plant (*FEER*, 24 June 1993).) The Kader factory was on CP-owned land, next to a company (Thai Chiu Fu Co. Ltd) that CP acknowledged owning, and which had a similar share-holding structure.

The point here is not to harp on CP's role in the Kader tragedy. Instead, it is to demonstrate that, whatever Wanlop may have said, the reality of CP control, of the group's definition, centres on Dhanin and Sumet. One can safely identify CP by, in addition to the names Chia Tai and Zheng Da, the presence of Dhanin and Sumet, and the core management team, as directors and as principal shareholders. The core management team, Dhanin's lieutenants, has for more than two decades comprised the following executives:

Thirayuth Pitya-Isarakul
Chingchai Lohawatanakul
Eam Ngamdamronk
Prasert Poongkumarn
Thanakorn Seriburi
Min Tienworn.

All but Eam are top shareholders in CP Group Co. Ltd; Prasert, Min and Thirayutt are on CP Group's board. All but Eam were principal shareholders of Honbo Investments. In addition, Dhanin, Sumet and their two brothers Montri and Jaran, and three other relatives, were the other principal Honbo shareholders. Despite denials by the group, it is hard to see why this share-holding structure, virtually the same as all other group operations begun since the mid-1980s, would constitute anything but a CP group operation.

Since the mid-1980s, a few more names have entered into the core management circle and thus also signal CP's ownership of companies:

Adirek Sripatak
Sunthorn Arunanondchai
Ajva Taulananda
Veeravat Kanchanadul
Korsak Chairasmisak.

In almost every clearly-identifiable CP firm, a mix of these names, along with Dhanin and Sumet, appear as directors and principal shareholders. Thus it should be fair to say that other firms not so clearly identifiable as CP, but with the same structure, are also part of CP. Furthermore, it is probably fair to say that what Dhanin and Sumet take part in is always CP, or represents CP interests. Neither appears to get involved in personal projects or take personally-held, small shareholdings in someone else's business.

Dhanin's and Sumet's constant presence signals another evolutionary change: that Chia Ekchor's family have taken control of the business, while Chia Siew-whooy's heirs are increasingly marginalized, both as directors and shareholders. Two or three of Siew-whooy's sons still take an active part, but Chia Ekchor's other sons, Jaran, the former chairman (now mostly retired) and Montri, the group's principal legal advisor,[9] still exert a greater degree of influence. In the third generation, Dhanin's and Sumet's sons are the main family members on the fast track to leadership. Perhaps another sign of Dhanin's side of the family taking over the group is the naming of the group division which oversees its medium and heavy industry investments in China: Ek-Chor Industries, named after their father.

In 1995, Dhanin spoke of retiring or working at a slower pace. There has been little sign of this, or of relinquishing control, as he and Sumet and the old lieutenants still actively manage most operations. Both he and Sumet have put their sons into the more recent of the group's businesses: super-store retailing, and the telecommunications and entertainment industries, both of which Dhanin apparently sees as key businesses in the group's future. None of the sons has accumulated enough experience or leadership ability to assume the role of CP's chief executive, and it is assumed Dhanin and/or Sumet will be in that position for at least five and possibly ten more years, if not longer.

Strategies for success

CP's commercial success in agribusiness in Thailand and, later, China and Indonesia, has depended upon the following key points.

Gaining adequate market share in mass-produced consumer goods to achieve price-setting power, while avoiding establishing a monopoly

CP wants to engage in markets of mass consumer items, to tap the rise of lower and middle-class disposable incomes as countries develop. Market share is the first goal when CP gets into a business, and CP tries to achieve roughly a 50 per cent share of any market it is in, so that the group can determine prices without this becoming a social or political liability. Competitors cannot sell if they price themselves higher than CP; if they undercut CP, they still cannot force CP out of the market because it necessarily supplies so much of demand. Yet CP makes a point of not trying to destroy competitors, but only to limit their market power.

Using market pricing power and vertical integration to control margins

The group maximizes its profits in the chicken market, for instance, through vertical integration. CP breeds chicks, produces feed for them, produces the pharmaceuticals they require, raises the chickens to maturity,[10] slaughters and processes the meat, and distributes the meat and eggs. Going even further, CP is one of the largest traders in ingredients for animal feeds, and develops and distributes hybrid maize seeds to farmers, who often commit to sell their crops to CP.

This has several benefits. First, because CP is the largest producer and supplier of inputs into the poultry industry, especially of feeds, and because its inputs are all of standard and reliable quality, CP is also the main supplier of inputs for competing chicken producers. Hence the group intimately understands competitors' costs and competitiveness. Being the dominant player in each stage makes CP the main price setter at every step of the production process, as well as in the final retail market. Most importantly, though, the group has control of its margins at every step of the ladder, on each and every input, and pricing power helps to ensure that those margins remain higher than any competitor's.

Using size to influence public policy in its favour

CP's size and pricing power brings it important political influence in a country like Thailand where the government is often too weak to control market forces itself. This power helps CP defend its own margins at any turn of the market. Crop and livestock prices, for example, are politically sensitive due to the effect on farm incomes and on urban consumer satisfaction. Farmers, especially, carry political power in Thai elections, and so traditionally, political leaders are sensitive to the need to protect farm incomes.

Thai farmers produce many of the main ingredients for the domestic production of animal feeds like CP's, but not all, and never enough. Imports are always required, especially of protein additives like maize, soy bean meal and fishmeal. To protect local farm incomes, duties are kept high on these imports. But if protection is inordinately high – if domestic prices for inputs are allowed to rise much beyond international market prices – the cost of producing poultry in Thailand can become uncompetitively expensive. Import duties on feed inputs must therefore be regularly adjusted and moderated to both protect the livelihood of local farmers and, conversely, to prevent imports from becoming too expensive and forcing up the costs of livestock and meat for consumers.

CP's role in this is that its own calculations on feed and downstream meat costs, and acceptable margins for production at various levels, are the principal referents for the government in determining import duties on feed ingredients. If CP says domestic feed inputs are too expensive relative to world costs, and that domestic supplies are too small, the government reacts by lowering import duties. Government calculations are based on figures supplied by CP; estimates of demand and supply come from CP; and government officials' explanations of why the duties rise or fall often refer to CP's own costs. In effect, the government needs CP to understand what is happening in the industry and how to adjust policy. Being indispensable helps CP protect its margins.

Using transfer pricing and other accounting techniques to mask real costs and margins, minimize taxes and accumulate capital

Even if CP is the main source of information the government uses to determine policy, the government does not likely know the full story. Vertical integration allows CP to use multiple invoicing and transfer pricing to hide costs and margins, and minimize taxes. The group maintains hundreds of companies, some operating and others simply shells, through which intra-group trade is processed. This is typical behaviour among large trading-based conglomerates, and is an important tool for building capital resources for further investment. CP's impressive mastery of this led one Thai central bank official to complain privately to the author that, of all Thai companies and business groups, CP is the only one that the central bank and the ministry of finance are unable to understand, in terms of capital resources, capital movement, and profits.[11]

Avoiding competition with other major Sino-Thai business groups

Until the economic boom which started in 1987 changed the business environment, the large Sino-Thai business families generally stuck to unwritten rules about directly competing with each other. For decades CP has stayed out of steel, the automotive industry, department store retailing, banking, liquor and soft drinks, sugar, tapioca and rice milling and trading, construction, and textiles – the main business areas of other prominent Sino-Thai families. Even as the boom caused markets to expand too rapidly for the old families to keep up themselves, and created new niches in old industries, CP mainly pushed into new businesses. Despite numerous opportunities, CP has respected the old rules.

In Thailand, CP still has not taken a position in banking, although opportunities have surfaced. The group has only quietly and gently gone into the rice business, and only for speciality products, even as other rice tycoons like Hong Yiah Seng and Soon Hua Seng have diversified out of the trade. CP entered construction only in 1995, still avoiding competition with civil works contractors like Italthai; and it has stayed away from general retailing, the province of the Chirathivat family's Central group, even while pushing into supermarkets, club superstores, and category killer stores, all new businesses for Thailand. CP did declare a tentative link with Central competitor The Mall in the mid-1990s, but this was real estate-based, targeted for outside of Bangkok, and at any rate, it appeared that the idea had lost steam by 1997. CP's respect for these divisions in Thailand is underscored by its willingness to enter most of these businesses in China: in the 1990s the group quickly entered banking, liquor, and general retailing, among others.

Tapping capital markets for expansion funds

In the 1980s, CP began to list certain agribusiness and trading units on stock exchanges in Indonesia, Hong Kong, Thailand and Taiwan. These were solid, ongoing businesses, and the group was able to raise a significant amount of capital from them, though it appeared cautious about opening itself up to public scrutiny. From this experience, however, CP became much more enthusiastic about the resources of capital markets by 1988–9, and moved to publicly list new, unproven businesses, such as Vinythai, Orient Telecoms and Technology, Ek Chor China Motorcycles, TelecomAsia, and Hong Kong Fortune. One listing, TelecomAsia, was so hugely successful that CP was able to keep a controlling 70 per cent share of a US$5 billion company without taking on any significant level of debt and at a net cost of roughly half the initial par price of the shares (Handley 1996).

There is a negative side, however, to the way CP has used capital markets to fund expansion. Since their listing, many of the CP subsidiaries have been significant disappointments to investors. Growth is slow, and earnings growth even slower, despite CP Group's rapid advancement into new and seemingly very profitable businesses. Share prices of the newly listed, non-agricultural businesses have performed badly, due to profits in each that were far lower than projected, or, in the case of Vinythai and TelecomAsia, due to large operating losses.

This has left stock analysts unanimously suspicious that the cream of profits in these listed agribusiness companies, and possibly the newer firms, is siphoned away for group needs through transfer pricing, and they complain that the company accounts and operations are never transparent (Friedland 1989; Handley 1990). The broader result is higher costs of funding for CP: investors are more doubtful whether their investments will provide adequate returns, making it difficult for CP to go back to the markets to raise more capital. Likewise, CP's maintaining a shield over its inner workings and financial structure makes bankers equally suspicious. As a result, although the group appears to have a pristine record in paying its debts, it also pays interest rates on bank loans 100–200 basis points higher than what is paid by more transparent Thai conglomerates like Siam Cement.

Building and using **guanxi** *to obtain concessions*

Dhanin is a master of the political connection: he does not appear to enter any situation without having political support sewn up on every side possible. His alliances in China, through everything from sponsoring trips and private projects to employing family members, span the range of Zhao Ziyang to Deng Xiaoping to Yang Shangkun. In Thailand, he is said to be the largest contributor to every political party. Honorary (paid) and full positions in his group have gone to top diplomats, the head of the military, the King's Privy Councillors, leading bureaucrats and family members of numerous politicians. Dhanin's caution in developing business in Myanmar and Vietnam, both countries with huge potential for CP's chicken and prawn agribusiness, have reportedly been due to the inability to eliminate all opposition to the group, not because those economies are under-achievers.

In Thailand, employees of CP include:
A former head of the Petroleum Authority
A former head of the national planning agency, NESDB
A former army chief and former prime minister
The wife of the current deputy prime minister
A former minister of finance
The wife of the army chief of staff
A former foreign minister and current privy councillor
The daughter of a former prime minister.

Growth and diversification goals and strategies: pursuing the *chaebols*

CP's modern phase of rapid growth and diversification coincided with Dhanin's rise as *de facto* chief executive officer in the 1980s, replacing Jaran. During the 1980s, CP continued to look for new sites to replicate its feed mill, poultry- and shrimp-raising, and food processing industries, including Vietnam, Myanmar, Mexico, Turkey, Spain, India, and so on. This expansion of its core business was not neglected. However, Dhanin led the group into industries completely new for the group, as if he felt that agribusiness and food processing no longer held much of a future for the group if it was to become a global player. Agribusiness was never forsworn, but it was not considered the path to real prominence and power.

Dhanin's apparent goals in diversification were reflected in an interview given to journalist Suthichai Yoon on the Nation News Talk programme in Bangkok in 1994. In it he expressed admiration for South Korea's *chaebols* and how the Korean government had assisted in building them. He then complained that the Thai government does not see the importance of building large *chaebol*-like companies (*Nation News Talk* 1994). Dhanin noted that after the Second World War, Korea was poor and its companies small, not unlike Thailand, but that through focused government effort, Korea was able to develop quickly and build powerful companies like Samsung, Hyundai and Daewoo. He added that small countries cannot compete with large ones like the US without having such large companies. To him, this explains why the Japanese are able to compete successfully against the US. Dhanin then said that CP cannot hope to grow so large in Thailand because of government unwillingness to support the group the way Seoul supported the *chaebols*. Alternatively, if CP must grow large on its own, Thailand is too small a platform to support it; on its own, CP has maximized its potential in Thailand already. 'If CP is only in Thailand, it cannot be big', he said. Thus CP looks to China as a platform for growth that can help make it a conglomerate with the size and strength of the *chaebols*.

Still, CP's diversification was first focused on Thailand, and derived from the group's acute understanding of consumer market behaviour in rapidly developing countries. CP first pursued food-related industries which had been proven in the US, and later Japan, Hong Kong and Taiwan. The target as before was penetrating middle-class consumer markets, getting a large market presence for price-setting power, and beating the competition on quality.

But the group made an important step in China in 1985, when it set up a motorcycle manufacturing joint venture with Shanghai's largest industrial firm, Shanghai Automotive Industry Corp. The joint venture, Ek Chor China Motorcycle Co., was later said by Dhanin to be the group's first step toward the goal of entering the automobile industry (*Nation News Talk* 1996). The next step appeared to come slowly, however, for it was only in 1994–6 that the group moved into manufacturing automotive parts in China and Thailand. This perhaps reflects a caution born of not having state backing and protection for such a project. Other groups and governments in Asia during the period, like Malaysia and Indonesia, were avidly forming ventures with existing major manufacturers in order to build their own car industries and acquire technology. None has shown unqualified success, if the cost of government support and the lack of major technology transfer is figured in. By 1997, when Asian car production capacity (and the world's at that) appeared to be far beyond demand, CP itself appeared only lightly committed to the industry, suggesting Dhanin had perhaps revised his ambitions in this regard.

Beyond that first plunge into motorcycles, CP's milestones of diversification include, by date of being initiated:

- Retail food outlets (Kentucky Fried Chicken, Five Star Roast Chicken, Chester's Chicken, and later others): mid-1980s
- Motorcycle manufacture (China): 1986
- Convenience stores (7-Eleven, Thailand): 1987
- Real estate (Siam Fortune, Hong Kong Fortune, CP Land; Thailand and China): 1988
- Retail supermarkets, superstores (Thailand):1990–3
- Petrochemicals (Vinythai: Thailand): 1990
- Beer production and distribution (China): 1990
- Non-motorcycle automotive (China, Thailand): 1990
- Telecommunications (Telecom Holdings, TelecomAsia, Oriental Telecoms, UTV; Thailand and China): 1990–1
- Cosmetics production and distribution (China): 1992
- Petroleum refining and retail distribution (Thailand, China): 1993
- Satellite operation (China/Asia): 1993
- Banking and finance (Vietnam Joint Agricultural Bank, TM Bank in China): 1993–5
- Superstores (China): 1994
- Non-motorcycle automotive (Thailand): 1995.

CP has entered many of these businesses not by plan but through entrepreneurial opportunism: the opportunity appeared, and the group grabbed it. These and other diversifications combine both internally generated initiatives, like the Thai telecoms project and the move into petrol stations in Thailand (Petro Asia), and ventures in which CP was sought out as partner, like the petrochemicals ventureVinythai, with Belgium's Solvay group. Some, like power generation, appear to be both: foreign partners sought CP's support for its apparent political muscle, and CP itself decided to go into this business and cast about for experienced foreign partners. Likewise for investments in food processing, as with a Japanese-invested food additives plant: the Japanese needed a good partner and the additives fit with CP's food processing. CP hoped to learn the technology; the Japanese gained access to CP's market and distribution networks.

Most of CP's China projects outside of agribusiness have been in partnerships or joint ventures there.[12] Local companies, like China Petroleum (Sinopec) have sought out CP as an expansion partner for its capital resources. CP also brought initial capital and marketing expertise to the Shanghai authority in control of developing the Pudong area, resulting in CP gaining priority access (itself and through a joint venture with the authority) to the area's prime land in the Liujiazui district. From these, in addition to financial benefits, CP has sought to obtain market access, some managerial control, and the benefit of future connections.

On the other hand, foreign companies have sought CP as a door-opener and a protector in China, and from these, CP has assumed the potential to gain access to the partner's technology and better management that could eventually be transferred to CP's own ventures.[13] In addition, many Thai companies have approached CP to provide access to China, and have formed ventures with CP. CP has mostly taken a less aggressive posture in these, not seeking benefits such as technology, and leaving management in the hands of the partner. Examples include Shanghai area joint ventures with Thai Gypsum Products and with Thailand's Natural Park Development Co. CP acts as a facilitating agent and a benevolent big brother in what are almost always very small ventures, insignificant in CP's world.

The industries noted above only cover the largest ventures actually started up. The impression of wanton diversification is better conveyed by scores of announcements of big projects that have yet to materialize, like power generation, industrial estates in the region, computer chip fabrication, restaurants in Europe, and heavy duty truck production, among others; and smaller investments which did materialize, such as factories making shoes, raincoats, clothing, toys and PVC pipes; or projects in television programming and production, studio recording, highway development and management, and luggage manufacturing.

Dhanin has spoken of other goals in diversification, 'industries of the future', that he would like to pursue. These include biotechnology, aerospace, electronics (computer chip production specifically) and deep sea mining (*Nation News Talk* 1996). Only biotechnology could be explored based on existing expertise in the CP group. Although the firm intentions of the group are not clear for the other areas, CP is known to have investigated investing in a new Thai airline; it has invested in a Chinese satellite company; and in 1996, company officials spoke of the possibility of building a computer chip fabrication plant in China.

As argued above, in order to implement this strategy of diversification and growth, quickly establishing their place especially in China, CP has turned more to reliance on connections than other resources in the 1990s. Other approaches, such as openly competing for deals, exploiting internal technological, market or management advantages, building large from small, buying up failed companies, or other methods of expansion and diversification are less apparent. In contrast, other large ethnic Chinese business groups like those of Hong Kong's Li Kashing or Malaysia's Robert Kuok have moved more slowly, making strategic investments mostly where they have a particular expertise or where they have made a particular commitment to diversification. Both also tap their good connections, but hardly to the extent of CP. Many of the major CP diversifications, however, have had nothing to do with internal advantages and everything to do with acquiring concessions, mostly through secretive negotiated means (not publicly contested): TelecomAsia, Vinythai, Don Muang Tollway, Thai LNG Co. (formed to import liquefied gas for use in power plants), Shanghai real estate, APT Satellite, and attempts to get into telephone networks in various cities in China.

A second emphasis in CP's diversification has been a trend towards employing large amounts of capital in real estate and associated developments. In both Thailand and China, CP has aimed at developing numerous large shopping and commercial complexes, targeting the rising spending power of the population as the economy grows. As CP officials describe it, these complexes are designed to include as major tenants CP-controlled businesses, such as its Lotus and Makro department stores, its fast food outlets, and even CP-invested multiplex cinemas. This can be construed as an extension of CP's original vertical integration approach. In most countries, however, the developers of such shopping centres and malls are not also their prime tenants. In CP's case, it is not clear whether the group has decided to stake its future more on its real estate business or is just facilitating its development in the retail marketing industry. It is not possible to determine how many resources CP is putting into this sector, because far more projects have been announced than are actually materializing, but it appears that CP has shifted towards emphasizing this area possibly more than any other of its new businesses.

Diversification and expansion: mixed results

CP's strategy of rapid diversification and growth has not been clearly successful. Their agribusiness continues to be very strong, and property investments appear to have been very lucrative. But in other areas, especially in China – a particularly difficult place to do business, even for CP – the results have been mixed at best. The problem is often that diversification has been based too much on entrepreneurial opportunism and obtaining concessions through connections, and too little on existing internal group skills and attentive, capable management.

Retailing in Thailand, an important thrust in the late 1980s, has been slow to bloom. CP's first moves, into 7-Eleven, Sunny's Supermarkets, Chester's Chicken fast food, Lotus Superstore and Makro, and other franchise operations, have not proven themselves. For all but Makro, there is significant competition. 7-Eleven has dominated its competition, but in pricing power, CP still is said to lack volume and strong margins. In 1993–4, a shake-up of the management suggested that overhead costs had been huge due to poor management. In addition, franchisees were unhappy, marginally profitable, and angry over other shops CP itself had opened. Sunny's Supermarket, launched in 1989, only opened four stores in six years, a period when the supermarket business in general grew rapidly in Thailand. In an interview, the manager of this business conceded that the launch had been poorly executed. Similarly, Chester's Chicken, a brand launched by CP to compete with Kentucky Fried Chicken and other fast food outlets, also only opened a handful of stores over several years.

By contrast, Makro has been very successful, but its management has been completely in the hands of the Dutch partners who own the Makro group. Nor have there been any real competitors coming into the market. Lotus, CP's own brand of (non-membership) superstore, started slowly and with poor management until CP recruited experienced managers from the US. Faced with strong competition from both foreign and local brands, Lotus' expansion has been slower and the stores less profitable than expected, according to industry analysts.

In China, the retailing business is also just getting started, and no details on the performance of Lotus and other outlets are known. Reports suggest that Lotus is quite successful in Shanghai, as is a seafood restaurant CP opened in the city. Significantly, however, in areas like Guangdong and Shanghai where CP has opened various outlets, competition is intense from international investors, and especially from Hong Kong and Taiwan retailers with much greater experience than CP.

CP's failed joint venture with the US's Walmart group must be noted. Walmart had long used CP to help source Chinese-made goods to sell in the US, and Walmart had hoped CP's access to and knowledge of China – and Thailand secondarily – would help the US group make a strong stand in China. However, Walmart's unwillingness to cede management control and technology to their partners, and the inability of both sides to match corporate cultures, led to a break-up just as they were beginning to open China and Hong Kong outlets in 1995. Walmart has entered China on its own, instead. As CP had hoped to gain a significant market position in China from its link-up with Walmart, having Walmart now as a competitor must count as something of a failure. CP sources say the collapse of the partnership stemmed very much from lack of CP management attention.

In industry, CP has been less successful. Its maiden venture into petrochemicals, Vinythai, a joint venture with Solvay in Thailand, has lost money for three years. Announced large petrochemical projects in Hainan, Shanghai and elsewhere have never materialized, and CP officials said in 1996 it would no longer pursue this industry. Prior to its listing on the New York Stock Exchange in 1994, Ek Chor China Motorcycles was said to be very profitable. After the listing, the share price languished along with the company's profits. Strong competition, inability to export a large number of the motorcycles, and Chinese government policy restricting motorcycle ownership, have limited the success of this business (*International Herald Tribune* 2 November 1995; various stock broker reports).

Other sectors

Telecommunications: CP's financing of TelecomAsia, the 1991 concession to install telephone lines in Bangkok, was hugely successful, making CP's own investment cost in the business minimal (Handley 1996). But since listing on the Thai stock exchange in 1993, the company has steadily lost money: costs have been double projections, income half, and CP's expectations that its political connections would allow it to add a lucrative cellular phone business to its concession have not been fulfilled. Even if CP's own costs were low, the business has not generated profits as expected, and to increase its value (by building up cable TV services, for example), investment must increase.

Likewise, CP's investment in the Chinese government-controlled APT Satellite has also been more or less a failure: one launch exploded; another was very late; competition is strong, and their technology is poor in comparison to other regional satellite firms, especially Hong Kong's Asiasat.

CP had expected it would obtain a major telecoms concession in Shanghai, especially for the Pudong district. This was an important goal for CP's partner in TelecomAsia, Nynex, because Nynex expected CP could take both into the lucrative China market. CP was extremely confident: when Beijing announced in mid-1993 that foreign companies would be barred from obtaining telecommunications concessions, CP told bankers in Hong Kong it had several concessions already and was raising financing for them (*FEER* 1 July 1993). Yet the important concessions never materialized, although CP continued to pursue a role in Shanghai telephone services in 1996, and had partnered with the Chongqing, Sichuan telephone authority on a local refurbishment plan which CP hoped would help it get a foothold in the business.

Petroleum: In 1993, CP announced with great fanfare a joint venture with China Petroleum Corp., the large refiner known as Sinopec. This was to launch CP's Petro Asia petrol stations in south China and also to build a large refinery. Four years later, only a handful of stations have been built and the refinery project appears to be stalled.

Energy: In 1995, CP partnered several local Thai and foreign firms to try to obtain a concession for a local power station. In a transparent public tender, their bid failed to make the short list. CP followed this by joining several local businesses to form a company for the import of liquefied natural gas, which came under question in early 1997 as government policy appeared to shift against the scheme. CP had also been linked with Norway's Statoil in a proposed venture in oil and gas exploration in Myanmar, but nothing came of this (*Burma News Net* 10 January 1996).

Toll road: In 1990, CP joined several other large, well-connected Thai groups as a minority partner to build Don Muang Tollway, a local toll road under the B-O-T concession scheme. The economics of the road were originally poor, according to various experts; but in the event, the project was also hurt by delays and cost overruns due specifically to poor management and inability to obtain easy financing given the risks. Once the road opened in late 1994, the company was unable to service interest payments on its debt from toll collections, and asked the government to bail it out. This proved politically difficult, and though the government did provide some comfort, the road continues to be a loss-maker.

A number of minor ventures of CP's have also flopped: China-based clothing and shoe factories, and Thai toy-manufacturing plants, for instance. In other ventures it is too early, or data was unavailable, to assess CP's performance.

Alliances

CP has generally avoided long-term alliances with other significantly large, ethnic Chinese business groups, even as it avoids clashing with them head on. One does not see, for instance, the Lamsam or Sophonpanich banking families taking a minority share in CP businesses, as they do in those of many of their clients. Nor does CP seem to take share-holdings in banks. CP clearly prefers to have management and financial control unless the venture is very small, such as those with other Thai businesses using CP's coattails to enter the China market.

One exception appears to have been a relationship with the President Group in Taiwan in the early-mid 1980s. What this relationship was is not known, but it gave CP some investment exposure to Makro in Taiwan, and CP subsequently partnered Makro (but not President) in Thailand. President and CP opened an instant noodle factory in China, but after that both opened other noodle plants without the other's involvement. Both compete in retailing in China.

Otherwise, CP's limited experience with other ethnic Chinese firms has not been good. One example is the above-mentioned Don Muang Tollway. In this case, CP did not keep management control, and lost tens of millions of dollars on the project due to poor management by some prominent partners (the Tejapaibul, Srifuenfung and Phanicheva families), who boldly asked CP to bail them out after the government declined to. Another example of a bad tie-up is Siam Fortune and Hong Kong Fortune, a joint venture in property development and management with the Univest (Boondicharoen) group, which ended in divorce, with the two sides splitting the properties. The Bangkok business community views this as the fault of the Univest side. Yet another link-up which went sour was with the Hong Kong family of Dennis Ting, which owns Kader Industrial, the toy maker. Following the tragic fire in the joint-venture Kader plant in Thailand, the Tings actively pushed the blame onto CP and denied culpability. Refusing to get into a finger-pointing war, CP was said to take responsibility for all compensation (but only secretly) when the Tings refused, and the relationship has predictably broken up.

A successful, but limited link-up has been with the M Thai group, of the Virametheekul family. M Thai has long had trading links with powerful Chinese military organizations such as China Northern Industries (Norinco), and imports Chinese military supplies into Thailand. Some Bangkok observers have said that M Thai's own connections have helped facilitate CP's growth in China. Dhanin's daughter married a Virametheekul son in 1994. Business links between the two, however, are not extensive. M Thai was able to start a local Chinese bank, TM Bank, in Shantou in 1992 with Thai Military Bank as partner. This did not develop well, and in 1996 CP took the bank over and moved it to Shanghai, with M Thai still a partner. In other areas, however, particularly M Thai's large real estate projects, CP appears not to be involved. On the other hand, the M Thai link probably helped facilitate CP's establishment of businesses in northern China with Norinco. Norinco is a partner in Ek Chor China Motorcycles' Luoyang manufacturing operations, and CP has a joint pharmaceuticals investment with Norinco.

However, the links with Norinco, which is much more powerful than CP, are limited; CP appears to shy away from too much dependence on very powerful Chinese industrial groups.

Partnerships with Western firms have been, as noted above, based on CP's desire for technology and management expertise. But CP's aim has been to transfer this as quickly as possible with the hopes of striking out on its own, rather than defending the long-term partnership. Hence partnerships in farm businesses from the early 1970s, with Dekalb Co. and Arbor Acres, both of the US, did not survive into the 1990s, though CP's own activities in the areas of the partnerships continued to grow.

CP's partnership with Nynex in TelecomAsia has been successful, but only due to Nynex's low expectations. Nynex allowed CP ownership control and financial responsibility, in return for equity, very basic shares of cash flow, and management service fees. Even then, at the beginning of the project CP tried to limit the number of Nynex staff involved, insisting that its own people (none of whom had any experience in the business) could manage the establishment of a two million line network. In the end, apparently after serious debate, CP had to accept Nynex control of project implementation, and triple the number of Nynex staff beyond what the group had anticipated.

Other alliances have been rocky. The falling out with Walmart is noted above. Rumours in Bangkok in April 1997 also suggested difficulties between CP and Makro, over management control and over Chinese investment plans. Makro was said to be unhappy with CP's emphasis on its own Lotus superstores in expansion in China. While both sides denied any problem, industry sources said there is some tension, the reasons unclear, between the two.

Management issues

Modernizing management is one of the important challenges facing CP as it grows and diversifies so quickly. This aspect has been neglected in favour of reliance on opaque accounting methods, quick-fire entrepreneurial opportunism, and use of connections to deal with the challenges of growth.

Up until the late 1980s, CP's management structure was very effective. Each operation, each farm was its own little company, and an individual was put in charge to make it work efficiently. Because the operations were small, more or less based on proven formulas, and controlled in part by the operation's dependence on other CP units for inputs and outputs, the manager had little room for error. Proof of his effectiveness was the ability to remit an adequate level of dividends upwards into group hands. Successful managers from this bottom level could rise upward in the group, but at a very slow pace, and their success was likewise related to protecting the operation's margins. This system worked well while the group remained focused on integrated agribusiness. New firms established within the sector were generally operations that would further enhance margins or build market share.

The system does not work so well in diversification into more modern industries where the ability to build on vertical integration and margin controls does not yet exist. Costs became vastly inflated in TelecomAsia, for example, and revenues remained far below expectations, because CP had no experience in this area, and could not isolate basic operations to build margins.[14] In the Ek Chor Motorcycle project, building market share appears to have been more difficult than planned, due to the existence of three much larger competitors and restrictive government policies. With petrochemicals, the group found out that it did not have the understanding of petrochemical markets or ability it needed to eke out margins through trading of petrochemicals. Unlike its start in agribusiness, it had no established trading role in the petrochemicals markets. Nor did the rationale of Asia's growing consumer markets creating a lucrative demand for petrochemicals work: petrochemicals are global commodities, and the key to success is not based on location, marketing or distribution, but in technology and management. CP had advantages in neither in this business. These problems likely derive from CP's inexperience in more sophisticated capital- and technology-intensive industries and its unwillingness to change its management structure. In addition, CP has forgotten that its success in agribusiness was first founded on strong market positions: trading dominance was established before the group went into manufacturing.

Top management is dominated by the core group of Dhanin, Sumet, and their lieutenants who have mostly been with the group since the 1950s and 1960s. These are all shrewd traders and back room deal-makers who know best how to establish market position and defend margins in their traditional business areas. However, they have shown little ability to uncover and manage all the risks in capital-intensive project-based expansions such as petrochemicals, telecoms or other infrastructure-based business. Their approach has instead reflected an attitude of landing the deal, and working out problems later – with the assumption that good friends in high places, and common business sense, will help to sort out problems and risks not anticipated prior to a project's launch. They believe that, if they dither over details and risks before taking on a project or concession, they will stagnate like Western businesses in Asia that take few risks and never get anywhere. The CP assumption has been that if the business is basically a lucrative one with strong potential as the Asian economies grow, then it is worth pursuing, and market growth will eventually cover unforeseen difficulties.

In many respects, CP is right about this. (Again, though, the group failed to realize the global commodity nature of petrochemicals, and might be doing the same in other energy-related businesses.) Even if CP takes this approach, however, it still needs strong management in new projects to anticipate problems and find ways of correcting them. In most of its new businesses, the group has strong competitors with experience, fighting for the same turf in China. CP's structure has not helped the group respond to these challenges. The group fails to promote youngish, perhaps Western-trained executives who might be able to add value to more diverse projects, and sticks to the older generation instead. It has also demonstrated limited willingness to hire outside experts, Asian or Western, who might be able to manage new projects more knowledgeably and efficiently once they are launched.

CP basically had Nynex build its TelecomAsia system for example, but once the system was in place, the firm only hired staff from the inept local telecoms monopoly, and a manager from another Thai state enterprise, to run the business. None could perform well. Likewise, the group's launch of Lotus was less successful than expected because of management's dependence on CP's own staff, who were inexperienced in this particular business, to run the company. In a turnaround that indicates CP's plight, the group did later hire top staff from Walmart to improve Lotus. As a result, Lotus has become more competitive, but industry sources suggest that, as long these experts are not given adequate authority – perhaps because CP still mistrusts foreigners and non-ethnic Chinese – Lotus's potential is still limited.

Part of the problem is Dhanin's preference for relying only on Chinese managers, to whom he can speak in his own language. But another is that his traditional style, and reluctance to delegate authority to anyone who has not spent a decade or more in the group, does not work well even with Chinese who have a more modern (or Western) style of management. For instance, a respected Chinese-American franchising operations expert was hired in 1990 to help develop franchise and retailing businesses. He left after a year, frustrated with the CP group's inability to adjust its business style to the requirements of the franchising business.[15] Also in 1990, CP hired the former head of the business school of National Taiwan University to rationalize its business structure to better manage the group's new diversification. He was hired, according to one source, more because he could speak Chinese to Dhanin than for proven ability. He had been an academic and administrator, but never a real commercial consultant. The consultant's efforts proved to be divisive within the group, and after five years, he was only successful in outlining a business structure, CP's 'nine business groups and two business lines', which had evolved that way anyway. The various groups continue to have overlapping responsibilities and illogical operations, by modern corporate management standards. For example, one shoe manufacturing operation was placed in the petrochemicals division, and frozen dim sum production came under the management of franchise retailing, while other food production was partly amalgamated with chicken and shrimp farming.

A professional Western management consultant who knows the CP Group well said that, although some in the group at lower levels realize the need for professional advice from outside, CP is still reluctant to open its doors to any management consultant with real expertise, just as it is unwilling to recruit experienced managers to operate any of the new or larger businesses. This must be set in contrast to the willingness of other ethnic Chinese businessmen in East and South-East Asia, including Li Kashing and Robert Kuok, to draw on a global pool of talent, Western or Asian, for their management or finance expertise. Even when CP has brought youngish professionally trained Asians into the group, they have often felt stymied by the CP bureaucracy and their inability to rise in the ranks. Many bright MBA-types have come and quickly left, unwilling to spend two decades within the group to gain responsibility.

This, one might suggest, constricts the CP Group's potential in that it allows new businesses to capture too much of the attention of top management, while its traditional agribusiness develops well on the old policies. CP has got as far as it has in part by allowing a few relatively young financial experts – Veerawat Kanchanadul in Bangkok, and a shrewd, independent banking expert in Hong Kong – to be involved in managing the group finances with the old financial controller, Min Tienworn. But even then, reforms and adjustments proposed by both the younger experts have often not been implemented.[16] But beyond that, management has remained extremely cautious about letting anyone new into the inner circle of knowledge and responsibility – all the while actively hiring or appointing to the group's boards high-level Thai and Chinese officials who can help in building political connections. This is an imbalance that will become more apparent as CP attempts to compete in capital-intensive businesses outside its areas of expertise.

Allegiances

CP's image in Thailand has always been that of ethnic Chinese who have not accepted or integrated themselves into local culture. This is in part an unfair stereotype: Bangkok is so heavily populated by ethnic Chinese, perhaps predominantly so, that for a century the city's culture has not been identifiable as 'purely' Thai. On the other hand, compared to other large Sino-Thai groups – Bangkok Bank (Sophonpanich) and Thai Farmers Bank (Lamsam), among others – CP has historically had little room in high corporate ranks for ethnic Thais, or Thais who have taken active part in public society and government; and the Chaozhou dialect, up until recently, has been the language of CP board meetings. Dhanin has always preferred to work with people to whom he can speak in the Chaozhou dialect, or in Mandarin. The group has not gone out of its way to improve its image in this regard.

Because it was so little understood (and it remains so), CP was alternately called an agent of Taiwan or the PRC in the 1980s. The feeling was that the resources it used to expand must have come from some external sponsor. No conclusive evidence was ever provided on either side, but it is unlikely that CP is firmly linked to either government. From the 1960s, Dhanin built important trading and investment relations with Taiwan, and CP has companies listed on the Taipei stock market. But in farming, manufacturing and distribution, CP is relatively small in Taiwan. At the same time, the group has always maintained trade relations with China. Yet these are not enough to support accusations that CP is a tool of Beijing. By their size, CP's first important investments in China demonstrated some hesitancy and caution: the group waited until the open-door policy, and limited its first investments to small ones, despite being at the head of the queue in Shenzhen and Shantou.

In effect, Dhanin and CP have behaved like many pragmatic South-East Asian Chinese businesses do: as a friend to both Taiwan and China, when it serves their purposes, and unwilling to get involved on one side or another of the political split between the two. (Thailand's official stance has generally been the same, for that matter.) Nevertheless, China's market has grown and offered greater opportunities in the past 15 years. Unsurprisingly, then, most of the ethnic Chinese firms in the region, and indeed South-East Asian governments, have leaned towards Beijing's camp, and CP is no exception. Conversely, CP is prominent enough, in China and in overseas Chinese communities, that it merits recognition by Beijing. Hence both Dhanin and Sumet are among the few advisors (totalling no more than five) to Beijing on Hong Kong repatriation issues who are not from either China or Hong Kong.[17]

Underpinning a current perception that CP has greater allegiance to China than Thailand is CP's ongoing sponsorship and promotion of Chinese culture in Thailand, importing Shanghai and Beijing opera troupes to perform, and other such activities. It has been less active in promoting Thai culture in China. Although within Thailand, CP makes regular contributions to various Thai cultural activities, to the palace, and to Thai temples, the perception is that it is still more interested in China's culture.

CP is clearly aware of the perceptions. It attempted to make a point with the Thai people during its launch of new businesses, a Lotus store and expanded motorcycle production facilities, in Shanghai in August 1996, when it invited popular Thai Princess Sirindhorn to inaugurate the new operations. The press announcement for the occasions read: 'Wherever CP Group goes to invest, we raise the Thai national flag to display our pride in being Thai.'

But around the same time, according to newspaper reports, CP was organizing a well-funded lobbying programme for China, which possibly says more about its interests than anything else. In mid-1996, Dhanin and Sumet donated several hundred thousand US dollars to the US Democratic Party, enjoying in return a White House meeting with President Clinton in which they reportedly discussed China's interests in US–China trade. In the scandal that resulted, one of the most notorious figures was a Thai lobbyist, Pauline Kanchanalak, an employee of Ban Chang Co. Ltd, a listed Thai firm that CP took control of in 1995. Around the same time, Sumet was organizing a China promotion and lobby organization, the 'US-China Institute', to have offices in Washington, Hong Kong and Beijing. Recruited to help organize and run the effort were Brent Scowcroft, the national security advisor to former president George Bush, and other former high-placed White House staffers (*Washington Times,* 30 June 1997).

More important than cultural affinities is whether, in building business and industry, Dhanin is more committed to China or Thailand. CP's assets in China are now equal to if not greater than their Thai assets, and the Chinese market offers more long-term opportunities. Obtaining concessions in China through political channels leaves CP more vulnerable to government pressure there. But the same is true in Thailand.

As a real multinational, CP can behave as a stateless member of the global economic community. But political perceptions of national interest and economic competition can evoke questions of loyalties. An example of the kind of conflict which can arise is in the way Chinese exports of chicken to Japan – a field led by

CP in China – have risen at the expense of Thai chicken exports to Japan – also dominated by CP. The Chinese cost base is lower, and CP can be said to be defending its margins. On the other hand, some Thai government officials have quietly accused CP of selling out the country. Given CP's continued capital investment in Thailand, however, and the continuing strength of the Thai food processing and export industry, the accusations do not easily stick. Suffice it to say that CP continues to put money into both economies – though much more in China.

Yet, if CP has attempted to identify itself with China, as a PRC business group, in order to grow quickly, it has not been fully successful. As noted above, China has not rewarded CP to the same extent that it has provided deals and concessions to, and used as tools, its own large conglomerates. CP has not been chosen to hold a stake on Beijing's behalf in any of the large Hong Kong companies, like Hong Kong Telecommunications or Cathay Pacific Airlines, that have been divested to powerful mainland China business groups. Nor has CP been given preference, if anything at all, in Chinese infrastructure projects. One can surmise that, even if CP were to attempt to identify itself with China, the group would not be accepted as a 'national' entity. Beijing sees CP as overseas Chinese, with divided loyalties.

Conclusion and forecast

CP was already a fairly strong business house in the region when current head Dhanin finished his schooling in the late 1950s. Its growth had come from steady acquisition and development of superior products and market position. In the 1980s, second-generation leader Dhanin launched the group on a course of voracious diversification, principally built on a strong storehold of cash, faith in consumer spending as economies grow, and a store of strong political connections. Dhanin's goal was to create, through the fast establishment of footholds in a wide panoply of industries in China, the basis for turning his group into something resembling a Korean *chaebol*. One strategy in doing this has been to have CP identified in China as a Chinese business, so that Beijing leaders would feel it in their interest to support CP's growth.

CP's expansion has reflected and fed into the popular myth of the group's constant success. This supposed success then gives credence to the popular belief in the irrepressible rise of ethnic-Chinese controlled South-East Asian conglomerates. It also underpins a belief in the strength of the model of Chinese family-controlled business. Although CP has indeed been successful, its own rapid expansion may challenge these popular myths. Because of the speed of the diversification, and seeming lack of focus, CP has run into problems making many of the newer projects work. Further difficulties stem from putting low emphasis on developing management capabilities, on nurturing partnerships, and on focusing on economic details of projects. Another problem is that CP has not truly built on its past strengths and experience. The group constantly appears to be starting entirely new businesses rather than trying to build on an existing assets and market position. This constant addition of green field start-ups puts pressure on management abilities.

The myth has it that CP is particularly and successfully intimate with the Chinese leadership. This may be true, but it has not garnered the company the favours it expected. China continues to give more support, of the kind that Dhanin would like to attract, to what are more clearly domestic business groups, like Norinco, China Resources, CITIC and others, in building powerful conglomerates.

Dhanin has remained sufficiently conservative that the missteps will not substantially weaken the CP Group overall. Agribusiness is still strong, real estate is performing well, and telecoms and retailing provide strong cash flow if not great profits. What I expect will happen is a moderating of CP's ambitions, a slowing of expansion and diversification, while it deals with problems in existing projects. The sharp fall in the Thai economy in 1997 will reinforce this. Perhaps, too, there will be a sell-off of poorly performing units that are not part of the group's core business. This would be likely if cash resources become tight for the group – which at this time is impossible to know.

For the next several years growth will be slow as the group tries to develop more professional management. To be successful will require trusting more experienced outsiders to run certain new businesses: so far, this seems to be happening only slowly. There will be less of an accent on *guanxi* and more on developing real business opportunities through the traditional strong market analysis and planning that was a feature of CP's agribusiness and food industry. The group also needs to develop more sophisticated and transparent financial management in order to tap global capital markets more efficiently, for further expansion.

Business-wise, in the medium term I would hazard a guess that the group gives up on petrochemicals, steps back from expansion in the overcrowded automotive industries, maintains telecoms, and accents biotechnology, real estate development and retailing, over the next several years. Telecoms will only develop further if CP manages to get a significant concession in China. Real estate could become a core source of earnings, which would make the group look more like a typical South-East Asian ethnic Chinese business group than a Korean *chaebol*.

If the goal of becoming a *chaebol* is pursued, CP will probably need to begin buying other companies and operations, rather than starting new ones, on their own or with partners. This will require more sophisticated financial management as well. The slowdown in the Thai economy offers such possibilities, if CP has the financial resources to take over certain heavy industries that are in trouble. So far there is no indication of this happening. Nor is there any indication that CP wants to be in the business of taking over existing Chinese state enterprises and rehabilitating them. Without becoming involved in take-overs like these, CP stands less of a chance of being successful in heavy industry.

Notes

1   Helene Vissiere, reporter for Enjeaux.
2   Such characterizations of CP, and the myth-making surrounding the company, are to be found in many places: see *International Herald Tribune*, 16 November 1995; *Far Eastern Economic Review*, 23 April 1987; *Far Eastern Economic Review*, 20 April 1989; *Time*, 10 May 1993; Pananond 1996; Phaiboontham 1996; see also John Naisbitt's *Megatrends Asia*. Other common contributors to the same image are CP's own publications and stockbrokers' reports on the group.
3   An unofficial history published by the *Thansetthakij* newspaper, based heavily on articles in a CP-backed farmers publication, provides some cursory details of the way the family business developed (Suwannaban 1993). According to one of the book's editors, when it was published, CP bought up more than half of the 2,500 copy print run, and what happened to the copies was never clear. The editor did not know whether CP had any particular disagreement with the book's content, which had been serialized in *Thansetthakij*. Almost all of the content had been taken from published sources, and CP apparently never made any complaint. To this day the book is very difficult to find.
4   Chia Ekchor (Ek Chiau, b. 1894) was the eldest son of a farmer and trader who died in 1912.
5   Another brother, Chia Siewpae, became an academic and eventually a lecturer at a Chiang Kai Shek-controlled academy in Sichuan, suggesting the family was originally somewhat well-off (Suwannaban 1993).
6   However, this writer has heard an unverified account that in the 1960s, CP was also, at least in part, encouraged and/or aided by the US government (and possibly the Rockefeller Foundation, at the time closely linked to US government activities) to build up modern chicken production to both enhance Thailand's economic modernization and to feed US troops increasingly present in Thailand and Indochina. Because the US Cold War-inspired presence in Thailand between the 1950s and 1970s (with the greatest growth in the 1960s) was responsible for the introduction to the country of much technology and business, and the creation of substantial fortunes in manufacturing, trading, and services, this account cannot be totally dismissed.
7   Sumet apparently has kept his Thai citizenship and wife at the same time, and may have a Chinese or Hong Kong passport as well.
8   As reported on corporate registration documents, Ministry of Commerce, Thailand.
9   As a partner in the Dharma Niti law firm.
10   By the end of the 1980s, CP decided that contract farming was far less efficient than owning its own farms, and over time gradually reduced the amount of poultry and other products sourced from contract farmers to a small percentage of what they process.
11   The suggestion of transfer pricing cannot be proven: it is a suspicion expressed by numerous bankers and stock analysts imputed from CP's rapid growth, and the growth in turnover in listed companies, against what is often the reporting of stagnant profit growth. Corporate analysts have also suggested that CP's structure, with scores of small companies under centralized administration but with a more haphazard structure of cross-shareholdings, and relations with both listed and unlisted CP companies, serves the need of obscuring transfer pricing and profits.
12   By this I mean partnerships in which the partner wields significant power. In CP's China agribusiness there are many partnerships with local units, but in these CP wields most if not all of the power, financially, managerially and in ownership.
13   In an interview with the author in 1996, one Hong Kong-based consultant working as an advisor to CP's partner on such a joint venture, a very technology- and management-intensive business, said they believed CP essentially wanted to learn the business quickly and then expand it on CP's own.
14   As noted earlier, however, CP covered its risks in this regard by a strong financing package for the project which left them with relatively little risk (Handley 1996). By 1997, however, even that cushion began to appear less secure than anticipated.
15   Interview with Tony Wong, March 1996.
16   In interviews with the author in 1989 and 1990, both spoke of ambitious restructuring intended to make the group more transparent and logical in management, which would enhance CP's

ability to raise funds cheaply in banking and capital markets. What both spoke of in detail has mostly never taken place (*FEER* 25 October 1990).

17 Dhanin is an advisor to the PRC on Hong Kong affairs, while Sumet is a member of the Preparatory Committee for the Hong Kong Special Administrative Region.

Bibliography

Charoen Pokphand Feed Mill (various years) *Annual Reports.*

Corporate Thailand (1996) *CP Kin Ruap Prathet Thai*, Corporate Thailand, May 1996, 36–86.

Friedland, Jonathan (1989) 'Seeds of Empire'. *Far Eastern Economic Review*, 20 April, 46–7.

Goldstein, Carl (1993) 'Full Speed Ahead'. *Far Eastern Economic Review*, 21 October, 66–70.

Handley, Paul (1990) 'Food for Thought'. *Far Eastern Economic Review*, 25 October, 56–8.

Handley, Paul (1993) 'Lines of Control'. *Far Eastern Economic Review*, 24 June, 60–70.

Handley, Paul (1996) 'Growing Fast, the CP Way'. *Institutional Investor*, October, 70–9.

Naisbitt, John (1996) *Megatrends Asia*. New York: Simon and Schuster.

Nation News Talk (1994) Nation News Talk (television programme) (by video tape in Thai).

Nation News Talk (1996) Nation News Talk (television programme) (by transcript translation provided by CP).

Pananond, Pavida and Carl P. Zeithaml (1996) 'The International Expansion Process of MNEs from Developing Countries: A Model and Empirical Evidence'. *Asia Pacific Journal of Management*, 15: 163–84.

Phaiboontham, Phiraboon (1996) *CP Group's Diversification: History, Strategies and Development Model*. Bangkok: Charoen Pokphand.

Suwannaban, Wichai (1993) *CP: Turakij Rai Phrom Den*. Bangkok: Thansetthakij.

TelecomAsia (various years) *Annual Reports.*

10 Telecommunications, rents and the growth of a liberalization coalition in Thailand

Sakkarin Niyomsilpa

The 1997 financial crisis in Thailand that precipitated the Asian financial crisis unravelled the growing tension between the changing nature of Thai society and the increasing pressure for economic liberalization in Thailand. Central to the 1997 financial crisis was the expanding political power and control of access to rents by political parties, many of which have been associated with provincial businessmen–cum–politicians, and the competition for rents by business interests. Since democratizing, Thailand has been characterized by coalition government and fierce competition among political parties amidst political uncertainty and cabinet shake-ups. Political cronyism and rent-seeking activities in Thailand since the late 1980s have been largely short-termist, aiming for quick business returns. As Thailand was absorbed into the globalization process and forced to liberalize its economy, the country began lifting restrictions on foreign capital transfers in the early 1990s, which led to the influx of cheap capital from abroad. The abundant supply of capital, together with the growing power of political parties and the competition for rents by business interests, resulted in unsustainable economic growth involving speculative activities, asset price bubbles, poor investments and consumption booms. As the financial imbalance and growing current account deficits demanded correction, the Thai government, captured by political crony-ism and business interests, was unable to prevent the country's financial collapse and economic recession.

By the time Thailand was struck by the financial crisis, the country was markedly different from the conventional academic view of Thailand as a bureau-cratic polity. Even before the financial meltdown, when Thailand experienced remarkable economic growth[1] and significant economic and social transformation,[2] the country was often described as having a bureaucratic state, in which corruption and rentier activities are centrally controlled by the bureaucratic elite. Riggs (1966) believed that Thailand would continue, without major changes, as a bureaucratic polity with a low level of industrialization and economic growth. The state-business relationship was described as an unequal exchange in which business was subject to state control and patronage. Keyes (1989) added that despite the tensions between progressive technocrats and conservative bureaucrats in Thailand, the country remained a bureaucratic polity. These scholars of the modernization school adopted a view that rents are extracted from the states in developing societies. Government intervention in the economy only encourages rent-seeking activities, which in turn undermine economic growth and social welfare by diverting resources from productive activities and encouraging inefficient operations. For less developed countries (LDCs) like Thailand, rents enjoyed by political agents associated with state bureaucracies have also been seen as the main factor slowing economic growth. Whereas economic agents in a pluralist state use political markets for economic ends, political agents in most LDCs are assumed to use economic resources to achieve political ends. Rent-seeking activities by state officials encounter little public scrutiny, and rents in developing countries are assumed to involve a relatively high proportion of GDP because of the lack of civil society.[3] In contrast, open competition in a democratic system increases the cost of rent-seeking activities, and thus discourages potential beneficiaries from seeking rents, thereby bringing down the prices of goods and services.

Thailand's political democratization – associated with the rapid economic growth since the late 1980s and 1990s – seems to contradict the notion that a bureaucratic polity marred by corruption and rent-seeking is unlikely to achieve economic success. The subsequent financial crisis in 1997 also repudiates the view that political pluralism in a democratic system will increase the costs of rent-seeking activities, and thus discourages potential beneficiaries from seeking rents. As it turns out, political democratization in Thailand, along with increasing economic liberalization, has been associated with rents and competition for rents. Many issues relating to the nature and role of the state, rents and rent-seekers need to be discussed. What is the role of the state in the economy and in rent creation and allocation? How has the political economy of Thailand changed over time and how have these changes affected the structure of rents and rent-seeking rights, and the state's control over rents? How has the coalition of interests emerged and evolved over time? What are the roles and power relations of businesses, political parties and bureaucrats within the coalition of interests?

In trying to address these questions, I will analyse the political economy of telecommunications liberalization in Thailand and draw lessons from this experience. The telecommunications sector provides us with a revealing case study of the changing political economy of rents and the rights structure caused by changing relations among newly emerging businesses, political parties and the bureaucracy in Thailand. The explosive growth of business groups, partly contributed to by the transfer of state rights to private capitalists, involving increasing competition for rents, and partly by technological changes that opened new economic opportunities for telecommunications businesses, resulted in the rapid expansion of the economic and political influence of telecommunications companies. Concurrent with the growth of telecommunications, the Thai state has experienced a greater fracturing of its bureaucracy, weakening effective control by the centre, leading to the formation of a shifting coalition favouring liberalization, whose members comprise businessmen, politicians and elements of the bureaucracy. As a result, telecommunications capital's influence over political factions and agents has grown, as such businesses have depended increasingly on rents and the creation of rent-seeking rights. Relations between the once-dominant bureaucracy and the newly ascendant private sector have been evolving in a way that will throw light on broader changes in state–society relations and the restructuring of rents and rights in Thailand since the 1980s. It should be noted that local business groups have enjoyed rent-seeking rights that pave the way for their capital accumulation and subsequent political involvement.

Despite the growing importance of telecommunications and its role in Thailand's changing political economy, this industry also has many distinct characteristics that differ from those of other business sectors. Drawing general conclusions about business–government relations in Thailand from the changing political economy of rents and rent-seeking rights in the telecommunications industry should be done with great caution. For example, the telecommunications revolution and the convergence of telephony, broadcasting and computer technologies during the past two decades have created a huge new demand for telecommunications products and services, enabling small players and latecomers to enjoy rapid growth in spite of limited resources and expertise. As most telecommunications businesses in Thailand have enjoyed quick profits from selling recently imported products and technologies to local consumers, the Schumpeterian model – applicable to many fast-growing industries like textiles, automobiles or petrochemicals – may be less relevant to telecommunications. Instead of investing their state-protected surpluses and rents into developing new technologies or products, most Thai telecommunications businesses have concentrated on securing new licences and on other rent-seeking activities. Whatever the waste due to rent-seeking, the transfer of rights from the state to private operators and the availability of new telecommunications technologies have made private operations more efficient and responsive to market demand.

This chapter is divided into three parts. The first discusses some influential interpretations of state–society relations in light of the politics of rent and the structure of rights in Thailand. The second part includes three case studies of telecommunications privatization that demonstrate how the politics of the telecommunications industry and rents associated with it have been transformed. All three cases show the growth of private sector rent-seeking in Thailand through the takeover of rights to appropriate rents from state agencies, and the use of bureaucrats and politicians to contest such allocations of rights. Importantly, both ethnic Thai and Sino-Thai businesses actively participate in the gradual privatization and limited liberalization of the industry without any sign of ethnic discrimination. Whereas the first case study suggests higher costs of rent-seeking activities without significant benefit for the state from the reallocation of rents, private competition for rents in the other two cases has resulted in relatively efficient rights allocation, mainly concurrent with and due to greater transparency of state regulatory power. The third part is the conclusion.

Contending views of rents and state–society relations in Thailand

'Bureaucratic polity'

Many postwar studies of the Thai state have been influenced by Riggs' (1966) bureaucratic polity model, characterized by bureaucratic political dominance as opposed to the insignificance or nonexistence of extra-bureaucratic political forces. State-business relations involved an unequal exchange in which bureaucrats determined the terms of the relationship, commanded regulatory powers, centralized the allocation of rights and controlled access to rents. This conception was rooted in the modernization school and, implicitly, the liberal tradition. Riggs and Huntington (1993) share a unilinear view of development in which all nations follow a similar trajectory, starting from being a 'prismatic society' and ending up as a Western-type democratic society. From the late 1960s, Riggs' analysis gained widespread recognition and acceptance, to such an extent that it virtually dominated political studies of Thailand.

The mass uprisings in 1973, however, raised questions about Riggs' analysis of the Thai political economy and the state's absolute control of the rights structure. Anderson (1977) and Girling (1981a, 1981b) argued that bourgeois and urban middle classes had emerged outside of the feudal-bureaucratic class. They maintained, however, that the bureaucracy still reigned supreme while social forces in civil society remained politically weak. Similarly, Trakoon (1982) and Prudhisan (1987) argued that the state's dominant role caused business to be engaged in 'pariah entrepreneurship' – 'pariah' because the mostly ethnic Chinese private sector remained politically subordinate to the mainly ethnic Thai bureaucracy. Other scholars, including Suchit (1987), Keyes (1989) and Likhit (1992), observed that Thai politics was largely dominated by the military.

Radical resurgence

The 1973 political opening not only forced reconsideration of Riggs' views of the centralized bureaucratic state, but also encouraged a revival of radical thinking about Thai politics and society.[4] A number of radical intellectuals applied dependency theory, which had gained international popularity during the 1970s, to analyse capitalist development in Thailand. Suthy (1980), Krit (1982) and Yoshihara (1988) perceived local capital as insignificant, or subservient to international capital, while the Thai state was characterized as an essentially comprador state lacking autonomy. These analyses overemphasized external factors, and as a result, could not explain Thailand's subsequent rapid industrialization and the growth of local capital.

Another radical current applied class analysis to study the bourgeoisie following the emergence of large Thai business groups. Apart from rejecting the emphasis on the core-periphery or dependency relationship, Thai class analysis also ruled out recognition of state autonomy and rejected the pluralist notion of a non-partisan state. Attention was instead paid to the alliances formed between capital and the state in the process of capital accumulation, and to the transformation of class structures. Thai class analysis contended that the state and its machinery were basically instruments of business for the allocation of rights as well as the creation and protection of rents. Economic development and industrialization were considered effects of state policies that served the interests of business. Kraisak (1984) and Suraphol (1987) viewed Thai capital as economically strong, if not politically dominant. Hewison (1987) stressed the role of domestic capital in pressing for import substitution during the 1960s and then export orientation industrialization policies in the subsequent period. Business influence was exercised through connections between capital and political-bureaucratic groups, interlocking shareholdings, family connections, and quasi-institutional relations (Hewison 1989).

Liberal rethinking

The re-emergence of radical writings on Thai political economy has been followed by a new wave of liberal-pluralist studies focusing attention on changing state-business relations and rights structures. These suggested that the rights structures were being altered in such a way that the state had not only lost effective control over rights creation and the allocation of resources and rents, but also had to share power with business as well as other emerging forces in society. Prizzia (1985), Pisan and Guyot (1986), and Mackie (1988) pointed out that Thailand had moved away from being a bureaucratic polity to becoming a more pluralistic society since the 1970s. Anek (1989) later argued that business was not only the strongest social force, but also shared power with the bureaucracy in economic policy-making; state-business relations were thus seen as balanced, close, and mutually supportive. Government-business relations were portrayed by pluralist scholars as involving political manoeuvring among bureaucrats, businessmen and politicians (Pasuk 1989; Anek 1989; MacIntyre 1990).

Despite their appealing explanations for the rising political influence of business, the line drawn between business and the state by some pluralist studies was sometimes too clear-cut. State-business relations were often viewed in terms of institutional connections, without much regard for the policies at issue. In addition, co-operation between technocrats and businessmen has often been interpreted as clear evidence of business influence, although the state includes many different bureaucratic agencies whose interests may or may not coincide. It is often difficult to say who leads whom when the interests of bureaucrats (or technocrats) and businessmen are aligned. Beneficiaries of particular rents can be numerous, and a coalition of rent-seekers comprising partners of equal – or differing – strength may develop.

The amalgam of political ideas

The increase in society-based political economy studies from the 1980s stimulated modifications in the theories of the different schools of political economy. Criticism by pluralist and class analysts forced the state-centric scholars to incorporate various pluralist elements to correct shortcomings in their analysis. A group of radical intellectuals also reformulated dependency concepts to combine various elements from different approaches to explain the industrialization of regions formerly regarded as part of the periphery. Meanwhile, class-based studies prompted pluralist scholars to differentiate between business groups with more or less political influence and economic power than others. Recent class analysts have applied pluralist ideas to their discussion of social interests. In effect, this eclectic amalgam of new ideas became common in studies of political economy in the 1990s.

A major revision of the state-centric approach in Thai studies started with Chai-Anan's concept of the 'three-dimensional state' (1990a, 1990b, 1990c, 1990d) to explain the persistence of bureaucratic power in an increasingly pluralistic Thailand. According to this concept, the Thai state adjusted to the changing political economy by creating new institutional structures to cope with the increasing influence of extra-bureaucratic forces. The success of the state in maintaining its dominant role was explained by its continued performance of three main functions, relating to security, development and popular participation. As the security dimension became increasingly de-emphasized, the Thai state expanded its institutional structure and role to cope with new development efforts and the increasing transfer of rights to private capital, as well as in response to growing demands for political participation by various interest groups. In providing new bureaucratic channels for high-level communication as well as access to rights creation and reallocation processes, state elites expected businessmen to refrain from lobbying through political parties and factions to advance their business interests.

Following scholarly criticism of the classical dependency school, a neo-dependency analysis proposed that economic development in the periphery or semi-periphery was possible because of co-operation between the state, the Thai bourgeoisie, and international capital, sharing profits and rents and facilitating capital accumulation. Patcharee (1985) saw the Thai political economy since 1978 as involving a 'triple alliance' in which the state promoted industrialization by encouraging and facilitating co-operation between Thai and foreign capital. Chairat (1988) has portrayed rural development policy in Thailand as the state's means of facilitating capital accumulation in the agrarian sector while maintaining state legitimacy. Viewing the Thai state as a major accumulator of capital, Suehiro (1989, 1992) has reasoned that capitalist development since the 1960s has been a product of the rights structure, which has allowed capital accumulation by state enterprises, TNCs and mainly Sino-Thai private businesses.

The increasing liberalization of Thai politics and the growth of business forces and civil society during the 1980s encouraged many scholars to integrate more pluralist perspectives into their analyses of state–society relations and the rights structure. Meanwhile, business interests have been seen as advancing their position from merely allying with the state to taking control of the state and rent allocation. Hewison (1992) has argued that the Chatichai government (1988–91) epitomized this capitalist ascendancy as it undermined some older norms of bureaucratic society, such as order, stability and hierarchy. According to Thirayuth (1993), while the mass uprisings in 1973 emancipated business from state control by ending the bureaucratic polity, the 1992 overthrow of the Suchinda regime marked the real beginnings of business leadership in Thai politics and society.

Whereas previous liberal-pluralist studies emphasized the expanding role of Bangkok-based business firms in economic policy-making and rent-seeking, the provincial businessmen-cum-politicians in the major political parties, often referred to as *jao pho*,[5] now command their attention. Sombat (1991), Pasuk (1993), Pasuk and Baker (1993, 1995) and Ockey (1993) have led the way with pioneering studies on the growing influence of these provincial *jao pho* in local and national politics. Pasuk and Baker distinguish between Bangkok-based businessmen, termed *jao sua*, and the provincial *jao pho* to compare their different character, interests and political roles. The *jao sua* ('Chinese tycoons') refer to the more established, urban-based entrepreneurs whose businesses are more likely to be outward-oriented and international in character. They often prefer a more open and liberal administrative environment, relatively free of controls and regulations. On the other hand, the *jao pho* operate simpler, often rentier businesses which require government licences or protection, and often target public resources, patronage and rents to further their business interests. Sidel (1996) has explained the rights structure of provincial *jao pho* as taking three main forms. First, *jao pho* often enjoy monopolies within certain territories of state-derived concessions, contracts, and franchises, as well as illegal rackets. Second, *jao pho* gain power and influence through their role as vote brokers and canvassers in elections, delivering parliamentary constituencies to Bangkok-based patrons, provincial patrons or to themselves, by means of vote-buying and coercion. Third, *jao pho* may informally, but effectively, take control of state agencies with coercive powers and thus monopolize organized violence within defined territories, for the purposes of capital accumulation, electoral manipulation and racketeering.

As Thailand has undergone some democratization and the restoration of parliamentary elections during the past two decades, the emergence of *jao pho* has led to the transfer of political and economic power and control over the state apparatus to elected officials who are linked to these *jao pho* businessmen-cum-politicians. As a consequence, the rights structure has been transformed to favour the *jao pho* and *jao pho*-linked businesses with more rents. Despite their increasing influence in national politics, however, the rights structure favouring the *jao pho* is facing challenges from the partially 'disenfranchised' *jao sua* business interests and the emerging civil society. On the one hand, increasing wealth in the provinces, as a result of Thailand's steady economic expansion, has attracted big capital from the city and even from overseas. On the other hand, the new rights structures due to the political ascendance of the *jao pho* has alarmed the *jao sua* businessmen and other social groups as democratization has raised issues of transparency and public accountability more insistently. It seems that rent-seeking and protection of the existing rights structure by *jao pho* businesses will become more costly as they lack the technological and financial advantages possessed by the *jao sua* in business competition, and because the fractured bureaucracy can and will no longer effectively protect many of their rights and rents. Interestingly, however, there are recent signs of political collaboration between the *jao sua* and *jao pho* businessmen in politics and business to reallocate the rights structure, as the economic cost of their competition proves too high, especially after the financial meltdown in 1997.

Telecommunications liberalization and the politics of rents in Thailand

The liberalization of telecommunications in Thailand has progressed with the changing political economy of the country. Telecommunications politics reflected changes in the political regime and government-business relations. Although traditional powers such as the military and bureaucratic agencies have continued to play some roles in telecommunications politics, other emerging forces and interests, which include political parties, business and labour, have also been influential in the telecommunications reform process. As a result, different political economy perspectives can be applied to telecommunications politics as it has continued to change. The traditional view of the bureaucratic polity was deemed relevant until the 1980s, with bureaucrats dominating state telecommunications agencies and exercising regulatory and managerial rights. The dependency perspective could be used to examine the supply side for the telecommunications industry before the 1990s when Thailand largely depended on Japanese and European companies for telecommunications supplies, technology and capital. However, limited privatization of the telecommunications industry in the late 1980s and early 1990s could be seen as the result of joint efforts between domestic businessmen and technocrats to revamp outmoded infrastructure and to capture the enormous rents potentially associated with the industry. Whereas class analysis maintained that the domestic capitalist class and the bureaucratic elite carried out the privatization programme for their common interests, the liberal-pluralist approach tended to view state policy as a response to the pressing demands and rent-seeking activities of business interests.

Generally speaking, the politics of telecommunications in Thailand reflects the growing power and influence of a loose coalition (which I term a 'liberalization coalition'), which consists mainly of businesses, the technocratic arms of the bureaucracy, and political parties. From the 1980s the reform agendas of the industry have changed from state monopoly to privatization to liberalization and increasing competition. Meanwhile, the interests and positions of state and non-state actors have changed as Thai governments oscillated between democratic and semi-democratic regimes. Turning to the rents debate, the liberalization of telecommunications in Thailand seems to have involved the growth of local capital and increasing competition over access to public resources (telecommunications infrastructure, networks and information) and the reallocation of surpluses. During the initial period, the military, state telecommunications agencies, and labour interests joined hands to block regulatory reforms and the restructuring of rights. But the fracturing of the bureaucracy, coupled with aggressive rent-seeking by private capital and (legal as well as illegal) rent transfers to the anti-reform coalition, weakened such opposition. The success of the liberalization coalition in dismantling the state monopoly of telecommunications – and associated rents – has been well-received as private competition, though limited to just a few operators, has boosted the industry's efficiency and brought down the prices of many services. As the pace of telecommunications development quickened and private operators increased, business interests sought to extend the privatization and reform of the industry, both through the liberalization coalition and by taking over state regulatory powers. By the mid-1990s, the politics of telecommunications had been considerably transformed and the rent structure redefined.

Three cases of telecommunications projects will be discussed below to examine the politics of telecommunications liberalization and associated rents.[6] All three cases involve projects awarded to the private sector under build-operate-transfer (B-O-T) schemes. The first is the case of the bureaucracy-dominated telephone directory project privatized during the Prem regime (1980–8). The second discusses the liberalization of mobile phone services, while the last involves concessions to build a three-million-line telephone network. These cases will link the advancing privatization and liberalization of the industry to rent-seeking politics and the growth of private capital, rather than the declining control of rights by the bureaucracy.

The telephone directory project

The telephone directory project is an example of rent-seeking involving the military, a state agency and foreign business. This case involved the transfer of the monopoly right to publish telephone directories from a state telecommunications agency (the Telephone Organization of Thailand, TOT) to a private company, although a rival was also keen to secure the right. As the bureaucracy began to lose unchallenged control over the allocation of rights, rent-seeking by both firms became more aggressive. Owing to the high costs of the intense competition for the rent (as state control of the right was not very effective), the publisher of the directory was unable to run a profitable operation and the state agency ended up losing potential benefits. There were indications that rent-seeking activities in this case involved the bribery and lobbying of public officials and politicians to defend or alter decisions and legislation concerning these rights.

This case shows how rent-seeking can lead to the creation of a new right and its transfer to a private firm. When the Telephone Organization of Thailand (TOT), the state agency responsible for domestic telecommunications, called for bids to publish telephone and business directories in 1984, the TOT did not actually have a monopoly right to publish the directories in the first place, let alone to award or transfer such a right to anyone.[7] But because of the TOT's comprehensive database of telephone subscribers throughout Thailand, TOT co-operation has been essential to produce a comprehensive directory. For this reason, the General Telephone Directory Company (GTDC) had entered into contracts with the TOT since 1968 to publish telephone and business directories free of charge using the TOT's information database. In exchange, the TOT received a share of the revenue generated by the GTDC's business advertising (*Prachachart thurakit,* 15 August 1989; *Siam Rath,* 21 July 1987). As rents from the business directory were growing with Thailand's business expansion, interest from other private firms was rising, as the TOT's contract with the GTDC would expire in 1985. Therefore, the TOT decided to establish a right to publish directories and to sell the monopoly right in order to maximize its revenues. Bids were then called in 1984 and a five-member selection committee was appointed by the TOT board to consider tenders.[8]

But when the committee short-listed two tenderers as potential publishers[9] for further negotiation, the military bluntly stepped in to help AT&T, another bidder who had failed to be short-listed by the selection committee. General Arthit Kamlang-ek, the army commander-in-chief and TOT board chairman, ordered the selection committee to review its previous decision. Such an order came as no surprise as Gen. Arthit was known to be close to a local business group serving as agent for AT&T telephone equipment (*Prachachart thurakit,* 3 October 1984). The selection committee unexpectedly reaffirmed its previous decision and once again disqualified AT&T. In a controversial move, the TOT board decided to overrule the selection committee and called for new bids that allowed AT&T to tender again.[10] As a result, AT&T was chosen the winner, with only 1,275 million baht of revenue promised to the TOT for the 1986–90 concession period.

As producing telephone directories does not require specialized technology that would involve intrinsic cost differences between firms, publication of multiple competing directories would raise unit costs. A monopoly right given to one private firm would therefore be more efficient, less wasteful and potentially maximize returns to the TOT. But there was much formal as well as 'informal' bidding for this project, which raised the incurred rent-seeking costs and involved wasteful competition among firms. Moreover, because of the state's inability to protect the licensee's monopoly right to directory publication, the monopoly could not be enforced for some time and rents were not fully captured. Rent-seeking in this case was partly due to the weakly established rights of the TOT. The initial short-listing of the previous two bidders was subsequently overturned by what appears to have been more effective rent-seeking by AT&T. AT&T not only succeeded in reversing the TOT's initial award, but also improved the terms of the award in its own favour – at the TOT's expense. The TOT's ambiguity over the monopoly rights was tested when the GTDC, the former directory publisher, decided to contest the award given to AT&T by continuing to publish telephone and business directories. AT&T then forced the TOT to take legal action against the GTDC and sought to revise its directory contract with the TOT. To resolve the problem of weak rights protection and to maximize rents, the TOT then proposed a new law to establish the monopoly right over telephone and business directories that would strengthen the monopoly right awarded to AT&T. Nevertheless, it took almost three years to settle the weak rights issue as the law was only passed by parliament in 1987. But the amended contract with AT&T was questioned by the Director-General of the Prosecutions Department, who warned of a significant reduction of TOT benefits, in contrast to AT&T's loosely defined obligations.[11]

Mobile telephone concessions

The original mobile telephone service concessions in Thailand provide a good example of an inefficient duopoly of state operating agencies giving way to aggressive private sector rent-seeking, resulting in the allocation of rights to private operators. Unlike the telephone directory project, rent-seeking costs for mobile telephone service rights did not lead to inferior private operations. On the contrary, private competition in providing mobile telephone services contributed to better services and lower prices while rents accruing from the provisions of these services rapidly built up Thai telecommunications conglomerates. In response to the state's failure to establish clear rights, and hence to prevent competition between two public agencies providing the same services, private rent-seekers established a liberalization coalition to restructure mobile telephone rights and to break the state duopoly. Since the nature of mobile telephone technology can encourage competition among service providers for higher quality services and lower tariffs, the allocation of rights to two private firms in Thailand led to the explosive growth of the industry. In sum, the divided or fractured bureaucracy, together with private sector rent-seeking, contributed to the restructuring of rights and the subsequent growth of the industry.

The major players in mobile telephone services consisted of many actors and interests both inside and outside of the state structure. Bureaucratic agencies included two state regulatory agencies (Telephone Organization of Thailand, or TOT, and the Communications Authority of Thailand, or CAT), a public planning agency (the National Economic and Social Development Board, or NESDB), and the Ministry of Transport and Communications (MOTC). Non-bureaucratic actors included two private business groups (the Shinawatra and UCOM groups, both Sino-Thai groups), and politicians. Rents in the projects derived from the duopoly rights of the two state agencies (TOT and CAT) sold to the two private concessionaires and the related rights created for a handful of mobile telephone equipment suppliers.[12]

The weak rights structure, created by the fragmented bureaucracy and outdated laws, was a major contributor to competition between the TOT and the CAT as the rapid advancement of cellular phone technologies produced overlapping responsibilities and duplication of services between the two state agencies.[13] Competition between the two agencies since 1987 precipitated a series of problems and hostility between them. For instance, the TOT introduced connection fees for its domestic network from the CAT in order to extract more rents, while imposing higher costs for CAT's mobile phone operations. Moreover, CAT's operations were further impeded by the TOT's inadequate allocation of telephone circuits, which undermined the agency's business expansion (*Phu jad karn* 18 December 1988). As neither political parties nor other state agencies such as the MOTC could exercise effective control over the military-dominated board of TOT, an efficient rights structure over mobile phone business could not be established.

A turning point in mobile phone politics came in December 1987 when competition between the TOT and CAT was encouraged and private partici-pation in mobile telephone services was endorsed by the cabinet (Cabinet Resolution, December 1987). Pressure from a liberalization coalition, which included private businesses, politicians and the NESDB, finally kicked off a surge of privatization of the telecommunications industry. As a result, the TOT granted a concession to the Shinawatra group, a family firm led by Thaksin Shinawatra, a northern Thai who had served earlier in the Police Department, in October 1990 to provide another mobile phone system, while still maintaining its previous system.[14] In response, the CAT awarded a similar concession in September 1991 to the UCOM group, a telecom firm headed by Boonchai Benjarongkul, whose family is of Chinese origin. The creation of rights to both Shinawatra and UCOM due to the rivalry between the TOT and the CAT also brought about a new kind of competition between the two private firms. With competition between the two private concessionaires,[15] rents generated from the mobile phone business were still so large that both Shinawatra and UCOM managed to build huge business empires covering a whole range of telecommunications services.[16] Mean-while, the TOT and the CAT enjoyed enormous rents from revenue sharing with the two private operators in addition to connection and annual fees charged to mobile phone subscribers. Rents appropriated by the private operators and the two state agencies can be seen in Table 10.1, which shows huge revenues generated from the mobile phone business in Thailand.

Despite the duopoly rights protected by their contracts with the TOT and the CAT, Shinawatra and UCOM have seen their privileges challenged due to technological changes and liberalization policies supported by politicians. Recent developments in digital technology have contributed to new kinds of mobile phone services and new interpretations of existing contracts.[17] As Shinawatra and UCOM rushed to expand into digital phone systems (see Table 10.2), other business groups, supported by politicians, also seized the opportunities provided by the new technology to reform the rights structure to justify opening up the mobile telephone market to new operators.[18] As rents created by the duopoly rights are still very large, rent-seeking efforts by other business groups to enter the expanding market are likely to increase. The growing power of political parties and businessmen-cum-politicians, in contrast to the declining role of bureaucrats, will provide access to new rent-seekers and should pave the way for the erosion, if not the breakdown of the duopoly rights protected by the TOT and the CAT.

Table 10.1 Thailand: revenue from the mobile telephone business, 1987–95

Year	Sales of phone sets [a]	Insurance fee [b]	Connection fee [c]	Annual fee [d]	Operating revenue [e]
1987	439	16	5	33	41
1988	603	22	8	45	96
1989	1,736	21	22	130	456
1990	3,386	42	42	254	1,185
1991	5,200	80	80	480	2,690
1992**	n.a.	789	263	1,580	2,131 *
1993**	n.a.	1,390	463	2,780	4,658 *
1994**	n.a.	1,900	633	3,800	9,237 *
1995** (Jan–Jun)	n.a.	2,811	937	5,622	n.a.

Sources: *Klang samong* 9:98 (November 1991); *Thai thurakit Finance* (16 December 1995); *Daily News* (22 January 1996); *Million Baht Information Thailand 1995*.

Notes: units in million baht
*   Combined operating revenue of AIS (Advanced Info System – Shinawatra group) and TAC (Total Access Communication – UCOM group) only.
**   The 1992–5 figures are based on the total number of mobile telephone subscribers.
a   The annual market value of mobile telephone sets sold.
b   The rate is 3,000 baht/phone.
c   The fee is 1,000 baht/phone.
d   The annual fee is 6,000 baht/phone.
e   Minimum revenue estimates from telephone calls made by users.

Table 10.2 Thailand: mobile cellular telephone services, 1986–94

System	Operator	Inauguration	1992 Subscribers	1993 Subscribers	1994* Subscribers
NMT 470	TOT	Jul 1986	47,000	48,500	48,500
AMPS 800 A	CAT	Feb 1987	46,300	46,300	46,300
NMT 900	AIS (20 yrs)	Oct 1990	120,000	238,000	420,000
AMPS 800 B	TAC (15 yrs)	Sep 1991	62,100	116,900	240,000
GSM 900	AIS	1994	0	0	25,000
PCN-1800	TAC	1994	0	0	35,000
Total			275,400	449,700	814,800
Subscription growth (%)			61.1	63.3	81.2

Sources: *Bangkok Post* (11 March 1994 and 7 February 1995); *TISCO Quarterly Report 95*; TOT; CAT; AIS; TAC.

Note: * Estimates.

The fixed-line telephone project

The third case study involves an auction for the right to construct and operate a three-million-line telephone network. The military, state telecommunications agencies, MOTC, political parties, and local and foreign businesses played major roles in determining the outcome in this case. Political manipulation and intervention by all these interests contributed to the political crisis that arose out of the US\$4 billion telephone project. At the beginning of this project, an 'efficient rights structure' (see Khan and Jomo 2000) was established through a natural monopoly right by the state that would generate legal revenue from the licensee and illegal bribes for 'gatekeepers'. An efficient state could maximize the former in the long run by providing conditions necessary for the healthy growth of the producer, rather than maximizing both types of revenue in the short term. By maximizing growth, the state would maximize its revenue over time. But as things developed, the Thai authorities concerned chose to transfer the right to an inexperienced contractor on poor terms that ran against the long-term interests of the state. Political uncertainty – caused by the increasing pluralism of Thai politics, the faction-ridden military and the emerging power of businesses and political parties – encouraged short-termism and rent-seeking.

Frequent changes in Thai politics and changing coalitions of interests influenced the politics of rent-seeking in major ways. When a coalition – comprising business groups and technocrats from a few public agencies – achieved enough influence to challenge the authority of the military, an attempt to reallocate the rights to the telephone project was made, resulting in a greater degree of transparency. The allocation of part of the contract to a different and perhaps more efficient supplier then followed. Spanning four governments from 1989 to 1992, the fate of the telephone project demonstrated different kinds of telecommunications politics, reflecting changes in the political regime and ongoing struggles among major interests and rent-seekers. During the Chatichai government, the project revealed the crucial role of politicians and technocrats from the MOTC in bringing about the first privatization of basic telecommunications services in Thailand. Later on, rent-seeking by a Sino-Thai business group would influence the cabinet decision and the fate of the project. The military's role and influence – and the bureaucratic corruption associated with it – changed dramatically soon after the coup in 1991, when conflict with interim Prime Minister Anand Panyarachun and many technocrats led to the elimination of the military from telecommunications politics in 1992 with its withdrawal to the barracks.

Politicians and privatization

The birth of the fixed-line telephone project, the first basic telecommunications services to be privatized in Thailand, was the product of joint efforts by politicians, MOTC technocrats, and foreign telecommunications businesses. When severe shortages of telephones during Thailand's economic boom from the late 1980s pressured the government to find a quick solution, Montri Pongpanich, the minister of transport and communications at the time, decided to allow the TOT to add three million more telephone lines in Thailand through a special method called the 'repeat order'.[19] Before the project started, however, intense lobbying from many foreign telecommunications giants[20] convinced the minister that more state revenue could be generated through open bidding that would allow private investments in and operation of the project.

Wanting to privatize the highly protected telephone market while the TOT board was headed by an army general, Montri decided to exclude the military from the project. He then formed an alliance with MOTC technocrats by appointing a committee chaired by the permanent secretary of the ministry to implement the project instead.[21] Such an action was very unusual and widely perceived as outright interference in a state enterprise's affairs.[22] The military's role in the TOT was further reduced when the army general angrily resigned from the board a few months later.[23] According to the standard procedure for large-scale investments, the bidding result would require initial approval from the TOT board prior to the minister's consent. The cabinet's green light was only needed for B-O-T projects funded by the state. But the minister chose to do otherwise, by first selecting the winner – and only then having the choice approved by the TOT board.[24] Undoubtedly, the selection of the Charoen Pokphand (CP) group, one of the largest Sino-Thai business conglomerates, by Montri's appointed committee, stirred up much criticism of ministerial bias and political intervention. The fact that CP was Thailand's largest agro-industrial conglomerate, without any telecommunications experience, did not help the minister.

Moreover, it was hard to justify CP's victory when CP's bid could not be shown to be the best offer compared to the other proposals in terms of revenue-sharing, concession period, or investment costs. Table 10.3 shows that Alcatel made the best financial offer for the one-million-line project (part of the entire three-million-line project) with 56 per cent revenue sharing with the state, compared to CP's 6 per cent offer, and 51 per cent proposed by Ericsson. Table 10.3 also shows that Alcatel offered the most revenue to the state, at 51 per cent, for the two-million-line Bangkok project, followed by Ericsson at 20 per cent, while CP proposed only 6 per cent. In addition, CP asked for the longest concession periods: 28 years for both projects, while Alcatel proposed shorter concessions of 15 years. In terms of costs, CP could have been ranked at the bottom of the list, since Ericsson and Mitsui required smaller capital investments for the one- and two-million-line projects, respectively. Incredibly, the selection committee ruled that all the proposals except for those of CP and Toyomenka were not qualified for the telephone project. CP remained a candidate for both the one- and two-million-line telephone concessions, and Toyomenka was another contender for the former.[25] Interestingly, all the rejected candidates were neither given a chance to revise their proposals nor to negotiate with the committee. Despite the political controversy and public criticism, CP was finally chosen to be the sole supplier for both the one- and two-million-line telephone projects.

Owing to the many different details of each proposal, it is virtually impossible to compare all the proposals on the same grounds. Identification of the most efficient producer would require careful social cost-benefit analysis of what each producer was offering and of costs. It is conceivable that the most socially desirable producer might offer low revenues to the state in the short term, since a large component of domestic production, such as telephone switches and transmission equipment, might require Schumpeterian incentives to rapidly build up the necessary technological and industrial capabilities. In the long run, Schumpeterian rents enjoyed by a local supplier could yield far higher returns to society – and even the state – as local industry would develop and the growth of domestic production could result in higher revenue. Therefore, using short-term tax revenue as the sole criterion for assessing the relative efficiency of a supplier might be inadequate for determining the best and most efficient contractor for the TOT. Due to the limited information available, this chapter cannot provide such a cost-benefit analysis to compare the proposals.

Table 10.3 Thailand: comparison of proposals for the three-million-line telephone project

One-million-line project in rural provincial areas

Bidder	CP	Mitsui	Ericsson	Toyomenka	Alcatel
Investment (mil. baht)	52,311.00[a]	–	26,530.54[b]	40,300.00[b]	35,024.00[c]
Concession Years	28	–	24	30	15
Revenue Sharing (%)	6[d]	–	51[e]	5[e]	56[e]
TOT Income 15 years	26,196.18	–	47,015.88	5,596.77	30,106.38
TOT Income 20 years	41,970.48	–	75,626.88	7,806.77	–
TOT Income 24 years	58,610.28	–	101,376.78	10,016.77	–
TOT Income 28 years	68,802.78	–	–	11,342.77	–

Two-million-line project in the Bangkok metropolitan area

Bidder	CP	Mitsui	Ericsson	Toyomenka	Alcatel
Investment (mil. baht)	96,951.00[a]	33,174.00[f]	53,755.48[b]	–	55,612.00[c]
Concession Years	28	20	24	–	15
Revenue Sharing (%)	6[d]	15	20[e]	–	51[e]
TOT Income 15 years	17,936.58	16,826.10	21,104.00	–	38,155.55
TOT Income 20 years	38,959.08	25,404.90	41,510.40	–	–
TOT Income 24 years	54,556.98	–	51,713.60	–	–
TOT Income 28 years	66,371.88	–	–	–	–

Sources: Compiled from TOT documents.

Notes
a   Three-time investment and modernisation of equipment every 10 years.
b   If tax privileges granted.
c   If tax privileges granted and no maintenance costs involved.
d   Or 30% of profit before tax.
e   Revenue sharing would be recalculated if no tax privileges granted.
f   One million lines only.

As all the proposals were not based on the same conditions (partly due to the ambiguous four-page terms of reference drafted by the selection committee), the committee ruled that other proposals did not qualify, leaving CP as the sole candidate for both the one-million-line and the two-million-line projects, and Toyomenka as the other contender for the former project. Alcatel was ostensibly disqualified for lack of commitment to technical maintenance, and its intention to apply for tax privileges. Ericsson also intended to apply for tax privileges and would not provide any revenue to the TOT during the first five years of operation. Mitsui would only invest in a one-million-line project in Bangkok, while two million more lines would only be added as real demand materialized during 1992–6. Although Toyomenka asked for tax privileges, it was allowed to compete with CP for the one-million-line provincial project as the committee wanted to have more than one firm in the reckoning, and Toyomenka was the least unqualified candidate of all those rejected. See Prime Minister's Office Bangkok: 1991.

Business and politics

The telephone project had progressively unravelled the close connections between business, rent and politics. The minister's controversial handling of the project and public speculation about the enormous rents involved led to cabinet intervention to take control of the project.[26] But when the minister threatened the withdrawal of his party from the government,[27] the ruling coalition's party leaders were forced to compromise and the cabinet eventually agreed to endorse the minister's decision.[28] The cabinet's approval of the project shortly after its initial objections stirred public criticisms of political corruption by the coalition parties. One MP alleged that a 13 per cent commission was paid to cabinet members for their approval of the project.[29] Some sources also claimed that commissions for the project given to politicians and government officials ran into billions of baht.[30] There was also a rumour that CP received improper assistance, resulting in its selection for both the one- and two-million-line projects.[31] These allegations suggest that the award of the contracts to CP involved high input costs, though such shady deals involved straightforward transfers rather than socially wasteful dissipated expenses.

Why was CP so influential? How and in what ways could the business group influence decision-making by government officials? Founded as a small seed and fertilizer trader in 1921 by a Chinese emigrant, CP has experienced phenomenal growth since the 1970s under the leadership of Dhanin Jiaravanon, the son of the founder, when vertical integration of its agro-industry businesses was implemented. By the 1990s, CP had been turned into a multi-billion dollar conglomerate that encompassed more than 200 subsidiaries in eight business areas across the region. Although perceived as influential because of its extensive political connections and the sheer size of its business, CP and its executives have been rather careful not to be seen to be engaging in political affairs. There is no evidence of strong CP political support for any particular party when the telephone project was conceived. Nonetheless, as CP began to expand into new business areas, activities involving state discretion would require high-level political support and more active lobbying to ensure business success.[32] The telephone project was a case in point, with the company's existing political connections used together with other measures to secure the contracts. The huge value of the project and the expected high rates of return were expected to open a new chapter for CP's high-tech business ventures, in response to the global and regional opportunities arising from the telecommunications boom. But the political controversy surrounding the project involving many public officials, increasingly attracted public attention to CP's close relationship with the state. As rumours about political corruption spread like wildfire and the image of Chatichai and his cabinet plummeted, the prime minister was forced to reshuffle his cabinet to improve the government's reputation, but to no avail. Conflicts with the military over the officers' transfers then triggered a peaceful coup on 24 February 1991, a few days before the telephone contract was to have been signed.[33]

The military–technocrat confrontation

The 1991 coup marked the return of bureaucratic power to Thai politics after years of political ascendance by political parties. After the coup, the military appointed Anand Panyarachun, a technocrat-turned-businessman, to head an interim government controlled by the military. However, political conflicts and competition between the military and technocrats soon arose when the telephone project was being reviewed. While the military tried to regain control of state telecommunications agencies like the TOT and CAT and their privatized projects, the technocrats moved to check military power and attempted to change the awarded rights to the telephone project.

In order to revise the draft telephone contract made during the Chatichai government, Prime Minister Anand formed an alliance with the technocrats, and appointed Nukul Prachuabmoh, a former governor of the Bank of Thailand (BOT), to head the Ministry of Transport and Communications. The new minister was instructed to review the telephone project with the objective of avoiding a private monopoly of the telephone network, while minimizing likely project delays. Many reform-minded technocrats were then brought into the TOT board to counterbalance the incumbent interests represented there.[34] While the technocrats attempted to take over the TOT board, the military also sought to secure its position in the state agency by sending the deputy army commander to chair its board.

This political fracturing of the Thai state intensified when the review of the telephone project proceeded. Apart from the TOT board, the military and the technocrats also strived to gain the upper hand in the review committee, which was set up by the Minister of Transport and Communications. When a technocrat from the Ministry of Finance was appointed head of the committee,[35] the committee was so divided that Prime Minister Anand had to intervene to set up another committee chaired by a deputy prime minister for the same task. The World Bank was asked to study the telephone project and to make policy recommendations. Meanwhile, the Anand cabinet tried to break down the monopoly rights given to CP and demanded that seven major conditions be fulfilled in any new agreement with CP; among these were avoidance of any private monopoly in the telephone network and a fair revenue-sharing arrangement.[36] But CP fought back to restore its monopoly rights by cultivating extensive connections with the military, thus heightening political conflict between the military and the Anand government, and forcing Anand to step in to lead the negotiation team himself.[37]

Since all government reports strongly opposed the old draft contract and recommended substantial revision, ranging from abrogation of the contract to splitting the project into smaller ones,[38] the government took the opportunity to redraft the whole contract to reduce the exorbitant rents that would have been enjoyed by CP.[39] The negotiation of the new contract was an arduous task, requiring six rounds of negotiations and so much political bargaining that Anand was said to have threatened to quit the government. At the height of his popularity, in contrast to the military's waning legitimacy, Anand managed to forge a political compromise with the military and CP that allowed CP the right to build and operate two million telephone lines in Bangkok on less generous terms.[40]

The military's new retreat

The award of the Bangkok contract to CP did not bring conflicts and competition between the military and the technocrats to an end. As private rent-seeking for the remaining one-million-line telephone project in the provinces continued, political infighting resumed, with the military-controlled board of TOT defying the government order to finalize the provincial contract during the term of the Anand government.[41] The TOT board was widely suspected of using delaying tactics to procrastinate until a new government, widely expected to be led by military figures, would take office after the general election in March 1992. The Minister of Transport and Communications transmitted a note to Prime Minister Anand, predicting that misconduct in the provincial telephone project would occur with 'co-operation from TOT officials at various levels' while honest board members would 'be removed in due time'.[42] In response to these worrying concerns, Anand sent a memo to the military leader as well as to the TOT chairman (also the deputy army commander), urging them to speed up the telephone project for the following reasons:

> (1) The TOT managing director had not done his duty, was irresponsible, and had delayed the selection process. As a result, the bid for the one million line telephone project could not be settled within the term of this government. (2) It is essential for both the government and the NPKC [the interim organization which had launched the 1991 coup] to regard this as an urgent issue which had to be settled before 22 March 1992 [the end of the government's term]. (3) I have spoken to Gen. Issarapong [TOT chairman] and Gen. Chatchom [TOT board member], and both had agreed to solve the problem. (4) I am afraid that this issue is a complex one involving irregular deals. Therefore, I would like the consideration of technical proposals and administrative processes to end as soon as possible in order that financial considerations can commence next week. (5) The reputation of this government and the NPKC, and the interests of the state and the people, depend on transparency, honesty, and justice.[43]

In addition to the above memo, the Anand cabinet also gave orders to the TOT to accelerate its bidding process and to adopt measures that would ensure transparency and fairness.[44]

As the 1992 election was soon followed by mass protests and political uprisings that sent the military back to the barracks and brought back the technocrats into office,[45] the negotiation of the provincial telephone project took a different turn and produced a more non-partisan outcome. It was reported that the chairman of the financial committee tried to ensure fairness by chaining the box containing the financial envelopes to pre-empt any attempt to swap financial proposals, such as was believed to have occurred with the previous telephone bidding.[46] As a result, TT&T, a consortium jointly owned by Thai and Japanese business groups, was awarded the provincial contract, with a revenue-sharing offer of 43.1 per cent for the state (compared to CP's revised Bangkok contract of 22 per cent). It was then calculated that the new deal with TT&T would increase state revenue by as much as 200 billion baht over the 25-year concession period. In theory, the revised Bangkok and provincial telephone contracts would together increase state revenue by 270 billion baht over the 25-year period.[47] Certainly, the provincial telephone project came to be regarded by the Thai media as one of the most transparent bids Thailand had ever had. However, the estimated windfalls from both the Bangkok and provincial telephone projects proved to be unrealistic, as both CP and TT&T could not achieve as much revenue as they had envisaged. Thailand's currency devaluation in July 1997 and the subsequent economic recession put both concessionaires into the red.

In sum, the three million fixed-line telephones saga exemplified the changing politics of telecommunications and rent-seeking in Thailand. At first, politicians, military officers and collaborating bureaucrats apparently granted monopoly rights to CP in exchange for immediate gains in the form of rent transfers, with scant regard for maximizing social benefits. But changing conditions for rent-seeking by the private sector, including the competition between the military and the technocrats, and the resurgent technocratic influence that followed, led to much more transparent and 'rational' allocations of rights, with seemingly more efficient suppliers being awarded the one-million-line provincial telephones contract. However, the increasing competition for rents, combined with the reallocation of rights and contract revision, substantially reduced the potential rents to be gained by CP and TT&T. The immense rents expected from the telephone projects were thus reduced in favour of greater revenue for the state, but the situation has changed significantly since the financial crisis struck Thailand.

Conclusion

Rents have played an important role in the politics of telecommunications liberalization in Thailand. The initial period of telecommunications privatization involved competition over access to and control of rents. Rents secured by Sino-Thai business groups have helped accelerate the capital accumulation needed for business expansion and development of the telecommunications industry. The increasing power of businessmen and politicians in the Thai political economy has boosted the political weight of the liberalization coalition and made the restructuring of rights possible. Driven by the growth of private sector rent-seeking and the public demand for transparency and clear rules, the liberalization coalition has endeavoured to alter the rights structure to allow more business groups to enter and compete in the market.

The three cases discussed above demonstrate conflicts and competition among bureaucratic and non-bureaucratic interests in Thai telecommunications politics during the 1980s and 1990s. The increasing privatization and liberalization of the telecommunications industry was due to the fracturing of the state, declining bureaucratic power and its less efficient rights structure and allocations on the one hand, and the growing political influence of business and more aggressive rent-seeking efforts on the other. The telephone directory contract involved ineffective rights creation and protection owing to divisions within the bureaucracy, which allowed the private monopoly to be challenged. Economies of scale favoured a natural monopoly to bring down unit costs. The high costs of rent-seeking and rent protection have caused considerable inefficiency. Both the mobile telephone case and the fixed-line telephone concessions show the growth of private sector rent-seeking in Thailand taking the form of private capitalists forming and influencing state (military, bureaucratic and political) factions to help restructure and secure rights. The second case shows private rent-seeking leading to more efficient services as artificial monopolies created by state agencies were broken down. The third case suggests that greater transparency in the allocation of rights could occur due to the growth of private rent-seeking and the increasing influence or power of coalitions favouring liberalization. The third case also provides a good illustration of changing telecommunications politics, from party-based politics under Chatichai to technocratic government under Anand. The return to democracy in Thailand after September 1992 resulted in more active roles for business in telecommunications politics and rent-seeking. The line drawn between businessmen and politicians has become even less relevant as more and more telecoms tycoons have directly joined or even formed political parties, especially since the mid-1990s.[48] However, this chapter does not cover telecommunications politics during the late 1990s.

With Thailand's transition from a bureaucratic-dominated state to a more plural society, business interests increasingly compete for power, rights and rents. The rapid growth of the telecommunications industry, partly as a result of increasing private rent-seeking in the changing political economy, is probably not typical of the growth of other industries. The divided state and the competing regulatory authorities that encouraged private rent-seeking in telecommunications probably raised input costs and undermined the Schumpeterian rent structure of some businesses. Because telecommunications technology has played a major role in the success of business operations, and most Thai telecommunications businesses are engaged in the application of technology rather than its development, Schumpeterian rents, which require efficient rights structures and protection, have not been decisive for business growth in Thai telecommunications.

There has been no attempt in this chapter to estimate the social waste due to rent-seeking in the telecommunications industry, but there is little evidence of significant waste as such beyond that associated with electoral politics. Instead, the considerable evidence of corruption would presumably involve transfers of various types. However, while there may have been little waste in terms of socially unproductive rent-seeking costs, rent-seeking was generally not efficient. Rights obtained were rarely secured, regardless of the cost of obtaining the rights, owing to the politically contingent and insecure nature of the rights regimes, which were generally vulnerable before rights were contractually secured (though apparently, not thereafter). Such ambiguity in securing rights probably encouraged protracted rent-seeking efforts, raising related costs and waste. In so far as the structuring of rights has been seen to be politically determined, it has increased the scope for and range of rent-seeking activities and efforts, in contrast to situations less prone to political influence. And as long as electoral politics are seen to be the primary, and even a legitimate means of rent-seeking in Thailand, this has to be the focus of future analysis in this area. But to the extent that electoral outcomes may be fluid – due to the constantly shifting coalitions of recent Thai party politics – or can be overturned by military intervention, the rights secured are likely to be seen as contingent and precarious, which, in turn, increases rent-seeking efforts and costs.

Notes

1 During 1951–91, Thailand's GDP per capita increased at an average rate of 4.3 per cent per annum, while annual economic growth from the introduction of the First National Economic Development Plan in 1961 through 1985 averaged an impressive 7.1 per cent (Warr 1993: 25; Wisarn 1989: Table 2.1).

2 The share of agriculture in GDP slipped from 32 per cent in 1965 to only 12 per cent in 1990, while industry expanded from 23 to 39 per cent during the same period. The proportion of the labour force employed in industry and services also rose to 30 per cent in 1990 (Warr 1993: Tables 1 and 8).

3 Gallagher (1991) has estimated that rents in some African countries were as high as 6–37 per cent of their GDP.

4 Many pre-1957 radical works, mostly in the Marxist tradition, were reprinted and widely read by scholars and university students. See details in Craig J. Reynolds and Lysa Hong (1983).

5 According to Pasuk and Baker (1995), the term *jao pho* refers to businessmen whose interests lie in certain types of economic activities, including resource exploitation, agro-industry, construction contracting, trading, auto dealership, whisky distributorship, real estate development, underground lotteries, smuggling, gambling and criminal activities.

6 This chapter uses a broad understanding of rent-seeking to focus on actions that seek to alter, enforce, maintain or circumvent government policies that entail transfers of resources or incomes. Tariffs, domestic monopolies, credit rationing, foreign exchange rationing, government allocation of resources, and bribery are means by which rents are appropriated. The government may also gain rents directly through the operation of public enterprises. Also, rents may be sought by politicians lobbying for particular legislation or monopoly rights. See Gallagher (1991).

7 According to the Telegraph and Telephone Act 1934, state monopoly in telecommunications did not cover non-infrastructure projects.

8 The call for bids attracted four tenderers: ATTI Media, AT&T International, Siam Telephone Directory, and GTDC.

9 The committee favoured Siam Telephone Directory and GTDC, and unanimously rejected the AT&T bid because of its violation of two important conditions indicated in the terms of reference: the tenderer must be a legal entity based in Thailand; and the tenderer must possess a permit for the publishing and advertising business (*Prachachart thurakit,* 22 April 1987).

10 The new terms of reference stipulated that if selected, the tenderer be given a 30-day period to meet the two previous conditions.

11 Official letter from Sujin Timsuwan, Director-General of the Prosecutions Department, to the TOT managing director, dated 22 September 1986.

12 For rents allocated to mobile telephone retailers, see Nartnapha (1991).

13 Although both agencies started mobile telephone operations in the 1970s, their competition was rather limited until 1987 when personal services began.

14 The CAT continued to operate AMPS MHz 800 (system A) services (interview with a CAT senior official, 24 February 1993).

15 Whereas Shinawatra received a 20-year concession from the TOT, Total Access Communication (TAC) only got a 15-year concession from the CAT and was charged a higher fee for using TOT networks. As a result, TAC customers were charged for incoming telephone calls while Shinawatra users were not.

16 For example, the net profits earned by Shinawatra went up from 952 million baht to 1.5 billion baht, 2.9 billion baht, and 3.6 billion baht during 1993–6. Meanwhile, UCOM's net profits jumped from 712 million baht to 2.0 billion baht, 2.6 billion baht, and 3.5 billion baht during the same period (*Bangkok Post,* 15 January 1996).

17 The launching of the 'Thaicom 1' satellite in late 1993 enabled Shinawatra to extend and improve its mobile telephone services, broadcasting, and other telecommunications businesses throughout Thailand and Indochina. The move encouraged UCOM to join Motorola's 'Iridium project' to provide mobile satellite services in the region (*Bangkok Post,* 28 January 1994). But the steep cost of the Iridium project and its low subscription rate made the project, one of the most expensive telecommunications schemes ever, bankrupt in 2000.

18 Further liberalization of mobile telephones would require an amendment of contracts that protect Shinawatra and TAC from more competition. See *Telecom Journal,* 2: 29 (16–31 December 1993) and 2: 35 (1–15 February 1994).

19 Initially, Montri came up with a vague idea of adding five million more telephone lines by the end of the Seventh Plan, i.e. by 1996. But the TOT later convinced the minister to scale down the project due to the lower demand forecasts and the agency's limited capacity to expand (Sakkarin 1995).

20 They included British Telecom, Mitsui, Toyomenka, Alcatel, and Ericsson. Interview with Dr Sitthichai Pokhai-udom, former CAT board member, and Mr Direk Jaroenphol, TOT deputy managing director.

21 The committee, appointed by Montri in 1990 to draft the terms of reference for the project and to select the winner, consisted of MOTC Permanent Secretary Sriphumi, Deputy Secretary Mahidol Jantarangkul, TOT Managing Director Paibul Limpaphayom, TOT Deputy Managing Director Olarn Pientham, PTD Director-General Sombat Uthaisang, and TOT Director, Police Major General Suchart Phueksakol.

22 Under government regulations, the TOT board is responsible for the whole bidding process by setting up various committees to ensure fairness and accountability. These committees are tasked to draft the terms of reference, carry out financial and technical biddings, and pick the winner.

23 Despite a rumour that Gen. Jaruay Vongsayan was frustrated by the lack of co-operation from TOT officials, his hostile relationship with Montri was believed to be the major cause of his resignation (*Prachachart thurakit* 22 March 1990; *Than setthakit,* 9 April 1990).

24 After the committee (appointed by the minister) reached the decision to select CP as the contractor, the result was submitted to Montri on 5 September 1990 for his endorsement before being reported to Prime Minister Chatichai on 11 September 1990. But the TOT board was asked to award the contract to CP on 13 September 1990 in order to conform to the TOT's regulation prior to the minister's formal approval. Finally, the government sent its note, dated 20 September 1990, indicating its decision to enter into contract with CP.

25 Alcatel was disqualified for its demand for tax privileges and lack of technical support. Ericsson also intended to apply for tax privileges and a five-year grace period for revenue sharing with the state. Mitsui planned to invest in only one million lines in the Bangkok project and would only add the other two million lines as demand increased. Toyomenka also asked for tax privileges, but was allowed to compete with CP for the provincial project, ostensibly because it was the least unqualified candidate of all those rejected. See Prime Minister's Office 1991 (Report on the Facts of the Three Million Line Telephone Project. Bangkok: 1991).

26 On 2 September 1990, Chalerm Yubamrung, minister attached to the Prime Minister's Office, and Sanoh Thienthong, deputy minister of interior, urged Chatichai and the cabinet to review Montri's decision, claiming that such a large project needed to be studied carefully (*Siam Rath sapdah wijarn*, 37: 18, 14–20 October 1990).

27 *Dok bia*, 9: 114 (December 1990).

28 But four observations were made by the cabinet as follows: 1) the private investor must not be allowed to cause damage to the public; 2) the future expansion of the project must be approved by the cabinet; 3) the investor must supply at least 50 per cent from domestic sources; 4) the NESDB and the Solicitor General's Office were asked to draft criteria and procedures for future privatized projects (Cabinet Resolution, 9 October 1990).

29 *Siam Rath sapdah wijarn*, 37: 18 (14–20 October 1990).

30 Whereas a foreign financial analyst said that 100 million pounds sterling was distributed among cabinet members and key government officials, an academic source claimed that the commission ran as high as four billion baht. Interview with a foreign financial analyst of a financial securities firm, 11 January 1993, and a telecommunications expert and former CAT board member, March 1993.

31 It was rumoured that CP's financial proposal was altered to make it marginally higher than Toyomenka's. Whereas Toyomenka proposed 19 and 21 per cent revenue sharing for the 20- and 25-year concessions respectively, CP offered 19.5 and 21.5 per cent for the same periods (interviews with a senior official of the Ministry of Science, Technology and Environment, and a reporter of *The Nation*, 6–10 March 1993).

32 As an example, military participation in a resort developed by the Jiaravanon family was seen as a kind of protection for encroachment into a national forest reserve area.

33 The major excuse for the coup was rampant corruption in public projects, particularly the telephone project.

34 The technocrats included well-known public officials such as Pisit Lee-atam, Roungroj Sriprasertsuk, Savit Bhotivihok, and Somchai Ruechupan.

35 Nukul chose M.R. Jatumongkol Sonakul, director general of the Department of the Comptroller General, to head the committee, although Gen. Chatchom Kanlong was nominated by the NPKC.

36 The seven principles are: first, the public must receive good services at reasonable prices; second, there must be no legal or *de facto* monopoly, either economically or technologically; third, the government must receive a fair share of revenues; fourth, the investment must be done by an experienced and creditable company; fifth, investors must shoulder the risks involved; sixth, the government would provide an exclusivity guarantee to the investor for an exact period; seventh, there must be no restrictions for future network expansion by the state (Cabinet Resolution, 18 June 1991).

37 The committee comprised Prime Minister Anand, Nukul Prachuabmoh, Gen. Viroj Saengsanit, Gen. Chatchom Kanlong, Narongchai Akrasaranee and Staporn Kavitanon.

38 The World Bank report, completed in May 1991, noted that the proposed project was 'a high risk one that is not the most advantageous one for the public or the Royal Thai Government'. The report attacked many weaknesses of the project and the old draft contract, ranging from the feasibility of the project to its likely private monopoly status.

39 They included shortening the exclusivity period, breaking up the project into at least two packages by geography with different investors, and revamping the revenue-sharing formula.

40 See the seven points of agreement between the committee and CP in Cabinet Resolution, 18 June 1991.

41 During the second week of March, while the technocrats on the TOT board tried to accelerate the bidding process by first comparing the financial proposals, their effort was thwarted by other military-backed board members (Roungroj Sriprasertsuk's memo to Minister Nukul, dated 13 March 1992).

42 Nukul's note to the prime minister, dated 16 March 1992.

43 Prime Minister Anand's note attached to Nukul's report on the progress of the telephone project, dated 11 March 1992.

44 Cabinet Resolution, 17 March 1992.

45 When Gen. Suchinda Kraprayoon assumed the premiership after the 1992 election contrary to his earlier promise not to become prime minister himself, pro-democracy groups demanded an elected prime minister and called for Suchinda's resignation. As the political crisis developed, a large crowd of half a million people, embracing all social and economic strata, occupied many roads in the old city of Bangkok. Confrontation between the pro-democracy protesters, led by Palang Dharma Party leader Chamlong Srimuang, and the Suchinda regime reached its zenith on 18 May 1992, when a violent military crackdown escalated the situation and provoked more riots and protests across Bangkok and other cities. The King then intervened and Gen. Suchinda was forced to resign from the government while an amnesty was granted to all the parties concerned. In order to ensure political and economic stability, former Prime Minister Anand Panyarachun was then handpicked by the King to head an interim government for a second time.

46 The financial committee became a political battleground between the technocrats, led by chairman Roungroj Sriprasertsuk, on the one hand, and the military's allies, comprising some senior TOT bureaucrats, on the other (interview with Mr Sarin Skulratana, director of the International Communications Division, and a former Nukul aide).

47 The MOTC's note to the Counter Corruption Commission (CCC), dated 28 September 1993.

48 For example, Thaksin Shinawatra, chairman of SHIN Corp., the largest telecom group in Thailand, became leader of the Palang Dharma Party in 1995 and later served in various cabinets before heading the Thai Rak Thai Party and then becoming Prime Minister in 2001. The UCOM Group also sent three senior executives of the company to run in the 1995 election including the younger brother of its President. Likewise, Adisai Photaramik of the Jasmine Group, a major shareholder of TT&T, joined the Thai Rak Thai Party for the 2001 general election and was appointed Minister of Commerce.

Bibliography

Anderson, Benedict (1977) 'Withdrawal Symptoms: Social and Cultural Aspects of the October 6 Coup'. *Bulletin of Concerned Asian Scholars*, 9(3) July–September.

Anek Laothamatas (1989) 'From Bureaucratic Polity to Liberal Corporatism: Business Associations and the New Political Economy of Thailand'. Ph.D. dissertation, Columbia University, New York.

Anek Laothamatas (1993) 'Thurakit bon senthang prachathippatai: thitsadee kab khwam-pen-jing' (Business and Thai Democracy), in Sungsidh Piriyarangsan and Pasuk Phongpaichit (eds) *Chon-chan-klang bon krasae prachathippatai thai* (The Middle Class and Thai Democracy). Bangkok: Chulalongkorn University, Political Economy Centre.

Bangkok Post, 28 January 1994, and 15 January 1996.

Chai-Anan Samudavanija (1987) 'The Bureaucracy', in Somsakdi Xuto (ed.) *Government and Politics of Thailand*. Singapore: Oxford University Press.

Chai-Anan Samudavanija (1989a) 'The Role of the Military in National Development', in Suchart Prasith-rathsint (ed.) *Thailand's National Development: Social and Economic Background*. Bangkok: Thai University Research Association.

Chai-Anan Samudavanija (1989b) *Khana kammakarn ratthamontri fai setthakit* (The Economic Cabinet). Bangkok: Thailand Development Research Institute.

Chai-Anan Samudavanija (1990a) 'The Future Study of the Civil-Military Relations'. *Journal of Social Sciences* 27(1–2), March–July.

Chai-Anan Samudavanija (1990b) 'Administrative Reform', in Suchart Prasith-rathsint (ed.) *Thailand on the Move: Stumbling Blocks and Breakthroughs*. Bangkok: Thailand Development Research Institute.

Chai-Anan Samudavanija (1990c) 'Thailand: Economic Policy-Making in a Liberal Technocratic Polity', in J.W. Langford and K.L. Brownsey (eds) *Economic Policy-Making in the Asia-Pacific Region*. Halifax, Nova Scotia: Institute for Research on Public Policy.

Chai-Anan Samudavanija (1990d) *Rath kap sangkhom: trailak rath thai nai sangkhom phahu siam* (The State and Society: The Three-dimensional State in Plural Siam). Bangkok: Chulalongkorn University Press.

Chai-Anan Samudavanija (1991) *Rath* (The State). Bangkok: Chulalongkorn University Press.

Chairat Charoensin-o-larn (1988) *Understanding Post-war Reformism in Thailand: A Reinterpretation of Rural Development.* Bangkok: DK Books.

Charoen Pokphand (1990) *Proposal on Joint Investment of the Telephone Expansion in Thailand.* Bangkok: Charoen Pokphand.

Colclough, Christopher (1993) 'Structuralism versus Neo-liberalism: An Introduction', in C. Colclough and J. Manor (eds) *States or Markets? Neo-liberalism and the Development Policy Debate.* New York: Oxford University Press.

Doner, Richard F. (1991) *Driving a Bargain: Automobile Industrialization and Japanese Firms in Southeast Asia.* Berkeley: University of California Press.

Gallagher, Mark (1991) *Rent-Seeking and Economic Growth in Africa.* Boulder: Westview Press.

Girling, John L.S. (1981a) *Thailand: Society and Politics.* Ithaca: Cornell University Press.

Girling, John L.S. (1981b) *The Bureaucratic Polity in Modernizing Societies: Similarities, Differences, and Prospects in the ASEAN Region.* Singapore: ISEAS.

Grindle, Merilee (1991) 'The New Political Economy: Positive Economics and Negative Politics', in G.M. Meier (ed.) *Politics and Policy Making in Developing Countries: Perspectives on the New Political Economy.* San Francisco: International Center for Economic Growth.

Haggard, Stephan and R. Kaufman (eds) (1992) *The Politics of Economic Adjustment.* Princeton, New Jersey: Princeton University Press.

Hawes, Gary and Hong Liu (1993) 'Explaining the Dynamics of the Southeast Asian Political Economy: State, Society, and the Search for Economic Growth'. *World Politics*, 45(4).

Hewison, Kevin (1986) 'Capital in the Thai Countryside: the Sugar Industry', *Journal of Contemporary Asia.* 16(1).

Hewison, Kevin (1987) 'National Interests and Economic Downturn: Thailand', in R. Robison, K. Hewison, and R. Higgott (eds) *Southeast Asia in the 1980s: The Politics of Economic Crisis.* Sydney: Allen & Unwin.

Hewison, Kevin (1989) *Bankers and Bureaucrats: Capital and the Role of the State in Thailand.* New Haven: Yale University Southeast Asian Studies Council.

Hewison, Kevin (1992) 'Challenges to the Thai State: From Capitalist to Bourgeois State'. Paper presented to the conference on 'Thailand: The State and Civil Society', 18 October, Australian National University, Canberra, organized by the ANU Thai Studies Group.

Hewison, Kevin (1993) 'Of Regimes, State and Pluralities: Thai Politics Enters the 1990s', in K. Hewison, R. Robison and G. Rodan (eds) *Southeast Asia in the 1990s: Authoritarianism, Democracy and Capitalism.* Sydney: Allen & Unwin.

Huntington, Samuel (1989) 'Techniques of Political Graft', in Arnold J. Heidenheimer, Michael Johnston and Victor T. LeVine (eds) *Political Corruption.* New Brunswick, NJ: Transaction Publishers.

Huntington, Samuel (1993) *The Third Wave: Democratization in the Late Twentieth Century.* Norman: University of Oklahoma Press.

Keyes, Charles F. (1989) *Thailand: Buddhist Kingdom as Modern Nation-State.* Bangkok: DK Books.

Khan, Mushtaq H. and Jomo K.S. (eds) (2000) *Rents, Rent-Seeking and Economic Development: Theory and Evidence in Asia.* Cambridge: Cambridge University Press.

Kraisak Choonhavan (1984) 'The Growth of Domestic Capital and Thai Industrialization'. *Journal of Contemporary Asia*, 14(2).

Kraiyudht Dhiratayakinant (1990) 'The Role of Private Sector in the Thai Economy: Now and in the Future', in Suchart Prasith-rathsint (ed.) *Thailand on the Move: Stumbling Blocks and Breakthroughs*. Bangkok: Thailand Development Research Institute.

Krirkkiat Phipatseritham and Kunio Yoshihara (1983) *Business Groups in Thailand*, Research Notes and Discussions Paper No. 41. Singapore: ISEAS.

Krit Permtanjit (1982) *Political Economy of Dependent Capitalist Development: Study on the Limits of the Capacity of the State to Rationalize in Thailand*. Bangkok: Chulalongkorn University, Social Research Institute.

Likhit Dhiravegin (1992) *Demi Democracy: The Evolution of the Thai Political System*. Singapore: Times Academic Press.

MacIntyre, Andrew (1990) *Business-Government Relations in Industrialising East Asia: South Korea and Thailand*. Australia-Asia Papers No. 53, Centre for the Study of Australia-Asia Relations, Griffith University, Nathan.

Mackie, Jamie (1988) 'Economic Growth in the ASEAN Region: the Political Underpinnings', in Helen Hughes (ed.) *Achieving Industrialization in East Asia*. Cambridge: Cambridge University Press.

Meier, Gerald (1991) 'Policy Lessons and Policy Formation', in G.M. Meier (ed.) *Politics and Policy Making in Developing Countries: Perspectives on the New Political Economy*. San Francisco: International Center for Economic Growth.

Nartnapha Rohitakanee (1991) 'Kha chao thang setthakit kab talad thorasap kluentee' (The Economic Rent in Mobile Telephone Market). MA thesis, Thammasat University, Bangkok.

Neher, Clark D. and Bidhya Bowornwathana (1984) 'Thai and Western Studies of Politics in Thailand'. Paper presented at the International Conference on Thai Studies, 22–24 August, Bangkok.

Ockey, James (1993) 'Capital Accumulation by Other Means: Provincial Crime, Corruption, and the Bureaucratic Polity'. Paper presented to 5th International Conference on Thai Studies, SOAS, London.

Pasuk Phongpaichit (1989) 'Technocrats, Businessmen and Generals: Democracy and Economic Policy-Making in Thailand'. Paper presented at the workshop on 'The Dynamics of Economic Policy Reform in Southeast Asia and Australia', 7–9 October, Centre for the Study of Australian-Asian Relations, Griffith University, Nathan.

Pasuk Phongpaichit (1993) 'Jao-pho lae thurakit thongthin: amnat nokrabob karn khorrapchan lae prachathippatai' (Jao Pho and Provincial Business: Power, Corruption, and Democracy). Paper presented to the conference on 'Businessmen, Technocrats, Politicians, and Generals: Corruption and Future of Thai Democracy,' 27 August, organized by the Political Economy Centre, Chulalongkorn University.

Pasuk Phongpaichit and Chris Baker (1993) '*Jao Sua, Jao Pho, Jao Tii*: Lords of Thailand's Transition'. Paper presented at the 5th International Conference on Thai Studies, SOAS, London.

Pasuk Phongpaichit and Chris Baker (1995) *Thailand: Economy and Politics*. Oxford: Oxford University Press.

Patcharee Thanamai (1985) 'Patterns of Industrial Policy-making in Thailand: Japanese Multinationals and Domestic Actors in the Automobile and Electrical Appliances Industries'. Ph.D. dissertation, University of Wisconsin, Madison.

Phu jad karn (1988) 18 December.

Pisan Suriyamongkol and James F. Guyot (1986) *The Bureaucratic Polity at Bay*. Public Administration Study Document, No. 51. Graduate School of Public Administration, NIDA, Bangkok.

Prachachart thurakit, 3 October 1984, 22 April 1987, 15 August 1989 and 22 March 1990.

Prime Minister's Office (1991) *Khor-thet-jing khrongkarn thorasap sarm larn lekmai* (Report on the Facts of the Three-Million-Line Telephone Project). Bangkok: Prime Minister's Office.

Prizzia, Ross (1985) *Thailand in Transition: the Role of Oppositional Forces*. Asian Studies at Hawaii, No. 32, Center for Asian and Pacific Studies. Honolulu: University of Hawaii Press.

Prudhisan Jumbala (1987) 'Interest and Pressure Groups', in Somsakdi Xuto (ed.) *Government and Politics of Thailand*. Singapore: Oxford University Press.

Reynolds, Craig J. and Lysa Hong (1983) 'Marxism in Thai Historical Studies', *Journal of Asian Studies*, 43(1), November.

Riggs, Fred W. (1966) *Thailand: The Modernization of a Bureaucratic Polity*. Honolulu: East West Center.

Sakkarin Niyomsilpa (1995) 'The Political Economy of Telecommunications Liberalisation in Thailand'. Ph.D. thesis, Australian National University, Canberra.

Siam Rath (1987) 21 July.

Sidel, T.J. (1996) 'Siam and Its Twin? Democratization and Bossim in Contemporary Thailand and the Philippines'. *IDS Bulletin*, 27(2).

Sombat Chantrawong (1991) 'Botbart khong jao-pho thongthin nai setthakit karnmuang thai' (The Role of Rural Godfathers in the Thai Political Economy). Paper presented to the seminar on 'Thai Political Economy in the 1990s', 20–21 November, organized by the Political Economy Centre, Chulalongkorn University.

Suchit Bunbongkarn (1987) *The Military in Thai Politics 1981–86*. Singapore: Institute of Southeast Asian Studies.

Suehiro, Akira (1989) *Capital Accumulation in Thailand*. Tokyo: Centre for East Asian Cultural Studies.

Suehiro, Akira (1992) 'Capitalist Development in Postwar Thailand: Commercial Bankers, Industrial Elite, and Agribusiness Groups', in R. McVey (ed.) *Southeast Asian Capitalists*. Ithaca, NY: Cornell University.

Suraphol Thamromdee (1987) 'Sociology of Development and Underdevelopment: Contribution to the Critique of Dependent Theory'. M.A. thesis, Faculty of Sociology and Anthropology, Thammasat University.

Suthy Prasartset (1980) 'The Impact of Transnational Corporations on Economic Structure of Thailand'. Paper delivered at Conference on Asian Research in the Global Context, Yokohama, 1–5 December.

Telecom Journal, 2 (29), 16–31 December 1993; and 2 (35), 1–15 February 1994.

Thak Chaloemtiarana (1979) *Thailand: The Politics of Despotic Paternalism*. Bangkok: Social Science Association of Thailand.

Than Setthakit (1990) 9 April.

Thirayut Bunmi (1993) *Chut plian haeng yuksamai* (Transition of Time). Bangkok: Winyuchon Publishing House.

Trakoon Meechai (1982) 'Khwam samphan rawang klum thurakit ekkachon lae kharajchakarn kab karnmuang thai' (The Effects of the Interactions between Business Groups and Bureaucracy on Thai Politics). MA thesis, Department of Government, Faculty of Political Science, Chulalongkorn University, Bangkok.

Wade, Robert (1990) *Governing the Market: Economic Theory and the Role of Government in East Asian Industrialization*. Princeton, NJ: Princeton University Press.

Warr, Peter (1993) *Thailand's Economic Miracle*, Thailand Information Paper No. 1, National Thai Studies Centre, Australian National University, Canberra.

Wasrunee Boonyawinaikul (1995) 'Collaboration between the Public and Private Enterprises: A Case Study of the Landline Telephone Network', M.A. thesis, Thammasat University, Bangkok.

Wattanachai Winichakoon (1992) 'Formation and Behaviour of Thai Industrial Capitalists: A Case Study of Charoen Pokphand'. MA thesis, Faculty of Economics, Thammasat University, Bangkok.

Wisarn Pubphavesa (1989) 'Review of Economic Development in Thailand', in Suchart Prasith-rathsint (ed.) *Thailand's National Development: Social and Economic Background.* Bangkok: Thai University Research Association.

World Bank (1991) *Thailand Telecommunications Mission-Aide-Memoir.* Bangkok: World Bank.

Yoshihara Kunio (1988) *The Rise of Ersatz Capitalism in Southeast Asia.* Singapore: Oxford University Press.

11 Japanese transnational production networks and ethnic Chinese business networks in East Asia[1]

Linkages and regional integration

Kit G. Machado

Significant increases in the size and scope of ethnic Chinese firms' activities in East Asia in the early 1990s, particularly their overseas investments, have received widespread attention. Analysts from the Australian Department of Foreign Affairs and Trade say that ethnic Chinese 'entrepreneurs are at the very heart of East Asia's economic boom' (1995: 1). They estimate that the latter 'have created investment flows within East Asia that may exceed flows from the Japanese, normally thought of as the region's largest foreign investors' (1995: 6) and contend that the 'extensive business networks [they control] stitch together the economies of the region' (1995: 1). Such analyses are often extravagant and misleading, and in many cases they are advanced in support of the erroneous proposition that Japan's regional economic predominance is being eclipsed. A well known American economist and his associate assert that '[t]he net result of these cross-border investment flows…has been the rapid emergence of a new Chinese-based economy that is the epicenter for industry, commerce, and finance in South-East Asia' (Weidenbaum and Hughes 1996: 16). A widely read popular writer on Asian affairs describes the ethnic Chinese as 'a separate world force [whose] leverage far exceeds that of Japan's corporate shoguns' (Seagrave 1995: 14–15). A *Far Eastern Economic Review* correspondent writes of the integrative role of ethnic Chinese economic 'networks based on bonds of clan or kinship, [which] span the region more effectively than any corporate system or web of bilateral ties could devise' and says that '[t]ies like these [make] this region more integrated and interdependent than it often seems in either political or diplomatic terms' (Vatikiotis 1996: 201). Commenting on such trends, a Berkeley Roundtable on the International Economy analyst asserts that 'Japanese firms already have lost their dominant position as carriers of Asian regionalization' (Ernst 1995: 45), and a German business journalist says that 'Japan's…control of Asia's economies is fading, and the…overseas Chinese are taking over the economic reins of the region' (*Wirtschaftswoche* 1996).

There is no doubt that the activities of business people from the relatively small ethnic Chinese community made a very large contribution to the East Asian economic boom of the 1980s and early 1990s. Some 50 million ethnic Chinese constitute less than 10 per cent of the population of East Asia outside of China. Unevenly distributed across the region, they make up close to 100 per cent of the population in Taiwan and Hong Kong, 78 per cent in Singapore, 28 per cent in Malaysia, 10 per cent in Thailand, and between only 1 and 4 per cent in the rest of the countries of South-East Asia – Indonesia, Burma, Laos, Cambodia, the Philippines, and Vietnam. In 1990, they produced 'an estimated GDP [of] about US$ 450 billion,...[which was] almost on a par with China's GDP of approximately US$500 billion,[2]...generated by more than twenty times the number of people' (Australia, Department of Foreign Affairs and Trade 1995: 1). With a US$9,000 GDP per capita, the ethnic Chinese community of East Asia ranked with lower end, high income countries of the time (e.g. Spain, Ireland). These results are clearly impressive, but the claim that ethnic Chinese business activities are becoming the leading integrative force in East Asia is equally plainly wrong. Japanese transnational corporations (TNCs) are pre-eminent in this regard.

Misreading of the integrative role of ethnic Chinese economic activity derives primarily from uncritical assessment of some of its widely noted features. The most important are: first, the sectoral distribution and character of ethnic Chinese businesses at home and abroad; second, some common organizational characteristics of ethnic Chinese businesses; and third, most importantly, the nature of the linkages among these businesses, and between these businesses and Japanese (and other) TNCs. Ethnic Chinese business activity at home is heavily concentrated in property and services, while only a minority is in manufacturing. A larger portion of ethnic Chinese overseas investment in East Asia is in manufacturing, but much of this is in small- and medium-sized enterprises (SMEs) in lower technology areas, rather than in the dynamic sectors central to the formation of production networks and integration of the region. Moreover, some of what is assumed to be ethnic Chinese investment in manufacturing, particularly in more dynamic sectors, actually originates with East Asian subsidiaries of Japanese (as well as other) TNCs or is proxy for or heavily dependent upon Japanese (or other) TNCs. Unlike Japanese TNC-centred production networks, which are based on long-term linkages in a division of labour in manufacturing, Chinese business networks are for the most part informal, personally based and rather fluid alliances in commerce and services. These tendencies are, in part, related to the family-centred organization of many Chinese businesses. In any case, faulty analysis of these points leads to exaggeration of the integrative role of ethnic Chinese overseas investment.

The purposes of this chapter are to: first, show the magnitude and sectoral distribution of ethnic Chinese businesses in their home countries and in East Asia; second, analyse differences in the characteristics of Japanese corporate networks and Chinese business networks and the linkages that continue to develop between them; third, assess the view that Japan's regional economic predominance is in decline; and fourth, comment very briefly on the significance of these matters for East Asian regionalism and industrial development. What follows is informed by theoretical work in international political economy concerning the transition that has been underway since mid-century between an 'international economy' of classic arms-length trading relationships and a 'world economy' comprised of transnational production networks (Cox 1987). Particularly valuable in relation to the issues raised here is the work of Gereffi (1995), who focuses on the ways that TNCs link local, national, and global economic activities through formation of production networks, which he calls 'global commodity chains' (GCCs). He distinguishes between 'producer-driven' and 'buyer-driven' GCCs. In the former, TNCs play the central role in controlling capital- and technology-intensive production systems (e.g. computers, motor vehicles, heavy machinery); in the latter, larger retailers, brand name firms and trading companies set up more decentralized networks for labour-intensive production of consumer goods (e.g. apparel, toys, housewares, consumer electronics) (Gereffi 1995: 115–16). Both kinds produce 'deep integration', as they functionally link internationally dispersed but coordinated production activities, whereas traditional forms of trade and other cross-border transactions produce only 'shallow integration' (Gereffi 1995: 138–9). While Japanese TNCs are primarily engaged in creating GCCs, thus fostering 'deep integration', in East Asia, much integrative activity of ethnic Chinese businesses is either participation in traditional type transactions that only produce 'shallow integration' or assumption of subordinate roles in GCCs controlled by Japanese (and other) TNCs.

Magnitude and sectoral distribution of ethnic Chinese business activity

At home

Table 11.1 gives the portion of listed companies controlled by ethnic Chinese and the numbers and market capitalization of the top 500 ethnic Chinese controlled listed companies in East Asian countries in 1994. It shows that ethnic Chinese controlled firms constitute a large portion of other than government and foreign owned listed companies in each of these countries. They comprised 50 per cent of the total in the Philippines and from 75 to 100 per cent in the other countries. It also shows that 57 per cent of the top 500 ethnic Chinese companies, accounting for 63 per cent of the total capitalization of US$424 billion, are based in Taiwan and Hong Kong and that another 27 per cent of these companies, accounting for 23 per cent of capitalization, are based in Malaysia and Singapore. In any case, it must be noted that only a minority of ethnic Chinese companies are publicly listed. As will be seen in another context, to the extent that these firms are parts of conglomerates, decisions about listing or not listing are largely strategic. Outside of these conglomerates, a very large portion of ethnic Chinese firms are small, family businesses mainly engaged in commerce.

The main activities of these top 500 companies and of the top 20 ethnic Chinese listed companies in each of the major East Asian countries are shown in Table 11.2. Fifty nine per cent of the main activities of the top 500 companies are in property, services, or non-manufacturing industry, while only 37 per cent are in manufacturing. The non-manufacturing to manufacturing ratio in the

Table 11.1 Portion of listed firms controlled by ethnic Chinese and number and market capitalisation of top 500 ethnic Chinese listed firms in East Asian countries, 1994

Country	Portion firms controlled by ethnic Chinese (%)*	Firms (Number/%)		Market capitalization (US$billion/%)	
Taiwan	100	159	(32)	111	(26)
Hong Kong	100	123	(25)	155	(37)
Malaysia	60	83	(17)	55	(13)
Singapore	81	52	(10)	42	(10)
Thailand	80	39	(8)	35	(8)
Indonesia	75	36	(7)	20	(5)
Philippines	50	8	(2)	6	(1)
Total	–	500	(100)	424	(100)

Sources: Numbers and market capitalization:Weidenbaum and Hughes 1996: 25,Table. Chinese Portion, Taiwan and HK: Assumed. Chinese Portion, Others: Shu En 1995: 34,Table 2-1.

Note
* Government and foreign firms excluded.

main activities of the top 20 companies in each country ranges from 98:2 in Hong Kong and 76:19 in Singapore to 40:53 in Indonesia and 40:58 in Taiwan. In only the latter two countries does manufacturing account for as many as half of the main activities of these companies. Furthermore, only half of the manufacturing activities of the top 500 companies are in medium and high technology sectors. By contrast, 54 per cent of all Japanese companies located elsewhere in East Asia are in manufacturing, and 70 per cent of them are in medium and high technology sectors (Toyo Keizai 1995: 34, Table 2). Not surprisingly, the share of medium and high technology manufacturing activities tends to be somewhat greater among the top 20 Chinese firms in most countries than among the larger group of 500 firms, but it is most notable in Taiwan (80 per cent). In any case, manufacturing companies probably comprise a smaller share of all ethnic Chinese companies than the 37 per cent they make up of the top 500 listed companies.

In East Asia

Because there is no complete listing of ethnic Chinese companies and their activities, analysts often rely on foreign direct investment (FDI) figures for the 'Chinese-descent countries' (Taiwan, Hong Kong, Singapore) as an indicator of ethnic Chinese investment (e.g. Australia, Department of Foreign Affairs and Trade 1995: 179,Table 9.1;Tanaka *et al.* 1992: 18,Table 5;Abegglen 1994: 197, Table 8-2). Many analysts also note that a sizeable portion of the smaller FDI figures for the ASEAN-4 countries is ethnic Chinese investment. Table 11.3 presents FDI flows for these countries as well as Japan and the US since 1988 (1979 for China). 1988 was selected as it was just before a major 'wave' of Japanese FDI crested and began to decline, and at the beginning of an upsurge in FDI from 'Chinese-descent countries'. It shows that the portion of combined FDI

Table 11.2 Main activities of top 500 ethnic Chinese firms in East Asia, top 20 in each East Asian country and all Japanese firms in East Asia (number/%)

Activity / Location	Top 500 Chinese firms in:	Top 20 Chinese firms in:							All Japanese firms in:
	East Asia	Thailand	Indonesia*	Malaysia	Philippines	Singapore	Hong Kong	Taiwan	East Asia
TOTAL **	**568** (100)	**57** (100)	**45** (100)	**54** (100)	**48** (100)	**42** (100)	**60** (100)	**43** (100)	**6,509** (100)
Agriculture, timber, mining	**19** (3)	**3** (5)	**3** (7)	**8** (15)	**2** (4)	**2** (5)	–	**1** (2)	**82** (1)
Property, services, non-mfg industry	**336** (59)	**35** (61)	**18** (40)	**32** (59)	**31** (65)	**32** (76)	**59** (98)	**17** (40)	**2,910** (45)
Property	156	16	5	13	14	15	23	–	101
Finance, investment, insurance	73	11	9	9	8	12	17	9	408
Trade, commerce	13	3	1	1	6	3	5	3	1,452
Other services	61	3	3	6	2	1	12	2	637
Engineering, construction	33	2	–	3	1	1	2	3	312
Manufacturing	**213** (37)	**19** (33)	**24** (53)	**14** (26)	**15** (31)	**8** (19)	**1** (2)	**25** (58)	**3,517** (54)
Low technology	*106* (50)	*8* (42)	*14* (58)	*4* (29)	*11* (73)	*2* (25)	–	*5* (20)	*1,069* (30)
Food, beverages, tobacco	42	2	5	–	9	2	–	2	204
Textiles, apparel	39	3	2	2	–	–	–	2	360
Wood products	–	–	2	2	–	–	–	–	45
Pulp, paper, publishing	13	1	2	1	2	–	–	1	64
Basic metals	9	2	–	1	–	–	–	–	212
Metal products	3	–	3	1	–	–	–	–	184
Medium & high technology	*107* (50)	*11* (58)	*10* (42)	*10* (71)	*4* (27)	*6* (75)	*1* (100)	*20* (80)	*2,448* (70)
Chemicals, rubber, plastic	24	3	3	–	2	2	–	3	622
Cement, glass, ceramics	17	1	3	–	–	1	–	2	108
Machinery	7	–	–	–	–	–	–	–	273
Transport equipment	7	3	2	1	1	2	–	2	337
Electrical, electronic products	42	4	2	1	–	1	–	10	800
Other	10	–	–	8	1	–	–	3	308

Sources: Top 500 Chinese: Australia, Department of Foreign Affairs and Trade 1995: 149, Table 7.2. Top 20 Chinese: Shu En 1995: 183–90, Tables 1–7.

Notes: * Top 19. ** Totals exceed the number of companies, as many companies engage in multiple activities.

Table 11.3 Sources of FDI in ASEAN-4, Vietnam and China (US$ billion/%)

Source	Destination*							
	ASEAN-4				Vietnam (88–95)		China (79–93)	
	(88–90)		(91–3)					
Chinese-descent countries	12.2	(23)	11.0	(18)	5.9	(43)	55.4	(80)
Taiwan	6.0	4.1	2.6	6.4				
Hong Kong	2.3	2.4	1.9	47.5				
Singapore	3.9	4.5	1.4	1.5				
ASEAN-4	n.a.		2.2	(4)	1.4	(10)	n.a.	
Japan	14.4	(27)	13.2	(21)	1.5	(11)	3.3	(5)
United States	4.0	(8)	7.3	(12)	0.3	(2)	3.7	(5)
Other	22.2	(42)	28.0	(45)	4.5	(33)	7.1	(10)
Total	**52.8**	**(100)**	**61.7**	**(100)**	**13.6**	**(99)**	**69.5**	**(100)**

Sources: ASEAN-4: 88–90: Sekiguchi 1991, 5: 91–3: MITI Malaysia 1994: 324–7. Vietnam: *Business Times* (Malaysia), 22 December 1995; *Agence France Presse*, 9 July 1995. China: Australia, Department of Foreign Affairs and Trade 1995: 198.

Note
* Figures for ASEAN-4 and Vietnam are approved investments, and for China actual investments. During the same period over US$200 billion in investment was contracted for in China. The portion accounted for by the 'Chinese descent countries' is about the same. Taylor 1996: 74, Table 3.2.

from the 'Chinese descent' and ASEAN-4 countries was over 80 per cent in China (80 per cent from the former plus the not available ASEAN-4 share) and 53 per cent in Vietnam, compared with just 5 per cent and 11 per cent from Japan. The combined 'Chinese descent' and ASEAN-4 portion in the ASEAN-4 countries was over 23 per cent in 1988–90 (the ASEAN-4 share is again not available) and 22 per cent in 1991–3, compared with 27 per cent and 21 per cent from Japan. Exemplary of the conclusion that is generally drawn from such figures is Abegglen's that 'the Chinese connection is critical to these economies' (1994: 196).

The FDI figures in Table 11.3 exaggerate the magnitude of Hong Kong, Singapore and ASEAN-4 countries' investment, and thus also that of ethnic Chinese investment from those countries. This is because they do not indicate the real national origins of a significant portion of this investment, hence obscuring the extent of 'round trip', foreign subsidiary, proxy and dependent investment that originates elsewhere. The Taiwan FDI figures also miss the latter, but understate Taiwanese investment overall for reasons to be mentioned in another context. The single biggest investment flow by far is that from Hong Kong to China. A portion of this is 'round trip' investment, meaning that it originates with firms in China but is coursed through companies set up for this purpose in Hong Kong in order to take advantage of various investment incentives (e.g. tax holidays) offered by the Chinese government to attract foreign capital. According to one Hong Kong study, at least 40 per cent of Hong Kong investment in China is of this nature, and 'China's banking groups are the biggest source of investment' (cited by Low *et al.* 1996: 7). Ethnic Chinese (and other) businesses in South-East Asia also use Hong Kong as a base for 'round trip' investment in their home countries, although certainly on a smaller scale than their counterparts in China.

A considerable portion of what is recorded as Hong Kong and Singapore FDI and some ASEAN-4 FDI is actually overseas investment by wholly or majority foreign owned subsidiaries based in these countries. A large portion of Singapore FDI is in this category. In 1993, 51 per cent of its stock of outgoing FDI and 27 per cent of its firms that had gone abroad were wholly or majority foreign owned (DoS, MTI, Singapore 1995: 44–7). Hence, at least half of the value and over a quarter of the cases of Singapore FDI at that time were investments by locally based foreign subsidiaries. A significant portion of Hong Kong investment, particularly in China, is in the same category. One Chinese source says that 30 per cent of Hong Kong FDI in China is of foreign origin (cited by Low *et al.* 1996: 7). Some of this originates with TNCs (Taylor 1996 gives a number of Japanese examples), but much of it originates with Taiwan based firms. The latter is not recorded as Taiwanese investment, but most of it is presumably included in the Hong Kong figures. This is misleading with respect to the national origin of such investment, but it gives an indication of aggregate ethnic Chinese investment from Hong Kong and Taiwan. In any case, the high incidence of regional investment by TNCs' affiliates in Hong Kong and Singapore follows from the fact that many TNCs, particularly those based in Japan, maintain regional operational headquarters in these countries. A study of 95 Hong Kong and Singapore based companies in Thailand found, for example, that 59 per cent of the former and 64 per cent of the latter were, in fact, controlled by third country firms, about three quarters of which were Japanese in each case (Low *et al.* 1996: 44, Table 8).

FDI made by less than majority TNC-owned or even wholly locally owned firms that are nonetheless dependent on TNCs for materials, technology, and/or marketing are often proxy and always to some extent dependent investments. Proxy investments are those in which TNCs opt to have such local partners accompany them to third countries, usually because they are suppliers or because they have special characteristics that in some way improve the TNCs' access to the host countries. Japanese TNCs, for example, often rely on the connections of local ethnic Chinese partners to ease the way for their ventures in China. Mitsubishi Motors Corporation (MMC) recently formed a joint venture with its Taiwan affiliate, China Motor Corporation, and a Chinese automaker to assemble vans in Fujian, with the engines, transmissions and other key parts coming from Mitsubishi. MMC's stated aim was to take advantage of China Motors' 'cultural familiarity with Fujian' (*The Nikkei Weekly,* 17 June 1996). Similarly, Neturen (steel rods/pre-stressed concrete), a Japanese firm with a minority interest in and exclusive rights to the technology used by affiliates in several East Asian countries, recently decided that its ethnic Chinese-owned Malaysian affiliate, Ulbon, should take the lead in a new China venture. Explaining this, the managing director said, 'For political reasons, [our] Taiwanese concern may not be able to play a vital role while Malaysia has the advantage over South

Korea and Japan in terms of language, [so] the venture…will be led by the Malaysian party' (*New Straits Times*, 5 February 1996). A Chinese scholar at a research institute in Japan refers to ethnic Chinese firms that play such roles as 'guides' for Japanese firms' overseas 'advance' (*nihon kigyo no kaigaishinshutsu no annainin*) (Shu En 1995: 139). Such dependent firms may also invest overseas purely for their own reasons. A number of wholly owned Singapore firms engaged primarily in original equipment manufacturing (OEM) for Japanese TNCs have, for example, relocated to Malaysia to reduce production costs. Their output now goes directly to Japan on an OEM basis from Malaysia instead of from Singapore. In any case, with respect to the issue at hand, it is misleading to count Japanese TNC subsidiary, proxy or dependent investment as FDI of the country where the investing firm is based (Bernard and Ravenhill 1995: 185–7) or as ethnic Chinese investment. All such investment extends and consolidates Japanese TNC-centred production networks.

Qualified by the foregoing considerations, the recent FDI figures given in Table 11.3 give a fairly accurate picture of the relative magnitude of aggregate ethnic Chinese and Japanese investment in China and Vietnam, where the 'Chinese-descent' countries and Japan became involved at about the same time. Japanese firms have, however, been investing in the ASEAN-4 countries much longer than 'Chinese-descent' countries (Singapore investment in Malaysia being a notable exception), so the relative magnitude of their overall economic presence in the ASEAN-4 remains somewhat larger than an examination of the recent figures alone would suggest. In either case, the portion of this investment that is in manufacturing varies by country of origin. A large portion of Taiwan and Hong Kong FDI in East Asia is in manufacturing, but in both cases, the bulk of it is in lower technology (e.g. textiles, apparel and footwear, plastics, electrical equipment) SMEs. Only 20 per cent of Singapore's overall FDI and 33 per cent of its FDI in Asia are in manufacturing, although it is close to or more than half in several ASEAN countries and China (DoS, MTI, Singapore 1996: 9–10). As already noted, however, large portions of both Hong Kong and Singapore manufacturing FDI are TNC subsidiary, proxy or dependent investments. Malaysian FDI is overwhelmingly in finance, insurance, real estate, and services (69 per cent), while only a very small portion is in manufacturing (7 per cent) (MoF, Malaysia 1995: 127).

Japanese TNC-centred production networks and ethnic Chinese business networks

Japanese TNC networks [3]

Japanese TNCs have, particularly since the mid-1980s, been fostering expansion and integration of regional production networks in East Asia on a sector-by-sector basis. Most of these are what Gereffi (1995) refers to as 'producer-driven' GCCs of the kind that produce 'deep' regional integration. The TNCs at the centre of these networks manage and coordinate the activities of production sites in many countries. The stages of manufacture of their products are carried out or the parts and components of their products are made in states at different levels of industrial development. The resultant intermediate goods are traded, increasingly on an intra-firm basis, for eventual incorporation into finished products. The latter are then sold both internationally and/or locally. These activities are organized both regionally and globally. In East Asia, they have been fuelled by the more than US$88.5 billion of cumulated Japanese FDI (1995 figures), particularly the US$34.6 billion in manufacturing since 1985, as well as sizeable Japanese technology exports to the region. These activities reflect what American economist Leon Hollerman (1988) calls Japan's effort to become a 'headquarters country' able to 'impose central management on a world network of joint ventures, subsidiaries, and affiliates…[and to]…co-ordinate the relations of its foreign clients with each other as well as with itself' (Hollerman 1988: xi). In this process, he explains, 'Japan retains for itself the higher value added operations that yield the best rates of return', while at the same time, 'export of plants and equipment [establishes a] dependency relationship [in terms of financing, maintenance, management, and distribution of output]...between Japan and its clients' (Hollerman 1988: 8–11). Assessing such developments, Hatch and Yamamura contend 'that Japan has embraced the Asia-Pacific region in a keiretsu-like production alliance…[in] a coordinated effort to lock up the productive resources of the world's most dynamic region' (Hatch and Yamamura 1996: 4–5). The result has been formation of a vertically integrated, hierarchical, Japan-centred East Asian regional division of labour.

Japanese corporate ties with and coordination of the activities of their regional subsidiaries are central to the production networks under construction in East Asia. Some 7,000 Japanese companies now operate in Asia, and about 5,000 of them have been established since 1985. A bit over half (53 per cent in 1994) are in manufacturing (Toyo Keizai 1995: 32–47), and these firms are key components of the expanding production networks. Many are SMEs that act as suppliers to locally based TNCs (Takeuchi 1993). Some are subcontractors to Japanese corporations in Japan that have followed them to regional production sites, set themselves up as local firms, and continued to supply these corporations' affiliates there. A recent survey found that in the Asian NICs and ASEAN states together, 30 per cent of Japanese affiliates used at least 20 local companies as subcontractors, and another 21 per cent used between 5 and 19 (MITI, Japan 1992: 141). Some of the latter are owned or controlled by Japanese TNCs, while others are partly or wholly locally owned licensees or subcontractors. Many of the foregoing are joint ventures or other kinds of tie-ups between Japanese and local ethnic Chinese firms. Tokunaga argues convincingly that if local firms, Japanese affiliated or not, are incorporated 'in a Japanese corporation's intra-company production network …[they are]…overseas production facilities of Japanese corporations'. He says that Japanese corporations may incorporate local firms in their networks by furnishing directors, technology, raw materials, parts or semi-finished products and by such practices as production sharing and renting or lending capital equipment and buying products back (Tokunaga 1992: 14–15).

Following from Japanese TNCs' strategy of decentralizing their global operations and giving them greater regional focus in order to improve their decision-making capacities, relations between firms in these production networks have been increasingly structured in a 'multi-layered' way. Many Japanese TNCs have established regional management systems in sub-regions of Asia. Singapore is, for example, the chief regional centre for South-East Asia (Rodan 1993). Affiliates of Japanese TNCs in some countries have also been used to establish their own affiliates in third countries. According to JETRO, by 1993, 47 per cent of Japanese affiliated firms in Hong Kong and 43 per cent in Singapore had established foreign affiliate networks in the region. While only 4 per cent of Japanese affiliated firms in Malaysia and Thailand have established affiliates in other Asian countries, 35 per cent of those in Thailand and 28 per cent in Malaysia plan to do so by the year 2000 (cited in UNCTAD/DTCI 1996: 47). Implementation of this strategy is, as has already been seen, misleadingly reflected in FDI statistics as an increase in Hong Kong and Singapore regional investment.

Japanese TNCs are the prime movers in the regional extension of production networks. But their efforts have been facilitated by both key ministries and agencies of the Japanese government as well as other Japanese private institutions. For example, MITI assists other Asian countries in their industrial planning efforts in ways favourable to Japanese TNC interests, and Japanese official development assistance (ODA) has been geared to investment promotion. Similarly, Japanese banks have branch offices throughout East Asia, and other Japanese financial institutions have established ties for joint lending with local finance companies and merchant banks. Some Japanese joint ventures in the region have also listed on local stock markets to boost local fund-raising, and Japanese securities houses have established a regional presence to facilitate this. International and domestic integrated inter-modal transportation systems, which coordinate all elements required for door-to-door physical distribution on a world-wide basis, have also been organized, both by Japanese transportation firms and on an intra-company basis (Tokunaga 1992: 25–30). All of the foregoing support expansion of regional production networks and advance ties between the regional and global divisions of labour.

Regional production networks are particularly well developed in dynamic, internationally competitive sectors, such as the electrical/electronics and motor vehicles industries. Electrical/electronics firms, such as Sharp, Hitachi, Matsushita, Toshiba, and NEC, and motor vehicle firms, such as Toyota, Mitsubishi, Nissan and Honda, which are among the world's top 100 TNCs (as measured by foreign assets) (UNCTAD/DTCI 1996: 30–2, Table I.12), all preside over extensive production networks in East Asia. For example, motor vehicle assemblers and parts and component makers affiliated with each of the major Japanese firms are increasingly integrated into production networks, which are in turn tied into their global networks. These involve the exchange of parts and components made in one country for use in several other countries. Japanese TNCs favour this approach partly because it permits economies of scale in parts and components making, something which is impossible to do in the many countries with small domestic markets. In any case, such activity is clearly reflected in increasing intra-firm trade. For example, combined transactions in Toyota's system for exchanging motor vehicle parts and components among its ASEAN affiliates (e.g. engine blocks from Indonesia, transmission parts from the Philippines, power steering components from Malaysia, engine parts and body stampings from Thailand) were US$25 million in 1993 (EIU 1993: 37), but had risen to US$160 million, on the basis of trade in just 12 parts and components, by the end of 1994. They were slated to grow to US$1.3 billion on the basis of trade in about 100 parts and components by 1998 (*The Nikkei Weekly,* 30 January 1995). Most of this will be intra-firm trade. Such increases clearly reflect the growth of production networks and East Asian economic integration.

Ethnic Chinese business networks

Most ethnic Chinese businesses in East Asia are family owned SMEs. Larger ethnic Chinese operations include a few large, specialized TNCs, but most are big, highly diversified conglomerates. Both of these latter types, however, tend also to be family owned. The diversified conglomerates are mainly groupings, sometimes quite large, of small companies operating in a variety of sectors, rather than vertically integrated, hierarchical firms specializing in a specific sector. Typically,

> core business groups [have] varying degrees of ownership in dozens, if not hundreds, of small- to medium-sized businesses…many of [which] maintain cross-holdings with other family-controlled firms. The resulting web of holdings when combined with the insertion of family members into key management positions, allows the family to maintain ultimate, albeit circuitous, control.
>
> (Weidenbaum and Hughes 1996: 57)

Many such conglomerates have 'modernized' their management in the sense that members of the current generation of the core family who have earned MBAs at Western universities have been given management positions and tend to employ contemporary Western management techniques. To the extent that associated firms engage in manufacturing, however, their actual operations tend to be less advanced. Weidenbaum and Hughes tell us, undermining their argument that ethnic Chinese business activity is the economic 'epicentre' of Asia, that these firms seldom 'produce consumer goods with a Chinese brand name…. [Rather], they make components, manufacture for others, and perform sub-assembly work'. More importantly, they say,

> the Chinese family business structure makes it extremely difficult to develop the high-tech products and systems that will provide the foundation for future business growth and national economic progress…, [and i]n the long

run,…adaptation [of more modern business techniques] will be essential to maintaining competitiveness in an increasingly high-tech global marketplace.
(Weidenbaum and Hughes 1996: 55–8)

One widely cited study, however, identifies the paternalism and personalism that have traditionally been sources of strength for Chinese family enterprises operating in individual countries as real problems for them if they attempt to transform themselves into effective transnational firms (Redding 1990).

Many ethnic Chinese conglomerates are, the Australian analysts say,

> [t]ypically…formed into a squat pyramid structure, with a family holding company at the apex, a second tier holding the group's most prized assets (which are usually privately held) and a third tier at the base comprising the group's publicly-listed companies,
> (Australia, Department of Foreign Affairs and Trade 1995: 4)

This, they explain, makes it easy for conglomerates 'to raise funds at the bottom of the pyramid from shareholders in the group's public companies', mainly through rights issues, and 'then pass these up the pyramid' (Australia, Department of Foreign Affairs and Trade 1995: 159). They also rely extensively on conglomerate associated private banks and loans on what have, in recent years, been the increasingly valuable holdings of their property divisions, to finance expansion. In any case, listed group manufacturing companies are also frequently supported by more numerous non-listed group service and supply companies. It is a common practice for the latter to tack on excessive margins and mark-ups, so as to maximize the profits in these privately held group firms at the expense of the listed firms (Interviews, Malaysia 1996–7). Not surprisingly, 'the market performance of these public companies is not necessarily a good indicator of the overall profitability of the array of public and privately held companies controlled by family members' (Weidenbaum and Hughes 1996: 104). The most notable divergence from the foregoing pattern is in Taiwan, where holding companies are not legally permitted, and associated companies are more likely to be linked horizontally through cross-share holdings and interlocking directorships.

When analysts of ethnic Chinese business activities describe them as networked across the region, they are referring to relationships that, in most instances, differ substantially from those characteristic of Japanese TNC networks. They are less commonly production networks based on a division of labour than, as the Australian analysts explain, co-operative informal business and financial ties based on 'common personal link[s] between…people who have long-standing, cross-boundary business relationships with one another'. These links 'may be family relationship[s], share[d] ancestral village[s] or region[s] in China, same surname[s], or possibly same school' but are most often based on shared dialects or sub-dialects', which may be 'formalized in international dialect associations, which function partly as social groups and partly as dialect-based international chambers of commerce' (Australia, Department of Foreign Affairs and Trade 1995: 32–3). Ethnic Chinese entrepreneurs rely on these networks to 'tap the latest market intelligence to mobilize capital at short notice and to occupy market niches where the highest profits can be made' (Australia, Department of Foreign Affairs and Trade 1995: 5). 'Such "networks" may not be active, but should a business opportunity arise, they can be activated to enable business opportunities to be quickly exploited in an environment of mutual "trust"' (Australia, Department of Foreign Affairs and Trade 1995: 32). For example, groups of Hong Kong and South-East Asian ethnic Chinese firms have even formed equity ties to cement their joint participation in such things as property development and infrastructure projects in China (*The Nikkei Weekly,* 24 May 1993). Ethnic Chinese wholesalers and retailers are also frequently parts of networked distribution systems. Participation in such cross-border networks has, of course, many advantages, most notably reduction of a variety of transaction costs and diversification of risks across countries.

The governments of Singapore, Malaysia and Taiwan have, in recent years, all put policies in place that actively encourage domestic firms to invest in neighbouring countries. These governments' efforts do not, of course, begin to match those of the Japanese government in this regard. In any case, Singapore's efforts to grow an 'external wing' on its economy and Malaysia's to promote 'reverse investment' have primarily been efforts to overcome the limitations of small domestic markets. Beyond its political motivations, Taiwan's 'south bound' policy was designed to promote rationalization of its industrial structure through export of labour-intensive, low-technology industries to South-East Asia. These undertakings created more structured relationships than those in the more common informal networks. In following this policy, for example, some larger Taiwanese firms took suppliers with them from home and extended their own production networks to South-East Asia. While maintaining ties with their parent firms in Taiwan, SMEs more commonly opted to rely on local, frequently ethnic Chinese, or otherwise unrelated Taiwanese firms as suppliers. According to Jomo, '[u]nlike small Japanese firms in a *keiretsu* network…, [such] Taiwanese business networks appear to be more open-ended, with membership and roles much more fluid over time without dissolving into purely arms-length market transactions' (Jomo *et al.* 1997: 49–50).

As noted, there are ethnic Chinese TNCs that are structured like their Japanese counterparts and engaged in specialized manufacturing activities. Even these tend to be family controlled, to be relatively smaller, and to have less extensive overseas networks. Table 11.4 lists the 15 specialized manufacturing Japanese TNCs that are ranked among the top 100 TNCs world-wide (measured by overseas assets). These firms play a key role in the formation of regional production networks. It also lists the six ethnic Chinese TNCs with these characteristics that are ranked among the top 50 TNCs based in developing countries. The largest, Taiwanese electrical equipment manufacturer Tatung, has total assets (US$4 billion) that are only a fifth the total assets of the smallest of the listed Japanese TNCs, Bridgestone (US$20 billion). Tatung's overseas work force of 9,800 is

Table 11.4 Japanese and ethnic Chinese specialized manufacturing TNCs – total assets (US$ bil) and workforce (1,000s)

Japanese TNCs	Total assets	Workforce	
		Total	Overseas
Toyota	116.8	172.6	27.6
Sharp	109.9	42.9	29.0
Mitsubishi	109.3	36.0	11.1
Hitachi	92.5	331.9	80.0
Matsushita Elect	92.2	265.4	112.3
Mitsui	82.5	80.0	23.6
Nissan Motor	80.8	143.3	34.5
Toshiba	63.2	190.0	38.0
Nippon Steel	51.3	50.4	15.0
NEC Corp	47.7	151.1	17.6
Sony	47.6	156.0	90.0
Honda	28.3	92.8	19.7
Kobe Steel	28.3	32.5	5.5
Canon	23.9	72.3	35.1
Bridgestone	20.1	89.7	52.0

Ethnic Chinese TNCs	Total assets	Workforce	
		Total	Overseas
Tatung (Taiwan)	4.0	27.8	9.8
Acer (Taiwan)	2.0	10.0	4.2
Formosa Plastic (Taiwan)	1.9	3.6	0.1
Amsteel Corp (Malaysia)	1.5	28.2	7.8
Charoen Pokphand (Thailand)	0.6	8.4	1.1
Creative Tech (Singapore)	0.4	2.7	0.9

Sources: UNCTAD/DTCI 1996: 30–5, Tables I.12, I.13.

also smaller than all save one of the Japanese TNCs. Most of the more specialized ethnic Chinese business groups in manufacturing that are too small to be included in the top 50 developing country TNCs, are engaged in lower technology sectors – food processing, agro-industry, and textiles and apparel. There are, of course, much larger ethnic Chinese controlled TNCs, but they are diversified conglomerates with limited or no involvement in manufacturing. The second ranked of the 50 top TNCs based in developing countries is, for example, Hong Kong's Hutchison Whampoa Ltd, which has total assets of US\$52.2 billion and a total work force of almost 27,000, of which 15,000 are located overseas. Its main activities are, however, not in manufacturing, but in property development, cargo handling, container terminals, trading, retailing, gas and oil, cellular and paging services, and electric power.

Linkages

Japanese (and other) TNC-centred production networks and ethnic Chinese business networks are extensively linked. It has long been and continues to be Japanese corporate strategy to establish ties with reliable and well-connected local businesses when they set up operations in other East Asian countries. This has, of course, very frequently led to linkages with ethnic Chinese businesses. The latter commonly require external support, particularly for marketing and/ or necessary technology, in their manufacturing ventures. After Taiwanese and Hong Kong firms, that had been suppliers to big retailers or brand name companies, relocated their production facilities to South-East Asia or China, they often continued to supply these principals from their new overseas bases, thus becoming 'middle men' in buyer driven GCCs (Gereffi 1995: 118). As Japanese TNCs and their subsidiaries and Japanese suppliers have extended operations in their particular sector across the region, they have integrated firms that are parts of many different ethnic Chinese business networks into their production networks through the establishment of joint ventures and other kinds of ties (e.g. technology agreements). As already noted, diversified ethnic Chinese business groups are likely to have manufacturing operations in several sectors, even though these are usually not their primary activities. Hence, at least at their peripheries, they are also likely to be incorporated into the production networks of multiple Japanese (and/or other) TNCs. Malaysia's Hong Leong Group, for example, while not primarily engaged in manufacturing, has a manufacturing division, with associated companies producing building materials, electronic products, steel and structural steel products, and motorcycles, the latter two in joint ventures with Marubeni Corporation and Yamaha Motors respectively. Hong Leong also produces Yamaha motorcycles in China. While these linkages are presumably mutually beneficial, Japanese technological superiority gives the latter the pre-eminent position in such relationships (Machado 1999).

Toyota's extensive regional production network, to which reference has already been made, provides an excellent example of the kinds of linkages that have been formed by all major Japanese firms in the motor vehicle sector (i.e., passenger car, commercial vehicle and motorcycle makers). Toyota Motors of Japan and Toyota's trading company (Toyota Tsusho) respectively hold shares in 17 and 61 companies in East Asia (of 59 and 106 world-wide). There is considerable overlap in these holdings because, in a number of instances, both firms hold a share in the same local companies (Toyo Keizai 1995: 181, 191–2), but the activities of Toyota Tsusho are not limited to the motor vehicle sector. Toyota Motors, like many Japanese TNCs, has a regional headquarters in Singapore, a wholly owned subsidiary, Toyota Motor Management Services Singapore. Toyota is linked to Bangkok Bank in Thailand, United Motor Works in Malaysia, Metrobank in the Philippines, Astra in Indonesia, and Kuozui Motors in Taiwan. All are, or were at the time the linkages were formed, at the centre of or components of ethnic Chinese business networks.

In Thailand, the ethnic Chinese Sophonpanich family owns the controlling share in Bangkok Bank, the largest commercial bank in South-East Asia with branches and interests in and ties to banking, financial service and commodity trading operations all over the world. Bangkok Bank initially had a sizeable share and still retains a modest holding in Toyota Motor Thailand (TMT). TMT, in turn, has shares in several of the other seven companies in Thailand associated with Toyota. Bangkok Bank's current primary interest in this relationship is reflected in the majority share its subsidiary, Bangkok Insurance, holds, along with TMT and Chiyoda Fire and Marine Insurance of Japan, in Bangkok Chayorain, a loss and damage insurance firm which serves TMT customers. As is typical in large, highly diversified ethnic Chinese conglomerates, other Bangkok Bank group firms are tied up with Teijin of Japan in Teijin Polyester (Thailand) (polyester fibres), Toray and Tomen of Japan in Thai Toray Textile Mills (polyester fabrics), and Nissho Iwai and Nomura Trading of Japan in Bangkok Steel (galvanized iron sheets and steel bars) (Inoue 1994: 179). In Indonesia, Toyota participates in a joint venture with an ethnic Chinese (originally, the Soerjadjaja family; now the very well-connected Prajogo Pangestu and Bob Hasan) controlled Astra Group firm in P.T. Toyota-Astra Motor. The Astra Group is more extensively involved in manufacturing than most ethnic Chinese conglomerates, so it is linked with a wider array of Japanese (and other) TNCs, including Daihatsu, Nissan, Peugeot, BMW, Honda (motorcycles and parts), Daikin (clutches), Kayaba (shock absorbers), Nippondenso (auto a/c), Izumi (pistons), Nippon Denchi (batteries), Mitsubishi Shoji (steel sheets), and Komatsu (heavy equipment) (Sato 1996).

Japan-based TNCs are more inclined to establish wholly owned subsidiaries or joint ventures with their own wholly owned local subsidiaries in the electrical/electronics sector than in the motor vehicle sector when they set up operations elsewhere in East Asia. These firms both import various parts and electronic and mechanical components and procure them locally. Higher technology parts and components (e.g. ICs, micro-motors, picture tubes) are most likely to be imported from Japan or procured locally from affiliates of other Japanese firms or, in some cases, Taiwanese, Singapore or Hong Kong firms. In 1996, for example, there were about 90 Taiwanese electrical/electronics firms operating in Malaysia (a few were joint ventures with Japanese companies, like micro-motor maker Mabuchi), most of which were supplying Japanese and other TNCs. Lower technology items (e.g. some plastic and stamped metal parts, speakers, and cable harnesses) are most likely to be procured from wholly local firms, a great many of which are owned by ethnic Chinese. When parts and components are procured from either kind of non-Japanese owned local firm, it is quite likely that they have been made on imported Japanese machinery, and with technical assistance and raw materials from the Japanese firm(s) being supplied. Beyond such manufacturing, Japanese electrical/electronics TNCs also completely subcontract out the production of some items to local firms, also often Chinese owned, on an OEM basis. Whether such linkages are formed between Japanese TNCs and local branches of large Taiwanese firms or smaller wholly local firms, the latter thereby become 'overseas production facilities' of Japanese firms (Tokunaga 1992: 14).

Japan's regional economic predominance in decline?

The notion that ethnic Chinese business networks are becoming a relatively more powerful integrative force in East Asia is commonly associated with the view that Japan's regional economic predominance is in decline. There is no doubt that Japan's economy has been plagued with troubles in recent years. The post-1985 Plaza accord rise in the value of the yen put considerable strain on Japan's export industries for a time, and the burst 'bubble' in stock and property prices adversely affected that country's banks and financial institutions. Japan's economy was in the doldrums through the first half of the 1990s, experiencing declining or flat domestic investment and growth rates below 2 per cent. Despite government efforts to bolster the economy, the signs of recovery since 1996 have been far from robust. It is, however, wrong to assume that these problems are translating into a corresponding measure of decline in Japan's basic economic strength. Moreover, one major response of Japanese companies to these problems has been to accelerate expansion overseas, particularly in Asia. As a result, Japanese TNCs have continued and even hastened their integration of East Asian economies.

Despite the extended slump, Japan's economy is, in important respects, doing very well. Fingleton points out that '[j]udged by wages, jobs, and export growth – probably the three most reliable and universally applicable tests of good economic housekeeping – Japan has outperformed all other major nations in the 1990s' (Fingleton 1997: viii). Japanese wages and exports per capita greatly exceed those of the United States. At 3.3 per cent, Japanese unemployment is well below US and very far below European rates. Of fundamental importance is the fact that 'Japanese corporations have typically been investing two to three times as much per worker as their American counterparts in the 1990s', which fosters growing productivity (Fingleton 1997: x). MITI is also greatly expanding its financial support for growth industries, focusing on fostering the commercialization of promising technologies developed by government and university research institutes (JPRI Staff 1996: 1) and reviving the practice of creating joint government-private sector consortia and research programmes to develop advanced technology (*International Herald Tribune,* 19 November 1996). In light of such evidence, pronouncements concerning Japan's relative economic decline seem exaggerated.

A big upsurge in Japanese FDI began in 1985 owing to the rising yen, but this peaked in 1990 and went into decline for several years as a result of the economic slump (Machado 1995). It began to rise again in 1993, however, and most importantly, it is being diverted from North America to Asia. Manufacturing FDI going to Asia exceeded that going to North America for the first time in 1994 and did so again in 1995 (UNCTAD/DTCI 1996: 47). This FDI has driven a steady increase in the portion of Japanese production taking place overseas, a trend which is expected to continue. Japanese government agencies report that companies manufactured more overseas than they exported from home for the first time in 1995 and that the ratio of overseas production to GDP hit a new high of 10 per cent the same year, a figure which is expected to double by 2010 (cited by Hirsh and Henry 1997: 13). This would bring Japan to about the current American ratio. In any case, Japan's leading firms in the electrical/electronics, chemical and motor vehicle sectors are the prime movers in this shift. It is particularly important to note, as Hirsh and Henry point out, that even if this 'hollows' the Japanese economy, Japanese TNCs

> will remain world pacesetters…, [for while t]he domestic economy…has all but lost important…segments like colour televisions, VCRs, [fax] machines, and cameras…, [the] global market share [of the TNCs] in these segments has not budged, thanks to their manufacturing networks outside Japan, mostly in Asia.
>
> (Hirsh and Henry 1997: 12)

Clearly, current Japanese economic problems, often cited as evidence of that country's declining position in East Asia, are actually increasing the integrative role of Japanese TNCs in the region.

Conclusions

This chapter has shown that the primary activities of ethnic Chinese businesses in their home countries are in property, services and non-manufacturing industries, while only a minority is in manufacturing. Ethnic Chinese manufacturers, particularly those in Taiwan and Hong Kong, have, however, in recent years become significant investors, particularly elsewhere in East Asia. A very small number of them are specialized, higher technology based TNCs, but most are SMEs in lower technology sectors. The latter firms tend to play limited or subordinate roles in the extension of regional production networks. Some of this investment, particularly in higher technology sectors from Singapore, Hong Kong and Malaysia, is actually proxy investment for Japanese (and other) TNCs. In both instances, ethnic Chinese businesses are often linked to Japanese production networks through joint ventures or supply, technology and/or marketing ties. In such cases they facilitate Japanese dominance of various manufacturing sectors, including the most dynamic ones that are of primary importance in furthering regional integration. Japanese domestic economic problems cited as evidence of that country's economic decline are accelerating these tendencies, not slowing them down. Japanese TNC-centred production networks, therefore, remain the predominant force in advancing 'deep integration' in East Asia. Ethnic Chinese networks, with a few exceptions, tend independently to advance only 'shallow integration' or to play a subordinate role in advancing 'deep integration'.

These matters are of particular importance because the emerging character of East Asian regionalism and the development trajectories of individual countries in the region are both very much shaped by the structure and dynamics of the increasingly complex web of global and regional production networks. I have argued elsewhere that in the absence of any formal arrangements, Japanese corporate organization extending throughout the region has become the central architectural feature of East Asian regionalism (Machado 1995), and that it forms the boundaries within which the national industrial development efforts of other regional states, to varying degrees, take place (Machado 1999). These boundaries are maintained primarily by the technological superiority of Japanese TNCs as well as by their market power and capital supply. One issue of importance is thus the extent to which the growing complexity of the regional division of labour represented by increased ethnic Chinese FDI translates into greater economic diversity and decentralization in the region. A more pluralistic, balanced and competitive environment might offer more alternative sources of capital and technology and more channels of access to markets, conditions that would alter the architecture of the region and improve the prospects for secure and self-sustaining (as opposed to dependent) industrial advance for states attempting to improve their relative standing in the division of labour. To date, however, the most that can be said is that some ethnic Chinese FDI makes modest contributions to such localization of the regional division of labour. At the same time, some of it tends in the opposite direction by extending and consolidating Japan-centred production networks.

Epilogue: impact of the East Asian financial crisis

The Japanese and ethnic Chinese economic activities outlined in this chapter, along with European and American activities, included a significant amount of indiscriminate lending and investment. This was particularly so in the late 1980s and early 1990s. Combined with equally indiscriminate local borrowing and acceptance of investment, this activity fed the asset inflation and industrial over-capacity which helped to produce the East Asian financial crisis that erupted in July 1997. This crisis affected the political economy of the region and its individual countries and firms in a multiplicity of ways. The aim here is simply to identify aspects of that crisis that are of particular relevance to tendencies outlined in this chapter.

The impact of the crisis on ethnic Chinese businesses varied greatly from country to country. It was especially severe in the two hardest hit countries, Indonesia and Thailand. The mid-1998 political upheaval in Indonesia was, most immediately, precipitated by the devastating consequences of the financial crisis and IMF imposed remedies. It was accompanied by mob attacks on Chinese shops, businesses, homes and individuals. These included, for example, attacks on offices of a bank as well as a Jakarta home owned by Liem Sioe Liong, a very close, long-time crony of then-President Soeharto and perhaps Indonesia's wealthiest businessman. Continuing political instability in Indonesia has undercut the sources of patronage for many of the ethnic Chinese businessmen who played such a central role in the New Order political economy under Soeharto.

Of more fundamental significance than cases in which ethnic Chinese businesses fell victim to crisis-induced domestic political conflicts are cases in which they have been displaced by or become subordinate to foreign capital in the unfolding of processes designed by the IMF to address the crisis. The IMF demanded austerity programmes and liberalizing structural reforms as conditions for its bailouts of Indonesia and Thailand (as well as South Korea). Given the asset and currency devaluations in these countries, IMF-prescribed reforms produced some shift in the ownership of assets from domestic (often ethnic Chinese) to foreign firms. A central IMF bailout condition in Thailand was overhaul of the banking system, in which 12 of the 15 commercial banks were long controlled by ethnic Chinese families. The Thai government relaxed ownership rules that limited foreigners to minority shares in banks and financial institutions, and the central bank required local banks to meet strict international capital adequacy standards under threat of government seizure. This threat was carried out several times. In some cases, raising the capital to meet the set standards required selling controlling stakes to foreigners, from both advanced industrial countries and from regional 'Chinese-descent' countries that had fared better in the crisis. In other instances, distressed companies, including some manufacturing firms, were acquired by foreign bargain-hunters. Such asset transfers have strengthened the position of foreign (including some ethnic Chinese) capital at the expense of local (often ethnic Chinese) capital in these countries.

In sharp contrast to Indonesia and Thailand, Taiwan weathered the regional crisis relatively well. Taiwanese firms were prominent among the bargain-hunters in the hardest-hit regional countries. The Taiwanese government has since 1994 been encouraging firms to reduce investment activity in China and to increase it in South-East Asia, primarily as part of an effort to increase Taiwan's regional influence. The crisis bolstered this south-bound strategy, as both private companies and the Kuomintang-affiliated China Development Corporation (CDC) began scouting for investment opportunities among the distressed companies of South-East Asia. CDC, for example, acquired a controlling share in a unit of Thailand's Bangkok Bank. Singapore firms also pursued investment opportunities among troubled firms in the region. Clearly, the East Asia crisis damaged the interests of some ethnic Chinese firms and created opportunities that have been exploited by others. Consistent with one of the main themes of this chapter, however, the businesses so affected were primarily either in non-manufacturing sectors (e.g. hotels, financial services) or lower technology, small and medium sized manufacturing firms that play no role or only a subordinate role in integrated regional production networks.

Japan remains deeply mired in the economic doldrums and gives no signs of a quick recovery. Nonetheless, many Japanese TNCs have capitalized on the far worse conditions elsewhere in the region, particularly in South-East Asia, to consolidate and deepen their production networks. Japanese firms have continued to pour money into the region, but after the financial crisis erupted in July 1997, their investment shifted from launching new undertakings to revamping existing ones. This primarily took the form of increasing their capital in existing joint ventures, particularly in the motor vehicle and electrical machinery sectors. At the same time, because of greatly diminished demand for the output of Japanese factories in a number of regional countries, they retooled and diverted their products from the local market to the United States and Europe. Such products include everything from auto parts and components to household appliances, electronics products and earthmoving equipment.

It was particularly in the hardest-hit countries, most notably Thailand, that Japanese TNCs bought larger shares in joint ventures from their local partners. In some cases, this was a response to a severe shortage of local credit, but in others, it was, according to JETRO (1999: Section 3, 1), for '…offensive reasons, such as taking advantage of eased investment regulations to seize majority stakes in local affiliates'. Japanese firms, for example, made 86 such capital increases in Thailand in 1997 and the first half of 1998. Japanese TNCs in several countries also found it advantageous and sometimes essential to increase local procurement during the crisis, and they thus in some cases bailed out bankrupt local suppliers. This, of course, meant extended control over such vendors. Moreover, Japanese firms have continued to relocate component production facilities from Japan, and in a few cases they have also relocated them from the US to several South-East Asian countries because of the greatly reduced costs of production at the latter sites occasioned by currency devaluations. A 1998 Nikkei survey, to which 188 companies operating in the region responded, indicated that many intended further to localize component production as a hedge against currency fluctuations (*The Nikkei Weekly*, 12 January 1998). Again consistent with one of the main themes of this chapter, it is clear that many Japanese TNCs took the crisis as an occasion to weave their Asian affiliates ever more tightly into their networks.

At the same time, increasing numbers of Japanese firms, including important manufacturers, and numerous local companies throughout East Asia are currently being woven into broader global alliances and networks as a result of European and American companies' mergers and acquisitions in Japan and the region. This has been particularly notable in the motor vehicle, telecommunications and financial sectors. High profile examples include the large stakes taken by Renault in Nissan and Daimler-Chrysler in Mitsubishi Motor Corporation. The outlines of these new and broader networks and the power relationships among the firms at their centres have yet to be charted. Japanese TNCs will, however, clearly play a less single-handedly predominant integrative role in East Asia in coming years than that portrayed in this chapter. Ethnic Chinese businesses will, for the most part, continue to play subordinate, rather than central roles in these emergent global networks for some time to come.

Acknowledgement

The research for this chapter was done with the financial support of the Fulbright-Hays Faculty Research Abroad Program and California State University, North-ridge and the institutional support of Institut Kajian Malaysia dan Antarabangsa (IKMAS), Universiti Kebangsaan Malaysia. This assistance is acknowledged with thanks. I am alone responsible for the substance of what follows.

Notes

1   This chapter was originally written as a paper for a conference held in late June 1997, just days before the onset of the East Asian financial crisis and reflects my assessment at that time. The epilogue was written in May 1998 and updated in July 2001.
2   These figures are based on the conventional measure of GDP rather than the Purchasing Power Parity (PPP) measure in use by the World Bank since 1993. Were the latter used, ethnic Chinese GDP would probably not be as close to China's as these figures suggest.
3   This section is abbreviated and updated from Machado, 1995.

References

Abegglen, James (1994) *Sea Change: Pacific Asia as the New World Industrial Center.* New York: The Free Press.

Australia, Department of Foreign Affairs and Trade, East Asia Analytical Unit (1995) *Overseas Chinese Business Networks in Asia.* Canberra: Department of Foreign Affairs and Trade, East Asia Analytical Unit.

Bernard, Mitchell and John Ravenhill (1995) 'Beyond Product Cycles and Flying Geese: Regionalization, Hierarchy and the Industrialization of East Asia'. *World Politics,* 47: 171–209.

Cox, Robert (1987) *Production, Power, and World Order: Social Forces in the Making of History.* New York: Columbia University Press.

DoS, MTI (Department of Statistics, Ministry of Trade and Industry) Singapore (1995) *Singapore's Investment Abroad – 1990–1993.* Singapore: DoS, MITI.

DoS, MTI (Department of Statistics, Ministry of Trade and Industry) Singapore (1996) *Singapore's Direct Investment Abroad – 1994.* Singapore: DoS, MTI, Occasional Paper 23.

EIU (Economist Intelligence Unit) (1993) *Japanese Motor Industry.* Fourth Quarter, 1993.

Ernst, Dieter (1995) 'Mobilizing the Region's Capabilities? The East Asian Production Networks of Japanese Electronics Firms', in Eileen Doherty (ed.) *Japanese Investment in Asia: International Production Strategies in a Changing World,* San Francisco: The Asia Foundation and Berkeley Roundtable on the International Economy.

Fingleton, Eamonn (1997) *Blindside: Why Japan is Still on Track to Overtake the U.S. by the Year 2000.* Tokyo: Kodansha.

Gereffi, Gary (1995) 'Global Production Systems and Third World Development', in Barbara Stallings (ed.) *Global Change, Regional Response: The New International Context of Development.* Cambridge: Cambridge University Press.

Hatch, Walter and Kozo Yamamura (1996) *Asia in Japan's Embrace: Building a Regional Production Alliance.* Cambridge: Cambridge University Press.

Hirsh, Michael and E. Keith Henry (1997) 'The Unraveling of Japan Inc.: Multinationals as Agents of Change'. *Foreign Affairs*, (Mar/Apr), 76(2): 11–16.

Hollerman, Leon (1988) *Japan's Economic Strategy for Brazil: Challenge for the United States.* Lexington, MA: Lexington Books.

Inoue Ryuichiro (1994) *Ajia no zaibatsu to kigyo* (Asia's Company Groups and Businesses). Tokyo: Nihon keizai shinbunsha.

International Herald Tribune, 19 November 1996.

JETRO (Japan External Trade Organization) (1999) *White Paper on Foreign Direct Investment, 1999.* Available www.jetro.go.jp/it/e/pub/whitepaper/invest 1999.

Jomo K.S. with Chen Yun Chung, Brian C. Folk, Irfan ul-Haque, Pasuk Phongpaichit, Batara Simatupang and Mayuri Tateshi (1997) *Southeast Asia's Misunderstood Miracle: Industrial Policy and Economic Development in Thailand, Malaysia and Indonesia.* Boulder, CO: Westview Press.

JPRI (Japan Policy Research Institute) Staff (1996) 'Government Investment in Commercial Technology'. *JPRI Critique*, (Nov) III(8): 1–2.

Low, Linda, Eric Ramstetter and Henry Wai-Chung Yeung (1996) *Accounting for Outward Direct Investment from Hong Kong and Singapore: Who Controls What?* Cambridge, MA: National Bureau of Economic Research, NBER Working Paper No. 5858.

Machado, Kit (1995) 'Japanese Foreign Direct Investment in East Asia: the Expanding Division of Labor and the Future of Regionalism', in Steve Chan (ed.) *Foreign Direct Investment in a Changing Global Political Economy.* London: Macmillan.

Machado, Kit (1999) 'Complexity and Hierarchy in the East Asian Division of Labor: Japanese Technological Superiority and ASEAN Industrial Development', in Jomo K.S. and Greg Felker (eds) *Technology, Competitiveness and the State: Malaysia's Industrial Technology Policies.* London: Routledge.

MITI (Ministry of International Trade and Industry) Japan (1992) *White Paper on International Trade – Japan 1992.* Tokyo: Japan External Trade Organization.

MITI (Ministry of International Trade and Industry) Malaysia (1994) *Malaysia International Trade and Industrial Report 1994.* Kuala Lumpur: MITI.

MoF (Ministry of Finance) Malaysia (1995) *Economic Report 1995/1996.* Kuala Lumpur: MoF.

New Straits Times, 5 February 1996.

The Nikkei Weekly, 24 May 1993.

The Nikkei Weekly, 30 January 1995.

The Nikkei Weekly, 17 June 1996.

The Nikkei Weekly, 12 January 1998.

Redding, Gordon (1990) *The Spirit of Chinese Capitalism.* Berlin: Walter de Gruyter. and Co.

Rodan, Gary (1993) 'Reconstructing Divisions of Labour: Singapore's New Regional Emphasis', in Richard Higgott, Richard Leaver and John Ravenhill (eds) *Pacific Economic Relations in the 1990s: Cooperation or Conflict?* Boulder, CO: Lynne Rienner Publishers.

Sato, Yuri (1996) 'The Astra Group: A Pioneer of Management Modernization in Indonesia'. The Developing Economies, XXXIV(3), September: 2476–80.

Seagrave, Sterling (1995) *Lords of the Rim.* London: Corgi Books.

Shu En (1995) *Kajinnettowaku no himitsu* (The Secret of Ethnic Chinese Networks). Tokyo: Toyo Keizai Shinposha.

Takeuchi Junko (1993) 'Foreign Direct Investment in ASEAN by Small and Medium Sized Japanese Companies and Its Effects on Local Supporting Industries'. *RIM: Pacific Business and Industries*, IV(22): 36–57.

Tanaka Yozo, Mori Minako and Mori Yoko (1992) 'Overseas Chinese Business Community in Southeast Asia: Present Conditions and Future Prospects'. *RIM: Pacific Business and Industries*, II(16): 2–24.

Taylor, Robert (1996) *Greater China and Japan: Prospects for an Economic Partnership in East Asia*. London and New York: Routledge.

Tokunaga Shojiro (1992) 'Japan's FDI-Promoting Systems and Intra-Asian Networks: New Investment and Trade Systems Created by the Borderless Economy', in Tokunaga Shojiro (ed.) *Japan's Foreign Investment and Asian Economic Interdependence: Production, Trade, and Financial Systems*. Tokyo: University of Tokyo Press: 5–47.

Toyo Keizai (1995) *Kaigai shinshutsu kigyo soran '95* (Overseas Business Survey, '95). Tokyo: Toyo Keizai Shinposha.

UNCTAD/DTCI (United Nations Conference on Trade and Development, Division on Transnational Corporations and Investment) (1996) *World Investment Report, 1996: Investment, Trade and International Policy Arrangements*. New York and Geneva: United Nations.

Vatikiotis, Michael (1996) *Political Change in Southeast Asia: Trimming the Banyan Tree*. London and New York: Routledge.

Weidenbaum, Murray and Samuel Hughes (1996) *The Bamboo Network: How Expatriate Chinese Entrepreneurs are Creating a New Economic Superpower in Asia*. New York: The Free Press.

Wirtshaftswoche, 29 February 1996 (cited in *World Press Review*, June 1996: 30).

Glossary

Baba   Straits-born Chinese in Malaysia and Singapore, once Malay-speaking and now usually English-educated.

Benteng   (fortress) Indonesia-first, protectionist policy (Indonesian).

Bumiputera   Malay and other indigenous ethnic groups in Malaysia, literally meaning 'son of the soil'.

Chaebol   giant family-owned conglomerate (Korean).

Cu ren   rough people.

Cukong   Sino-Indonesian businessman who gives up a share of profits for political protection; suppliers of unofficial funds.

ekonomi kolonial   (dependent) colonial economy.

ekonomi nasional   (well-developed, self-reliant, diversified, integrated) national economy (Indonesia).

endaka   high (appreciating) yen (Japanese).

Ganqing   feeling; intimacy; relationship.

Geren guanxi   individual relationships.

Guanxi   networks of inter-personal relationships; particularistic relationships.

Hong bao   red packets of gift money.

Hui   variously translated as credit society, loan society, co-operative loan society, mutual aid club, rotating credit association.

Huo ji   apprentice or shop assistant.

Jao pho   rural 'god-fathers'; provincial businessmen (Thai).

Jao sua   large modern enterprises; Bangkok-based businessmen (Thai).

Jia   'family'/'house'.

Jia shi   'family matters'.

Kampung   village.

Kan dian   looking after the shop.

Keiretsu   group of inter-linked Japanese companies.

Keku nailao   'working hard to overcome difficulty'.

Kongsi   multi-member Chinese business organizations; originally huge partnerships, outgrowths of the voluntary associations and 'secret societies' of China's coastal cities; shares purchased with capital or with the promise to provide labour.

Kretek   clove cigarette (Indonesian).

Laoban   boss.

Laoqian gongsi   'trolling-for-money companies'.

Lunhui   credit rotation by prior agreement.

Mestizo   children of mixed marriages between 'aliens' (e.g. ethnic Chinese) and indigenous people (Philippines).

Pasisir   guest; passenger; customer (Indonesian).

Peranakan   early Chinese settler immigrants and subsequent generations who have assimilated (Indonesian).

Pribumi   indigenous ethnic groups (Indonesian).

Renqing   mutual obligations among relatives or friends.

Shou qi   the experience of being mistreated or bullied.

Taipan   wealthy, powerful owners of Chinese conglomerates.

Tong   same or common.

Tongshi   co-workers; colleagues; comrades.

Tongxiang   persons from the same native place.

Tongxue   classmates; schoolmates.

Totok   relatively recent unassimilated ethnic Chinese immigrants (Indonesian).

Tou shou   foreman, responsible for running a shop in consultation with the owner.

Towkay   tycoon; shopkeeper (Malaysia); businessman.

Tukushengyi   'businesses of the original storehouse'; monopolists.

Wayang   show (stage performance, movie, shadow play, etc.).

Xiao   small; term of (filial) deference.

Xiao shen yi   small business.

Xinyong   trust.

Yaohui   credit rotation by chance, e.g. by casting dice or drawing lots.

Yingchou   entertainment.

Zhuan xin   focus or single-mindedness.

Zu   patriline.

Zuo shen yi   'the way of commerce'; 'doing business'.

Index

Note: Page locators followed by (*N.*) refer to the notes following the chapters, e.g. indigenism 43(*N.* 17); Page locators followed by (*Table*) refer to the tables within the text, e.g. foreign direct investment figures 216(*Table 11.3*).

accounting systems 163–4
agribusiness 155, 156–7, 162–3, *see also* Charoen Pokphand Group (CP Group)
airline business 97, 100, 123
Alcatel 196
Ali Sadikin 111
alliances: business 138–43, 143(*Figure 8.1*), 149(*N.* 6), 172–3, 176–8; marriage alliances 100; patronage-based alliances 2–3, 129, 147, 176–8
America *see* United States; the West
Anand Panyarachun 136, 199–200
Anek, Laothamatas 186
ASEAN economies 74, 105, 125(*N.* 1)
assets, from Thai politicians 130(*Table 8.1*)
associations (*kongsi*) 36, 38–9, 235
Astra Corporation 111–12, 113, 226
AT&T telephone equipment 191
auction 14, *see also hui*
Australia, Department of Foreign Affairs 211, 222, 223

B. Grimm-Siemens partnership 139
Babas 21, 235
Bangkok Bank 120, 121, 142, 226
Bangkok Land group 120
Bangkok Post (newspaper) 136
banking operations: Indonesia 111; Japan 220; Philippines 95, 96–7, 98, 123; Singapore 119; Thailand 120, 226, 230
Bardsley, Alex 3–4, 26–41
Becker, Gary 17

beer industry 7
Benteng (fortress) policy 21, 235
BGs (business groups) 119–20
bidding and tenders 191, 195–7, 197(*Table 10.3*), 200–1
Bob Hasan 107, 110, 111, 116, 226
BOI (Board of Investment, Thailand) 132, 133, 134, 147
Boonchai Benjarongkul 135, 193
Borisut Kansinphila, and Chanphen Wiwatsuhseri 132
Bourdieu, Pierre 81–2
bourgeoisie 20, 185
BT-CP joint venture 136, 138
Buddhism 20
build-operate-transfer (B-O-T) method 135–6, 171, 190, 196
bumiputra 114, 116
bureaucracy 182, 185, 187
Burma 106
Burma News 171
business: alliances in Thailand 138–43; capability 147–8; Chinese idiom of 34–41; ethics 15, 33; ethnic Chinese activity in Southeast Asian business 26–34, 213–18, 214(*Table 11.1*), 215(*Table 11.2*), 228–9; European practices 37, 39; international 98, 113, 133, 139; organization of 16–18; proposals 191, 195–7, 197(*Table 10.3*); reform and restructuring 131; small-scale 4–5, 40–1, 74, *see also* diversification of business; networking; state–business relations
business groups (BGs) 119–20; Thai (TBGs) 131, 132–3, 138–43, 140–1(*Table 8.4*), 192, *see also* companies; conglomerates; corporations; family-based enterprises;

firms, top ranking; local firms; small
   and medium size enterprises (SMEs)
businessmen (*jao sua*) 188–9

Callis, Helmut G. 93
capital: and class 92–3; concepts of
   26–34, 81–2, 85, 120; ethnic Chinese
   control of 29–32; foreign 129, 131,
   142, 230; local and international 185,
   230; and power 78; social/cultural 12,
   15, 177; tripod structure of Thai capital
   131–2
capitalism: Confucian, and ethics 52–4;
   guerrilla capitalism 22, 41; historical
   background of Chinese 3–4, 10–11,
   13, 35–41
car assembly 98
cassava trading 112
chaebols (family-owned conglomerates) 7,
   166, 178, 179, 235
Chai-Anan Samudavanija 187
Chairat Charoensin-o-larn 187
chambers of commerce 36, 100, 103(*N*. 7),
   222–3
chance (*yaohui*) 14, 236
Charoen Pokphand Group (CP Group) 7,
   113, 120–1, 125; business strategies
   162–5; diversification and expansion
   166–71, 174, 178; family issues and
   ownership 159–62; history and growth
   153–9; management 155, 161, 173–6,
   179; myth of success 178–9; political
   patronage and connections 129, 133,
   134, 136–8, 153–4, 176; strategic
   alliances 142, 172–3, 176–8; Thai
   telecommunications projects 196, 198,
   199
Chatichai regime 134, 135, 188, 195, 202
Chearavanont family 7, 155, 159–62
Chew, Daniel 54, 56–7
Chia Ekchor 133, 155, 156, 159, 161–2
Chia Oai Peng 14
Chia Siew-whooy 155, 156, 159, 161–2
Chiang Mai 144, 146
chicken farming *see* poultry farming/trade
children 13–14, 56, 65, 67–9, 82–3
China: and the CP Group 154–5, 157,
   158, 166, 169–70, 176–7, 179; imperial
   and communist eras 35, 106, 156
Chinese capitalism *see* capital; capitalism
Chinese culture *see* Confucian ethics;
   Confucianism
'Chinese-descent countries' 214
Chinese (people) *see* ethnic Chinese

'Chineseness' 3–4, 27–9, 42(*N*. 10)
Chinese–Filipino business families 5–6,
   92–102
Chong Yew Tong 62–9
Chop Hock Guan 62, 63–4, 66
Christensen, Scott R. 129, 139
cigarette manufacture 95, 97, 100
Ciputra 111
citizenship law 93–4
class: bourgeoisie 20, 185; capitalist 92–3;
   professional middle 118
clientelism 7, 130, 138
Clifford, James 52
co-operative loan society (*hui*) 14, 235
cockfighting 153
colonialism: and division of labour 4;
   European and Japanese 20; US colonial
   rule in Philippines 93, 122, *see also*
   European colonialism
Communications Authority of Thailand
   (CAT) 135, 192–3
communications industry 77, 143, 144, *see
   also* telecommunications industry
   (Thailand)
companies: CP Group's foreign
   partnerships 167–8; Dutch and English
   East India Companies 28; *laoqian
   gongsi* ('trolling-for-money
   companies') 80, 236; top 500 ethnic
   Chinese controlled 213–18, 214(*Table
   11.1*), 215(*Table 11.2*), *see also* business
   groups; conglomerates; corporations;
   family-based enterprises; firms, top
   ranking; local firms; small and medium
   size enterprises (SMEs)
competition 192–3
computer industry 143, 144
concessions (*sampathan*) 134–8, 139, 146,
   see also rent-seeking
Confucian ethics 15, 33, 52–4
Confucianism: business and family ethos
   4–5, 58–61, 69–70; Chinese values and
   capitalism 2, 10–15; in East Asian
   economies 18–19; the non-
   homogeneity of Chinese business
   people 21, 105–6; re-assessment of
   15–16; and social organization 33–4
conglomerates: *chaebols* 7, 166, 178, 179,
   235; ethnic Chinese 213–18, 214(*Table
   11.1*), 215–16(*Table 11.2*), 221–2; in
   Indonesia 107–14, 108(*Table 7.1*); in
   Malaysia 114–18; in Philippines
   122–3; in Singapore 118–19; Sino-
   Indonesian 107–14; in Thailand

119–22, *see also* business groups; companies; corporations; family-based enterprises; firms, top ranking; local firms; small and medium size enterprises (SMEs)

control *see* labour resources; ownership; power

corporations: Thailand 132–4, 147–8; *tukushengyi* (monopolists) in Malaysia 78; Western-style corporate forms 4, 39, 40, *see also* business groups; companies; conglomerates; family-based enterprises; firms, top ranking; local firms; multinational corporations (MNCs); small and medium size enterprises (SMEs); transnational corporations (TNCs)

Cox, Robert 213

Coyiuto, Roberto 123

CP Group *see* Charoen Pokphand Group (CP Group)

credit networks 14–15, 37, 39, 45(*N.* 51)

credit society (*hui*) 14, 235

cronyism 15, 100, 110–12, 123

Crouch, Harold 107, 114, 116–17, 118

cukongs (unofficial funds) 21, 107, 235

'cultural determinism' 5

cultural/social capital 12, 15, 177

culture, Chinese *see* Confucian ethics; Confucianism

Daim Zainuddin 116

daughters 84, 85, 101–2

de Certeau, Michel 66

decision-making 18

'deep integration' 229

dependency theory 187, 189

Depression (economic, 1930s) 39

deregulation 148

Dhanin Chearavanont 120–1; business and management style 165, 174, 175, 176–7, 179; career 1, 153, 156, 159–62, 178, *see also* Charoen Pokphand Group

Dharmala Group 112

digital technology 193

Dirlik, Arif 52

discrimination: economic 17, 86–9; Spanish colonial legislation 92

diversification of business 97–9, 159, 166–70, 174

domestic capital 30–1, 230

Don Muang Tollway 171, 172

Doner, Richard F. 130; and Ansil Ramsey 130, 131, 138, 148

duopoly rights 192, 193

Dutch colonial era 109

Dutch East India Company 28

East Asian economy *see* economy

East India Company (English) 28

economic boom (1987–97) 7, 129, 130, 147–8, 211–12

economy: ASEAN economies 74, 105, 125(*N.* 1); constraints set by 73–4, 109–10; East Asian crisis (July 1997) 1, 26, 182, 229–32; East Asian economic miracle 2, 16, 129; Japan's economic predominance and financial crisis 227–8, 231–2; modernity and hybridity 74–5; Philippines 93–4, 122; preferential treatment 17; and socio-economic organization 36–40; Thai economic growth 129, 131–2, 132(*Table 8.2*); Thai financial crisis (1997) 179, 182, 201

education 13, 85, 101–2

Eka Cipta Wijaya 111, 124

emigrant Chinese 13, 35, 38

employees *see* labour resources; resistance

employers (*towkays*): shop owners in Sarawak 56, 61, 64, 65, 67–9; truck transport owners in Malaysia 78–9, 81, 86–9

energy industry 171

engineers 146, 147

entertainment (*yingchou*) 79, 236

Ericsson 196

ethics *see* Confucian ethics; values

ethnic Chinese: activity in Southeast Asian business 26–34, 213–18, 214(*Table 11.1*), 215(*Table 11.2*), 228–9; business networks and Japanese TNC networks 218–27; characteristics and differences in 1–2, 6, 105; and CP Group 172–3, 178; and economic boom 211–12; political exclusion of 18; in post-Marcos Philippines 92–3; shop ownership in Sarawak 55–6, 60–9; Sino-Indonesian conglomerates 107–14, 124–5; in Thailand 185; and transnational corporations 223–5, 224(*Table 11.4*)

ethnicity: and Chinese capital in Southeast Asia 18–22, 86–9; concepts of 'Chineseness' 3–4, 27–9, 42(*N.* 10)

ethnographic research 76–7

European business practices 37, 39
European colonialism 20; concepts of
    Chinese ethnicity 28–9; Dutch
    colonial era in Indonesia 109; legal and
    administrative systems 35–6, 118;
    racialism and social mobility 33, 35;
    Spanish colonialism 92, 93, *see also* the
    West
exclusion, political 18
expansion 164–5, 169–70, 178, 227
experts *see* professionals
exports: the CP Group 159;
    manufactured goods 125

familism 4–5, 17–18, 52–70, 81–8;
    lineage system 35, 37–8
family: children 56, 65, 67–9, 82–3;
    daughters 84, 85, 101–2; the *huo ji*
    system 61–3, 65–6, 235; inheritance
    84; kinship 17–18; marriage alliances
    100; no universal characteristics 74;
    non-family members 61–6, 82, 83, 84;
    the patriline 82–6; sons 8, 67–9, 84,
    87, 101; succession and leadership 101,
    155–6, 159–60; values and ethos
    58–61, 69–70; wives 55–6, 67–8
family-based enterprises: Chinese traders
    in Karjan (Sarawak) 54–70; Chinese–
    Filipino business families 5–6, 92–102;
    and Confucianism 57–9; the CP
    Group 154–5, 155–6, 159–62, 178;
    ethnic Chinese in East Asia 221–5;
    family-sourced labour 2, 38–9;
    historical background 3, 13–14, 15, 22,
    92–3; Indonesia 124; small-scale
    Chinese businesses in Malaysia 73–89;
    and Thai corporate organizations 134,
    143, 146, *see also* business groups;
    companies; conglomerates;
    corporations; firms, top ranking; local
    firms; multinational corporations
    (MNCs); small and medium size
    enterprises (SMEs); transnational
    corporations (TNCs)
Far Eastern Economic Review (*FEER*) 144,
    161, 171, 211
FDI (foreign direct investment) figures
    214–18, 216(*Table 11.3*), 227–8
Federation of Chinese–Filipino Chamber
    of Commerce 100, 103(*N. 7*)
feed meal 133
FEER (*Far Eastern Economic Review*) 144,
    161, 171, 211
Filinvest 98

Filipino Chinese *see* Philippines Chinese
financial management 176, 179
financial operations: Japan 220;
    Philippines 95, 96–7, 98, 123;
    Singapore 119; Thailand 120, 226, 230
Fingleton, Eamonn 227
firms, top ranking: ethnic Chinese
    213–18, 214(*Table 11.1*), 215(*Table
    11.2*); Japanese 220–1; Thai 131–2,
    132(*Table 8.2*), 148(*N. 1*), *see also*
    companies; conglomerates;
    corporations; family-based enterprises;
    local firms; small and medium size
    enterprises (SMEs)
first-tier East Asian NIEs 18–19
fixed-line telephone project 194–201
flotations 113
food processing business 95, 97, 98
foreign capital 30–1, 129, 131, 142, 230
foreign companies 167–8
foreign direct investment (FDI) figures
    214–18, 216(*Table 11.3*), 227–8
Fortune Tobacco 95, 97, 100
Foucault, Michel 66
Freedman, Maurice 14
Fukuyama, Francis 11

ganqing (intimacy of relationships) 12, 235
Gatchalian, William 123
Gates, Hill 10
GCCs (global commodity chains) 213,
    225
gender *see* family; patriarchal power;
    women
Gereffi, Gary 213, 218, 225
global commodity chains (GCCs) 213,
    225
globalization 2, 52, 229, 231–2
Gokongwei, John (Jr) 93, 94, 100, 101,
    122, 123
Gokongwei family 94–5, 96–7, 98
golf, as business model 41
Gomez, Edmund Terence 116
Gondokusumo, Soehargo 112, 124
gossip 68–9
Gotiaco, Pedro 95
Gotianun, Andrew 93, 94, 98–9, 122, 123
Gotianun family 95, 96, 98–9, 100, 101–2
government, Thailand: Anand
    Panyarachun 136, 199–200, 202;
    Chatichai regime 134, 135, 188, 195,
    202; coup of 1991 199–200;
    democratization and economic
    liberalization 1, 182, 183, 186, 187–8,

189–90, 202; intervention 129–31, 132, 135–8; regimes 188, 190, 198–9, 199, *see also* infrastructure; non-governmental institutions; state
Gramsci, Antonio 29
Greenhalgh, Susan 54, 56, 58
guanxi (interpersonal relationships): and the CP Group 153–5, 158, 165, 168–9, 179; historical background 5, 12; 'political *guanxi*' 2; and small-scale Chinese businesses 75, 79–81, 222–3; Thaksin Shinawatra 145–6
guerrilla capitalism 22
Guomindang government (Taiwan) 11

Hamilton, Gary 31
Handley, Paul 7, 153–79
Harvey, David 82
Hatch, Walter and Kozo Yamamura 219
Hewison, Kevin 30, 120
hierarchy, Confucian 16
high performing Asian economies (HPAEs) 129, 131
Hirsch, Michael and E. Keith Henry 228
Hodder, Rupert 69
Hollerman, Leon 219
Hong Kong 11, 19, 157, 216, 217, 225
Hong Leong Group 225
House of Investments 95, 100
HPAEs (high performing Asian economies) 129, 131
hui (credit or loan society) 14, 235
human resources *see* labour resources
huo ji (shop assistant) system 61–3, 65–6, 235
Hutchison Group 142, 225
hybridity 74–5

identity: of ethnic Chinese 27–32; and nationalism 36
IMF (International Monetary Fund) 230
immigrants, Chinese: in Korea and United States 58, 59; *peranakan* and *totok* 109, 124, 236; in Philippines 93–4, 122, *see also* emigrant Chinese
importers 133
indigenism 4, 31–2, 43(*N*. 17)
individual, and the state 53
Indonesia 6, 105–6; *Bentang* (fortress) policy 21; and the CP Group 157–8; the East Asian economic crisis 230; and Malaysia 114–18; New Order 106–7, 107–8, 110, 112, 157, 230; and Philippines 122–3; and Singapore

118–19; Sino-Indonesian conglomerates 107–14, 124–5; and Thailand 119–22
industrial development 131, 143–4, 148, 170
informal arrangements (economic and business) 17
infrastructure (administrative) 118, 129
inheritance 84
insurance companies 94, 95, 99, 123, 226
integration 229; vertical integration 162–3, 219, 222
inter-ethnic redistribution agendas 3
international business 98, 113, 133, 139
International Herald Tribune 154, 170, 228
International Monetary Fund (IMF) 230
interpersonal relationships *see guanxi*; trust
investment 217–18, 228–9; off-shore investment 119, 124–5, 146
Islam 21

Jakarta Stock Exchange (SEJ) 118, 118(*Table 7.3*)
jao pho (rural 'godfathers') 188–9, 235
jao sua (modern enterprises/businessmen) 188–9, 235
Japan: colonialism 20; and the CP Group 158–9, 177–8; economic predominance and financial crisis 18, 227–8, 231–2; multinational corporations (MNCs) 129; transnational corporations (TNCs) 8, 212, 213, 217–21; transnational production networks 211–13
Japan External Trade Organization (JETRO) 231
Jaran 156, 157, 160, 161, 162, 166
JETRO (Japan External Trade Organization) 231
jia shi (family matters) 60, 235
Jomo, K.S. 1–9, 2, 10–22, 223

Kader Industrial (Thailand) 160–1, 172
Kahn, Herman 52
kan dian (watching the shop) 4, 64–6, 67–9, 70, 235
Kanjanapas family 120
Kapitan China 35, 36
Karjan (Sarawak) 54–70
Kasian Tejapira 28
Keyes, Charles F. 182
Khoo Kay Peng 116
kinship 17–18

KLSE (Kuala Lumpur Stock Exchange) 118, 118(*Table 7.3*)
Koh, Tommy 52–3
kongsi (associations) 36, 38–9, 235
Korea: *chaebols* 7, 166, 178, 179, 235; Chinese immigrants in 58; Korean workers in Japan 53
kretek (clove cigarette) industry 112, 124, 126(*N.* 8), 236
Krirkkiat, P. and Kunio Yoshihara 119–20
Kuala Lumpur Stock Exchange (KLSE) 118, 118(*Table 7.3*)

labour resources: and economic diversity 229; family-based business in Sarawak 56, 61–9; historical background 4, 12, 38–9; small-scale Chinese businesses in Malaysia 77, 79, 84, 85–6; workers and Confucian ethics 53
Lamsam family 120, 139
land reform (1949–53) 54
language: and Chinese ethnicity 27, 109, 124; and management styles 175, 222–3
laoqian gongsi ('trolling-for-money companies') 80, 236
large-scale enterprises 119
legal systems 17, 35–6
legislation 93–4
legitimacy 32–3, 34
Leung Hon-chou 53
Li, Tania M. 14
liberalization, economic and political 182, 187–8, 202
Liek How Seng 63–4, 65, 67–8
Liem Sioe Liong 107, 110, 111, 113, 116, 124–5, 126(*N.* 8 and 10)
Light, Ivan and Edna Bonacich 58, 59
Lim, Linda Y.C. 2
Lim, Mr 86–9
Lim Thian Kit 116
Limlingan, Victor Simpao 15
lineage system 35, 37–8; familism 4–5, 17–18, 52–70, 81–8
linkages 212–13, 225–7
Lippo group 111
loan society (*hui*) 14, 235
local firms 130, 225, 227, *see also* business groups; companies; conglomerates; corporations; family-based enterprises; small and medium size enterprises (SMEs)
logging/logging camps 62, 63
Lotus Superstore 169, 170, 173, 175

Loxley Group 138, 139
Loy Hean Heong 116
lunhui (prior agreement) 14, 236, *see also hui*

M Thai 172
Machado, Kit 8, 211–32
Mackie, Jamie 6, 95, 102(*N.* 3), 105–25, 186
macro-economic stability 129
McVey, Ruth 29, 30–1, 32, 73
Mahathir Bin Mohamad, Dr 6, 115, 116
Makro 169, 170, 172, 173
Malayan Insurance Company 94, 95, 99, 122
Malaysia: anti-Chinese discrimination in 13, 86–9; compared with Indonesia 114–18; equity ownership stipulations 2; Japanese TNCs and ethnic Chinese linkages 225–6; New Economic Policy (NEP) 21, 87–8, 114, 116; political power 6; small-scale Chinese businesses in 73–89
male domination *see* patriarchal power; patriline; power
management: the CP Group 155, 161, 173–6, 179; modern/Western-style 133, 146, 174–5; professional managers 6, 99, 101, 102, 124, 148; reform and restructuring 131, 134, 148, 221–2; surveillance 5, 65, 66–9, 70
manufacturing 94, 95, 97, 98, 212, 228; exports of manufactured goods 125; mass-produced goods 163; motor vehicle manufacture 98, 111–12, 166–7, 220, 225–6, 231; regional production networks 219; tobacco and cigarette manufacture 95, 97, 100
Marcos, President Ferdinand 93–4, 112, 122, 123
Marcus, George 57
market networks 37, 40–1, 130, 162–3, 164–5
marriage alliances 100
mass-produced goods 163
Mauro, Paolo 130
May Fourth Movement (1919) 16
meat consumption 158
mestizos 92, 102(*N.* 1), 236
methodology, research into small-scale Chinese businesses in Malaysia 76–7
Metrobank 96, 97, 98, 99, 123
middle class 118
migrants 35

the military 115, 133, 136, 139, 142, 199;
    support for business tenders 191,
    200–1
MITI (Ministry of International Trade and
    Industry) Japan 220, 227–8
MNCs (multinational corporations) 129,
    131, 132, 148
mobile telephone concessions 192–4,
    194(*Table 10.1*), 202
mobility: and power 88; upward social
    33, 35
modernity 52, 74–5
money: historical background of Chinese
    capitalism 10–11, 37; 'rice-eating
    money' 79, 86
monopolies: rights to, and rent-seeking
    190–2, 195; state-licensed 38–9, 133,
    135–6
monopolists (*tukushengyi*) 78, 236
Montri Pongpanich 195, 196
motor vehicle manufacture 98, 111–12,
    166–7, 220, 225–6, 231
motorcycle manufacture 166, 225
multinational corporations (MNCs) 129,
    131, 132, 148
mutual aid 11–12, 16–17; *hui* (club) 14,
    235; *renqing* (obligations) 12, 236

The Nation 153, 154
Nation News Talk 154, 166
nation and state, concepts of 31–2, 36
nationalism 36
NEP (New Economic Policy), Malaysia
    21, 87–8, 114, 116
networking: business networks 130,
    211–13; cronyism 15, 100, 110–12,
    123; ethnic Chinese business and
    Japanese TNCs 212, 218–27; social
    networks 2; transnational 8, 40–1,
    211–13, *see also* credit networks;
    market networks
New Economic Policy (NEP), Malaysia
    21, 87–8, 114, 116
New Order (Indonesia) 106–7, 107–8,
    110, 112, 157, 230
New Straits Times (journal) 218
newly industrializing economies (NIEs)
    18–19
Ng, Lilian 35
Ngiu Ah Khew 62–3, 65–6, 67–8
NIEs (newly industrializing economies)
    18–19
The Nikkei Weekly (journal) 217, 221, 223,
    231

non-governmental institutions 130
Nonini, Donald M. 5, 73–89
Norinoco 172–3
Nynex 173, 175

Ockey, James 188
off-shore investment 119, 124–5, 146
Ong, Aihwa 52
opium farms 38
ownership, and ethnic Chinese control of
    capital 29–32, 43(*N.* 18)

Palanca, Ellen H. 94, 123
PAP (People's Action Party) 119
'paper millionaires' 116
Papua New Guinea 14
'particularistic relationships' *see guanxi*
partnerships 167–8
Pasuk Phongphaichit 188; and Chris
    Baker 132, 188; and Sungsidh
    Piriyarangsan 130
Patcharee, Thanamai 187
paternalism 54
patriarchal power 5, 14, 82–6
patriline 82–6
patrimony (Indonesia) 110–11, 113–14
patronage-based alliances 2–3, 129, 147,
    176–8
peasant economies 37
People's Action Party (PAP) 119
peranakan (Chinese immigrants) 109, 124,
    236
personal contacts *see guanxi* (interpersonal
    relationships)
petrochemicals industry 131, 132, 171,
    174, 179
petty accumulation trap 75, 84–6
Phacharaphon Changkaew 139
Philippines Chinese 5–6, 92–102,
    126(*N.* 17)
Pisan, S., and James F. Guyot 186
pluralist societies 3, 186
Police Department (Thailand) 144
policy factors 3, 163; business-friendly
    state policies 4, 132, 148
political economy, Thailand 183–4, 187,
    189
political elites: Filipino 6, 99–100; Thai
    130
political protection: Sino-Indonesian
    businesses 6, 107–8, 110–11, 116; Thai
    businesses 129–31, 147–8
political systems: decentralization and
    local government 101; Malaysian 114,

see also political elites; state–business relations; state; state–business relations

political systems (Thailand) 6–7, 121, 129–31, 134–8, 146–7; bureaucracy 182, 185, 187; and business 198; democratization/liberalization 1, 182, 183, 186, 187–8, 189–90, 202; political crisis 194–5, 230, *see also* political elites; state; state–business relations

politicians: assets 130(*Table 8.1*); personal relations with 146–7

population: Malaysian Chinese 114, 115–16; Sino-Indonesian 108–9

poultry farming/trade 133, 139, 157–8, 158–9, 162, 177–8

power: and family-based business relationships 61, 65–9; and inequality 73; political 6–7, 147; small-scale Chinese businesses in Malaysia 75, 77, 82–6; and wealth 32

Prachachart thurakit 191

Prajogo Pangestu 111, 113, 226

Prem regime 190

pribumi conglomerates 113, 116

price setting 162–3, 163–4

prior agreement (*lunhui*) 14, 236, *see also hui*

privatization/private firms: joint government programmes 228; Thailand 7, 131, 135–8, 137(*Table 8.3*), 202; and rent-seeking 184, 189–90, 192, 195, 202

Prizzia, Ross 186

production *see* manufacturing; regional production networks; transnational production networks

professionals 146, 147, 174–5; managers 6, 99, 101, 102, 124, 148

proportionality 114, 115–16

proposals, business 191, 195–7, 197(*Table 10.3*)

protection *see* political protection

Protestant ethic 10, 28

Prudhisan, Jumbala 185

Qing dynasty 35

Ramos, Alfredo 123

Ratanarak family 120

RCBC (Rizal Commercial Banking Corporation) 95, 99

real estate 95, 98–9, 123, 169, 179

Redding, Gordon 5, 41, 53, 81, 222

regional production networks 8, 218–20, 225–7

Rejang trading system 54–5, 56–7

relationships *see guanxi*; trust

religion: and capitalism 10, 20–1; Chinese 16

renqing (mutual obligations) 12, 236

rent-seeking 7–8, 129–31, 132–4, 138, 147–8; political interventions 182–3, 189–201; state–society relations 185–9, 195, 202

resistance 66–9, 86

retail trade 94, 119, 169

Riady, Mochtar 111, 113

'rice-eating money' 79, 86

Riggs, Fred W. 182, 185; and Samuel Huntington 185

risk 12, 37; the CP Group 174; and credit networks 39

Rivera, Temario C. 5–6, 94, 122, 123

Rizal Commercial Banking Corporation (RCBC) 95, 99

road construction 171

Robison, Richard 29

Roman, Emerlinda *et al.* 96

Sahaviriya Group 134, 149(*N.* 3 and 4)

Said, Edward W. 52

sakdina 30

Sakkarin Niyomsilpa 7, 182–203

Salim Group 113, 119, 126(*N.* 10)

sampathan (concession granting) 134–8, 139, 146

Sarawak 5, 14, 54–70

Schumpeterian models 184, 197, 202

Scott, James 66

Seagrave, Sterling 211

Searle, Peter 116–17

Second World War 37, 39; postwar economy in Philippines 94, 95; pre-war economy in Indonesia 110

seed distribution business 120, 153, 155, 156

SEJ (Jakarta Stock Exchange) 118, 118(*Table 7.3*)

'shallow integration' 229

shareholding 160, 161, 222

Shieh, G.S. 11

Shinawatra family 144, 146

Shinawatra (SHIN) Group 7, 120, 139, 142, 143–7, 145(*Table 8.5*), 193

ShoeMart 95, 98, 101

shops/shophouses 55–6, 62

short-termism 15, 22

Siam 35, 39, 42(*N.* 10), *see also* Thailand
Siam Cement 129, 133, 134
Siam Group 133
Siam Rath 191
silk industry 144, 146
Sinar Mas-BII (Bank International Indonesia) 111
Singapore 14, 21, 52–3, 118–19, 217, 230–1
Sino-Indonesian conglomerates 107–14
SM Prime Holdings 96
small and medium size enterprises (SMEs) 11, 109, 212, 221–5, *see also* family-based enterprises
SMEs (small and medium size enterprises) 11, 109, 212, 221–5
social mobility 33
social organization: Chinese, and business organization 40, 55–70, 102; Chinese, and the state 34–6, 106–7; culture and Confucianism 33–4; socio-economic organization 36–40; socio-political contexts 6, 108–9; state–society relations in Thailand 185–9
social/cultural capital 12, 15, 177
socialism 36
Soeharto, President 6, 106–7, 107–8, 110, 111, 116; children/relatives of 111, 112, 113, 158
Soeryadjaya, William 111–12, 113, 126(*N.* 9)
Sombat, Chantrawong 188
sons 8, 67–9, 84, 87, 101
Sophonpanich family 120, 226
Sorakan Adunyanon 144, 145
Southeast Asian diaspora: Chinese cultural factors 12–15; ethnicity and Chinese capital 18–22
Spanish colonial rule 92, 93
spatiality 83–4, 84–5
staffing 175
state: and Chinese social systems 34–6; and the individual 53; and nation, concepts of 31–2; policies and intervention 129–31, 132, 135–8, 223; state–society in Thailand 185–9, *see also* political systems; state–business relations
state–business relations: CP Group 153–4, 163, 176–7; historical background 3, 11–12, 20–1; Japan 220, 227–8; Malaysia 114–15; post-Marcos Philippines 92–3, 99–101; Singapore 118–19; Sino-Indonesian 108–9, 109–14, 116–17, 124; state-led economic growth 86–9; state-licensed monopolies 38–9, 133, 135–6; Thailand 129–31, 132, 135–8, 147–8, 182–4, 189–201, *see also* political systems; state
state-owned enterprises (Thai) (TPEs) 131, 132
steel industry 131, 134
stereotyping, racial 8, 15
Stock Exchange of Thailand (SET) 120
stock exchanges 96, 118, 118(*Table 7.3*), 120, 124
stock market 96, 142, 146, 164–5
strategic alliances (*phanthamit thurakit*) 138–43, 143(*Figure 8.1*), 149(*N.* 6)
subcontracting: the CP Group 158; historical background 5; small-scale Chinese businesses in Malaysia 75, 79–81; to Japanese corporations 219
Suchinda regime 188
Suehiro, Akira 7, 29–30, 120, 129–48, 187; and Makoto Nambara 131, 133
sugar production 92, 98
Sumet Chearavanont 158, 160–2, 174, 177
Suwannaban, Wichai 156
Sy family 94–5, 96, 101
Sy, Henry 93, 94, 100, 101, 122

taipan families (powerful conglomerate owners) 95–102, 111, 122–3, 236
Taiwan 11, 54, 172, 176, 223–5, 230
Tan, Lucio 93, 94, 95, 96, 97, 100, 122–3
Tan, Mely G. 10, 13
Tan, Vincent 116
Tan Chee Beng 12, 13, 14, 15
Tan Yu 123
Tatung 223–5
tax: evasion 100; farming 134–5; incentives 129–30, 133
technical knowledge 145, 148, 157
technocrats (MOTC) 195, 196, 199
technological innovations 77, 88, 134, 184, 193
Tejapaibul family 120
telecommunications industry (Thailand) 7–8, 120, 121, 131, 134–43, 137(*Table 8.3*), 143(*Figure 8.1*); the CP Group 170–1, 179; political economy of 183–4; rents and the growth of a liberalized coalition 182–4, 189–202
telephone directory project 190–2, 202

telephone line installation project 134, 170, 192, 194–202, 197(*Table 10.3*)

Telephone Organization of Thailand (TOT) 134, 135, 137(*Table 8.3*), 138, 190–3, 195–6

telephone services (Thailand) 134, 135, 136, 170–1, 202

tenders and bidding 191, 195–7, 197(*Table 10.3*), 200–1

tertiary services 119, 125

textile industry 130, 131, 132

Thai business groups (TBGs) 131, 132–3, 138–43, 140–1(*Table 8.4*), 192

Thailand 182–203; business capability 147–8; Chinese capital in 21; Chinese migrants in 35, 106, 119–22, 125; the CP Group 154–5, 158–9, 164, 166, 169–70, 177–8; economic crisis and political power 182–4, 230, 231; Japanese TNCs and ethnic Chinese linkages 226; political power/system 6–7, 121, 183; the Shinawatra Group 7, 120, 139, 142, 143–7, 145(*Table 8.5*); telecommunications industry 138–43, 143(*Figure 8.1*), 149(*N.* 6), 183–4, 189–202; tripod structure of capital 131–2, 187, *see also* government, Thailand; rent-seeking

Thaksin Shinawatra 8, 143–7, 145(*Table 8.5*), 193

Thanayong Group 142

Thansetthakij (newspaper) 156, 180(*N.* 3)

Third Wave 144

Thitayut Bunmi 188

Thomas, Nicholas 60

thrift 13

T'ien Ju K'ang 14

TNCs *see* transnational corporations (TNCs)

tobacco and cigarette manufacture 95, 97, 100

Toffler, Alvin 144

Tokunaga, Shojiro 219

TOT (Telephone Organization of Thailand) 134, 135, 137(*Table 8.3*), 138, 190–3, 195–6

totok (recent Chinese immigrant) 109, 124, 236

tou shou (foreman) 63, 65, 235

towkays (managers): shop owners in Sarawak 56, 61, 64, 65, 67–9; truck transport owners in Malaysia 78–9, 81, 86–9

Toyota 225–6

trade: intra-firm trade 221; Rejang trading system 54–5, 56–7

Trakoon, Meechai 185

transfer pricing 163

transnational corporations (TNCs): ethnic Chinese 223–5, 224(*Table 11.4*); Japan 8, 212, 213, 217–21, 224(*Table 11.4*), 225–7

transnational practices 75, 83, 84–5, 86–9

transnational production networks 8, 40–1, 211–13

tripod structure, of Thai capital 131–2

truck transport industry 76, 77–81, 86–9

trust (*xinyong*) 11–12, 17, 236

tukushengyi (monopolists) 78, 236

Ty family 95

Ty, George S.K. 93, 94, 95, 97, 98, 99, 122, 123

UCOM Group 135, 139, 142, 193

Unger, Danny 131

UNICORD Group 133

United States: Chinese immigrants in 58, 59; colonial rule in Philippines 93, 122; and CP Group 157, 170, 177; and Japanese economy 227, 228

Universal Robina Corporation 95, 96, 97

upward mobility 33, 35

values: Chinese 2, 10–15; East Asian 53; family 58–61, 69–70, *see also* Confucianism

Vatikiotis, Michael 211

vertical integration 162–3, 219, 222

Virametheekul family 172

visual power 66–9

wages 61–2, 68, 79

Waldinger, Roger 58

Walmart 170

Wanlop Chearavanont 159, 160

Warr, Peter 129

Washington Times 177

wealth, and power 32

wealth, 'old' and 'new': Indonesia 110; Malaysia 94, 102(*N.* 3), 114, 115, 116–17; Philippines 122

Weber, Max 10

Wee, Vivienne 28

Weidenbaum, M., and S. Hughes 77, 79, 211, 221–2

Wertheim, W.F. 28–9

the West: business alliances with Western firms 173; economic withdrawal 39;

Western-style corporate forms 4, 40, 133; Western-style democracy 185; Western-style management 133, 146, 174–5, *see also* European colonialism
Wirtschaftswoche (journal) 211
women: and inheritance 84; wives 55–6, 67–8; younger women 83
Wong, Ramon H.K. 95
Wong Siu-lun 5, 53
workers *see* labour resources
World Bank, *The East Asian Miracle* (1993) 129, 131
Wu, David Y.H. 14

xinyong (trust) 11–12, 17, 236

Yao Souchou 5, 52–70
yaohui (chance) 14, 236, *see also hui*
Yeung 2
yingchou (entertainment) 79, 236
Yoshihara Kunio 27, 29, 30, 94, 111, 124
Yuchengco, Alfonso 93, 99, 101, 122, 123
Yuchengco, Ernesto Tiaoqui 94
Yuchengco family 94, 95, 96, 97, 99, 101

zhuan xin (single-mindedness) 59–60, 236